D1562404

Media Commercialization and Authoritarian Rule in China

In most liberal democracies, commercialized media is taken for granted, but in many authoritarian regimes, the introduction of market forces in the media represents a radical break from the past, with uncertain political and social implications. In *Media Commercialization and Authoritarian Rule in China*, Daniela Stockmann argues that the consequences of media marketization depend on the institutional design of the state. In one-party regimes such as China, market-based media promote regime stability rather than destabilizing authoritarianism or bringing about democracy. By analyzing the Chinese media, Stockmann ties trends of market liberalization in China to other authoritarian regimes in the Middle East, North Africa, Sub-Saharan Africa, and the post-Soviet region. Drawing on in-depth interviews with Chinese journalists and propaganda officials as well as more than 2,000 newspaper articles, experiments, and public opinion data sets, this book links censorship among journalists with patterns of media consumption and the media's effects on public opinion.

Daniela Stockmann is Assistant Professor of Political Science at Leiden University. Her research on political communication and public opinion in China has been published in *Comparative Political Studies*, *Political Communication*, *The China Quarterly*, and the *Chinese Journal of Communication*, among others. Her 2006 conference paper on the Chinese media and public opinion received an award in Political Communication from the American Political Science Association.

Communication, Society and Politics

Editors

W. Lance Bennett, *University of Washington*
Robert M. Entman, *The George Washington University*

Editorial Advisory Board

Scott Althaus, *University of Illinois at Urbana-Champaign*
Larry M. Bartels, *Vanderbilt University*
Jay G. Blumler, *Emeritus, University of Leeds*
Michael X. Della Carpini, *University of Pennsylvania*
Doris A. Graber, *University of Illinois at Chicago*
Regina Lawrence, *University of Texas at Austin*
Paolo Mancini, *University of Perugia*
Pippa Norris, *Harvard University*
Barbara Pfetsch, *Free University, Berlin*
Philip Schlesinger, *University of Stirling*
Gadi Wolfsfeld, *Hebrew University of Jerusalem*
John Zaller, *University of California, Los Angeles*

Politics and relations among individuals in societies across the world are being transformed by new technologies for targeting individuals and sophisticated methods for shaping personalized messages. The new technologies challenge boundaries of many kinds – between news, information, entertainment, and advertising; between media, with the arrival of the World Wide Web; and even between nations. *Communication, Society and Politics* probes the political and social impacts of these new communication systems in national, comparative, and global perspective.

Other Books in the Series

Eva Anduiza, Michael James Jensen, and Laia Jorba, eds., *Digital Media and Political Engagement Worldwide*
C. Edwin Baker, *Media Concentration and Democracy: Why Ownership Matters*
C. Edwin Baker, *Media, Markets, and Democracy*
W. Lance Bennett and Robert M. Entman, eds., *Mediated Politics: Communication in the Future of Democracy*
Bruce Bimber, *Information and American Democracy: Technology in the Evolution of Political Power*

Series list continues following the Index.

Media Commercialization and Authoritarian Rule in China

DANIELA STOCKMANN

CAMBRIDGE
UNIVERSITY PRESS

University Printing House, Cambridge CB2 8BS, United Kingdom

Cambridge University Press is part of the University of Cambridge.

It furthers the University's mission by disseminating knowledge in the pursuit of education, learning and research at the highest international levels of excellence.

www.cambridge.org
Information on this title: www.cambridge.org/9781107469624

© Daniela Stockmann 2013

First published 2013
Reprinted 2013

A catalogue record for this publication is available from the British Library

Library of Congress Cataloging in Publication data
Stockmann, Daniela.
Media commercialization and authoritarian rule in China / Daniela Stockmann.
    p.   cm. – (Communication, society and politics)
Includes bibliographical references and index.
ISBN 978-1-107-01844-0 (hardback)
1. Government and the press – China.   2. Journalism – Political aspects – China.
3. Newspaper publishing – Economic aspects – China.   4. Press and politics – China.
5. Freedom of the press – China.   I. Title.
PN4748.C5S76   2012
302.230951–dc23   2012021708

ISBN 978-1-107-46962-4 Hardback

To my parents

"It takes an awful long time to not write a book."
Douglas Adams

Contents

List of Figures

List of Tables

Acknowledgments

My father escaped from East Germany in the fall of 1965. Without a single word to his family, he went "on vacation" to Hungary. He had made contact with a group of anarchists and had planned to cross the border to Austria. After spending hours squeezed into a hidden compartment of a VW station wagon he safely arrived in the West where his dream was to study medicine and play American Rock'n Roll music.

Had I grown up in East Germany, like my father, I probably wouldn't have shown much interest in Leninist political systems. But because I grew up in West Germany stories about my father's escape and life in East Germany triggered my curiosity about what it meant to live under authoritarianism. By way of many detours this eventually led to my interest in Chinese politics.

This book, then, is about the relationship between people living under authoritarian rule and the state. Its focus is on the Chinese media as an example of how political communication works under authoritarianism, particularly single-party states. As I discovered while doing research for this book, many other authoritarian states have followed a strategy similar to China's by introducing market forces into previously tightly controlled state media.

When I started this project I was convinced that the introduction of such market forces had diversified and liberalized the Chinese media. My initial plan was to examine how *commercial* liberalization of the media could contribute to *political* liberalization and possibly democratization; but the more data I gathered, the more evidence I found that the reverse was the case: while market forces brought about greater space for news reporting, this space turned out to the advantage of the regime, under the condition that institutions tighten the leash on the media when necessary. Overall, the balance between liberalization and control promoted regime stability rather than diluted it.

I do not claim that these conclusions are "objective." My goal in writing this book has been to examine the empirical facts in order to obtain answers to the questions raised by market liberalization of media in authoritarian regimes. However, my standard to evaluate the empirical evidence has been significantly shaped by my own training and personal experiences on three continents – North America, Asia, and Europe. On each of these continents I was fortunate to have an amazing number of colleagues and friends who listened to my ideas, raised interesting questions, and gave feedback on my work. Rather than listing all of them individually here, I prefer to thank them in person. Instead, I want to use this space to express my deepest gratitude to those whose guidance and feedback have laid the foundation for the approach laid out in this book.

One of the best decisions I ever made was to continue my studies of political science in the United States. At the University of Rochester I took my first course on Chinese politics with Melanie Manion. This was an eye-opening experience. Melanie encouraged me to dare to ask the big questions that allow us not only to better understand China and Chinese politics but also the broader political science discipline. I admire her courage and honesty and strive to meet the same high standards of quality in my research as she embraces in her own.

At the University of Michigan I have encountered an extraordinary scholarly community open to diverse ideas and approaches. Michigan has the reputation of focusing on quantitative methods, but I have experienced it as a place that encourages the choice of research methods depending on the question that is asked; the emphasis is on obtaining the right answer to an interesting question, not the method itself. Among the larger Michigan community my special thanks go to my dissertation committee members Ken Lieberthal, Mary Gallagher, Don Kinder, Mark Tessler, and Iain Johnston.

As my dissertation committee chair, Ken has guided me through the process of transforming an initial idea into a feasible research project of substantial interest to a broad range of people. His tough questions were the ones that should be asked before a dissertation is finished and have tremendously improved the overall argument of the book. I have always admired Ken for his ability to capture big trends in China as a whole without losing sight of its diversity.

In a similar way Mary encouraged me to see the bigger picture, not only inside China but also of China in comparison to other countries. Working with her helped me see state–society relations in a new light. I am particularly grateful for her offer to add questions to the Survey on Labor Law Mobilization (LLM) and her continuing support on all aspects of scholarly life well beyond graduation.

Don reminded me at a critical point that our purpose as scholars is not to seek evidence to support the conclusions we want to draw, but to instead let rules about research design and methodology guide our judgment of what constitutes trustworthy evidence. His comments inspired me to think creatively about solutions to problems associated with research design and about how political communication in authoritarian contexts differs from democratic ones.

Mark's feedback helped me to view this project in a broader context comparing China with other authoritarian states. What struck me in particular was how many issues were similar in China and the Middle East, while they ultimately led to different outcomes during the Arab Spring. Mark's friendly reminders to look into generalizability helped unravel how the specifics of regime type explained this puzzle.

Working with Iain on various projects has been an extremely pleasant and enriching experience. With Iain I share a fascination for the Chinese language and I learned much from his profound knowledge and insights on how language figures into public opinion and foreign politics. Without his offer to share questions on the Beijing Area Studies (BAS) survey this book would only tell part of the story.

In addition to my academic training in the United States, my experiences in China have significantly shaped the content of this book. From 1997 onwards I have made almost yearly trips to China. These many visits, during which I was affiliated with the School of Communication and Journalism at Peking University, have laid the groundwork for this book. For generous support during fieldwork in Beijing and Chongqing I am grateful to the Harvard-Yenching Institute and the Center for Chinese Studies at the University of Michigan. For sharing data or data reports I am grateful to Barbara Gedde, Jason Brownlee, Mark Frazier, Ku Lun-wei, Deborah Cai, Yu Guoming, Jonathan Hassid, Xiao Qiang, CTR Market Research, AC Nielsen, the HuiCong Media Research Center, and Kaiyuan (CPCR).

At Peking University I was fortunate enough to be taken under the wing of Chen Changfeng, who embraced me as one of her own students. As my *daoshi* she opened my eyes to the key approaches and academic discussions in communications in China. I am especially grateful to Changfeng for always taking me seriously despite my simplified explanations of this research in Chinese. Through her I also came across many new friends within the broader communication and journalism community, and my conversations with them have greatly refined my understanding of China. One of them, Zhang Jie, deserves separate mentioning here.

Over many years now Zhang Jie and I have been engaging in an ongoing discussion about research methodology developed abroad and its application to China. By asking me to present my work to her colleagues and students at Communication University of China, Zhang Jie shed light on different Chinese scholarly perspectives on my research, often perceiving the research methodology applied in this book as distinctively "Western." In contrast to some of these perspectives, I do not see the scientific methods applied in this book as incompatible with a Chinese view or as preventing researchers from understanding China. In my opinion, social science research methods are aimed at understanding attitudes and behavior of human beings. In this book I show that readers in China turn out to act just like audiences in other countries once we adjust the methodological tools to the specifics of the Chinese environment. That does not mean that there is not anything distinctively Chinese about China. Of course there is, just as any country is ultimately special and unique from all others. However, I do not believe that social science research methods prevent us from understanding these differences.

Three Chinese scholars whose works are exemplary of such an approach and served as an inspiration for this book are Shen Mingming, Tang Wenfang, and Shi Tianjian. I am thankful to Mingming for providing me with the opportunity to collaborate with the Research Center for Contemporary China, where I learned how to adjust concepts and measures developed abroad to the Chinese context in practice. As I started writing, I was glad to meet Wenfang and TJ. Their encouragement to pursue this research and explore new avenues for social science inquiry came at the time when it was most needed. I am deeply saddened that TJ passed away before he could see this book's publication. In his own work, TJ found the right balance between employing sophisticated social science methods while also stimulating substantive scholarly discussions among China scholars, Americanists, and comparativists alike. He was a true Confucian scholar and greatly revered among the Chinese scholarly community.

Back in Europe, I discovered that such successful communication between area specialists and the broader political science discipline requires reaching out to different scholarly communities. In most European countries, Chinese studies developed as a separate discipline, with university structures that foster separation rather than integration into the social sciences. When this research grew from a dissertation into a book at Leiden University, I profited tremendously from discussions with these two distinct communities, each of them providing space for scholarly development within an extraordinary collegial atmosphere.

With its stronghold in the study of political parties, my Leiden colleagues in political science inspired and helped form my ideas about the analytical framework as "Downs with Chinese characteristics." Conversations with my colleagues from Chinese studies made me more aware of the norms that guide the decisions of research in the social sciences and how they shape my understanding of China. While at Leiden University I have also had the help and assistance of a large number of suberb research assistants from Leiden, Communication University of China, Harvard, and Cornell University. I thank Wang Mingde, Li Zheng, Jin Xi, He Yewen, Zhang Yunqing, Song Yao, Cao Manwen, Ai Dan, Cai Jingyi, Zhou Moli, Cheng Yuan, Li Ang, Jin Yanchao, Sun Jia, Zhang Qian, Zhai Peng, Andrew Miller, Marat Markert, Andrew Wagner, Emily Zhang, and Roelof Lammers.

This book, then, grew out of my ongoing journey "commuting" between three continents. The people who had to endure the most during my constant travels are, of course, family and friends. Fortunately, I can say that it was my family's own "fault" that I took this road. My parents Connie and Claus taught me how to find my own path in life and triggered my curiosity for exploration. I am also grateful to my parents-in-law Erika and Gerhard Hoppe for being truly interested in my ideas and for having the life-changing idea to go to China. My deepest thanks goes to my husband Carsten for making me laugh every day since we started this journey together.

Berlin
July 2012

Abbreviations

BAS	Beijing Area Studies Survey
BBS	Bulletin Board System (chat forums)
CATA	Computer-Aided Text Analysis
CCP	Chinese Communist Party
GAPP	General Administration of Press and Publication
GPS	Random Sampling according to the Global Positioning System
ISDN	Integrated Services Digital Network
KMT (in Taiwan)	Kuomintang or Nationalist Party
LLCATA	Labor Law Computer-Aided Text Analysis
LLM	Survey of Labor Law Mobilization
MAELEZO	Information Services Department of Tanzania
MCT	Media Council of Tanzania
NATO	North Atlantic Treaty Organization
PD	Propaganda Department
PPS	Random Sampling according to Probability Proportional to Size
PRC	People's Republic of China
PRI (in Mexico)	Institutional Revolutionary Party
RCCC	Research Center for Contemporary China
RMB	Renminbi
SARS	Severe Acute Respiratory Syndrome
SMS	Short Message Service
SOE	State-Owned Enterprise
SPPA	State Press and Publication Administration (now General Administration of Press and Publication [GAPP])
USCATA	United States Computer-Aided Text Analysis
WTO	World Trade Organization

List of Chinese Newspapers and Other Media Sources

English	Pinyin	Chinese Characters
21st Century Economic Report	*21 Shiji Jingji Baodao*	21世纪经济报道
Beijing Daily	*Beijing Ribao*	北京日报
–	*Beijing Yule Xinbao*	北京娱乐信报
Beijing Evening News	*Beijing Wanbao*	北京晚报
Beijing Morning News	*Beijing Chenbao*	北京晨报
Beijing News	*XinJingbao*	新京报
–	*Beijing Shangbao*	北京商报
Beijing Times	*Jinghua Shibao*	京华时报
Beijing Youth Daily	*Beijing Qingnianbao*	北京青年报
Business Times	*Caijing Shibao*	财经时报
Business Watch Magazine	*Shangwu Zhoukan*	商务周刊
Caijing Magazine	*Caijing*	财经
Chengdu Business News	*Chengdu Shangbao*	成都商报
Chengdu Evening News	*Chengdu Wanbao*	成都晚报
China Daily	*Zhongguo Ribao*	中国日报
China Economic Times	*Zhongguo Jingji Shibao*	中国经济时报
China Newsweek	*Zhongguo Xinwen Zhoukan*	中国新闻周刊
China Radio International	*Zhongguo Guoji Guangbo Diantai*	中国国际广播电台
China Times	*Huaxia Shibao*	华夏时报
China Womens' News Daily	*Zhongguo Funübao*	中国妇女报
China Youth Daily	*Zhongguo Qingnianbao*	中国青年报
Chinese Business Paper	*Huashangbao*	华商报
Chongqing Business News	*Chongqing Shangbao*	重庆商报
Chongqing Daily	*Chongqing Ribao*	重庆日报
Chongqing Economic News	*Chongqing Jingjibao*	重庆经济报
Chongqing Evening News	*Chongqing Wanbao*	重庆晚报

(continued)

The list includes newspapers mentioned at least twice in the text.

(continued)

English	Pinyin	Chinese Characters
Chongqing Labor News	*Chongqing Gongrenbao*	重庆工人报
Chongqing Morning News	*Chongqing Chenbao*	重庆晨报
Chongqing Times	*Chongqing Shibao*	重庆时报
Chongqing Youth Daily	*Chongqing Qingnianbao*	重庆青年报
Economic Daily	*Jingji Ribao*	经济日报
Economic Observer	*Jingji Guanchabao*	经济观察报
Financial News	*Jinrong Shibao*	金融时报
Fujian Daily	*Fujian Ribao*	福建日报
Global Times	*Huanqiu Shibao*	环球时报
Guangming Daily	*Guangming Ribao*	光明日报
Guangzhou Daily	*Guangzhou Ribao*	广州日报
–	*Huaxi Dushibao*	华西都市报
–	*Jiankangbao*	健康报
–	*Laodong Wubao*	劳动午报
Legal Daily	*Fazhi Ribao*	法制日报
Legal Evening News	*Fazhi Wanbao*	法制晚报
Liberation Daily	*Jiefang Ribao*	解放日报
Lifestyle	*Jingpin Gouwu Zhinan*	精品购物指南
Nanfang Sports	*Nanfang Tiyu*	南方体育
New Women (Paper)	*Xin Nübao*	新女报
New World	*Xin Shijie*	新世界
People's Daily	*Renmin Ribao*	人民日报
People's Liberation Army Daily	*Jiefangjunbao*	解放军报
Reference News	*Cankao Xiaoxi*	参考消息
Science and Technology Daily	*Keji Ribao*	科技日报
Shanxi Evening News	*Shanxi Wanbao*	山西晚报
Soccer News	*Zuqiu*	足球
Southern Daily	*Nanfang Ribao*	南方日报
Southern Metropolis Daily	*Nanfang Dushibao*	南方都市报
Southern Weekend	*Nanfang Zhoumo*	南方周末
Tianjin Daily	*Tianjin Ribao*	天津日报
–	*Titan Zhoubao*	体坛周报
–	*Wenhui Bao*	文汇报
Workers' Daily	*Gongren Ribao*	工人日报
World News Journal	*Shijie Xinwenbao*	世界新闻报
Xinhua News Agency (Xinhua)	*Xinhua She*	新华社
Xinmin Evening News	*Xinmin Wanbao*	新民晚报
–	*Zhongguo Jingyingbao*	中国经营报

I

Propaganda for Sale

Have you ever had a newspaper stand yell at you? In the streets of Beijing, newspaper stands used to be heard first, and then seen. A monotonic voice from a tape recording shouted out names of newspapers to pedestrians – a form of advertisement that could be heard from far away. This innovative advertising form revealed one important element about the changing media environment in China: media outlets had to market themselves to audiences to finance news production. This type of advertising before the Olympics in 2008, and newspapers turned to visual advertising to stay competitive. Today, a typical Chinese newspaper stand carries at least twenty-five different newspapers and about as many magazines. Newspapers come in different colors, sizes, and styles. They try to attract potential consumers with slogans such as "We Make a Newspaper That Is Close to YOU!" or "The Paper That Talks Responsibly about Everything!"

In most liberal democracies, such advertising is taken for granted, but in China and most other authoritarian states, this transformation represents a radical break from the past. In the past thirty years, the Chinese state has marketized its news media. In doing so, China follows a general global trend toward economic media reform that has not been confined to democracies. This is significant because regime type and regulatory practices of the media industry have traditionally been regarded as linked. In many nondemocratic states, the media used to be state-owned and financed with state subsidies. However, since the late 1970s until the first decade of the 21st century, most authoritarian regimes have opened their media markets.[1] In East Asia, for example, Vietnam is following the lead of China, encouraging media organizations to

---

[1] By "authoritarian regime" or "authoritarian state," I refer to political systems that are neither characterized by free, fair, and competitive elections, nor politically liberal. In 2001, 71 of 192 countries in the world could clearly be classified as authoritarian, and 17 were ambiguous. Larry J. Diamond, "Elections without Democracy: Thinking About Hybrid Regimes," *Journal of Democracy* 13, no. 2 (2002): 21–35.

finance themselves through advertising. In Latin America, General Pinochet liberalized the financing of television before Chile's transition to democracy in 1988 (Tironi and Sunkel 2000). In North Africa and the Middle East, Morocco and Egypt have partially privatized former state radio and television stations (Amin 2002). The trend toward marketization of the media is evident in a substantial number of authoritarian regimes.

What are the effects of these trends on the continuation of authoritarian rule? Do marketized media outlets report more politically diverse messages? If not, how is the state able to synchronize media messages despite marketization? What are the effects of these changes in the media industry on the credibility of media under authoritarianism? Finally, what consequences do these dynamics have for the ability of the state to promote support for government policies? This book explores these questions with respect to Chinese media, placing China into a broader comparative context. The answers that emerge in this book explain why scholarship about the consequences of media marketization in China and other authoritarian states has come to two opposing conclusions: one emphasizing liberalization, and the other emphasizing control. Media marketization in authoritarian states contains both liberalization and control and leads to different outcomes, depending on whether the state can maintain the delicate balance between the two.

Media Marketization and Political Change

During his visit to China in 2009, President Obama gave the highly marketized *Southern Weekend (Nanfang Zhoumo)* an autograph, congratulating the paper "for contributing to the analysis and flow of vital political information. An educated citizenry is the key to an effective government, and a free press contributes to that well-informed citizenry."[2] Showing support even more directly, former Soviet President Mikhail Gorbachev bought shares of the Russian newspaper *Novaya Gazeta* in 2006 to help publicize "pluralism in opinions," subverting the uniform information flow under the Putin regime.[3] Marketized media are often portrayed as forces that contribute to a free press and possibly democracy in authoritarian states.

The idea that the mass media play an important role in regime change is not exactly a new one. Since the 1960s, political scientists have expressed the view that the media play a facilitating role in destabilizing authoritarian regimes and contribute to a sociocultural framework favorable to liberal democracy. Lerner (1964) argued that access to the mass media would encourage citizens to become politically active, thus promoting democratization. With the decline of modernization theory in the late 1960s, skepticism grew regarding

---

[2] China Digital Times (*Zhongguo Shuzi Shidai*), http://chinadigitaltimes.net/2009/11/propa ganda-department-bans-obama-interview/, accessed October 27, 2011.
[3] Gorbachev Foundation, http://www.gorby.ru/en/presscenter/publication/show_25172/, accessed November 6, 2011.

the argument that greater access to the media alone would have the power to bring about regime change (Mowlana 1985). However, when the opening of media markets provided citizens in authoritarian regimes with more information sources, the media reemerged as a factor in scholarship on regime transition in the 1990s. Television reporting was said to have a signaling and accelerating effect on public protests in Eastern Europe in the late 1980s, playing a part in the breakdown of the Soviet Union (Huntington 1996). Similarly, the Internet has been described as space for the development of civil society and as an alternative news agency that is able to subvert state control over the flow of information (see, for example, Howard 2010). Numerous studies of the role of the media during democratization argued that criticism voiced in independent media outlets erodes a regime's legitimacy (see, for example, Rawnsley and Rawnsley 1998; Lawson 2002; Olukotun 2002). Greater diversity of information is also said to transform political culture and foster the emergence of a public sphere (see, for example, Bennett 1998; Eickelman and Anderson 2003). The link between the media and political liberalization is also evident in works that use freedom of the press as one indicator for liberalization of a political system (Diamond 2002).

This discussion has concentrated on the potential liberalizing role of the media in nondemocracies, and arguments in favor of corporate and global media in authoritarian regimes are often inverse to conclusions drawn in a liberal democratic context, in which the same forces are often regarded as reducing the quality of democracy, as discussed by Graber (1990). Only recently have scholars studying media in authoritarian regimes devoted more attention to the possibility that corporate and global media might function as a reactionary force that strengthens authoritarian rule.

Along with increased interest in sustained authoritarianism or "authoritarian resilience," new research has led to a more profound understanding of variations within the authoritarian context and to the recognition that transition theory–driven analysis of authoritarian regimes may be misplaced (see, for example, Carothers 2002; Levitsky and Way 2002; Nathan 2003). Not all authoritarian regimes are in a (gradual or rapid) transition toward democracy. Many authoritarian regimes, including China and Russia, are ambitiously pursuing institutional and political changes that cement leaders' political power rather than dilute it. In both countries, the media have played a crucial role in this process of power consolidation.

Such arguments often return to past theories on authoritarianism and totalitarianism. The highly influential *Four Theories of the Press* (Siebert et al. 1956 [1973]) claimed that authoritarian states would use the media to stabilize the regime, whereas totalitarian regimes would also rely on the media to proactively transform society. More recent works that explore the role of media in sustained authoritarianism often tie the increasing corporate and global nature of the media to political and economic elites (White et al. 2005; Zhao 2008). These arguments often mirror critiques by Habermas (1962 [1990]) and others positing that marketization has transformed media into a place of cultural consumption manipulated by corporations and dominant elites.[4] This is a back-lash against the assumption that global and corporate media would have a lib-eralizing effect on authoritarian systems as states are no longer able to tightly control information flows at home.

This book adds to this discussion because it examines the *circumstances* under which marketization of media benefits authoritarian rule and the *mechanisms* that tie state, media, and audiences together. Media marketization provides incentives for media practitioners to overstep boundaries of news reporting, leading to tensions between media and the state. However, one-party regimes, such as China, are better able than other authoritarian states to maintain the capacity to enforce press restrictions with the help of institutions in charge of monitoring news content. Moreover, political leaders are able to take advantage of market mechanisms because doing so reduces the exercise of coercion through these institutions to a minimum. Because audience demands induce media practitioners to produce news favoring the political goals and policies of the leadership, there is less need to issue instructions. The interac-tion between institutions and the market synchronize political messages in the news in support of the regime.

At the same time, however, media marketization makes a big difference to the people living under authoritarian rule. Marketized media brand themselves as trustworthy representatives of ordinary citizens, leading to greater credibil-ity in the eyes of audiences. This credibility boost entailed in media marketi-zation promotes consumption and persuasiveness – especially among potential political activists. As a result, media marketization strengthens the ability of one-party regimes to disseminate information and shape public opinion in a way conducive to their rule.

In examining the mechanisms linking media marketization with the pro-duction of news and the credibility of media outlets, this book expands the discussion of sustained authoritarianism beyond the focus in current research on seemingly democratic institutions, such as elections, dominant parties, and legislatures (see, for example, Schedler 2002; Brownlee 2007; Gandhi 2008). In addition, stable one-party systems also achieve their dominance through manipulation and control over many other institutions that do not necessar-ily appear democratic, including the media. Recent studies on media under authoritarianism confirm that there is significant variation in the ability of authoritarian states to restrict press freedom and access to information (Egorov

---

[4] Often unnoticed by those citing Habermas' work on the public sphere, he argued that media marketization eroded the public sphere that developed between the 17th and the 19th centuries among the bourgeoisie in the United Kingdom, France, the United States, and Germany. Later, he differentiated between different ways of communicating that could either benefit or undermine democratic decision making. Commercial interests in the mass media are engaged in "strategic communication," primarily aimed at manipulating public opinion and thus unable to function as an instrument for the formation of political views among citizens in a democratic public sphere. Jürgen Habermas, *Theorie des Kommunikativen Handelns* (Frankfurt am Main: Suhrkamp, 1995 [2009]).

et al. 2009; Norris and Inglehart 2009). Much of this variation can be explained by the institutional design of the political system: one-party regimes, such as China, are better able to restrict information flows, using marketized media to their advantage.

This book also goes beyond the current emphasis on media independence and press freedom by focusing on the ways in which citizens interact with media when living under authoritarian rule. Increased interest in recent years in understanding the effects of media on public opinion under authoritarianism constitutes a great advancement over the assumption that people's opinions reflect the nature of media content in nondemocracies (Kern and Hainmueller 2009; Norris and Inglehart 2009). In part because of the difficulties in obtaining suitable survey data, these studies often measure media influence by means of media consumption, which constitutes only one of several factors that together produce attitude change (see, for example, Zaller 1992; Baum and Groeling 2009). This book takes into account that people not only need to be exposed to political messages but also need to encode and retain the information they receive from the mass media. Its core finding is that the commercialized look or branding of marketized media induces readers to perceive media sources as more credible. Drawing on insights from a large body of literature on public opinion and political communication, I demonstrate that variation in media credibility leads to different patterns of consumption and persuasiveness among Chinese audiences.

In addition, this book adds a dynamic element to the discussion: although the scholarly debate focuses on only two possible outcomes – regime stability or democratization – here I examine a case in which marketized media bring about political change without democratization. In China, the introduction of market mechanisms leads media to undergo cycles of liberalization and retrenchment, whereby the state walks a fine line between tolerating space to respond to market demands and controlling media content. In the long term, these dynamics appear to lead to greater openness of space in news reporting and cautious adjustments of central policy positions to popular demands. At the same time, they do not produce greater pluralism of political voices in media, as state media accommodate market demands while maintaining a roughly uniform information flow. This book uncovers these dynamics in state–society relations from the perspective of "responsive authoritarianism."

Finally, this book offers insight regarding when media marketization is likely to stabilize and destabilize authoritarian rule. Media does not necessarily have the power to bring about regime transition on its own, but can serve as a catalyst for the breakdown of the authoritarian state. By comparing China with other authoritarian regimes, I identify the conditions under which market mechanisms in media tend to promote regime stability. These conditions tend to be present in one-party regimes, including single-party states and electoral-authoritarian states that are ruled by one hegemonic party, and possibly even with certain circumstances ocurring in liberal democracies. In comparing China with other authoritarian regimes, this book specifies the political context under which market-based media promote political support.

Approach to State–Society Relations

In liberal democracies, scholars, journalists, and politicians often doubt that people living under authoritarian rule genuinely support the goals and policies of their political leaders. In most accounts of state–society relations in comparative politics, citizens are either coerced into complying with authoritarian rule or are "bought off" by economic means. In contrast, this book focuses on the ways in which authoritarian states use media to stabilize their rule, whereby media communicate information between citizens and political elites. Political communication takes place in both directions – from the top-down, but also from the bottom-up.

One of the core problems of authoritarian rulers is their difficulty in obtaining societal feedback about their policies because citizens are hesitant to voice their true opinions under dictatorship (Wintrobe 1998). Despite this difficulty, many authoritarian states have developed "input institutions" that allow them to respond to societal forces in ways that facilitate their continuing rule (Shi 1997; Nathan 2003). Electoral authoritarian states that were dominated by one hegemonic party, such as the Institutional Revolutionary Party (PRI) in Mexico, the United Malays National Organization (UMNO) in Malaysia, or the Kuomintang (KMT) in Taiwan, could rely on elections as an instrument for obtaining information about the party's mass support and its geographic distribution (Magaloni 2006). In China those kinds of input institutions include village elections, petitioning, public deliberative meetings (*ting zheng hui*), legal cases, protests, social organizations, the Internet, and, I argue, marketized media.

These input institutions open up social space, which creates tension between the provision of societal feedback and the threat of social disorder and authoritarian collapse. Thus they require the state to walk a fine line between allowing social space to emerge and keeping the resulting tensions under control. Weller (2008) and Reilly (2012) have described these dynamics as "responsive authoritarianism," emphasizing that societal forces can be beneficial to authoritarian rule as long as the state is able to sustain the delicate balance between tolerance and control. In other words, state and societal forces can mutually reinforce rather than undermine each other.

This book expands on the problem of tension between societal space and state control under responsive authoritarianism. Chinese media provide an excellent window into these dynamics because they serve a dual function: on the one hand, they are supposed to function as the party's "eyes and ears" by communicating information (feedback) from the "masses" to the party; on the other hand, they serve as a mouthpiece of the party that disseminates information about the political goals and policies of the government and as a propaganda instrument aimed at changing people's political beliefs. The findings in this book demonstrate that market mechanisms have improved the ability of Chinese newspapers to fulfill these seemingly contradictory functions.

Media marketization constitutes one solution to the dictator's dilemma in that it allows authoritarian rulers to obtain feedback about public opinion (i.e., opinions of a particular subset of citizens) while simultaneously enhancing the ability of the regime to guide public opinion in a direction that is beneficial to the rule of the Chinese Communist Party (CCP).

In exploring the dual functions of Chinese media, this book provides insight into a number of questions raised by responsive authoritarianism. One such question concerns mutual benefit of state and societal forces: if these relations are not zero-sum, when do Chinese media represent the state and when do they represent society? With respect to news reporting, I suggest distinguishing between issues and topics that are open or closed. When media face competing demands of propaganda authorities and audiences, they tend to reflect the position of the state, and when interests converge, they tend to be representative of both state and society.

A second question refers to the need to clarify the motivations of political elites for responsive authoritarianism. Although recent studies agree that, at least for the moment, the opening of space for societal actors works in favor of CCP rule, the intentions of the Chinese party-state in opening up space for societal actors remain unclear. Although the ability to receive feedback clearly constitutes an important factor, to a certain extent, the Chinese state has also been motivated to reform state media to support economic reforms and to address budget deficits. Media marketization constitutes a less expensive alternative to the distribution of rents that solve the dictator's dilemma, explored in detail in Chapter 2.

Finally, it is important to understand which societal voices are accounted for when giving feedback to political elites. In the case of marketized media, the most influential audiences can be found in cities with more strongly marketized media located on the east coast, but within those cities, marketized media turn out to be surprisingly inclusive and incorporate a broad range of social strata. Fortunately for the state, the same audiences to which media are most responsive are also the ones that tend to be most easily persuaded by political messages in the news.

At least for now, responsive authoritarianism helps the CCP to maintain its rule, but it also poses a risk for the survival of the regime. The Chinese leadership must maintain the delicate balance between opening space for societal engagement and protecting the party from its possible negative effects. Where the tipping point lies depends on the capacity of the Chinese leadership to balance these. As we will see, China's capacity to maintain the balance between state and societal forces is not specific to China, but reflects dynamics that can be observed in one-party regimes more broadly.

Defining Media Marketization

When authoritarian states decided to reform state media in the late 1970s, they decided to deregulate, commercialize, and (partially) privatize media outlets. These terms are frequently used interchangeably, but they refer to different aspects of media economic reform. I refer to these three developments together as *media marketization.*

Deregulation describes the process of diminishing intervention by the state in media organizations. It involves a shift of the role of the state from one planning communication to one that manages the parameters of an "open ecology of communication" (Mulgan 1991: 142). In the media, deregulation is visible in such areas as licensing, personnel appointment, management, and business operations. Deregulation is sometimes referred to as *decentralization* by China scholars, but here I use a different term to stress its link to a general global trend toward deregulation in media industries (Park and Curran 2000).

As the driving force behind marketization, *commercialization* produces a shift from being managed with the primary goal of serving the public (as defined by the state) toward being managed primarily for profit. As media shift from being fully funded by state subsidies toward being primarily funded by advertising, media outlets become more dependent on audiences because advertisers care about the size and characteristics of media audiences. Commercialization thus leads to greater responsiveness of media to audience demands because advertising constitutes the main source of profit for media.

Privatization is the process of transferring property from public ownership to private ownership. Privatization can be partial or complete. In China, for example, investment is allowed for up to 49 percent of capital, with the remainder belonging to the CCP. On the whole, Chinese media organizations are partially privatized.

Among these three processes, commercialization – also referred to in the title of this book – forms the "engine" behind media marketization. Although deregulation allows media to respond to market forces and partial privatization creates further pressure to make a profit through advertising, commercialization ties media to audiences with important consequences for state–society relations, as discussed in this book. As such, the impact of the marketization of media is distinct from that of communication technology, such as the Internet, and the terms should not be used interchangeably. There is, however, evidence that the institutional design of authoritarian states interacts with new communication technology in similar ways as market forces in media.

Not much detail is known about the pattern of media marketization in authoritarian states. There is some evidence, however, that authoritarian regimes have been most progressive with respect to deregulation and commercialization, but more hesitant to privatize state media. For example, Jordan and China both allow nonstate parties to hold shares of media outlets, but restrictions remain that allow the state to keep a majority of shares. Morocco and Egypt have been relatively progressive when it comes to private ownership.[5] The general pattern of media reform in authoritarian regimes is characterized

---

[5] In addition, there is a tendency among authoritarian states to constrain the influx of foreign investment and international information sources into the local media market. China's restrictions on foreign media organizations and efforts to censor the Internet are no exception. For

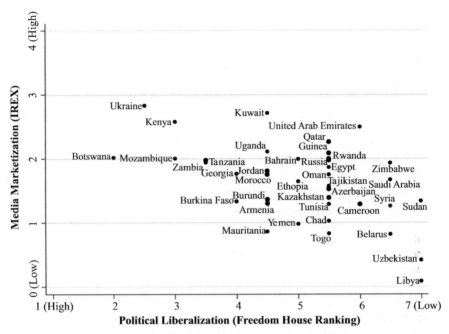

FIGURE 1.1. Scatterplot of Media Marketization and Political Liberalization. *Source:* Freedom House and IREX, 2005–2008.

by deregulation, commercialization, and partial privatization of local media markets, while at the same time keeping restrictions on press reporting.

Figure 1.1 illustrates the relationship between media marketization and political liberalization. The y-axis shows the degree to which local media in the Middle East, Africa, and the post-Soviet region are marketized, according to International Research and Exchanges Board (IREX) data; the x-axis displays political liberalization, according to the Freedom House rankings.[6] Countries that are the least and the most politically liberalized also tend to have less and more marketized media, respectively. However, most countries in the middle hold market influences in media fairly stable at medium levels.

The Chinese media system, not covered by IREX, constitutes an example of a state characterized by medium levels of media marketization, comparable to the United Arab Emirates (UAE), located in the upper right of Figure 1.1. In 2007, most media outlets in the UAE were able to finance themselves independently through advertising. However, the government held shares of

example, Iran has relied on technological solutions to restrict the influx of outside information through the Internet. Similarly, foreign media organizations self-censor news reporting in Singapore and Malaysia as they run the risk of being denied access to flourishing media markets. For a comparison across countries see Hans-Bredow-Institut. *Internationales Handbuch Medien (International Handbook Media)* (Baden-Baden: Nomos Verlagsgesellschaft, 2002).

[6] For details on IREX and Freedom House data and coding, see Appendix D. The IREX data display the most recent year available as of 2009.

private or owned profitable media, and the government maintained the ability to indirectly subsidize certain media. In comparison to China, Freedom House ranked the UAE slightly better in terms of its degree of political liberalization, ranking China as not free, with a score of 6.5. Therefore, China would be located to the right in Figure 1.1, above Saudi Arabia as a highly marketized but politically closed state.

In authoritarian states that have undergone media marketization, media have been affected by deregulation, commercialization, and privatization to varying degrees. As a result, news media types, which include newspapers, magazines, television, radio broadcasting, and the Internet, differ in terms of the extent to which they have been marketized. In Morocco, for example, more newspapers are privately owned than radio stations. Similarly, in China, private investment is more common in magazines than in newspapers.[7]

In addition to differences *between* media types, there is also variation *within* media types. According to a study by Ayish (2002), three models of television evolved in the Middle East, represented by, for example, the Syrian Satellite Channel; Abu Dhabi Satellite Television, based in the United Arab Emirates; and Al-Jazeera, based in Qatar. These television channels differed in terms of their level of marketization and were available to media audiences in many authoritarian regimes during the Arab Spring movements that began in late 2010, as commercial satellite television had become popular and transcended national boundaries.

The present study shows that similar developments can be observed in China. Citizens in urban China have access to newspapers that differ in terms of how strongly they have been affected by media marketization. The emergence of this pattern has transformed the nature of political communication between the state, media institutions, and citizens.

Analyzing the Effects of Media Marketization

This book examines the effects of newspaper marketization on the production of news and media credibility of Chinese newspapers. Research on these effects must address (1) the relationship between the Chinese state and journalists, and (2) the relationship between readers and newspapers. The book is divided into two empirical parts corresponding to these relationships.

In a first step, I examine the relationship between the state and media practitioners, which gives insight into the production of news. Based on in-depth interviews with senior editors, reporters, and propaganda officials, as well as content analysis, I explain how the interaction between market mechanisms

---

[7] In Morocco 78 percent of newspapers were owned by private companies in 2002. In comparison, only one of two national radio stations – the favorite medium of Moroccans – was private. Hans-Bredow-Institut. *Internationales Handbuch Medien (International Handbook Media)* (Baden-Baden: Nomos Verlagsgesellschaft, 2002). For more information regarding private investment in Chinese newspapers, see Chapter 3.

and institutions, most importantly the Propaganda Department, allows the Chinese state to synchronize news content and retain roughly uniform political messages in the news. My emphasis is on issues of concern to the central party-state. As we will see, the state selectively tolerates responsiveness to market demands, while also controlling this emerging social space by means of institutions. The emerging dynamics allow marketized media to function as input institutions.

To most scholars of Chinese media, the role of media as the eyes and ears of the party is limited to internal reports (*neican*) on stories that reporters are not allowed to publish.[8] These are confidential reports prepared for leaders of a corresponding rank that often contain material too sensitive for publication. My argument here is that the introduction of market mechanisms into newspapers has provided public officials with an additional tool for obtaining societal feedback.

Journalists have gained greater autonomy for news reporting to be able to respond to audience demands. Media practitioners tend to perceive more marketized newspapers as having more space for news reporting than less marketized papers, and these papers systematically differ in terms of the selection of topics and tone in news reporting. There is also evidence that journalistic space has increased over time. These findings are consistent with the view that marketization has brought about semi-independent media outlets (see, for example, Huang 2000), but they also differ from these accounts by stressing that the state allows this space to emerge primarily when the interests between state and society converge.

Because audiences do not always demand news stories that conform to the official line of the state, market mechanisms create tension between media practitioners and propaganda officials, and this tension manifests itself in the "glass walls" of Chinese journalism that are socialized by means of the political structure in which newspapers remain embedded. Like Cook (1998), I find that the unspoken rules that guide journalistic practice in media create structural biases in the news that favor public officials. Journalists feel that topics become more restricted as audience demands provide incentives to write stories that undermine the position of the central government. By selectively opening and closing space for news reporting depending on how demands by the state and market relate to each other, the Propaganda Department produces roughly uniform political messages while minimizing state control over newspapers. Because this space is dynamic and constantly negotiated, public officials learn about market demands from newspapers in the absence of directives or by comparing across newspaper types. Even though space for news reporting remains restricted, the positioning of nonofficial newspapers within this space provides them with cues about the nature of public opinion.

---

[8] Journalists are still encouraged to submit such reports on sensitive topics, but because of the secrecy of the Chinese bureaucracy, it remains unclear who reads those reports and how they figure into policy making.

Like Zhao Yuezhi (1998), I argue that the CCP places greater emphasis on public opinion guidance than on obtaining feedback, but my findings also indicate that the selective toleration of open space for news reporting contributes in important ways to the ability of newspapers to function as mouthpiece and propaganda instrument. This is so for two reasons:

First, there is simply no need to control news reporting if audience demands already provide incentives for journalists to report in line with official policies. News content can be roughly uniform while coercion exercised over newspapers is kept to a minimum, saving resources on the part of the state. In contrast to previous studies that focused on conglomeration and salary bonuses of media staff, this book stresses the role of audience demands as a key component of commercialization – the engine behind marketization that allows media to attract advertising (and investment) as alternative sources of funding, thus replacing state subsidies.

In addition, the creation of semi-independent space for news reporting significantly shapes the perception of newspapers in the eyes of readers. This book goes beyond previous studies on Chinese media that usually stop at analyzing news content. The second empirical part of the book lays out this active engagement of Chinese audiences, which Yu (2009) termed "media citizenship."

In the second step of the analysis, I examine the interaction between readers and newspapers. Based on a field experiment, a natural experiment, and survey data from urban China, I analyze how media marketization changes people's perceptions of media sources and in particular the credibility of media sources in the eyes of audiences. The newspaper types that are created during the process of media reform are associated with different levels of media credibility that have important consequences for consumption and persuasion of media audiences.

Official newspapers function as communication devices for official discourse and mouthpieces for disseminating the position of the government. Readers of official papers tend to work at party or state units or belong to social groups that have incentives for staying informed about the official discourse among elites. During big events of national or local importance, average citizens may also read these papers to learn about the position of the government. However, reading official papers does not necessarily imply that citizens find them credible. Readers of official papers are more resistant to political messages, especially when they are highly attentive to those issues.

By contrast, nonofficial newspapers are regarded as belonging to a social sphere disassociated from the state. In fact, these papers contain a lot of politically relevant information, but their perceived apolitical nature and closeness to society enhances their credibility in the eyes of ordinary people. Nonofficial papers are regarded as representatives of "ordinary people" and are believed to be more likely to publish a full, uncensored story. When people disagree with the dominant political message in the news, they turn to nonofficial papers because they expect those to diverge from the official line. However, because nonofficial papers usually follow the restrictions imposed by propaganda officials, these papers end up being more effective than official papers in changing people's opinions in favor of the official line demanded by the state. Readers of nonofficial papers are more susceptible to messages contained in the news than readers of official papers.

It is therefore precisely the perceived disassociation with the state that makes nonofficial newspapers more credible in the eyes of readers. Nonofficial papers gain a reputation for representing the public as opposed to the state by means of branding strategies, such as advertising, design, and columns that emphasize service to the reader, and news coverage of big media events despite state restrictions. This commercial look aids in creating the perception of media outlets as trustworthy representatives of ordinary citizens. Together, these two features increase credibility in the eyes of citizens, which aids the state in reaching citizens and guiding public opinion through marketized newspapers by boosting consumption and persuasion.

In part, nonofficial newspapers can function as effective propaganda instruments because of the lack of alternative sources of information. Many media scholars have argued that media access matters for media selection and media effects. My findings confirm that most people do not avoid using news media sources, even if media are controlled. For most citizens, getting some information is better than not being informed at all. Only those with very strong beliefs contradicting the position of the government tend to abstain from using news media sources. However, even among the most discontented citizens, complete avoidance of the news media is only temporary, because a shift in attention toward other issues in public discourse provides strong incentives to return to previous consumption habits.

Access, however, is only part of the story. Chinese citizens are not necessarily influenced by media outlets, even if they are highly dependent on media sources. Instead, their likelihood to resist or be convinced by media depends on the credibility of the source. This may explain why previous findings on the relationship between media exposure and political beliefs in China have been inconsistent, arguing that Chinese citizens either believe or disbelieve domestic media sources (Chen and Shi 2001; Kennedy 2009; Shi et al. 2011). After taking into account differences in terms of credibility across newspaper types, media effects are large and significant. With respect to the issues and cities examined here, media are found to have a stronger impact on political attitudes than a person's personal experience or national identity.

From the perspective of the state, the division of labor between official and nonofficial newspapers is a useful one because it allows the media to function as input institution, mouthpiece, and propaganda instrument. Figure 1.2. illustrates these relationships. Together, the combination of synchronization of news and the credibility boost contained in media marketization results in greater responsiveness and persuasiveness of news, here termed "propaganda for sale." Note that the Chinese term for propaganda (*xuanchuan*) is similar

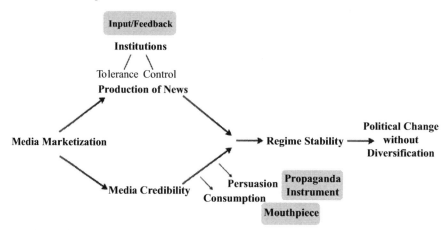

FIGURE 1.2. The Impact of Media Marketization on the Production of News and Media Credibility in China.

in meaning to the English term *persuasion* and does not carry a negative connotation for native Chinese speakers.[9]

Propaganda for sale strengthens the ability of media to communicate societal feedback to authoritarian leaders and disseminate information about the position of the government on political issues and aids in guiding public opinion in a direction favorable to CCP rule. By improving the ability of media to fulfill these functions, market mechanisms contribute to the stability of the regime. The most important condition for maintaining this system of responsive authoritarianism in Chinese newspapers is for the state to retain the capacity to walk the fine line between toleration and control of societal space such that the news product remains roughly uniform.

This book complements a large body of literature on authoritarian transition and revolutions that emphasizes the capacity of the state to prevent the collapse of the regime. Drawing on scholarship on the durability and formation of one-party regimes, I find that the CCP is not alone in its ability to use marketized media in its favor. A cross-country comparison of authoritarian states in the Middle East, Africa, and the post-Soviet region demonstrates that one-party regimes, more generally, have greater capacity to effectively use marketized media as an instrument for prolonging their rule. At the same time, marketization promotes media credibility across different forms of authoritarian rule. Therefore, the effects of media marketization depend on the regime type: in the absence of rule by one party, as is, for example, common in the Middle East, market-based media are likely to place pressures on the authoritarian state to prevent authoritarian collapse, whereas countries in which one party

---

[9] See Chapter 7 for details.

monopolizes power, including electoral-authoritarian states common, for example, in Sub-Saharan Africa, are better able to maintain stability.

It would be wrong, however, to conclude that successful use of the media as an instrument for regime stability implies absence of political change. Over time, the dynamics of responsive authoritarianism in Chinese newspapers appear to have led to cautious adjustments of the CCP's political positions as disseminated by newspapers. Information flows remain roughly uniform while also accommodating audience demands, thus bridging the gap between citizens and the state when their political positions diverge from one another. Market-based media may increase the responsiveness of authoritarian rulers while also preventing pluralism and disintegration.

These benefits of marketization for the Chinese state have been and continue to be discovered by pragmatic adaptation to changing circumstances. The Chinese state initially decided to reform the state media and undergo marketization as a result of budget deficits. Advertising was regarded as the only alternative to keep a very expensive media system running. Over time, the government has discovered that marketization of the media can work in its favor rather than undermining it. Through trial and error, the Chinese state has learned how to use market mechanisms to its advantage. Propaganda officials are not always aware of the causal mechanisms that hold this system together or how this system develops in the long run. However, they are very aware that the glue that holds this system together remains their ability to guide media to form a politically correct "main melody" (*zhu xuanlü*) in China's 1,938 newspapers, 9,884 periodicals, 227 radio stations, and 247 television stations.[10]

Comparing Evaluations of Labor Law and Sentiment toward the United States

In China's large and rapidly changing media market, it is not easy to address the relationship between the state, newspapers, and readers. The approach that I have taken here is to systematically study the preceding relationships within two issues relevant for a growing number of protests by workers and nationalists in recent years. Both of these issues include subtopics that are more and less sensitive in the eyes of journalists, but they differ regarding how novel the subject matter is to citizens. The first difference is important regarding the first empirical part of the book on the production of news, and the second is important regarding the second empirical part of the book on media credibility.

In the case of labor, the government aims to protect social groups that have not fared well during the reform era from abuse in the workplace with a labor law and an improved legal system that is intended to address worker grievances. In the 1990s, urban workers, particularly in the state sector

---

[10] Data relate to the end of 2010, retrieved from the General Administration of Press and Publication (GAPP) and the National Bureau of Statistics websites at www.gapp.gov.cn and www.stats.gov.cn, accessed November 10, 2011.

(state-owned enterprises, or SOEs), experienced delays in wages, pensions, and unemployment benefits, as well as sharp declines in health benefits (Lewis and Xue 2003; Giles et al. 2006). In addition, migrant workers are particularly vulnerable to abusive workplace practices because of their inferior status as holders of agricultural *hukou*, or residency permits, which do not entitle them to the same public goods as residents with urban *hukou* (Solinger 1999). In contrast to SOE workers, who feel entitled to better treatment as a result of their status in a socialist system, protests by migrant workers tend to be driven by exploitation and a feeling of being treated like second-class citizens (Lee 2007; Hurst 2009).

These grievances pose a serious challenge to the Chinese state because labor security and favorable treatment of workers used to be part of the unwritten social contract between workers and the state during the Mao years. To actively build a rule of law in China and mobilize workers to use the law as a weapon against abuse in the workplace, the government has launched a legal dissemination campaign in which labor law and the legal system are supposed to be presented as an effective weapon of the weak (see, for example, Exner 1995; Stockmann and Gallagher 2011).

In the case of nationalism, the CCP has been trying to address the decline of socialist ideology with a stronger emphasis on nationalism as the ideological basis for regime legitimacy, and negative sentiment toward foreign countries boosts nationalist credentials.[11] In the 1990s, Jiang Zemin promoted patriotic education as a means to foster popular identification with the party (S. Zhao 1998).[12] However, nationalism has become a double-edged sword for the Chinese leadership, as state-initiated nationalism developed a dynamic of its own. Popular nationalism has gone beyond the boundaries of the official discourse and contains criticism of the CCP and its foreign policy stance, thus posing pressures and constraints on Chinese foreign policy.[13] Nationalist outbursts have sporadically taken place throughout Chinese modern history, but they

[11] Social identity theory suggests that the construction of in-group identity generally leads to the construction of different and often devalued notions of out-group identity. See Henri Tajfel, *Social Identity and Intergroup Relations*, European Studies in Social Psychology (Cambridge: Cambridge University Press, 1982), and John C. Turner, *Rediscovering the Social Group: A Self-Categorization Theory* (Oxford: B. Blackwell, 1987).

[12] In the 1980s, campaigns against spiritual pollution and bourgeois liberalization also contained antiforeign and patriotic elements. However, Hughes (2006) has shown that the patriotism articulated by political elites during the 1980s did not encourage the involvement of Chinese publics as much as it did in the 1990s. See Christopher Hughes, *Chinese Nationalism in the Global Era* (New York: Routledge, 2006).

[13] For a discussion of these pressures and constraints, see Kenneth Lieberthal, "Domestic Forces and Sino-U.S. Relations," in *Living with China: U.S./China Relations in the Twenty-First Century*, ed. Ezra Vogel (New York: Norton and Company, 1997), Joseph Fewsmith and Stanley Rosen, "The Domestic Context of Chinese Foreign Policy," in *The Making of Chinese Foreign and Security Policy in the Era of Reform, 1978–2000*, ed. David M. Lampton (Stanford: Stanford University Press, 2001), James Reilly, *Strong State, Smart State: The Rise of Public Opinion in China's Japan Policy* (New York: Columbia University Press, 2012).

have escalated since 1996.[14] As a result, the central government has taken actions to "massage" antiforeign sentiment by means of media.

Contrary to popular belief, my interviews with media practitioners and examination of handbooks used in journalistic training by media outlets do *not* suggest that the government is proactively timing the production of negative images of the United States to prime attitudes among the population for discrete policy initiatives. Rather, the government attempts to shift public perceptions of the United States in a positive direction to cool off popular nationalism. Similar actions have been taken regarding the image of Japan in the Chinese press (Reilly 2012).

When massaging public perceptions of the United States and creating positive evaluations of labor law, the regime has relied on the media as an important tool for propaganda. In both cases, media practitioners describe the official line of the central government such that news stories should depict labor law and the United States in a positive (or less negative) light, although they are eager to point out that both issues are relatively open. Thus the central government aims to portray labor law as an effective weapon of the weak and to restrain negativity toward the United States, although this official line does not necessarily need to be actively enforced by propaganda authorities.

China's legal dissemination campaign has been initiated by the state, but there is also a genuine demand for legal information and negative news reporting among Chinese audiences that goes hand in hand with the goals of the central leadership. To most Chinese, labor law is a fairly unfamiliar concept that has been under revision since its introduction in the mid-1990s. Passed in 1995, the National Labor Law was the first comprehensive labor law in PRC history and built the foundation for later regulations. Ordinary citizens seek legal news to learn about the reformed dispute resolution process, to keep up with China's socioeconomic transformation, and because of its sensationalist and tragic content (Stockmann and Gallagher 2011). Therefore, with most news tied to labor law, demand for information among media audiences and the official line of the government for the media converge, and a new set of beliefs is created because of lack of previous information.

With respect to attitudes toward American politics, the relationship between the position of the government and audiences is more complicated. The Chinese public holds bifurcated views of the United States. On the one hand, the United States is admired for its level of development, its openness, its social

---

[14] For example, the May 4th movement in 1919 started with an anti-Japanese student demonstration against the Shandong resolution of the Versailles Peace Conference. Similarly, on December 9, 1935, students marched in the streets to urge the government to resist Japanese invasion. See Dingxin Zhao, *The Power of Tiananmen: State-Society Relations and the 1989 Beijing Student Movement* (Chicago: University of Chicago Press, 2001). However, since 1996, nationalist protests have become more regular; see James Reilly, "China's History Activism and Sino-Japanese Relations," *China: An International Journal* 4, no. 2 (2006), Jessica C. Weiss, "Powerful Patriots: Nationalism, Diplomacy and the Strategic Logic of Anti-Foreign Protest," *PhD diss.*, University of California, San Diego, 2008.

individualism, its opportunities for economic advancement, and the efficiency of its bureaucracies. Often the United States is the unspoken comparison against which China's backwardness is measured. On the other hand, many of the same people view the United States as hegemonic, aggressive, and arrogant in terms of foreign policy (M. Zhao 2001). Shambaugh (1991) therefore named the image of the United States in China as "Beautiful Imperialist." Bifurcated views are also reflected in a distinction that is made between Americans as people and the United States as a state, with the latter (or its leaders) rather than the former being the object of criticism. This is true for even less well-educated urban residents, who differentiate between people and state (Johnston and Stockmann 2007).

The Chinese leadership cultivates a positive relationship with the United States. With respect to many news reports on American business, culture, and society, propaganda officials do not have to intervene to promote an official line. They primarily impose constraints on news reporting related to the United States as a state rather than as a people, because the government often holds a more lenient stance on foreign policy toward the United States than the Chinese urban public. When taking steps to cool down popular nationalism, political leaders attempt to change deeply held beliefs genuinely held by Chinese citizens.

This approach toward restraining negative news reporting on the United States by the central government can change during crisis. When there is tension in Sino-US relations, the propaganda authorities may *tolerate* criticism of American foreign policy expressed in media, as happened, for example, during the anti-American protests in 1999 (Reilly 2012). Often, Chinese officials explain that public anger directed at foreign countries could easily turn against the regime if suppressed. In addition, the leadership may be divided about its own foreign policy stance (Reilly 2012) or aim to signal to foreign governments that its hands are tied domestically (Weiss 2008). Yet such an opening of space for criticism, if allowed, is only temporary to avoid further threats to social stability. Once protests have erupted, the government usually calls upon the Chinese public to calm down and let the government handle the crisis (Stockmann 2010a; Reilly 2012).

The government walks a fine line between tolerating expressions of negativity in times of crisis and simultaneously appeasing public anger to prevent future conflict in the long term by means of more positive (or less negative) news reporting on foreign countries that are closely tied to Chinese nationalism, such as the United States and Japan. Instead of creating a new set of beliefs on issues that ordinary citizens care about, here the official line of the government conflicts with less malleable beliefs of media audiences who are attracted by critical news reports about American politics.

Overall, the two issues examined in this book are highly relevant to the continuation of CCP rule. Variation in terms of sensitivity across topics within issue areas and differences in novelty across issue areas lead to a number of propositions regarding the production of news, media credibility, consumption, and persuasion, which are explored in detail in Chapter 2.

Data

The evidence presented in this book is based on diverse research methods, qualitative and quantitative, to capture variation in media marketization, the diversity of political news content, and media credibility, consumption, and persuasion. Here I only briefly summarize the data sources and the broader research design. More details are included in a methodological essay entitled "Notes on Data and Research Design" in Appendix A of this book.

While doing fieldwork, I have spent extensive time in Beijing and Chongqing, conducting in-depth interviews in Mandarin Chinese with forty-six editors, journalists, media researchers, and officials within the propaganda *xitong*.[15] My conversations took place between August 2004 and August 2005 and covered *Xinhua News Agency (Xinhuashe)*, *People's Daily (Renmin Ribao)*, *Workers' Daily (Gongren Ribao)*, *China Daily (Zhongguo Ribao)*, *Economic Daily (Jingji Ribao)*, *Global Times (Huanqiu Shibao)*, *Reference News (Cankao Xiaoxi)*, *World News Journal (Shijie Xinwenbao)*, *Beijing Youth Daily (Beijing Qingnianbao)*, *Legal Evening News (Fazhi Wanbao)*, *Beijing Times (Jinghua Shibao)*, *Beijing News (XinJingbao)*, *Chongqing Daily (Chongqing Ribao)*, *Chongqing Evening News (Chongqing Wanbao)*, *Chongqing Times (Chongqing Shibao)*, and *Chongqing Business News (Chongqing Shangbao)*, among many others.[16] These interviews were invaluable for developing a typology of newspapers and for learning about self-censorship in the Chinese media. I also complemented these interviews with journalistic handbooks used for training of reporters and updated my factual knowledge of media developments in a rapidly changing society during annual fieldwork trips. To ensure anonymity, I do not reveal names of interviewees, but I try to give as much background information as possible.

To further understand the relationship between the Chinese state and journalists, I systematically sampled and analyzed newspaper content that corresponded to the issues under investigation in this study. To improve reliability and comparability of newspaper content, I used Yoshikoder, which is, to my knowledge, the only content analysis software that can handle Chinese characters. Measurement of key concepts was developed based on extensive qualitative reading of newspaper articles. The resulting data sets cover more than 2,000 articles and are available at www.daniestockmann.net for further investigation.

To investigate the relationship between readers and newspapers, I rely on two randomly sampled public opinion surveys of high quality, both conducted by the Research Center for Contemporary China at Peking University. The Beijing Area Studies (BAS) survey was modeled after the Detroit Area Studies and strictly sampled according to probability proportional to size (PPS), a form

---

[15] *Xitongs* are groupings within the bureaucracy that together deal with a policy area.
[16] To facilitate reading for non-Chinese speakers, I use English titles of newspapers, when available. Pinyin is included on each paper's first mention in the text. A list of newspapers in English, Pinyin, and Chinese characters is included at the beginning of this book.

of stratified random sampling. The Survey of Labor Law Mobilization (LLM) employed the global positioning system (GPS) sampling technique and was one of the first surveys conducted in China that included migrant workers, a large social group normally excluded when sampling is conducted based on lists of registered households, as in the BAS. The LLM included four cities, Chongqing, Wuxi in Jiangsu, Shenyang in Liaoning, and Foshan in Guangdong province. Interviews were conducted face to face by trained interviewers and resulted in data that are representative of their sampling population.[17]

To draw causal inferences on media selection and media effects, I rely on an experimental research design. To separate the effect of the style of reporting from the newspaper's brandname (label) on the ability of newspapers to persuade readers, I conducted an experiment with ordinary citizens in Beijing relying on experimental vignettes. A *vignette* is a short story about a political event that differs only in terms of the treatment – in this case, the frame of a news article and a reference to a specific newspaper at the beginning of the text. Respondents were randomized, thus making the most likely causal source of the choice the attribute manipulated by the vignette. Results are consistent with the statistical findings, thus supporting an interpretation of correlations as media effects.

In addition, I rely on a quasi-experimental research design to examine media selection as well as media effects. A *quasi-experiment* draws an analogy between a situation in real life and an experiment. One potential weakness of the experimental method is that people are placed into an artificial situation that may not correspond to their real lives. The BAS survey data provided a unique opportunity to observe how people's attitudes and behavior change under natural circumstances. Unexpectedly, the anti-Japanese protests erupted about halfway through conducting the survey. After the first protest, the government attempted to appease angry citizens through the means of the mass media. This "treatment" allows us to observe how citizens react to changes in news content, both in terms of which media outlets they select and how they are influenced by mass media.

To further test generalizability of the key research findings, I also conducted a cross-regional comparison of twenty-four Chinese provinces, municipalities, and autonomous regions, as well as a cross-country comparison of thirty-eight authoritarian states at different levels of media marketization between 2001 and 2009. The results strengthen the conclusion that the relationship between media marketization, the production of news, and media credibility in China can be observed more broadly and is applicable to other one-party regimes.

Overview of Chapters

To give us a foundation for our inquiry, this book opens with the introduction in Chapter 1, followed by an explanation of the theoretical framework to

---

[17] The LLM response rate in the city of Chongqing was 73% (n=1,019); in Foshan, 72% (n=1,029); in Wuxi, 73% (n=1,029); and in Shenyang, 72% (n=1, 035). The BAS response rate was 56.1% (n=617).

examine responsive authoritarianism in Chinese newspapers and the political and institutional context in which Chinese newspapers operate.

Chapter 2 engages common understandings of state–society relations under authoritarianism based on coercion and exchange of economic benefits. It exposes the absence of public opinion in such understandings and addresses this shortcoming with an alternative approach. Media marketization provides one solution to the dictator's dilemma by decreasing the use of coercion and by providing societal feedback.

Chapter 3 lays out the pattern of marketization among newspapers and the institutional structure in which they remain embedded. In doing so, it lays out the circumstances under which the media industry has been deregulated, commercialized, and partially privatized. Within this broader institutional framework, there is room for variation. Chinese media practitioners distinguish between three types of newspapers, called official, semiofficial, and commercialized papers. Semiofficial and commercialized papers are often grouped as nonofficial; they tend to be more marketized and enjoy greater autonomy than official papers. The remaining chapters use this typology of newspapers to examine the impact of marketization of Chinese newspapers.

Chapters 4 through 6 form the first empirical part of the book, exploring the effect of media marketization on the production of news. Chapter 4 explains how the institutional mechanisms identified in Chapter 3 influence the production of news by creating informal rules for news reporting. When journalists perceive readership demands to conflict with the position of the government, news reporting becomes more sensitive between topics within issue areas. Chapter 5 examines how the interaction between institutions and the market translates into news reporting. An examination of how changes in rules enforced by institutions induce changes in news content corresponding to readership demands over time demonstrates that newspapers respond to readership demands when rules conveyed by means of institutions are lifted, but comply with state restrictions when criticized by political leaders. Systematic comparison between topics within issue areas exposes how strategic toleration and control of social space in media aids in synchronizing news content. The first empirical part ends with Chapter 6, which discusses the implications of these findings for discursive space in Chinese media more broadly. Although Chapters 4 and 5 are specific to labor law and the United States as well as Beijing and Chongqing, Chapter 6 explores how these findings apply to domestic and international news reporting, other regions, levels of government, crisis situations, and over time.

Chapters 7 through 10 form the second empirical part of the book, which focuses on the effects of media marketization on media credibility and its consequences. Chapter 7 explains which newspapers Chinese media practitioners and readers consider to be credible and why. By means of marketing strategies, nonofficial newspapers "brand" themselves as trustworthy information sources that represent ordinary people, whereas official newspapers have the reputation of representing and propagating the voice of the state. Together, these media labels boost credibility of nonofficial papers and undermine credibility of official papers.

Chapter 8 deals with the consequences of media credibility for the selection of newspapers. Based on a quasi-experimental research design, I provide further evidence for the higher credibility of nonofficial newspapers compared with official ones. Most of the time, readers seek nonofficial papers to obtain credible information. People read official papers only if they have an incentive to learn about the position of the government or when the costs of obtaining these papers are low. The newspaper types that are created during the process of media marketization allow official papers to function as mouthpieces, whereas nonofficial papers aid in guiding public opinion.

Chapter 9 examines the impact of marketization of newspapers on media influence. Readers tend to be more easily persuaded when reading nonofficial newspapers, and they tend to be more resistant when reading official newspapers. Because nonofficial papers usually follow the restrictions imposed by the Propaganda Department, nonofficial papers are actually more effective than official papers in changing people's opinions in favor of the official line demanded by the state. The effect of media credibility contained in media labels is the strongest when individuals are highly attentive to issues. At the same time, readers are more easily persuaded by newspapers with respect to labor law than regarding the United States because they are less familiar with the issue of labor law.

Similar to the first empirical part, the second empirical part ends with a chapter that places findings in Chapters 7 through 9 into a broader context. Chapter 10 discusses variation between regions, uncovering a credibility gap across Chinese media audiences, and discusses its implications for consumption and persuasion of newspapers in comparison with other media types. In doing so, this chapter develops a profile of the most active media citizens in China. In contrast to common accounts of Chinese media, I do *not* detect a bias toward an emerging middle class among media citizens, but I find that "issue publics," comprising those who are the most informed and aware about an issue, shape engagement with media outlets. The evolution of these issue publics is, however, biased toward issues of concern to people living in urban, more developed regions, and particularly "globalized" citizens located in Beijing, Shanghai, and Guangzhou.

Chapters 11 and 12 form the concluding chapters of the book, comparing China with other authoritarian regimes. If we want to understand when media marketization undermines regime stability, we need to pay attention to differences across authoritarian regimes and to which features and changes in political systems can influence the capacity of authoritarian rulers to effectively synchronize media messages. Chapter 11 focuses on the role of one-party rule in establishing this capacity, whereas Chapter 12 examines the role of exogenous shocks and skills of political elites to keep the balance between toleration and control at the core of responsive authoritarianism.

2

Instruments of Regime Stability and Change

How can some authoritarian regimes arrive at high levels of support for the government's goals and policies without openly enforcing their preferences on citizens? It seems obvious that propaganda may explain why citizens under authoritarian rule support their leadership, but this view is not widely accepted by researchers of authoritarian politics and democratization. This chapter explains why existing research has refrained from explaining regime support based on propaganda and lays out a theoretical framework for examining the relationship between media and public opinion under authoritarianism. I argue that marketized media provide one solution to the so-called dictator's dilemma by providing information about citizen views and increasing the credibility of media in the eyes of citizens. In doing so, marketization allows the media to function as both input and output institutions, although the ability to guide public opinion always remains more important to authoritarian leaders than obtaining societal feedback. When balancing the two, control remains more central than liberalization in maintaining stability.

Note that I use the term *citizen* here despite a continuing discussion among China scholars regarding whether the use of this term is appropriate in the Chinese context, as it is often associated with rights consciousness (Goldman and Perry 2002). I do not intend to solve this debate here. Instead, I prefer to refer to citizens to stress that media audiences play an active role in seeking, choosing, and screening media sources under authoritarianism. In doing so, my understanding of the term is based on the concept of "media citizenship," which is used as a synonym for active involvement in public discourse (Yu 2009).

Coercion, Public Opinion, and Regime Stability

A state is the apparatus used for exercise of public power (Way 2006). States "aim to transform population, space, and nature under their jurisdiction into the closed systems that offer no surprises and that can best be observed and controlled," Scott (1998: 82) reminds us, highlighting the coercive nature of the state. When aggregating facts, collecting documents, and creating statistics, state organizations impose structure on a more complex reality and gain control over social, economic, and political processes.

Yet the exercise of power by means of coercion and monitoring has its limits. The use of coercive power requires a large expenditure of resources to obtain modest and limited amounts of influence over others; it is costly and ineffective (Tyler 2006). However, if citizens accept or positively evaluate the government and its policies, the state can rely less on coercion and monitoring. The larger the proportion of the citizenry who defer to a government, the smaller the effort the state must expend to achieve its policies and programs (Hardin 2007).

A number of political attitudes are particularly beneficial to governance, including legitimacy, political trust, and regime support.[1] These political beliefs build loyalty among citizens and thus allow states to endure deteriorating circumstances that would otherwise lead people to look for political alternatives (see, for example, Weatherford 1984; Anderson et al. 2005). To speak in the words of Hirschman (1970: 81), loyalty to an organization is "at its most functional when it looks irrational, when loyalty means strong attachment to an organization that does not seem to warrant such attachment." Because loyalty helps political leaders maintain political and social order within a state, it is to the advantage of the state to rely on public relations strategies and persuasion to actively foster loyalty among citizens.

Yet once we want to take into account the role of media, it becomes difficult to link these general attitudes to the content covered by reporters. News stories usually deal with specific events and issues that rarely explicitly discuss the broader political system. To establish a relationship between public opinion and news content, we therefore must turn to specific issues. In China, the

---

[1] Most scholars employ a working definition that originates with Weber's notion that legitimacy becomes valid when its rationale resonates among the expectations of the subjects about how the government should claim its legitimacy such that the subjects are willing to obey its rule. This concept has been criticized for its tautological nature and lack of falsifiability. Therefore, many scholars prefer to examine regime support and political trust. According to Mishler et al. (2006), support for a regime exists if a political equilibrium has been established whereby both governors and governed accept a regime type as "the only game in town" among political alternatives. Political trust constitutes a basic evaluative orientation toward government, incorporating feelings of attachment or loyalty to the political system (diffuse support) on the one hand and specific evaluations of political leaders or policies (specific support) on the other hand. See Max Weber, *Wirtschaft Und Gesellschaft* (Tuebingen: Mohr, 1921 [1980]), David Easton, *A System Analysis of Political Life* (Chicago: University of Chicago Press, 1965), Adam Przeworski, *Democracy and the Market: Political and Economic Reforms in Eastern Europe and Latin America*, Studies in Rationality and Social Change (New York: Cambridge University Press, 1991), Susan Pharr and Robert Putnam, *Disaffected Democracies: What's Troubling the Trilateral Democracies* (Princeton: Princeton University Press, 2000), William Mishler, Richard Rose, and Neil Munro, *Russia Transformed* (New York: Cambridge University Press, 2006), Russell Hardin, "Compliance, Consent, and Legitimacy," in *The Oxford Handbook of Comparative Politics*, ed. Carles Boix and Susan Stokes (Oxford: Oxford University Press, 2007).

central government has developed concrete propaganda strategies to influence public opinion about certain issues with the explicit purpose to keep social order.

The CCP itself is clearly concerned about its ability to stay in power. The emphasis on "Harmonious Socialist Society" during the Hu-Wen administration constitutes an attempt to deal with the rising number of riots, protests, and petitions that have been fueled by growing inequality and discontent brought about by the economic reform process.[2] These protests tend to be localized and directed against local officials rather than the political system (see, for example, Blecher 2002; Lee 2007), but their enormous growth poses a serious challenge, if not a threat, to CCP rule. The CCP even openly acknowledged facing a legitimacy problem by opening up elite discourse about their nature and possible cures in 2005 (Gilley and Holbig 2009).

The issue areas covered in this book are linked to protests that the CCP itself regards as worrisome for the stability of the regime. To further explain this rationale, it is helpful to briefly consider how Chinese political leaders view the role of media within the broader political system.

According to Marxist–Leninist communication theory with Chinese characteristics, public opinion is channeled through the means of the media "from the masses to the masses," whereby Party officials refine the scattered and unsystematic ideas of ordinary people and then propagate concentrated and systematic ideas until the masses embrace them as their own and behave accordingly. In an endless spiral, policies are improved over time. The mass line, first introduced by Mao Zedong in his 1943 essay "Some Questions Concerning Methods of Leadership," still provides the basis for the role of media as a propaganda instrument within the Chinese political system that allows it to simultaneously function as input institution for societal feedback and mouthpiece of the CCP (Chen 2002; Chen 2003b).

After the Cultural Revolution, Deng Xiaoping reemphasized that such propaganda works need to be based on truth: "our propaganda needs to stop causing phenomena among the masses that don't suit reality" (Chen 2003b: 324). "If we [the state] as individual work units really manage to explain the problems the country faces clearly to the masses and thus win their empathy and understanding, we will also be able to overcome serious hardships" (Chen 2002: 55). According to an official slogan, journalism should be "close to reality, close to daily life, and close to the masses" (*tiejin shishi, tiejin shenghuo, tiejin qunzhong*).[3]

---

[2] Specific counts of these incidents differ, but show a rapidly rising trend. See, for example, Murray Scot Tanner, "China Rethinks Unrest," *The Washington Quarterly* 27, no. 3 (2004), Jianrong Yu, *Diceng Lichang (The Perspective of the Lower Class)* (Shanghai: Shanghai Sanlian Shudian, 2011).

[3] See, for example, "Guanyu Xinwen Caibian Renyuan Congye Guanli de Guiding (Shixing) (Regulation Regarding Managing News Media Staff)," General Administration of Press and Publication (GAPP), March 22, 2005. Available at http://www.zessp.org.cn/resources/ShowArticle .asp?ArticleID=1489, accessed January 28, 2012.

One means to reduce the gap between the Party and the people is a greater toleration for investigative journalism, referred to as public opinion supervision (*yulun jiandu*). Li Ruihuan, head of the Central Leading Group for Propaganda and Ideological Work in 1989, stressed that newspapers should include (limited) criticism, otherwise they would appear "boring, dull, listless and weak" (Chan 2007: 554).

Since the 1990s, the CCP has emphasized public opinion guidance (*yulun daoxiang*) aimed at matching public opinion with elite preferences through media. First introduced by Jiang Zemin in 1994, this concept places emphasis on preventing public opinion from becoming disadvantageous for "the Party and the people." That is, media should not publish content that conflicts with the "spirit of the Party center and contemporary policies." If news reports do not match propaganda, such "mistakes" need to be stopped from spreading further. Also, if public opinion differs from the spirit of the center, the Party should implement guidance to bring public opinion back on track (Chen 2002: 90).[4] Rather than arousing and suppressing public opinion, public opinion guidance relies on insights from marketing and public relations to shape public opinion (Chan 2007; Brady 2008). Greater conformity with the official position of the state on specific political issues does not necessarily lead to legitimation, political trust, or support for the regime as a whole, but it builds a broader foundation on which to govern and decreases potential for conflict between citizens and the state, thus stabilizing society and securing the rule of the CCP.

In addition to public opinion guidance aimed at the general population more broadly, Chinese leaders have also developed propaganda strategies aimed more specifically at potential protesters, assuming that a change in people's beliefs will directly translate into political behavior. For example, a central-level official in the Propaganda *xitong* explained to me: "If something goes wrong Chinese emphasize education: first you need to change thought (*sixiang*), then you resolve the problem."[5] An important "cure" for the rising number of protests is to manipulate the beliefs of potential protesters. Many propaganda activities are aimed at "weak groups in society" (*ruoshi qunti*), such as, unemployed and migrant workers or young people, often referred to as strongly nationalistic "angry youth" (*fenqing*).[6]

---

[4] Regarding communism in Eastern Europe, Ekiert (1988) pointed out that declared policy goals were extremely vague and varied among the elite itself. Chapter 6 explores factionalism, as well as the mechanisms that establish norms among media practitioners. See Grzegorz Ekiert, "Conditions of Political Obedience and Stability in State-Socialist Societies: The Inapplicability of Weber's Concept of Legitimacy," *Working Paper Series, Center for Research on Politics and Social Organization* (Cambridge, MA: Harvard University, Department of Sociology, 1988).

[5] Interview in Beijing (#30). See also Chapter 4.

[6] On references regarding the CCP's emphasis on weak groups and young people, see, for example, "Hu Jintao Zai Ershi Guo Jituan Lingdaoren Di Liu Ci Fenghui Zuo Zhuanti Fayan (Hu Jintao's Theme Speech at the 6th Meeting of the G-20 Leaders)," Xinhua Net, November 4, 2011. Available at http://news.xinhuanet.com/politics/2011-11/04/c_111146786.htm, accessed December 23, 2011.

Social science research has disputed that political attitudes are the main cause driving political action, emphasizing other factors, such as socioeconomic status or political mobilization. More recently, however, there has been a revival of the argument that political attitudes motivate political behavior. When citizens clearly think and care deeply about an issue, they form real attitudes that energize a broad range of political action, including working in a political campaign, persuading others to vote, or joining an organization (Burns and Kinder 2005). Borrowing from Abelson (1988), Kinder (2006) refers to those strong attitudes as "conviction"; Fiorina (2002) observed that people feel intensely about those attitudes that motivate them to act and that intensity is associated with extreme political beliefs.

People who hold these strong attitudes belong to what Converse (1964) called "issue publics." An issue public is composed of those who are highly informed and aware of an issue. This group of people is *not* equivalent to the highly educated; citizens can overcome lack of education by acquiring knowledge about an issue they care about (Converse 1964). People who belong to issue publics are more likely to possess stable attitudes held with conviction, to express opinions, and to take part in politics (Kinder 2006).

For simplicity, the CCP prefers to think about potential protesters in terms of sociodemographic categories, but here I distinguish between people who are more attentive and knowledgeable toward an issue and thus likely to belong to issue publics. Media contribute to regime stability by changing attitudes among issue publics in a direction that is favorable for the CCP, thus guiding public opinion and appeasing potential protesters.

There is, of course, an ongoing discussion regarding whether we should use the term *public opinion* to refer to attitudes expressed by people living under authoritarianism, which in itself could fill an entire book. Here, I use Converse's (1987) definition of public opinion as the aggregate of individual attitudes within a particular social group whereby each individual's attitude is weighted equally. Such a definition does not assume that these individuals are living in a democracy, have access to a public sphere, or have influence on politics. I explicitly do not use the term *political culture* because this term refers to enduring values and beliefs about politics that are less malleable than some of the political attitudes studied in this book. Instead, I examine political attitudes that the CCP itself considers to be important to maintaining its rule, arguing that public opinion plays an important role in state–society relations under authoritarianism.

The Absence of Public Opinion in State–Society Relations under Authoritarianism

The classic view of state–society relations under authoritarianism emphasizes that authoritarian rulers stay in power by means of repression, whereas democracies reduce repression by means of liberal democratic institutions (Friedrich and Brzezinski 1956). Indeed, it is a well-established fact that nondemocracies tend to spend more on the military, to rely more on imprisonment and the death penalty, and to restrict press freedom and other civil liberties (see, for example, Mulligan et al. 2004; Norris 2006; Egorov et al. 2009). There is, however, a great deal of variation among nondemocracies in how much coercion authoritarian leaders use to maintain their rule. For example, the Soviet Union is often cited as an example of a highly repressive regime, whereas the Russian Federation established afterward is considered to rely less on coercion to maintain its rule (see, for example, Mishler et al. 2006). The most common explanation for this variation among authoritarian states relies on exchange of economic benefits in return for political support.

Authoritarian rulers overpay supporters among political elites and/or the larger populace. Dictators "buy" the loyalty of a group when they give those who belong to that group more than they can expect to obtain under a different regime. One way to obtain loyalty among supporters is to distribute economic resources in the form of private or public goods, thus binding rulers and supporters to each other (Stokes 2005; Hicken 2006; Grzymala-Busse 2007).[7] Another way is to lower tax rates (Ross 2001; Bueno de Mesquita et al. 2003) or to distribute wealth more equally among society. In places where income distribution is more equal, such as Singapore, citizens may have less demand for democracy because there is less need for credible institutions to redistribute wealth among citizens (Acemoglu and Robinson 2006).[8]

According to this understanding of state–society relations under authoritarianism, compliance with the policies and goals of authoritarian rulers is explained by a combination of repression and economic factors. Wintrobe's (1998) model of dictatorship sums up this view by stating that there are people who are strongly repressed under a dictatorship and those who are highly overpaid. In between, there are people who are somewhat repressed and somewhat overpaid, and the stability of the regime depends on whether they side with either the repressed or the overpaid group.[9] This view assumes that people

---

[7] Public goods provision under dictatorship has also been rationalized based on self-interest of political leaders. See Mancur Olson, "Dictatorship, Democracy, and Development," *American Political Science Review* 87, no. 3 (1993).

[8] The empirical evidence on the relationship between economic inequality and democratization is contradictory: Przeworski did not detect any relationship or find that inequality destabilizes dictatorships and democracies, depending on the measure for economic inequality; Boix reports results in which economic inequality reduces the likelihood for democracy; Acemoglu and Robinson argue that countries are most unstable at medium levels of income inequality. See Adam Przeworski, *Democracy and Development: Political Institutions and Material Well-Being in the World, 1950–1990*, Cambridge Studies in the Theory of Democracy (Cambridge: Cambridge University Press, 2000), Carles Boix, *Democracy and Redistribution* (New York: Cambridge University Press, 2003), Daron Acemoglu and James A. Robinson, *Economic Origins of Dictatorship and Democracy* (New York: Cambridge University Press, 2006).

[9] Other formal models of dictatorship rely on a similar categorization of societal divisions. See Barry R. Weingast, "The Political Foundations of Democracy and the Rule of Law," *American Political Science Review* 91, no. 2 (1997), Bruce Bueno de Mesquita et al., *The Logic of Political Survival* (Cambridge: The MIT Press, 2003).

living under authoritarian rule would prefer to live under a different political system (i.e., democracy), but decide to comply with authoritarian rule either out of political fear or economic interests. Citizens' true beliefs about the policies and goals of authoritarian leaders, as well as their views of the political system more broadly, rarely figure into accounts of authoritarian politics or theories of regime change.

This understanding of state–society relations sharply contrasts with more in-depth studies by area specialists that highlight the importance of public opinion as one important source of regime stability (see, for example, Mishler et al. 2006). In new democracies, the population also often continues to support different types of authoritarian regimes (Rose et al. 1998; Chang et al. 2007). Although numerous empirical studies have demonstrated the importance of support for democracy and liberal-democratic values for the consolidation of democracy after the breakdown of authoritarianism, it is often assumed that public opinion emerges as an important factor only after the breakdown of authoritarian rule. The role of public opinion in authoritarian politics is often dismissed, citing the dictator's dilemma.

The Dictator's Dilemma

The dictator's dilemma as formulated by Wintrobe (1998) refers to the problem of knowing how much support an authoritarian leader has among the general population, as well as among elites. The use of repression breeds fear on the part of people living under authoritarian rule, and this fear breeds reluctance on the part of the citizenry to state their true opinions when they are dissatisfied with policies. Because the dictator cannot rely on the information provided by subordinates, he suspects that people are opposing his rule and are planning his overthrow, leading to even greater repression, thus magnifying the problem. The main solution to this problem is the distribution of economic benefits to supporters because such overpayment allows him to reduce coercion while also securing compliance among subordinates out of economic interests.

Explicitly or implicitly relying on the logic of this dilemma, it is often assumed that people living under authoritarianism do not state their true opinions in public (see, for example, Kuran 1991). There is, of course, evidence that people living under such a regime exaggerate their support for the regime while keeping their true opinions to themselves. For example, Havel (1978) described life under communism in East Central Europe as living within a lie, and Scott (1985) observed that Malaysians resorted to hidden transcripts to resist domination rather than openly expressing discontent. Clearly people do not always report their true opinions on politically sensitive questions, but does this mean that we can disregard categorically the opinions of citizens living under authoritarian rule, as the dictator's dilemma would suggest?

Later in this chapter, I comment on the role of political sensitivity in creating potential bias for the empirical findings presented here, but before discussing specifics of the research design, I first lay out a theoretical framework for studying media and public opinion in China. I propose that the predominant view of state–society relations under authoritarianism as a function of coercion and exchange of economic benefits may have been applicable in the past, but does not conform to recent trends in media systems. Marketized media provide another solution to the dictator's dilemma, in addition to the distribution of economic benefits to supporters.[10] Today, many nondemocratic leaders can rely on marketized media as a means for obtaining immediate feedback about the policy performance of the government, and market mechanisms can aid the state in achieving compliance among journalists while reducing the need to rely on repression. Media marketization has changed the dynamics of state–society relations, benefiting authoritarian rule under some circumstances and undermining it in others.

Marketized Media as a Solution to the Dictator's Dilemma

The media system that the CCP built in the 1950s resembled in many ways the traditional model of state–society relations under authoritarianism discussed previously. As explained in detail in Chapter 3, it was characterized by a system of institutional and financial control mechanisms that influenced the organization, personnel, and editorial process inspired by the Soviet Union. These measures were aimed at *political control*, here defined as the way in which officials in the party or state administrative organs influence the selection, framing, or wording of news stories. Because of a strong reliance on institutions, observers have often emphasized the coercive nature of media systems in Leninist states. For example, in 1947 the Hutchings Commission's *Four Theories of the Press* described the Soviet media system as a totalitarian media system characterized by "state owned and closely controlled media existing solely as arm of the state" (Siebert et al. 1956 [1973]: 6).[11]

However, it was highly expensive to fund an administrative bureaucracy in charge of organizing and monitoring media, especially because news production and salaries of media personnel also needed to be subsidized. As described in detail in Chapter 3, this system had become unsustainable in the early years of economic reform, and the Chinese state introduced media marketization. Although the basic institutional framework through which the Party exercised political control under a socialist planned economy still remains in place today, the marketization of the media has resulted in an increase in the autonomy of newspapers and greater space for news reporting. This greater media

---

[10] Another solution to the dictator's dilemma is elections in hegemonic-party systems, as they provide information about supporters and opponents of the regime. See Beatriz Magaloni, *Voting for Autocracy: Hegemonic Party Survival and Its Demise in Mexico* (New York: Cambridge University Press, 2006).

[11] Many have criticized *The Four Theories of the Press* for being too simplistic, for not conforming to reality, and for its normative bias. Herbert I. Schiller, *Mass Communications and American Empire* (New York: A. M. Kelley, 1969), Yuezhi Zhao, *Media, Market, and Democracy in China: Between the Party Line and the Bottom Line* (Urbana: University of Illinois Press, 1998), Myung-Jin Park and James Curran, *De-Westernizing Media Studies* (London: Routledge, 2000).

independence and freedom becomes visible when comparing across newspaper types and across open and closed topics.[12]

Media marketization has brought about different types of newspapers that differ in terms of how strongly they are marketized. Chinese media practitioners and citizens distinguish between three types of newspapers, referred to as *official, semiofficial,* and *commercialized* papers. Commercialized papers are at the front line of marketization, whereas official papers lag the farthest behind. Semiofficial papers lie somewhere in between these two extremes. Semiofficial and commercialized are also grouped as *nonofficial papers.* Because of their differing degree of marketization, official papers are the most tightly controlled by the state, followed by semiofficial papers; commercialized papers are the most autonomous within the broader boundaries for news reporting set by the Chinese state. As explained in Chapter 3, individual papers do not always fit neatly into these categories, but media practitioners make sense of a complicated media environment by distinguishing between different types.

When marketizing media, the Chinese state had to give media outlets space to compete with one another for the attention of audiences. Wu (1994), a former journalist at the *People's Daily,* has described this opening of space as moving away from "pouring" to a "birdcage" and finally to "kite flying." The pouring pattern described the top-down flow of information whereby the Propaganda Department (PD) and political leaders pour water (ideas) into a cup (the journalist's brain). The birdcage pattern described the ability of the journalists to select from speeches, directives, and documents of the leadership as birds flying in a cage. When journalists select topics themselves, they can fly in the sky with just a string in the hands of the Party.

To hold the strings on the kite of journalists, Chinese propaganda authorities have tried to restrict competition among media outlets on more politically sensitive topics, while allowing competition on less politically sensitive topics. Individual news stories line up on a dimension of political sensitivity associated with certain norms in journalistic behavior that determine whether reporters can cover a story and self-censorship in the case of coverage. I refer to stories that can be covered, but need to be self-censored, as *closed topics,* whereas I refer to stories that can be covered without any restrictions as *open topics.*[13] Officially, nonofficial papers are supposed to cover open topics and official papers closed topics, but in practice, papers do not always stick to this division of labor, as shown in Chapter 5.

This distinction between open and closed topics, official and nonofficial newspapers, is important because it allows us to understand how the interaction between state and market forces leads to compliance of journalists with an

---

[12] Due to the lack of time-series data, I focus on a comparison of newspaper types and issues at around 2005. Chapter 3 explains how newspaper types correspond to different stages in media reform, supporting the conclusions that the relationship between reporters and audiences across types may also reflect changes in this relationship over time.

[13] *Taboo topics* and their role in the production of news are discussed in detail in Chapters 4 and 5.

"official line" defined by the state. As we will see, media marketization may lead to greater autonomy of media outlets and even greater media freedom, but this liberalization does not necessarily lead to diversification of political messages in the news.

State and Market Forces in the Production of News

To understand how state and societal forces interact with each other in the production of news, I took instructions from the literature on political parties.[14] Made famous by Downs (1957), spatial theory of party and voter behavior assumes that parties will choose policy positions on a left–right continuum that minimize the distance between themselves and voters. Parties competing for votes can either move toward or away from each other. By increasing policy distance, they encourage voters to vote for the competing party; by accommodating the competitor, they attract voters (see, for example, Shepsle 1991; Kitschelt 1995). Which of these two strategies a party adopts depends on the number of parties and issue areas (see, for example, Meguid 2005).

In studies of media markets, the spatial dimension does not necessarily have to be the left–right continuum, but can also span between soft and hard news content (Hamilton 2004).[15] In the context of news production in China, newspapers align themselves in relation to an official line defined by the state, which demands a positive spin on a news story, whereas audiences often prefer "negative news" – an expression of critical news reporting. Of course, there are more nuances to differences between what journalists refer to as propaganda and "real news," many of which are discussed in Chapters 4 and 5, but at the most fundamental level, this continuum spans between positive and negative news reporting. Later in this chapter, I explain in detail the positions of the state and audiences on each of the issues explored here. For now, we explore the theoretical relationships and mechanisms influencing the production of news.

Let us first investigate where official and nonofficial newspapers will position themselves when demands between state and audiences converge. In such a situation, there is no need to issue restrictions for news reporting and to control media content because market demands already pull content in a desired direction. The state does not need to rely on coercive measures to control media content because media practitioners already produce roughly uniform messages in the news, assuming a position that is to the advantage of political leaders. In the absence of tension between demands by the state and audiences, there

---

[14] My goal here is to flesh out the rationale for systematic differences in news reporting across newspaper types, *not* to develop a testable formal model.

[15] There is no commonly accepted definition of "hard news" and "soft news." Features of soft news common in definitions include a more personal and colloquial language as opposed to a more institutional and distant one, as well as a set of story characteristics, including sensationalism and the absence of a public policy component. See Matthew A. Baum, "Sex, Lies, and War: How Soft News Brings Foreign Policy to the Inattentive Public," *American Political Science Review* 96, no. 1 (2002).

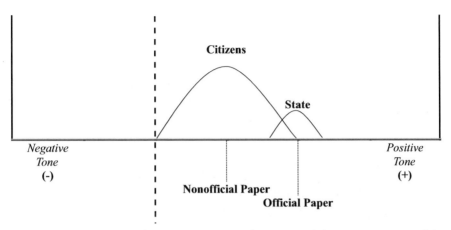

FIGURE 2.1. Positioning of Newspaper Types When Demands between Citizens and the State Converge.

is little need for the state to issue instructions for news reporting to reporters, which leads reporters to consider such topics as "open."

Figure 2.1 illustrates this first situation, whereby audience and state demands converge with one another. The horizontal scale represents tone of news reporting, ranging between negative and positive tone; the vertical scale displays the number of ordinary citizens and public officials, each of them normally distributed with means relatively close to each other. I refer to *media citizens* here, which includes only a subset of the population, and the term *state* to highlight that public officials may adopt a political standpoint in their role as representatives of the state that can differ from their preference as media citizens. To facilitate explanation, Figures 2.1 and 2.2 display a single-peaked, normally distributed shape of citizen and state preferences.[16] The curved line to the left indicates how much space the state would be willing to grant to media outlets.

Let us assume that there are only two newspapers, an official paper that is more tightly controlled by the state and a nonofficial paper that is more autonomous from the state. If both papers were marketized to similar degrees, they would locate themselves at the position preferred by the median citizen, as predicted by the median voter theorem. In this case, marketized papers can maximize their audience, whose size and characteristics matter for advertisers and investors. However, because they are not equally dependent on audience demands, the nonofficial paper will attempt to capture the median citizen, whereas the official paper will position itself at the median preference of the state.

In Figure 2.1, space for news reporting would theoretically be restricted, but these restrictions never need to be enforced because nonofficial newspapers will

---

[16] For a review on how changes in the underlying distribution of audience preferences may affect the positioning of parties (or papers), see Lawrence Ezrow, "The Variance Matters: How Party Systems Represent the Preferences of Voters," *Journal of Politics* 69, no. 1 (2007).

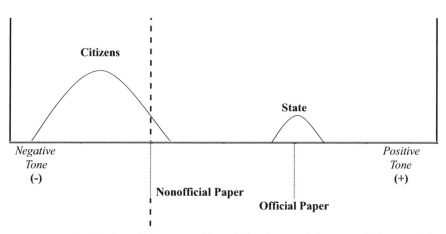

FIGURE 2.2. Positioning of Newspaper Types When Demands between Citizens and the State Diverge.

position themselves close to the median citizen within the boundaries for news reporting. Nonofficial papers will produce stories that conform to the official line by following market demands. Because journalists never experience the "glass walls" of news reporting, they feel generally free to report the news without interference by the state.

These dynamics fundamentally change once reporters feel pressure from audiences to cover the news more negatively than space for news reporting allows. Figure 2.2 illustrates this second situation, whereby the median citizen lies now outside of the boundaries for news reporting. Ideally, nonofficial newspapers would place themselves at the position preferred by the median citizen, but because they are held back by propaganda authorities, they align themselves as close as possible within the space deemed acceptable to the state. The state restricts how distant newspapers can locate themselves away from the position of the state, but within these boundaries, there is variation in news reporting. As long as nonofficial papers are kept on a relatively short leash, the state can achieve roughly uniform messages in the news, whereas there is still some but limited variation in positive and negative reporting between official and nonofficial papers. Because journalists now experience boundaries for news reporting, they feel constraint by the state, considering the topic as closed.

Note that this theoretical framework is based on a number of assumptions, and each of these assumptions is carefully examined in the empirical chapters. A first assumption is that nonofficial newspapers tend to be more responsive to audience demands than official papers. Of course, audience demands are not the only factor that figure into the production of news in China, but perceived audience demands constitute the most important factor besides demands by the state (see Chapter 3). The degree of marketization among papers also roughly corresponds to their degree of autonomy from the state (see Chapter 3), and Chinese journalists usually follow demands of audiences when space for news is unrestricted, whereas they tend to comply to the rules when space for news reporting is restricted (see Chapters 4 and 5). With respect to the issues examined here, journalists also seem to have a fairly accurate assessment of the kind of news stories readers actually would like to read (Chapters 4 and 5), and readers prefer to read papers that are more likely to conform to their own political beliefs (see Chapter 8). Similarly, power is never absolute, and Chinese reporters employ creative means to constantly push the boundaries set by the state, but instructions tend to be enforced rather than broken (see Chapters 5 and 6). Stories about nonofficial papers going against the official line become big events precisely because they constitute exceptions rather than the norm (see Chapters 6 and 7).[17]

How do journalists learn about the restrictions set by the propaganda authorities? I employ an organizational approach to understanding journalistic practices. Timothy Cook (1998: 84) regarded media as institutions defined as "taken-for-granted social patterns of behavior," which extend over space and endure over time. He argued that the unspoken procedures, routines, and assumptions that guide journalistic practice in the American media create structural biases in the news in favor of powerful officials.[18] Similarly, Chinese journalists have conceptions about whether and how they *should* or *should not* cover news stories, whereby they distinguish between open and closed topics. Self-censorship depends strongly on a feeling of political sensitivity, which is socialized over time. The institutional structure in which Chinese newspapers are integrated builds rules for which topics are more and less politically sensitive, open and closed. Guidelines for news coverage are constantly adapted to an ever-changing news environment and communicated directly from propaganda officials to senior media personnel, who pass them on to journalists. Journalists learn rules for political sensitivity through announcements of senior staff, by trial and error, through journalistic training, and in social networks with peers.

And how do media practitioners learn about demands by media citizens? Most newspapers, even official ones, are sold at newspaper stands, although official papers still primarily rely on subscription by government institutions. Many nonofficial papers have set up their own distribution channels to increase sales and rely on market research companies to study audience characteristics and sales patterns (Chapter 3). As we will see, Chinese readers demand stories that they find credible, and the credibility of the story depends to a large extent on whether it conforms to their preexisting beliefs (see Chapters 7 and 8).

---

[17] I do not assume that political leaders have one cohesive view. Chapter 6 examines in detail factionalism, fragmented authoritarianism, and leadership cycles.

[18] There is an ongoing debate in the United States about whether and how politicians can influence news reporting. See, for example, Gregory Bovitz, James N. Druckman, and Arthur Lupia, "When Can a News Organization Lead Public Opinion?," *Public Choice* 113, no. 1–2 (2002), Lance W. Bennett, Regina G. Lawrence, and Steven Livingston, *When the Press Fails: Political Power and the News Media from Iraq to Katrina* (Chicago: University of Chicago Press, 2007). In China the symbiotic relationship between media and government is more visible than in other countries. For details, see Chapters 3 and 10.

By following which stories sell better than others, editors develop a sense for what kinds of stories audiences find attractive.

* * *

As a result of the interaction between state and market forces, media marketization allows the state to synchronize news content while also limiting the exercise of coercive instruments to those cases in which audience demands challenge boundaries for news reporting set by the state. This increase in autonomy of media outlets opens up space for societal forces, most importantly media citizens, to influence the content of public discourse publicized in the media. In the context of Chinese media, this space is often described as "semi-independent" (see, for example, Huang 2000). Public discourse in China is semi-independent, because the state restricts space for media reporting, but within that space there is variation among media outlets in terms of how much they depend on the state. In addition, space for societal influence is created by selectively opening space for news reporting when market mechanisms pull content into the desired direction. At the same time, the state's tolerance has its limits once media messages start to undermine the official line of the state. In this semi-independent space for public discourse, the Chinese media tend to be biased in favor of the regime; however, news reporting that supports government policy not only serves the state but also reflects societal demands when the state allows media to respond to them. As long as the state can walk the fine line between selectively opening and closing space for news reporting while ensuring a roughly one-sided flow of information, state and market forces can mutually reinforce each other.

In balancing liberalization and control, responsive authoritarianism in Chinese media provides a solution to the dictator's dilemma whereby compliance is achieved less by means of coercion and more by the interplay between institutions and the market. If this is true, the dictator's dilemma would predict that subordinates, in this case media practitioners, would be less hesitant to voice their true opinions about public affairs to superiors. Indeed, there is some evidence that senior media staff engage in arguments with PD officials when they disagree with instructions issued to them; propaganda officials are very concerned about conflict they experience with media staff (Chapters 4 and 6).[19] It is this conflict, however, that allows political leaders to learn about public opinion by means of marketized media.

Space for news reporting is dynamic and constantly negotiated between media practitioners and public officials. News reports about current events have to appear in a timely manner, which leaves little time for the state to edit content before it is publicized. Electronic media have placed additional pressure on traditional media outlets to publicize news quickly. Therefore, restrictions on

---

[19] Senior staff were probably more hesitant to voice disagreement during the Mao years, although we lack interview data with senior staff during this period. For a detailed account of media control before the reform period, see Zhao, *Media, Market, and Democracy in China: Between the Party Line and the Bottom Line.*

news reporting are usually issued after specific events have occurred. However, in the absence of directives, marketized media follow demands of the market, and public officials decide to either restrict these reactions or allow them to freely unfold themselves, depending on the official line. Thus the first reaction by marketized media and discussion about state restrictions (if they take place) often provide public officials with cues about how public opinion relates to the specific goals and policy positions of the government.[20]

A second way in which audience opinion is transmitted to officials is by means of nonofficial papers, which are regarded as being *closer* to public opinion than official papers. Officials are media consumers themselves – public officials read commercialized papers in addition to official ones (Chapter 8); they are also likely to read the news online (Stockmann 2011a).[21] When President Hu Jintao met with "netizens" on People.com in June 2008, he stated: "Often when I go online I do so to first read the domestic and international news, second to learn which issues and opinions netizens are concerned about, and third to learn what kinds of opinions and suggestions netizens have about the work of the Party and state (*dang he guojia*)."[22] Most of the news stories available online constitute either reprints of or remain similar in content to nonofficial papers, the main difference being that netizens also have the option to comment (see Chapter 6). Marketized media provide public officials with an additional tool to obtain information about the nature of public opinion, in addition to daily short reports (*jianbao*) by the PD and internal reports (*neican*) by reporters that often contain material too sensitive for publication.[23]

As we will see, the audiences to which nonofficial papers are responsive are not representative of Chinese society as a whole, but instead reflect a certain segment of the population: their readers.[24] To understand which segments of Chinese society exert influence on news reporting and media effects, the next section turns to the relationship between media outlets and audiences.

Responsive Authoritarianism and Media Citizenship

Thus far, I have emphasized the ability of the Chinese state to ensure rough uniformity in the news through the interaction between institutions and market

---

[20] Similarly, electronic communication technologies, such as the Internet, constitute information sources for citizen beliefs. For a more detailed discussion of the implications of the book's findings for the Internet, see Chapters 6 and 10.

[21] On the use of the Internet as a source of public opinion among political elites, see Susan Shirk, "Changing Media, Changing Foreign Policy," *Japanese Journal of Political Science* 8, no. 1 (2007), Xu Wu, *Chinese Cyber Nationalism* (Lanham: Lexington Books, 2007). Other sources on the nature of public opinion include, for example, intelligence agencies, such as the Public Security Bureau; survey data collected by government agencies, such as the Statistical Bureau; and the petitioning system.

[22] http://www.people.com.cn/GB/32306/81152/7409486.html, accessed November 9, 2011.

[23] Due to the secrecy of these reports, it is difficult to assess how influential they are in policy making. Additional feedback mechanisms that do not involve media are mentioned in footnote 21 above.

[24] In line with my definition of public opinion, I consider public opinion to be representative if it accurately reflects the aggregate of individual attitudes within a social group.

forces. In some ways, I have provided a view of the semi-independent space for newspapers similar to a "glass being half empty." Clearly, there has been some systematic difference with respect to the core political messages, here measured in terms of tone in news reporting, but this variation has remained constrained. Yet once we put ourselves in the shoes of Chinese readers, we find that audiences, in fact, regard space for public discourse as "half full" rather than "half empty."

Layers of Public Discourse and Media Labels

As pointed out by Fraser (1993) and Lee (2002), it may be helpful to think of public discourse as consisting of multiple spheres rather than one single, comprehensive sphere.[25] Stratified societies in which the institutional framework generates unequal and hierarchical relationships between social groups can give rise to multiple spheres or layers, which are in contestation rather than deliberation with one another as less empowered groups are trying to challenge the sphere of more empowered groups.[26] Like Zhao (2008), I found that Chinese public discourse in newspapers primarily consists of two main layers composed of official and nonofficial papers, but my emphasis here is on how these layers are perceived by media users and the consequences of these perceptions rather than the dynamics and boundaries between them.

Official newspapers create a sphere for communication among elites, but they also overlap with a second layer of public discourse that prodes communication between elites and the broader populace, referred to as "ordinary citizens," or *laobaixing*. First and foremost, official papers allow political elites to communicate with each other by announcing the goals and policies of state and Party units at different levels of government. Local governments also use official papers to display their support or lack of support for cadres higher up in the administrative hierarchy through articles in official papers. For example, provincial Party papers were more likely to publish articles on the Three Represents campaign launched by Jiang Zemin in 2000 if the local Party secretary or governor belonged to Jiang Zemin's faction (Shih 2008). Yet in addition to communication among elites, official papers also signal to ordinary citizens

---

[25] The term *public* can take on many meanings, including being state-related, being accessible to everyone, being of concern to everyone, or pertaining to a common good or shared interest, and each of them may exclude subordinate groups. See Nancy Fraser, "Rethinking the Public Sphere: A Contribution to the Critique of Actually Existing Democracy," in *Habermas and the Public Sphere*, ed. Craig Calhoun (Cambridge: MIT Press, 1993). Here I am using the term to refer to media discourse on politically relevant issues, even though, as shown in Chapter 4, these issues may become depoliticized in an authoritarian environment.

[26] Thinking about public discourse in China as layers allows me to simply distinguish between different societal forces that find ways to enter public discourse without making any claims about the quality of communication that takes place in marketized media. Habermas views commercial interests in the mass media as a form of "strategic communication," primarily aimed at persuasion and manipulation and thus unable to function as an instrument for the formation of political views among citizens in a public sphere. See Jürgen Habermas, *Theorie Des Kommunikativen Handelns* (Frankfurt am Main: Suhrkamp, 1995 [2009]).

where the government stands. Since official papers function as mouthpieces, citizens perceive official papers as representatives of state and Party units at different levels of government; they also describe them as propaganda organs that self-censor information to guide public opinion (Chapter 7). From the perspective of ordinary citizens, this sphere is built around the core of the regime; it contains issues and topics that are central to the goals and policies of political elites.

By contrast, nonofficial newspapers belong to a social layer that is disassociated from politics. Citizens identify more strongly with marketized papers, which are perceived as representatives of "ordinary people." They describe news reporting in nonofficial papers as more objective and truthful because these media outlets are more likely to overstep boundaries for news reporting set by the official layer of public discourse and talk about "social problems" that are less political. It is, in fact, not true that this social layer is truly apolitical – nonofficial papers cover a fair amount of politically relevant stories, as shown in Chapter 5. However, it is precisely the depoliticization of this social sphere that allows these papers to engage in public discourse. As Weller (2008) noted, the social sphere in an authoritarian state can become vital to politics, but it must remain apolitical to survive, even if the authoritarian state makes use of this social sphere to get feedback on its policies and leadership in the manner described previously.

I refer to the preceding perceptions of official and nonofficial newspapers as *media labels*. Media labels serve as shortcuts or heuristics that allow citizens to make sense of a more complicated media environment.[27] In the American context, media labels are associated with political ideology. For example, Fox news is considered to be conservative, whereas CNN is regarded as liberal, even though in practice neither Fox nor CNN continuously broadcast conservative or liberal messages (see, for example, Peffley et al. 2001; Baum and Gussin 2007; Baum and Groeling 2009). In China, the brand identities associated with official and nonofficial papers lead to differing levels of credibility in the eyes of readers. Because nonofficial papers are considered as experts of ordinary citizens' concerns and trustworthy in their news reporting, they tend to be perceived as more credible as compared with official papers.

These media labels seemingly contradict the previous section describing how the interaction between institutions and the market synchronizes the core political messages contained in the news. How are these labels created if the political messages contained in the news tend to be roughly uniform in practice?

First, as explained in the previous section, newspaper types systematically differ in terms of tone, whereby nonofficial papers tend to position themselves

---

[27] Shortcuts or heuristics help people to overcome lack of information. See, for example, Samuel L. Popkin, *The Reasoning Voter: Communication and Persuasion in Presidential Campaigns* (Chicago: University of Chicago Press, 1991), Arthur Lupia, "Shortcuts Versus Encyclopedias: Information and Voting Behavior in California Insurance Reform Elections," *American Political Science Review* 88 (1994).

closer to audiences and official papers closer to the state. However, space remains tightly restricted and does not allow the distance between official and nonofficial papers to grow too far apart from each other. Therefore, nonofficial papers rely on marketing techniques to distinguish themselves from official papers, including advertising, corporate identity, design, and reporting on big events and controversial topics to push the boundaries for new reporting set by the state. Nonofficial papers do sometimes contest and alter the official line of the state, which aids in establishing themselves as credible sources of information and in voicing public opinion. As a result, media labels are rooted in the interactive semiautonomous layers of public discourse in China, but differences across newspaper types are also exaggerated by the branding strategies of media outlets.

These findings point toward a new direction for studying the causes of media labels. Ideological reputations of media outlets are not solely created based on the content of news stories published in the media, as shown in Chapter 7. Instead, media outlets also engage in branding strategies that aid in building the reputation of media outlets. There is some evidence that American media outlets engage in similar strategies, such as, for example, designing special sections to meet the interests of readers (Attaway-Fink 2005).

Before we turn our attention to the consequences of media labels, let us consider for a moment spaces for views that contest the limits set by the state. Of course, voices that provide countervalent political information exist in China and are circulated on the Internet and even in (often unlicensed) publications.[28] These "subaltern counterpublics," to speak in the words of Fraser (1993: 124), function as spaces of withdrawal and regroupment as well as bases for resistance directed toward the dominant discourse. However, newspapers and other traditional media outlets rarely take on such functions, although nonofficial papers contest the limits for space of news reporting, as in the case of the thirteen newspaper editorials explored in Chapter 6.

Consequences for Media Consumption

Media labels have important consequences for what kinds of newspapers citizens decide to read and which ones they find convincing. To understand when, how, and why media labels are important, we need to first take a look at the broader picture.

An authoritarian media environment is characterized by an intense one-sided message with periods in which countervailing messages appear in the mass media, but usually do not gain in intensity – unless the regime undergoes transition (see Geddes and Zaller 1989). Such an environment can also occur in liberal democracies, although in most democracies, information rarely stays completely one-sided over a long period of time (Zaller 1992). For example,

---

[28] For a research note and annotated bibliography of illegal and underground poetry, see Maghiel van Crevel, "Unofficial Poetry Journals in the People's Republic of China," available at http://mclc.osu.edu/rc/pubs/vancrevel2.html, accessed December 23, 2011.

American media reporting on the US invasion of Iraq in 2003 generally followed the official government line, despite evidence disputing official claims available to reporters (Bennett et al. 2007).

In such a one-sided information environment, people's access to and choice of political information is limited. Access to information and media choice have profound consequences for political learning, although there is an ongoing debate regarding when, how, and why greater access and choice lead to polarization (see, for example, Norris 2001; Prior 2005). Because authoritarian regimes are more likely to impose barriers on access and restrict press freedom (Egorov et al. 2009; Norris and Inglehart 2009), studies on media use and persuasion in authoritarian and democratizing regimes often implicitly or explicitly rely on ideas originating in dependency theory.

Dependency on media sources follows from the perceived lack of available functional alternatives. The more functional alternatives there are for an individual, the lesser the dependency on and influence of a particular media source (Rubin and Windahl 1986). Uncertainty in the political environment can further increase dependency because it generates heightened anxiety among citizens. Therefore, citizens are more likely to turn to mass media as a source of information and in doing so are more easily influenced by the mass media (Ball-Rokeach and DeFleur 1976). Indeed, Loveless's (2008) study of media use during democratic transition in East-Central Europe confirmed that citizens of countries undergoing transition tend to be heavy media users. Based on a comparative study of ninety-five countries, Norris and Inglehart (2009) detected that media exposure was positively related to beliefs and values conducive to authoritarian rule, provided that countries imposed barriers to access to information. By emphasizing access to information, they implicitly assume a relationship between dependency and media effects.

In China, limited access contributes to a certain dependency on domestic information sources, but even when having access to nonmainland sources of information, only a small minority turn to those alternatives (Shi et al. 2011; Stockmann 2011a). Barriers imposed on access can only partially explain who, when, and why people seek media sources and whether they are influenced by what they read, watch, or hear in the news.

Drawing on insights from theories of "selective exposure" (Festinger 1957; Frey 1986), I argue that Chinese readers attempt to seek information that is consistent with their own beliefs. Lack of alternative sources of information prevents people from avoiding domestic media outlets entirely and increases the likelihood that people encounter information that differs from their own beliefs. Only those with very strong beliefs contradicting the position of the government choose to abstain from using media sources. Yet even for these highly committed citizens, complete avoidance of the news media is only temporary as public discourse shifts to other issues, providing incentives to return to previous consumption habits (Chapter 8).

With respect to newspapers, readers' choices depend strongly on media credibility. Chinese readers seek the most credible information source in their attempt to seek information consistent with their beliefs. Much research in social psychology and communications has shown that consistent information and perceptions of its bias, trustworthiness, and quality tend to be correlated with one another (see Chapter 8). Similarly, Chinese readers seek nonofficial newspapers in an attempt to obtain information consistent with their beliefs, even though the tone in news reporting does not match their own evaluations (Chapters 8). These papers are also perceived to be more trustworthy and representative of public opinion as compared with official papers (Chapter 7). Once we take into account media labels, we can detect a significant relationship between media credibility and media selection.[29]

Nonetheless, the function of official newspapers as mouthpieces make them useful for readers. In an authoritarian regime, information about the goals and policies of the government can be crucial because individuals tend to be more vulnerable to state intervention in their private lives as compared with individuals living in democracies. Political elites, the more affluent, and the more educated are particularly likely to turn to official papers, but even ordinary citizens can turn to official papers during important national or local events, even if these papers contradict their beliefs and lack credibility (Chapter 8).

Overall, Chinese media users prefer to read credible news, and media labels serve as shortcuts that aid ordinary citizens in obtaining information they consider to be closer to their own opinions. Nonofficial papers tend to be better at satisfying these demands. Here, my findings differ considerably from arguments made by Chinese officials and media practitioners working for official media outlets. Allegedly, the rise of "fake news" in more highly marketized media outlets has decreased the credibility of these outlets over time, and audiences perceive official papers as more trustworthy. Although fake news constitutes a problem among some media outlets, it does not seem to have greatly influenced media labels, according to my research findings (Chapter 7).

Consequences for Persuasion

Many scholars have speculated that the media play a key role in creating support for the regime and building regime legitimacy in China (see, for example Nathan 2003; Brady 2008), but others suspect that people "read between the lines" and may not be easily manipulated by state propaganda (see, for example, Shue 2004). To understand who, when, and why Chinese are persuaded by media, we need to consider the broader information environment, individual characteristics of the receiver of the message, source perceptions, and features associated with the content of the message.

---

[29] This may explain why other studies based on more general measures for media trust have detected only a weak positive relationship between media skepticism and exposure. See Yariv Tsfati and Joseph N. Cappella, "Do People Watch What They Do Not Trust? Exploring the Association between News Media Skepticism and Exposure," *Communication Research* 30, no. 5 (2003).

In terms of the broader information environment, Geddes and Zaller (1989) argued that people living under authoritarian rule in Brazil were more susceptible to political messages as a result of the predominantly one-sided information flow. Indeed, this book confirms that a dominant message in the broader information environment facilitates persuasion. In contrast to Geddes and Zaller, however, this book finds that susceptibility of Chinese audiences also depends on the extent to which the audience is already familiar with the issue covered in the news. In issue areas in which the state attempts to change deeply held beliefs, audiences tend to be more resistant, as compared with novel issues about which citizen audiences are more malleable. Highly aware Chinese may be more suspicious of media when the state is trying to actively change deeply held beliefs, such as sentiment toward foreign countries, rather than when it intends to actively build new opinions, such as, for example, a legal consciousness that previously did not exist.

In addition, individual-level differences turn out to be powerful in explaining why some people are persuaded by media messages originating in Chinese media sources. Apart from greater exposure to media – so far, the predominant indicator of media effects in China – a person's level of awareness and attention makes a significant difference in terms of how strongly a person can be influenced by media content. This book replicates the influential exposure–acceptance model, according to which a person's likelihood of being persuaded by a piece of information depends on that person's likelihood of receiving and accepting messages. Zaller (1992) proposed that people differ in the care and attention they invest in politics as well as in their ability to maintain political information, manifesting itself in differences in political knowledge. Zaller argued that these differences have important implications for the ability of media to change people's opinion. Poorly informed citizens are less likely to receive and maintain news media messages because they are less aware of politics. More informed citizens are more likely to receive and store political information conveyed through the mass media, but they are also more resistant to media messages that are inconsistent with their own predispositions. Consistent with the exposure–acceptance model, I find that media credibility associated with media labels makes Chinese more susceptible or resistant to media messages. Marketized media have promoted the ability of the regime to persuade citizens because of the credibility boost that media marketization entails.

Drawing on insights from social psychology and political communications, I find that Chinese newspaper brands are more influential than the framing of a news report in lending credibility to a news story. The commercialized brand of a newspaper induces readers to identify more strongly with the paper and to consider it more trustworthy, thus increasing the persuasiveness of the message (Chapter 7). As explained previously, the brand is the product of marketing by media outlets that is also transmitted by means of content, but the brand turns out to be more influential than style in persuading readers. As predicted by the exposure–acceptance model, these source effects are particularly strong among issue publics.

Why Evaluations of Labor Law and Sentiment toward the United States?

To a certain extent, the issues examined in this book were chosen because I had the opportunity to collaborate with ongoing research projects that focused on these issues. However, the similarities and differences between these issues also provided an excellent opportunity to examine the causal mechanisms and conditions that link market mechanisms to the production of news and persuasion of media audiences.

The issue areas covered in this book are linked to protests that the CCP itself regards as core to its own survival. On these issues, the central government has developed concrete instructions for news media in the form of an official line aimed at creating support for the goals and policies pursued by the CCP to prevent further threats to stability and CCP rule. In the case of labor law, the central government aims to provide workers with a weapon against abuse in the workplace to channel angry workers into the legal system and keep them from protesting in the streets. In the case of the United States, the central government "massages" negative sentiment toward the United States as a state (not as a people) to gain flexibility in foreign policy making and to limit protests by angry nationalists that could easily turn against the regime (see Chapter 1).

Furthermore, I explicitly decided to focus on nonsensitive but politically relevant issues. Any changes in media content that occurred as a result of media marketization should become most evident in the open realm. If political messages are relatively uniform even if journalists feel unconstrained, this constitutes a "most difficult" test of the hypothesis that media marketization brings about diversity in news content by increasing the distance between public opinion and the official line.

In spite of the previously mentioned similarities, there are also differences within and across these issue areas. As explained in Chapter 1, demands by the central state and audiences differ by topic within each issue area. In the case of the United States, audiences demand critical news of American politics, but not so much of American society and culture; in the case of labor law, audiences have an appetite for sensationalist and "negative news" on labor protests and labor disputes, but they primarily want to learn how to be better able to use the law as a weapon against abuse in the workplace. At the same time, the central government demands a positive spin on stories that may undermine the goals and policies of public officials by publishing too much criticism of American politics and too many negative news stories on labor protests and labor disputes. These differences between open and closed topics within each issue area allow us to examine the relationship between market demands, the official line of the central government, press restrictions, and news content.

Therefore, the first empirical part on the production of news is based on a comparison between topics within each issue area. If we find that propaganda authorities use the same underlying logic to synchronize social and international news in such different issue areas as evaluations of labor law and sentiment toward the United States, we can be more confident that audience demands play an important role in the management of media outlets rather than considerations specific to domestic or international politics.[30]

The second empirical part on media credibility and its consequences is based on a comparison between issue areas. A key difference between evaluations of labor law and sentiment toward the United States constitutes the extent to which citizens are already familiar with the issue. In the case of labor law, the central government is attempting to create a new set of beliefs regarding the law and legal system, whereas it aims to change beliefs that are more central to people's "belief systems" in the case of the United States (see Chapter 1).[31] These features affect the nature of audience demands, whereby citizen demand about labor law is more about what the law could be, and demand about the United States is more about what people already believe, which may affect the ability of the government to persuade citizens by means of media, as explained earlier in this chapter. Differences in the novelty of the issue allow us to capture a possible interaction between features associated with the issue and the significance of media credibility in persuasion: on novel issues, media credibility may play a less significant role than on issues with which audiences are already highly familiar.

Specifying Empirical Propositions

The theoretical framework outlined in this chapter leads to a number of empirical propositions about when, how, and why media marketization aids in the synchronization of news and promotes media credibility, with important consequences for consumption and persuasion.

Let us first consider these propositions with respect to the production of news. The interaction between market mechanisms and political institutions in charge of editorial supervision of news content should produce a roughly uniform news product. If the state selectively opens or closes space for news reporting depending on whether audience demands converge or diverge from the official line, we would expect that topics within each issue area become more sensitive as audience demands conflict more strongly with the position of the central government (see Chapters 4 and 5).[32]

At the same time, we should find that the tone of news reporting is, on average, positive on both issues, but we should also detect systematic variation

---

[30] These considerations are explored in more depth in Chapter 6.

[31] According to Converse, as a set of ideas and attitudes in which the elements are bound together by some form of constraint or functional interdependence. That is, belief systems are based on a logical framework in which a change in one idea element results in changes elsewhere in the configuration. Belief systems differ in terms of the types of issues that they encompass (range) and the resistance of idea elements to changes in information (centrality). See Philip E. Converse, "The Nature of Belief in Mass Publics," in *Ideology and Discontent*, ed. David Apter (New York: Free Press, 1964). On the centrality of sentiments toward social groups, see Donald R. Kinder, "Belief Systems Today," *Critical Review* 18, no. 1–3 (2006).

[32] Chapter 4 lays out why international news tends to be less politically sensitive as compared with domestic news, independent of audience demands.

between official and nonofficial newspapers as more marketized media outlets enjoy more autonomy from the state. Nonofficial papers should consistently be more negative in tone than official papers because they cater toward tastes of Chinese audiences for negative news (see Chapter 5).

As far as causal mechanisms are concerned, I have proposed previously that norms of journalistic reporting are socialized by means of institutions and that newspapers respond to consumption patterns of their readers. If that is true, reporters should develop different norms for journalistic reporting for more and less sensitive topics (see Chapter 4), and these norms should change once the state imposes or lifts instructions: if space becomes more closed over time, reporters should abstain from following market demands; if space becomes more open over time, they should follow market demands (see Chapter 5). Media practitioners learn about these demands based on sales patterns (see Chapter 3), and these sales increase if stories are closer to reader demands (see Chapters 7 and 8).

Once we turn to the effect of media marketization on the relationship between media citizens and the news product, we would expect that media marketization increases the credibility of newspapers, despite rough uniformity in the news (see Chapters 7, 8, and 9). If it is true that branding strategies of newspapers exaggerate the existing differences between newspapers in terms of the core political messages in the news, we should find that persuasion depends more strongly on the media label attached to a news story as opposed to framing (see Chapter 7). In terms of the effects of media credibility on consumption, citizens should be more likely to read nonofficial papers in their attempt to seek credible information sources, even if political messages contained in the news are inconsistent with their previously held beliefs (see Chapter 8). With respect to persuasion, readers should be more susceptible to positive messages on labor law and the United States when reading nonofficial papers as opposed to official papers, and these effects should strengthen as a person's awareness and attention toward these issues intensifies (see Chapter 9). Also, due to differences in terms of the novelty of the issue, we should also detect greater resistance to positive messages among readers of official papers when examining sentiment toward the United States than evaluations of labor law (see Chapter 9).

A Note on Political Sensitivity and Social Desirability Bias

A key hurdle for studying public opinion in nondemocratic contexts is that even high-quality survey data are often considered to be biased in favor of the official government line because citizens may be afraid of reporting their true opinions. Political sensitivity is, of course, a concern for anyone studying Chinese politics, but there are three reasons to be confident that this bias is not driving the results of the research findings presented here.

First, scholars studying public opinion in China emphasize that respondents generally feel free to express their opinions under circumstances consistent with the survey data used in this book (Shi 1996; Tang and Parish 2000). Although evidence for guessing socially desirable answers was detected, an experiment with 210 adult Beijingers with diverse social backgrounds surprisingly did not detect *any* evidence for bias in survey responses driven by political sensitivity (Stockmann et al. 2011). A careful examination of survey data conducted by the Research Center for Contemporary China (RCCC), the research institute implementing the BAS and LLM, Ren (2009) found that Chinese who are concerned about political sensitivity tend to choose the non-response category rather than reporting biased responses. In the BAS and LLM, the number of respondents excluded from the statistical analysis due to nonresponse is very small, strongly reducing the likelihood that the general research findings would change if all respondents reported their true opinions.[33]

One reason for the low number of nonresponses may be a result of the focus on nonsensitive but politically relevant issues for this study to increase my confidence in the research findings. Although public opinion polls are conducted on core political issues, such as evaluations of political leaders and governmental institutions, obtaining those data is difficult and arguably overstated because those kinds of survey questions are more politically sensitive. Regarding issues viewed as not politically sensitive, citizens are more likely to report their true opinions in public opinion surveys, thus reducing social desirability bias.

Second, I rely on multiple measures to examine journalists' assessments of space for news content, complementing in-depth interviews with handbooks for journalists that are published by newspapers to be distributed to entering journalists and by communication scholars to improve training of young journalists. These sources of information are aimed at a Chinese audience for training purposes and are unlikely to suffer from social desirability bias.

Third, if it is true that most respondents adjust their opinions in favor of the official government line, we would expect to observe that those respondents exposed to official media outlets also report opinions that correspond to media content. In contrast, I found that those who read official media outlets tend to report opinions that *contradict* the official position of the state, especially as a person becomes more attentive to the issue (see also Chapter 9). Therefore, we can be confident that social desirability bias does not drive the results on media effects.

---

[33] Only 7 of 617 BAS respondents did not respond to the question used to measure sentiment toward the United States; only 6 of 4,112 LLM respondents refused to evaluate labor law; 178 indicated they did not know how to evaluate labor law (726 were not asked the question because they had never heard the term *labor law* before). Missing values increase when adding more independent variables in multiple regressions, but the main results remain stable when reducing control variables in the model. Due to the stability of the regression results and small number of missing values, I decided not to use multiple imputation of nonresponses to replicate the research findings.

Limitations and Elaborations

Before we move on to examining the empirical findings for the theoretical framework laid out in this chapter, I wish to clarify some aspects of my argument. First, I agree with Przeworski (1991: 54) that some "authoritarian regimes have been illegitimate since their inception, and they have been around for forty years." My argument is that some regimes can make use of market mechanisms in media while reducing coercion and state subsidies to achieve compliance among reporters. However, these regimes need to retain a certain degree of control to use media marketization to their advantage. Because one-party regimes are better able to maintain this capacity, they may enjoy higher levels of public support for their policies while also receiving input from citizens about their policies through marketized media. Over time, these two-way influences are likely to induce political change without democratization. Just as liberal democracies are more dependent on public opinion because they can rely less on coercion, public opinion may play a stronger role in one-party regimes with highly marketized media as compared with other states that did not undergo media reform or that lack the institutions to use market mechanisms to their advantage. Those kinds of regimes are probably more dependent on coercion and economic factors, maintaining their rule despite low levels of regime support.

Furthermore, a common criticism of arguments that take into account political views of citizens living under authoritarian rule is that they imply false-consciousness arguments. Originating in Marxist theories, *false consciousness* is defined as "the holding of false beliefs that are contrary to one's own social interest" (Jost 1995: 400). The belief must be false in the epistemological sense of being contrary to the fact, and it must be harmful in the sense that it fails to reflect one's own personal or group interest. None of these criteria apply to the core argument made in this book.

Media labels constitute shortcuts that aid people in making sense of a more complicated environment. The reputation of marketized media as being more trustworthy and closer to society comes about as a result of a combination of news content and the branding strategies of media outlets. Thus these beliefs are rooted in real differences between media outlets in terms of tone, selection of topics, corporate identity, style, and design. Chinese are conscious of the fact that media are tightly controlled by the state, but among the media sources available to them, they find marketized media more credible – in part because marketized media are closer to citizens' own ideas about what constitutes truthful information, and they do reflect public opinion when audience and state demands converge. Because it is difficult to decipher when the state issues restrictions and when not, people use media labels as shortcuts that are transferred into news content even if the reporter did self-censor herself while producing the news story.

This book does not make any normative claims about what may be in the interest of Chinese citizens because any such claims ultimately depend on the highest value chosen: if one seeks to improve Sino-US relations to avoid future conflict between the two countries, one may very well conclude that effective persuasion by means of mass media is in a person's (or China's) interest; the opposite conclusion can be reached when favoring the breakdown of CCP rule in China. Without glancing over the negative aspects of the system, this research reveals that authoritarianism is multifaceted rather than binary. I hope that the differentiated and counterintuitive findings presented here will raise awareness of how our own normative values can distort the way we view the world beyond liberal democracy.

3

Types of Newspapers in China

In 1978, the CCP made a decision with profound consequences for the Chinese media system. At the Third Plenary Session of the Eleventh National Party Congress, the CCP dropped its emphasis on class struggle as part of a broader attempt to correct specific theories and practices of the Cultural Revolution. Under the leadership of Deng Xiaoping, the government relaxed control over domestic and international flows of information to foster initiative, innovation, and economic growth. Media were intended to serve both the state and the market.

In this atmosphere of economic reform and opening to the outside world, local media outlets started to experiment with alternative sources of funding. Advertising appeared for the first time on Shanghai television and in the Shanghai-based *Liberation Daily* (*Jiefang Ribao*) in 1979.[1] Similar initiatives soon followed in other localities, although the central government did not legalize advertising until a trial version of regulations on advertising management was enacted in 1982.[2] For a long time, however, policy makers did not make public statements about media marketization. It was not until 1992 that Liang Heng, an official responsible for newspaper management at the State Press and Publication Administration, acknowledged for the first time the commodity nature of the press and announced the imperative of "eventually pushing

---

[1] Cao (1999) dates the first commercial after the Cultural Revolution back to January 4, 1979, in the *Tianjin Daily* (*Tianjin Ribao*), 24 days before Shanghai television. However, this information conflicts with most other sources. See Junhao Hong, "The Resurrection of Advertising in China: Developments, Problems, and Trends," *Asian Survey* 34, no. 4 (1994), Peng Cao, *Zhongguo Baoye Jituan Fazhan Yanjiu (China Newspaper Group Development Research)* (Beijing: Xinhua Chubanshe, 1999), Chunlei Hu, "Zhongguo Baoye Jingji Fazhan Jin 20 Nian Chengjiu (The Achievement of the Chinese Newspaper Industry in the Course of the Past 20 Years)," in *Zhongguo Baoye Nianjian (China Newspaper Industry Yearbook)* (Beijing: Zhonghua Gongshang Lianhe Chubanshe, 2004).

[2] Conversation with Shen Yuanyuan, expert on Chinese regulation of advertising, December 8, 2011.

newspapers to the market" (Y. Zhao 1998: 50). After the Fourteenth Party Congress in 1992, the CCP proclaimed the increase of efficiency, reduction of government subsidies, reduction of staff members, commercialization, and restructuring of the whole culture and arts sector as a policy goal (Brady 2008).

The decision to initiate marketization of the media was not entirely voluntary. Budgetary constraints forced the state to cut media subsidies as early as 1978 (Y. Zhao 1998). The previous system under which media outlets had been fully financed by the state had simply become unsustainable. Many innovations in the Chinese press have been initiated by media outlets at the margins of the system in their pursuit of increasing profits. The government's new approach was to pursue a path of experimenting with marketization of the media while at the same time maintaining the mouthpiece role of the media for the CCP through means of an infrastructure in form of institutions. Ideologically, the role of Chinese media within the political system outlined in Chapter 2 continued throughout the reform period.

This chapter traces the process of marketization of Chinese newspapers. I start with an overview of the institutional environment within which newspapers have undergone reform, thus laying out the circumstances under which marketization has taken place. The CCP maintains an institutional framework through which it is able to exert a considerable amount of control over the organization, personnel decisions, and the editorial process of newspapers. Mann (2008) regarded such institutional structures as *infrastructures* that increase the state's capacity to logistically implement political decisions. Such infrastructures aid the state to reach compliance among journalists, as discussed in the previous chapter. Although this institutional structure has been adjusted to changing circumstances over time to maintain its infrastructural capacity, the CCP has also relaxed coercion exerted through these institutions to allow media to respond to market demands. As the Chinese state deregulated, commercialized, and partially privatized newspapers, political leaders have sacrificed much of their capacity to exchange economic resources for compliance among journalists as media became more independent from the state in terms of business management and finances. As a result of these developments, different types of newspapers emerged in the Chinese media sector that differ in terms of their degree of marketization and are associated with different stages of media reform.

Newspapers within the Chinese Propaganda Apparatus

As a Leninist political system, the Chinese state comprises territorial divisions at the center, province, city, county, township, and village levels. It is composed of numerous government and Communist Party units (commissions, ministries, bureaus, and departments) at the national level, which replicate themselves in a vertical chain through lower levels of government. Individual units receive administrative guidance from above, but they are also subject to the leadership of the local governments to which they belong.

Newspapers are integrated in this broader political structure at their level of government. To obtain a license, all newspapers must find a sponsor. The sponsor's rank determines the administrative rank of the newspaper as well as its scope of circulation.[3] For example, so-called Party papers (*dangbao*) are registered under a CCP party committee and function as the mouthpiece of the Party at the respective level of government.[4] The *People's Daily*, for example, is sponsored by the Central Propaganda Department under the CCP Central Committee. Accordingly, the paper is supposed to represent the viewpoints of the Chinese national leadership. It can also be read at work units all over the country. The *Beijing Daily* is registered with the Propaganda Department under supervision of the CCP party committee at the Beijing municipal level.[5] Accordingly, it focuses more on issues that the Beijing leadership considers to be important. Its distribution is restricted to Beijing.

Through the means of the sponsor, state and Party units can also directly influence personnel appointments and dismissals of senior staff at newspapers. For example, the editor of a newspaper registered with the provincial-level All-China Federation of Women is appointed by its sponsor, but needs to get approval from the local Party authorities and then receive confirmation from the next higher Party unit, the CCP Central Committee (Houn 1958–59). At the central level, directors (*shezhang*), editors-in-chief, deputy editors-in-chief, and editorial committee members of central Party papers are included in nomenklatura lists (Burns 1994; Chan 2004). Appointments are encouraged to be Party members (Brady 2008). Indirectly, PD officials can also influence personnel decisions in other newspapers by pressuring sponsors to reprimand or dismiss senior personnel.[6] In more serious cases, the General Administration

---

[3] There are some exceptions to this rule. For instance, *Beijing Times* in the *People's Daily* group would have the right to circulate nationally, but only circulated in Beijing as of 2005. *Southern Weekend* is managed to circulate nationally, although registered with the Southern Daily Group (*Nanfang Baoye*) at the Guangdong provincial level.

[4] The institution I refer to as sponsor is the *zhuban danwei*. Also, there is a second institution *zhuguan danwei*. The *zhuguan danwei* is the institution that applied for the paper's license. It is either a body above the level of the sponsor or the same body. According to GAPP's Regulation for Publication Management (*Chuban Guanli Tiaojian*), the sponsor needs to have a leadership relationship to the newspaper as opposed to professional relations. In other words, sponsors can issue binding orders to their newspapers. My interviews indicate that this does not happen frequently unless the PD is equivalent to the sponsor. See also Honglei Ju, "Zhongguo Baoye De Fagui Yu Zhengce (Law and Policies Relevant to the Chinese Newspaper Industry)," in *Zhongguo Baoye Nianjian (China Newspaper Industry Yearbook)* (Beijing: Zhonghua Gongshang Lianhe Chubanshe, 2004).

[5] Conversation with journalist of an official paper, December 2009. See also Guoguang Wu,"Command Communication: The Politics of Editorial Formulation in the People's Daily," *China Quarterly* 137 (1994).

[6] As employees in public institutions (*shiye danwei*), media staff are subject to administrative reprimands, including, in the order of seriousness, warnings (*jinggao*), demerit (*jiguo*), major demerit (*jidaguo*), demotion (*jiangji*), dismissal from post (*chezhi*), or discharge from employment (*kaichu*). Reprimands may negatively affect promotion. See "Xingzheng Jiguan Gongwuyuan Chufen Tiaoli" (Regulation Regarding Disciplining of Civil Servants), State Council,

of Press and Publication (GAPP) and the PD may temporarily halt publication to educate media staff in politically correct news reporting or even permanently close the newspaper.[7] In response to reporting about Hunan gangster Zhang Jun, for instance, *Southern Weekend*'s editor-in-chief Jiang Yiping, chief editor Qian Gang, and news director Zhang Ping, as well as two additional staff members, were removed under pressure from the Central PD in May 2001.[8]

Licensing policies are implemented by the GAPP (Xinwen chuban zongju), formerly the State Publication and Press Administration. This institution is responsible for drafting and enforcing regulatory press policies, including licensing, investigation, and prosecution of illegal publications. By making decisions about when, where, by whom, and how many newspapers can be founded, the CCP is able to determine the organization of the newspaper industry and its ties to the political structure.

Apart from the GAPP, which is part of the state administrative system, the CCP also established PDs (Xuanchuanbu) under CCP Party committees at every level of government. This institution is at the heart of the Chinese propaganda system. The PD is a very secretive body, and its internal structure and decision-making process are not entirely clear to outsiders. In general, the PD is in charge of guiding and planning China's ideological development, thus having leadership relations with a number of institutions relevant to propaganda work, including the GAPP (Brady 2008). At the central level, the minister of the PD (during the Hu-Wen administration Liu Yunshan) usually also serves as a member of the Politburo, and it has become conventional since 1992 that he also serves as the deputy head of the Central Leading Group of Propaganda and Ideological Work, ranked second after the Leading Group head (during the Hu-Wen administration Li Changchun), also a member of the Standing Committee of the Politburo, the most powerful policy-making body in the Chinese political system (Shambaugh 2007). Most relevant for newspapers is the PD's involvement in editorial oversight and personnel appointment.

News bureaus of PDs are involved in editorial supervision exerted in the form of pre- and postpublication censorship.[9] In practice, censorship primarily takes place before publication; it involves a combination of standing rules, documents, and instructions from the Party propaganda authorities, and informal norms and content regulations within newspapers, explained in more detail in Chapter 4. Instructions by the PD are binding, as most newspapers have

---

April 4, 2007, http://www.gov.cn/flfg/2007–04/29/content_601241.htm, accessed December 22, 2011.

[7] Interviews with female researcher and female central-level official in the propaganda *xitong* in Beijing (#19, 33).

[8] Reports suggested the political climate had partially led to Zhang Jun's greed and violence. In a one-party regime such as China, only one party is to blame for the political climate. See Ashley Esarey, "Speak No Evil: Mass Media Control in Contemporary China," in *Freedom House Special Report* (Freedom House, 2006).

[9] In principle, sponsors also have the responsibility to engage in postpublication monitoring. However, none of my interviewees or existing studies mention that this has been practiced.

lower administrative rank.[10] If a newspaper is found to have been engaged in unethical practices, such as carrying fake news, surreptitious advertising, or publication of pornographic or politically problematic content, PD officials contact senior editors and can, if several warnings do not suffice, resort to more severe measures affecting employment of media staff.

The power of the PD and GAPP is further supported by the absence of a rule of law that protects freedom of press. In the abstract, the constitution affirms the right of Chinese citizens to freedom of speech. However, laws and regulations impose content restrictions regarding such broad subjects as national security and state secrets.[11] Regulations governing newspapers continue to oblige newspapers to uphold the Party principle, comprising three components: (1) the news media must accept the CCP's guiding ideology as its own; (2) media outlets must propagate the Party's programs, policies, and directives; and (3) media outlets must accept the CCP's leadership and stick to the Party's organizational principles and press policies.[12] According to the US Congressional Executive Commission on China, most cases of imprisoned journalists are based on convictions related to laws on national security and state secrets. In 2010, China had thirty-four imprisoned journalists, according to the Committee to Protect Journalists (CPJ). This constituted less than 1 percent of China's total number of news media workers, encompassing approximately 700,000, according to the GAPP.

Although the possibility of being charged for leaking state secrets deters some journalists from politically sensitive news reporting, a far more common source of legal constraint for Chinese journalism is defamation litigation. In 2004, Chinese courts heard 5,195 defamation cases (Liebman 2011b). Media lose most defamation cases brought against them by officials, party-state entities, corporations, courts, and judges in response to critical coverage, most of the time leading to financial awards against the media.[13] This supervision by

---

[10] The Central PD does not have authority to issue binding orders to central Party papers such as the *People's Daily* or the *Guangming Daily* (*Guangming Ribao*). See also Wu, "Command Communication: The Politics of Editorial Formulation in the People's Daily," Yuezhi Zhao, *Media, Market, and Democracy in China: Between the Party Line and the Bottom Line* (Urbana: University of Illinois Press, 1998).

[11] See, for example, Baoshou Guojia Mimi Fa (Law on Protecting State Secrets), 1998, art. 20 (stating that media publications and broadcasts shall not reveal state secrets); Criminal Law of the People's Republic of China, 1997, art. 398 (barring divulgence of state secrets). See Benjamin J. Liebman, "Watchdog or Demagogue? The Media in the Chinese Legal System," *Columbia Law Review* 101, no. 1 (2005).

[12] Baokan Guanli Zanxing Guiding (Interim Rules on the Administration of Newspapers), December 25, 1990, arts. 7, 8. See Ibid and Zhao, *Media, Market, and Democracy in China: Between the Party Line and the Bottom Line*.

[13] Interviews with male lawyer and male journalist of commercialized paper in Beijing (#26, 27). See also Benjamin J. Liebman, "The Media and the Courts: Towards Competitive Supervision?" *China Quarterly* 208 (2011b). On court cases involving the media, see Haitao Liu, Jinxiong Zheng, and Rong Shen, *Zhongguo Xinwen Guansi Ershi Nian, 1987–2007 (Twenty Years of Chinese News Lawsuits, 1987–2007)* (Beijing: Zhongguo Guangbo Dianshi Chubanshe, 2007).

the courts has positive and negative effects on media reporting. On the one hand, it increases media attention to collect evidence to support a story and abstain from fake news reporting, as in the case of the 2007 "fake dumpling case," when a report aired on Beijing television claimed that dumplings were sold filled with cardboard (Liebman 2011b). On the other hand, reporters are often unable to win defamation cases, even if they have collected evidence. To avoid financial risks, reporters may refrain from publishing some investigative or critical stories (Esarey 2006). In response, the Chinese Journalists Association has attempted to persuade the Supreme People's Court to issue a new interpretation of defamation that would provide journalists with greater protection (Liebman 2011b).

* * *

Overall, Chinese newspapers are embedded into the broader Chinese political structure and are subject to the PD and GAPP. This basic institutional framework was established in the 1950s and was reestablished after the Cultural Revolution. During the reform period, the CCP adjusted this institutional framework to maintain its capacity to retain a one-sided information flow in the news. Through the means of the PD and GAPP, the Party continues to exert a very considerable amount of political control over the organization, personnel, and editorial process of newspapers. The power of these institutions is strengthened by the absence of a media law that protects freedom of press in China. The next section shows how these institutions prevented the loss of political control over newspapers when introducing market forces.

Pushing Newspapers to the Market

Chinese newspapers underwent deregulation, commercialization, and partial privatization. To support the marketization of newspapers, the GAPP and PD has shifted from managing media at the microlevel to the macrolevel, guiding its overall development rather than managing the specifics (Brady 2008). Deregulation is visible in the decentralization of control by the GAPP and PD over the organization and personnel decisions among newspapers. In addition, Chinese newspapers have become profit-making enterprises in which investment is permitted to a limited extent.

Deregulation of Licensing and Personnel Management
In 1979, Hu Yaobang, then director of the Central PD, encouraged media to become more proactive and original while also strengthening the collective leadership of the Party. Party committees at lower levels of government were urged to establish new newspapers to increase the flow of information for economic development and to rebuild the propaganda system after the end of the Cultural Revolution (Esarey 2005). Following Hu's calls for deregulation, the GAPP, then the Publication Bureau under the Ministry of Culture, started

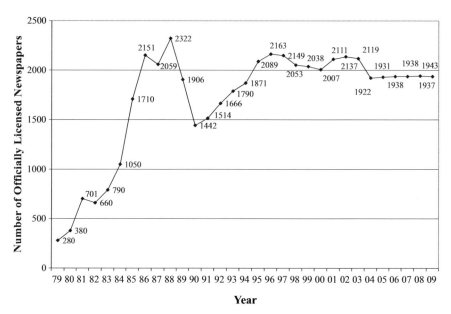

FIGURE 3.1. Number of Officially Licensed Newspapers, 1979–2009. *Source: Chinese Journalism Handbook.*[a]

[a] Measures before and after 1995 are not entirely consistent as a result of inconsistencies in the *Chinese Journalism Handbook*. Between 1979 and 1994, I added the number of Party and nonofficial papers to retrieve the total number of newspapers. Between 1985 and 1989, the sum of these papers is higher than the total number of officially licensed papers. The two measures match between 1990 and 1994.

to issue more licenses. The number of officially licensed newspapers increased from 186 to 1,943 between 1978 and 2009, peaking shortly before the 1989 Tiananmen crisis (see Figure 3.1). In the late 1980s, the government began cutting back the number of daily newspapers. In 1987, the Central PD and GAPP (then named State Press and Publication Administration) asked newspapers to reregister, allowing the state to suppress publications that had "committed political mistakes" or were of low quality (Esarey 2005: 44). However, national reregistration had only limited impact compared with the massive closures of daily newspapers during Deng Xiaoping's crackdown on widespread media support during the 1989 Tiananmen demonstrations. After 1990, the GAPP started to issue more licenses, although at a much slower pace than during the 1980s. Licensing slowed down after a decision was made to rule out the creation of more newspapers in January 1994 to deal with illegal selling of registration numbers, parallel to a licensing stop of ISBN numbers in the publishing industry (Chan 1993; China News Analysis 1995; Schell 1995). After a sudden rush to get approval for a new registration number right after 1994, the number of newspapers remained relatively stable after 1996. By 2003, the number of newspapers had reached almost the same level as in 1986, but this number slightly decreased afterwards.

This growth has primarily taken place among newspapers that are both local in focus and not under direct supervision of a Party committee. The rise of evening papers (*wanbao*) in the 1980s and metro papers (*dushibao*) during the late 1990s has been largely to the disadvantage of the formerly mentioned Party papers (*dangbao*),[14] which are under *direct* supervision of a CCP party committee at the national or local level, and "political organ papers" (*jiguanbao*), which are under *direct* supervision of a governmental institution.[15] This vertical decentralization of media power from the national center to the locality mirrors the power redistribution from the highest decision-making bodies to local governing bodies within the political system.

Although the policy change in the 1980s to issue more licenses was not free of political barriers, the increase in the total number of newspapers had far-reaching implications: on the one hand, competition intensified as the number of players grew in the emerging media market. On the other hand, China's newspaper industry increased in size and became fragmented, posing a challenge to monitoring by the state.

In response, China improved monitoring of the proliferation of nonofficial newspapers by upgrading the Publication Bureau under the Ministry of Culture to first-tier status under the direct supervision of the State Council. The institution was also renamed the State Press and Publication Administration (Xinwen chuban shu) (SPPA) in January 1987. In the Chinese political system, authority is passed top-down; raising the administrative rank of government bodies tends to improve the organizations' ability to have authority over lower levels of government. In other words, the upgrading of the SPPA reemphasized political control. In 2001, the SPPA was further elevated to ministerial-level status and renamed the GAPP (Xinwen chuban zongshu).

In addition, the GAPP encouraged newspaper conglomeration to tighten control over the organization of newspapers.[16] Starting in 1996, the *Guangzhou Daily* (*Guangzhou Ribao*) was the first to organize a newspaper conglomerate. Officially, bigger and stronger organizations were created in the face of anticipated foreign competition (Hu 2003). Indeed, in some cases conglomeration strengthened a press group to the point that it sometimes established a monopoly over the local media market. This was, for instance, the case in Shenzhen, in which the Shenzhen Special Economic Zone Daily Group held a monopoly in the city's newspaper market (Li et al. 2006). However, even in

---

[14] Some papers at the national level are often referred to as Party papers although they are not under direct supervision of the central Party committee: *Guangming Daily*, *China Daily*, and *Economic Daily*. They can be considered "quasi-Party papers."

[15] Based on my interviews and conversations with media practitioners, there is some confusion about whether or not Party papers are included in the category of political organ papers or whether they are a separate category. To simplify my explanations, I use separate categories.

[16] Conglomeration refers to the formation of a large corporation by the merging of separate firms or entities.

more competitive markets, conglomeration had organizational advantages: it represented a way for the Party to regain control over an increasingly fragmented press structure. An estimated 15 percent of the total publications, many of them commercialized papers, were dismantled or merged into press groups.[17] With Party papers as the core, the state expanded political control over nonofficial papers. Although conglomerates vary in terms of their internal organization, they tend to be hierarchically structured with the Party paper at the top (Zheng 2003; Song 2004). In 2002, thirty-four of a total of thirty-nine newspaper conglomerates were headed by a Party paper.[18] Conglomeration clearly had the advantage to strengthen the position of Party papers in the newspaper market and to tighten political control over nonofficial papers.

Overall, the CCP has continued to rely on infrastructures to exercise political control over the organization of newspapers through the means of the GAPP. Licensing policy had been quite open throughout the 1980s, but the state has tried to reestablish more effective political supervision by means of upgrading the administrative rank of the GAPP, a licensing stop for newspaper registration numbers, and conglomeration. These measures have slowed down and confined previous developments to fragmentation of the newspaper industry, but they have not put an end to the general trend toward greater deregulation.

Apart from licensing, deregulation is also visible with respect to supervision of personnel. Over time, the CCP has shifted its emphasis from directly managing media staff through Party membership and the nomenklatura system to relying on more flexible personnel management based on contract and exchange, which were seen as being more suitable to the market.

The formal rule that top leaders of Party papers had to be Party members has been abolished, although in practice, nominees tend to be Party members.[19] A survey of journalists conducted around 1994 revealed that 54 percent of reporters were Party members, though this percentage has declined to 38 percent in Guangzhou since then (Chen et al. 1998; Lin 2010). Yet even if

---

[17] Newspapers were forced to either achieve complete financial autonomy or merge with central and provincial Party organs in 1999. They faced closure if circulation was less than 30,000 and if Party organs were unwilling to take them over. A case in point is the forced merger of the lucrative *Xinmin Evening News* (*Xinmin Wanbao*) with the party-controlled *Wenhui Bao* in Shanghai. See Yuezhi Zhao, "The State, the Market, and Media Control in China," in *Who Owns the Media: Global Trends and Local Resistance*, ed. Pradip Thomas and Zaharom Nain (Penang, Malaysia: Southbound, 2005).

[18] There are four other forms of newspaper groups that are not regarded as conglomerates: *Renmin Ribao She, Beijing Qingnianbao She, Jinwanbao*, and the *Jisuanji Shijie Chuanmei Jituan*. See China Newspaper Industry Yearbook, *Zhongguo Baoye Nianjian (China Newspaper Industry Yearbook)* (China: Zhongguo Gongshang Lianhe Chubanshe, 2004), 386–405.

[19] Interview with male editor of semiofficial paper in Beijing (#25). See also Ju, "Zhongguo Baoye De Fagui Yu Zhengce (Law and Policies Relevant to the Chinese Newspaper Industry)." Some of my interviewees speculated that the leadership of nonofficial papers was composed of fewer Party members, but most of the editors and directors I interviewed indicated that the majority of the editorial board were Party members – even in nonofficial papers.

Party membership continues to be influential, this does not ensure full ideological conformity anymore. Although still promoting socialism with Chinese characteristics on the outside, the CCP is now accepting a broad range of members, many of them entrepreneurs and technocrats, in an effort to secure the future of the CCP in a society that places much emphasis on economic success. Newspapers are increasingly managed by leaders who do not have a political agenda, but who care about the success of the newspaper.

Apparently, top leaders were worried about loosening their grip over senior personnel, resulting in recentralization of control over cadre management in the propaganda *xitong* in the 1990 central nomenklatura list.[20] In the Chinese political system cadres are appointed based on nomenklatura lists. It is unclear how later reforms of this nomenklatura system of cadre management, such as the downsizing of the bureaucracy in 1998, has impacted newspapers.[21] According to my interviews, investors now play a key role in appointments of editors-in-chief and other senior personnel of newspapers.[22]

Apart from Party membership and changes in nomenklatura lists, a key change in personnel management has been the abolishment of permanent employment and introduction of a performance-based contract system, which provides incentives for media practitioners to comply with journalistic standards, in part, set by the PD. Editors at the top level of Party papers continue to have political ranks as cadres, but are now paid under a journalism professional rank system rather than a "cadre pay schedule" (Chu 1994). Heads of press groups, editors-in-chief, and deputy editors-in-chief are well paid in comparison with average incomes, and promotion to these positions is based on considerations regarding consumer satisfaction in addition to compliance with demands by the propaganda authorities (Esarey 2005).

Similarly, many newspapers tie journalists' income to the quantity and quality of their output. For example, staff of the *Chongqing Business News* are

[20] The CCP moved leadership positions in various central radio and television broadcasting stations located in Beijing, and positions in the Chinese Journalists Association, from the secondary list to the job title list. Leadership of selected propaganda bureaucracies was managed directly by the Politburo itself. According to the 1990 nomenklatura list, the following staff members of newspapers were centrally managed by the CCP: *People's Daily*: director (*shezhang*), deputy directors, editor-in-chief, editorial committee members, head of the discipline group; *People's Daily*, overseas edition: editor-in-chief; *Guangming Daily*, *Economic Daily*, and *China Daily*: editor-in-chief, deputy editors-in-chief, editorial committee members. Publishing houses of print media were listed as local organizations, whose appointments could be vetoed by the Organization Department, including, for example, *Workers' Daily*, *China Youth Daily* (*Zhongguo Qingnianbao*), or Xinhua. See John P. Burns, "Strengthening Central CCP Control of Leadership Selection: The 1990 Nomenklatura," *China Quarterly* 138 (1994).

[21] The 1998 nomenklatura list moved Xinhua to the category that had to report directly to the center. See Hon Chan, "Cadre Personnel Management in China: The Nomenklatura System, 1990–1998," *China Quarterly* 179 (2004).

[22] Interview with male editor of nonofficial paper in Chongqing and female journalists of official paper in Beijing (#9, 42).

required to pay fines if they come late to a meeting – their income is strongly tied to performance.[23] In addition to negative incentives in the form of fines, there are also positive economic incentives in the form of performance bonuses, now quite common in Chinese media more broadly. Performance bonuses tie the popularity of reports among audiences and the number and length of stories that are broadcast or published (see, for example, Esarey 2005). They can reinforce compliance with PD instructions, as those provide disincentives for publishing a story or report about a topic in great length.

The new contract system gave media outlets more leeway in personnel appointments and tied promotion more strongly to performance. Emphasis on performance provides financial incentives for compliance with PD instructions, but it also added consumer satisfaction as an important standard. A study of 123 Chinese journalists with an expertise in international news reporting conducted by People's University of China in the fall of 2010 revealed that only a small minority of media practitioners believe that factors other than the government or demands by media audiences influence their reporting about foreign actors.[24] Similarly, Lin's (2010) study of journalists in Guangzhou found that the majority of journalists thought their own organization placed a strong emphasis on increasing revenue and felt constrained by considerations regarding readers' preferences. As we will see in later chapters, such a shift toward emphasis on the market can play out to the benefit of the state when demands converge, but otherwise gives rise to tension between media practitioners and propaganda officials.

To reinforce its grip over media personnel, the CCP tried to reinforce monitoring through licensing of press cards of which the GAPP has been in charge since 1987. In 1989 and again in 2004, all legally employed journalists in China had to reapply for press cards issued by the GAPP.[25] To obtain this press card, reporters are required to take a training program in official ideology, media

---

[23] Interview with male editor of nonofficial paper in Chongqing (#42).

[24] Twenty-nine and a half percent of editors and journalists name the nature of the relationship between China and the foreign actor, another 13.11% the Chinese government and senior-level media staff; because the Propaganda Department demands that the Chinese media report about foreign affairs from the perspective of the Chinese government, together the perceived influence of the state on media reporting adds up to about 43% (the perceived influence of the government is much higher among second [11%] and third important factors [29.5%] in influencing reporting). Another 27% name readers and media audiences as influential. Only 16.4% selected attitudes of other media, and only 4% the news worthiness of the story as being influential in how they report about foreign politics. These data are part of a research project on Chinese views of the European Union funded by the 7th framework programme of the European Commission run by the University of Nottingham in collaboration with the Chinese Academy of Social Sciences, People's University of China, Leiden University, Jakobs University Bremen, and Chatham House.

[25] "Xinwen Chubanshu Guanyu Chongxin Hefa Jizhezheng de Tongzhi" (Announcement Reapplying for Legal Press Cards), SPPA, April 10, 1989, and "Guanyu Hefa Qikan Xin Ban Jizhezheng de Tongzhi" (Announcement on Reapplying for Press Cards for Journalists of Periodicals and Journals)," GAPP, July 8, 2004.

policies and regulations, journalism ethics, and Marxist-Leninist communication theory (Zhao 2008). The state can "weed out undesirable workers" by requiring reporters to obtain press cards (Hassid 2008: 427). Still, there are a large number of freelance and part-time journalists employed without press cards (Hassid 2012).

The formalization of government certification of journalists has also not been able to stop the emergence of new journalistic standards for news reporting (Lin 2010; Hassid 2012). Communist professionals who see their role as mainly serving as the CCP's mouthpiece are shrinking in numbers. Now Chinese newspapers employ journalists that see their role in a variety of ways, some of them primarily interested in making money, some of them claiming to represent the voice of the people, and some of them – according to Hassid (2012), only a small number – dedicated to independent, unbalanced reporting.

Just as in the area of licensing, the CCP has decreased its involvement in personnel management while also making attempts to reinforce authority over media practitioners over time. Most importantly, the CCP deregulated licensing of newspapers and decentralized personnel management, although it also introduced press cards as a mechanism to screen personnel and utilizes financial incentives to ensure compliance with PD instructions. Although the new generation of editors and journalists wants to avoid political trouble to retain their jobs, their salaries and promotion are often tied to the success of their papers, which have become more dependent on audiences as a result of changes in business management and finances of papers.

Commercialization and Partial Privatization

On the eve of the reforms, all newspapers were owned by the state and all aspects of newspaper business operations and finances were administered by the state. Newspaper staff did not need to be concerned about newspaper management and finances. When a paper wanted to purchase a new printing press, it had to apply to the state for the full amount. Distribution was handled by the post office. About 90 percent of all printed copies went to subscribers, which were for the most part work units.[26] Newspapers relied exclusively on state subsidies.

Yet as part of the early economic reform policies, the central government pursued economic decentralization under the leadership of Deng Xiaoping, which led to redistribution of wealth from the central government to local governments, enterprises, and individuals. As a consequence of these developments, the share of revenues going to the central government dropped. Government funds could provide only about 9 percent of the funds necessary for technological development of the newspaper sector (Y. Zhao 1998). All media, especially broadcasting for which expenses are particularly high, suffered severe financial difficulties.

---

[26] Only about 10% of the production was distributed to newspaper stands. Roderick MacFarquhar, "A Visit to the Chinese Press," *China Quarterly* 53 (1973).

At the same time, the public's demand for more and better media services grew. Along with China's economic growth, citizens had more money to spend on culture and entertainment, and business took advantage of increased consumption by advertising their products (Hong 1994). The rapid growth in the number of media consumers provided an opportunity for a growing advertising industry to make money and for new media outlets to be funded by sources other than state subsidies.

Once media outlets started to experiment with advertising as early as 1979, the government adopted a policy of gradually cutting subsidies and encouraging commercial financing. Production materials such as newsprint and ink, which had previously been allocated by the government, were gradually left to the invisible hand of the market. Some newspapers had already lost all subsidies in the early 1980s (Y. Zhao 1998). Soon businesses could buy advertising space virtually anywhere in a newspaper. In July 1993, the state further cut state subsidies and ordered financial reorganization of all top Party papers (Hong 1994). By the end of the 1990s, the majority of media outlets had become not only financially self-sufficient but also profitable.

In the 1990s, the growth of the media sector attracted nonstate capital, although the government did not officially allow outside investments in newspapers before the early 2000s.[27] Although there remain restrictions – the share of nonstate investment in media outlets must not exceed 49 percent – the state has partially transferred property from public to private ownership.[28] An increasing number of businesses and private individuals have invested in publications. For example, the Peking University Jade Bird Group invested in the *Beijing Times*, which became a major player in the Beijing newspaper market.[29] Similarly, the Shanxi China Sage Group belonging to the Association of Returning Overseas Chinese invested in a number of newspapers, including the *Chinese Business Paper* and *Chongqing Times*.[30] Beijing Youth Daily Group was the first press group to be listed on the stock market in Hong Kong in December 2004.[31] Its ability to deepen privatization remains limited,

[27] For example, *Sichuan Sports News* was established with investment from a musical instrument manufacturer as early as 1993. See Zhao, *Media, Market, and Democracy in China: Between the Party Line and the Bottom Line*. For more examples see Qinglian He, *Zhongguo Zhengfu Ruhe Kongzhi Meiti: Zhongguo Renquan Yanjiu Baogao (Media Control in China: A Report by Human Rights in China)* (New York: Human Rights in China, 2003).
[28] "Guanyu Guifan Xinwen Chubanye Rongzi Huodong De Shishi Yijian" (Opinion on the Implementation of Regulations on Financial Activities of the Publication and Press Industry), GAPP, July 25, 2003.
[29] Interviews with male editor of nonofficial paper in Chongqing and male editor of commercialized paper in Beijing (#41, 10).
[30] Interviews with two male editors of nonofficial papers in Chongqing (#37, 38).
[31] Interview with male editor of semiofficial paper in Beijing (#21). Although *Beijing Youth Daily* was first among newspapers, the Hunan Broadcasting Bureau listed parts of its business on the Shenzhen stock market in 1999. The *Guangzhou Daily* also applied to be listed on the stock market but did not receive permission on its first try. See Qingnan Shentu, "2004 Nian Baoye Touzi Xin Tedian (New Characteristics of Investment in the Newspaper Industry in 2004)," in

however: according to GAPP regulations, even Chinese investors can collectively only hold up to 49 percent of a given enterprise.[32] Foreign investments remain restricted to magazines and the Hong Kong–based Phoenix TV.[33] Although all media thus remain state-owned, the CCP has prepared itself for greater capital investment in domestic media outlets. In 2001, the central government transformed state assets into Party-owned assets, reflecting the new strategy to turn the media into more commercially minded organizations while simultaneously benefiting the CCP (Hu 2003).

Despite the general trend toward greater financial independence, those publications under Party or governmental units (Party and political organ papers) continue to receive indirect state subsidies. They can largely rely on subscriptions by government offices at all levels of government.[34] According to the 2003 Code on Practical Regulations, all groups using public funds must apply them first to Party papers and periodicals, especially central-level publications (He 2003). Governmental units also have incentives to subscribe to Party and/or political organ papers, as those are considered to publish their respective institution's position and are up to date with respect to the newest policy developments.[35]

Conglomeration has also indirectly subsidized Party papers, as profitable papers – in many cases, evening papers – were incorporated into one organization. For example, the Chongqing Daily Group was founded in 2001, but expenses and income of the *Chongqing Daily* only broke even in 2004.[36] As the state phased out subsidies, the capital had to be accumulated by more profitable papers in the conglomerate, in this case mostly the *Chongqing Evening News*. This relieved pressure on Party papers to soften their news content to generate income. In addition to enhancing organizational control, as outlined

---

Zhongguo Baoye Nianjian (China Newspaper Industry Yearbook) (Beijing: Zhonghua Gongshang Lianhe Chubanshe, 2004), Zhao, "The State, the Market, and Media Control in China."

[32] "Guanyu Guifan Xinwen Chubanye Rongzi Huodong De Shishi Yijian" (Opinion on the Implementation of Regulations on Financial Activities of the Publication and Press Industry), GAPP, July 25, 2003.

[33] Interviews with male news assistant of foreign newspaper, male editor-in-chief of an official paper, four male editors of commercialized papers, male market researcher of advertising, male head of press group, and male editor of semiofficial paper in Beijing and Chongqing (#4, 7, 10, 15, 21, 25, 27, 35, 42). Phoenix TV is a satellite television joint venture between Rupert Murdoch's Star TV, Liu Changle, an overseas Chinese entrepreneur, and the Bank of China.

[34] Nevertheless, official papers are sold at newspaper stands, although fewer copies are usually sold compared with nonofficial papers. Since late 2004, the *People's Daily* can also be bought at newspaper stands. Interviews with male editor of semiofficial paper and female specialist on newspaper distribution in Beijing (#8, 34). For reliable data on newspaper retail sales, see CPCR, "Zhongguo Shichanghua Baokan Guanggao Toufang Cankao 2005 (I) (Market Intelligence Report on China's Print Media Retail Distribution)," (Beijing: CPCR Kaiyuan Celüe [Opening Strategy Consultation], 2005).

[35] Interview with male editor of semiofficial paper in Beijing (#13).

[36] Interview with two male staff members of advertising sections at nonofficial and official papers in Chongqing (#36, 44).

earlier, conglomeration thus also affected control over business management of newspapers.

One legacy from the planned economy retains the newspapers' status as public institutions (*shiye danwei*), resulting in eligibility for tax exemptions according to Chinese tax law. As public institutions, they concentrate on the production and provision of public goods and services, while also operating like businesses, raising revenue through market-oriented activities that can become a lucrative source of income for local governments (Esarey 2005; Zhao 2008). Due to tax breaks, newspapers exaggerate their advertising income in official documentation to appear competitive in the market.[37]

Along with changes in finances, newspapers moved away from a state-planned system of operations. As early as 1978, the Ministry of Finance approved the introduction of a business management system at the *People's Daily* and a number of other newspapers published in Beijing. They were forced to save money by streamlining operations and were subjected to cost analysis, profit targets, and government taxation (Y. Zhao 1998). Newspaper management became more innovative and diverse over time, sometimes inspired by business trips to Europe and the United States.

Along with these changes in business operations, new structures were built to attract readers and advertisers. Many newspapers have established independent, more efficient distribution channels now, as opposed to relying on the post office as the main distributor (Chen 2004; Hu 2004). They have also set up advertising departments that either collect information about readership backgrounds themselves or contract out such data collection to market research companies. Through these channels, newspapers obtain circulation data and readership statistics, which have become increasingly important when competing for advertisers. Authentic circulation rates are kept as an internal secret known by senior staff and advertising experts, but are inflated to outsiders to appear more competitive.[38]

To provide advertisers with more reliable statistics, a growing number of market research companies and academics have collected data on newspaper distribution, audience demographics, and retail sales data at newspaper stands. These data vary in quality, focus on the more developed cities in China, and are only rarely obtained through representative samples of the population or panels.[39] Advertisers ultimately care about reaching particular target audiences,

---

[37] Due to inflated advertising income reported by newspapers, I rely on media practitioners' expert assessments to develop a typology of newspapers. In addition, in Chapter 10, I rely on advertising revenue reported by the advertising industry which has less incentive to overreport its income due to tax policies.

[38] Based on my interviews and conversations. See also Ying Zhao, "Two Circulation Audit Cases in China – Circulation Audit Development in China and Its Future," *China Media Research* 3, no. 1 (2007).

[39] Based on conversations with thirteen academic and market research companies in Beijing in 2005. For examples of research on distribution and audience background among respected scholars and market researchers, see *Chinese Advertising Yearbook 2004* (*Zhongguo Guanggao Nianjian 2004*) (China: Xinhua Chubanshe, 2004).

but statistics on audience background are presented as a percentage of inflated and foggy circulation numbers. Therefore, advertisers have pressured print publications to voluntarily enter organizations that audit circulation, such as China's first own audit research center, *Guoxin*, established in 2005 (Y. Zhao 2007).

In part due to the secrecy of authentic circulation rates and lack of reliable data, journalists themselves only have very general ideas of their own readers. A comment by a reporter at *Chongqing Evening News* illustrates the general perception that journalists have about readers: "of course, what places food on the table at our organization is not the management by the Party, but the market. That's the reader – 'ordinary people' (*laobaixing*) – and the advertising client."[40] Phone calls, letters, emails, or text messages are seen as indicators of consumer preference that drive circulation levels.[41] Editors talk about differences across readership in terms of percentages of paid subscriptions in comparison with sales at newsstands, whereby greater reliance on distribution through newsstands leads to more aggressive news reporting, as readers may change their consumption habits from one day to another.[42] Of course, advertising staff had more concrete understandings of their readership background, distinguishing mostly in terms of age, education, and profession, but none of the journalists or editors I interviewed brought up detailed demographic characteristics. They mostly cared about circulation as an indicator of attractiveness to ordinary citizens.[43]

Overall, this emphasis on audience demands exemplifies the key feature of media commercialization and media marketization more broadly. As advertising becomes the main source of revenue for newspapers, media practitioners also become more responsive to readers. Today, Chinese media practitioners don't talk about "the masses" anymore – they use the term *audience*.

* * *

In response to budgetary deficits, the Chinese state has supported the introduction of market mechanisms in the media industry with deregulation of licensing, personnel management, and business operations. Relaxation of licensing policies, increased emphasis on performance, and reliance on advertising and investment caused newspapers to rely on market competition for their survival and prosperity rather than solely on the newspaper's hierarchical location

---

[40] Interview with male journalist of nonofficial paper in Chongqing (#39).

[41] Interview with female journalist of official paper and male editor of commercialized paper in Beijing (#9, 27). See also Esarey, "Cornering the Market: State Strategies for Controlling China's Commercial Media."

[42] Subscription rates can be divided into work units and personal subscriptions. Some nonofficial papers, such as *Beijing Youth Daily*, can rely on high personal subscription rates, but those are the minority, as it is uncommon for Chinese readers to subscribe to newspapers outside of the work unit. Interview with male editor of official and semiofficial paper in Beijing (#8).

[43] This was true also for publications specializing in international news. Editors and journalists may have more concrete ideas about reader background when working for publications geared toward business, such as, for example, *Caijing Magazine* (*Caijing*).

within the political system and its connections with the state. Because audience characteristics and size attract advertisers and investors, the greater profit orientation of newspapers has increased their responsiveness to readers.

At the same time, media marketization took place within an institutional structure that allowed propaganda authorities to intervene in the organization, personnel decisions, and editorial process of newspapers. This basic institutional framework has remained in place, but it has also adjusted to changing circumstances over time to prevent the erosion of state influence over newspapers, as happened shortly before the 1989 Tiananmen demonstrations. As coercion exerted through institutions relaxed, the state found new ways to exchange economic resources for compliance with PD instructions, which is one solution to the dictator's dilemma, discussed in Chapter 2. Performance bonuses for media staff complement, but do not substitute, the institutional structure the CCP created to monitor and control the production of news.[44] On the whole, media marketization has brought about greater autonomy for newspapers, although the state has maintained the capacity to exert considerable control over newspapers through institutions, most importantly the Propaganda Department, if it makes it a priority. Officially, this policy is formulated so that the editorial process is under the supervision of the Party, whereas business and finances are not.[45]

These changes have created a peculiar structure in the Chinese newspaper market. The Chinese newspaper industry is highly localized and fragmented by cities. Because licensing policies require sponsorship, most newspapers register with local institutions, which in turn has consequences for their distribution. Each city in China, even small towns, has its own newspapers. Although some newspapers are available all over China, which media sources people seek and how they view the media themselves depends primarily on the location.

In addition, advertisers are most interested in consumers primarily located in urban areas, thus creating incentives for newspapers to focus on readers located in the cities. In the countryside, readership had declined to approximately 20 percent by the early 1990s. Villagers complain that newspapers are often delivered late. Not surprisingly, television and radio constitute the preferred media in the Chinese countryside.[46] In contrast, more than 80 percent of people in the cities read newspapers, as indicated by the BAS and LLM surveys. As

---

[44] Chapter 11 discusses authoritarian states that rely more strongly than China on distributing economic resources to media by means of indirect state subsidies.

[45] Interviews with male central-level official in the propaganda *xitong*, male director of a major press group in Beijing, and male editor of nonofficial paper in Chongqing (#30, 21, 42). See also Hu, "Zhongguo Baoye Jingji Fazhan Jin 20 Nian Chengjiu (The Achievement of the Chinese Newspaper Industry in the Course of the Past 20 Years)."

[46] Conversations with villagers in the Beijing area. For survey results, see Xuehong Zhang, "Wo Guo Nongcun Xinwen Chuanbo Xianzhuang Yanjiu (A Study of Media Communication in China's Rural Regions)," in *Zhongguo Chuanbo Xiaoguo Toushi (A Perspective on Media Effects in China)*, ed. Chongshan Chen and Xiuling Mi (Shenyang: Shenyang Chubanshe,

the Internet grows, newspapers will continue to remain important information sources in China. As explained in Chapter 6, online news websites are tied to traditional media outlets and often reprint newspaper articles.

Because newspaper markets differ across cities, the remainder of this chapter outlines the structure of newspaper markets in Beijing and Chongqing in the eyes of local media practitioners. These are experts on their local media markets who describe general differences between newspaper types to make sense of a highly complex media environment, although, of course, they differ from one another somewhat in their individual perceptions. The next section explains how media practitioners categorize newspapers in these two cities.

The Structure of Newspapers in Chinese Cities

One day I was sitting with Jiang, a journalist famous for investigative journalism, in a cafe in Beijing.[47] I kept asking very specific questions about individual newspapers' relationship with the government. At one point Jiang started to get a bit impatient answering my detailed questions. "I will tell you a story," he said. "I'm sure then you'll understand the relationship between newspapers and the state. Once upon a time the emperor had two sons. One (apparently illegitimate) grew up as an average guy; the other one was brought up as the heir to the throne. Both of them opened food stands selling baked sweet potatoes to people in the street. Both depended on selling sweet potatoes for their living, but the average guy knew if he couldn't sell any, he would not be able to survive. The heir to the throne, however, didn't have to make as much of an effort selling potatoes – he knew he could always depend on the emperor if he was in need."[48]

Jiang's story illustrates that media reform has systematically changed the way in which different kinds of newspapers relate to the state. The "heir to the throne" and the "average guy" described by Jiang are equivalent to two newspaper types, referred to as *official* (*guanfang de baozhi*, also called *dangbao*, *jiguanbao*, or *dabao*) and *commercialized* (*shichanghua de baozhi*, also called *xiaobao*, or *dushibao*) by Chinese journalists and editors. Often they also raise a middle category, described as *semiofficial* (*banguanfang de baozhi*, also called *wanbao*), which fits in between the other two extremes.[49] Semiofficial

---

1989), Chongshan Chen and Wusan Sun, *Meijie – Ren – Xiandaihua (The Media – People – Modernization)* (Beijing: Zhongguo Shehui Kexue Chubanshe, 1995).

[47] Jiang is a pseudonym to guarantee anonymity of the interviewee.

[48] Interview with male journalist of semiofficial paper in Beijing (#30).

[49] The term "semiofficial media" (*banguanfang meiti*) received 157,000 hits when searching the Chinese online search engine Google, and 26,400 when searching Baidu. Accessed December 2, 2011. For references to newspaper types among Chinese scholars, see, for example, Cungang Wang, "Gongzhong Dui Zhongguo Waijiao De Canyu Jiqi Yingxiang: Jiyu 2003 Nian De San Ge Anli De Yanjiu (The Participation and Influence of the Public on Chinese Foreign Affairs: Three Case Studies from 2003)," *Waijiao Pinglun (Commentary on Foreign Affairs)* 3 (2010).

and commercialized papers are also described as nonofficial papers, although everyone agrees that truly nonofficial papers do not exist in China.

In my interviews, I first asked whether the journalist had heard these terms before. If yes, I asked what these terms meant. The first reaction to my question often was as follows: "In fact these expressions are not fully accurate. In reality, China does not have a fully commercialized and truly private media – all media are ultimately owned by the state."[50] Despite state ownership, however, reporters were eager to explain that newspapers systematically differed on several dimensions that correspond to the infrastructures of political control outlined earlier, including institutional affiliation, finances, and management and personnel. What media practitioners had in mind when categorizing newspapers into different types turns out to be closely associated with different degrees of media marketization and perceived autonomy from the state.

Institutional Affiliation

Media practitioners often use a newspaper's sponsoring institution to determine its type. Editors and journalists describe Party and political organ papers consistently as official papers; other papers are either placed in one alternative group or divided into two more groups.[51] If editors and journalists distinguish between semiofficial and commercialized papers, they attribute the main difference to the internal structure of the conglomerate. Semiofficial papers are incorporated as "son-papers" into a hierarchical structure within a press group, headed by an official paper as "mother paper."[52] Commercialized papers are either not incorporated into a press group or are often part of one within which they have more equal status. Thus the first factor that defines the structure of local newspaper markets is the organizational features of the papers in the market, most importantly their institutional affiliation and the internal structure of the respective conglomerate.

Finances

Media practitioners agree that official newspapers finance themselves mainly through advertising, but 24 percent are convinced that official papers still receive state subsidies, although the amount has decreased and is expected to diminish over time. Thirty-two percent believe that official papers are indirectly subsidized, as they can largely rely on subscriptions by government offices at all levels of government. By contrast, nonofficial papers rely largely on sales at newsstands – only a small minority, such as, for example, *Beijing Youth Daily*, manage to obtain private subscriptions, as those are uncommon in China.

---

[50] Thirty-five percent of interviewees brought up this point.
[51] Interviewees #10, 13, 27, 28, 46 only distinguished between two; interviewees #33, 38, 42, 43 distinguished between three groups.
[52] Alternatively, mother-papers are often called "big papers" and son-papers "small papers." These terms can be misleading: "small" papers are often more widely circulated than "big" papers.

Nonofficial newspapers cannot rely on a steady income through subscriptions by work units.

In addition, media practitioners associate marketization with nonstate investment and profit making; 38 percent of media practitioners brought up this point. Nonofficial newspapers supposedly attract a greater audience and thus more advertising. By contrast, official papers either incur a loss or, at the most, break even, but fortunately, they can overcome financial difficulties with the profits of the more marketized "son-papers" within the same press group. However, although official papers can survive through indirect state subsidies and nonofficial papers are not as fortunate, there are also differences across nonofficial papers: semiofficial papers finance themselves solely through advertising but are not partially privatized. Commercialized papers must also satisfy investors, who place additional pressure on editors and managers to make a profit.

Management and Personnel

Media practitioners also bring up differences in management style and personnel of official and nonofficial papers. Sixty-two percent describe the style of official papers as "traditional." According to this view, the institutional sponsor is strongly involved in management and personnel appointments; salary and promotion are not tied to performance, and journalists primarily take the state's position into account as opposed to that of their readers.

By contrast, commercialized newspapers are seen as being primarily oriented toward their readership. They intend to "make a paper that readers would like to read," "satisfy readers' demands," "stand for the point of view of their readers," and have the intention to "inform and give advice."[53] These papers therefore also conduct research on their consumers. To increase profits, the paper is run like an enterprise and less like a state organ.

Semiofficial papers fall somewhere in between these extremes. They operate like official papers but "look commercialized on the outside" and "have no real drive to change."[54] Although they care about profit making, they also have the security that their institutional sponsor won't "let them die."[55] As a result, they are seen as being less likely to overstep boundaries set by the PD.

Naturally, changes of management style are associated with changes of personnel in terms of political leadership, attitudes, and age. Media practitioners point out that the leadership of official and semiofficial papers was solely composed of political officials and/or Party members, whereas the highest leadership of commercialized media were not always public officials and/or party members. At lower levels within the institution, staff members of official papers at all levels had titles that resembled those in government institutions.

---

[53] Interviews with male editor of semiofficial paper in Beijing and male editor of nonofficial paper in Chongqing (#13, 40).

[54] Interviews with two male editors of nonofficial papers in Chongqing (#41, 42).

[55] Interview with male editor of nonofficial paper in Chongqing (#40).

Those "who do not act like public officials" became more numerous as the newspaper's degree of commercialization increased.[56] "Acting like a public official" was associated with not writing "real news" and copying from official documents.[57] Despite greater professionalism, editors and journalists at nonofficial papers, particularly commercialized papers, tended to be younger, more inventive, and more open to change and regard themselves as the voice of ordinary people.[58] Hassid (2012) describes these two types of journalists as Communist and advocacy professionals.

In sum, media practitioners associate official newspapers with greater involvement of the state in management and stronger connections between staff members and the government. Nonofficial papers are seen as being run like an enterprise that is more responsive to readers.

Newspaper Types in Beijing and Chongqing

After media practitioners had explained their own understanding of newspaper types to me, I presented them with a list of newspapers in Beijing and Chongqing, asking them to categorize individual newspapers according to their own understanding as laid out in the preceding section. Later I assigned each newspaper type a number and averaged across the responses. The result of this first question is presented on the x-axis in Figures 3.2 and 3.3, revealing the degree of media marketization across newspaper types, whereby official papers lag behind in terms of the extent to which they have undergone marketization, followed by nonofficial papers. Official papers still receive certain state subsidies, semiofficial papers finance themselves exclusively through advertising, and commercialized papers finance themselves with advertising, but they also receive some investment.

The answer to a second question I asked is displayed on the y-axis in Figures 3.2 and 3.3. In addition to categorizing individual newspapers in terms of types, I also asked editors and journalists whether individual papers were more open (*kaifang* or *fangkai*) or closed (*baoshou*) in reporting.[59] As before, I

---

[56] Interviews with two male editors of nonofficial papers and male specialist on advertising at an official paper in Chongqing (#40, 42, 44).

[57] Interviews with male freelance journalist formerly working at an official paper in Beijing, female journalist of official paper in Beijing, and male editor of nonofficial paper in Chongqing (#3, 8, 42). See also Wu, "Command Communication: The Politics of Editorial Formulation in the People's Daily."

[58] Interview with male editor of nonofficial paper in Chongqing (#35). According to the Chinese journalism network, the age of staff in thirty nonofficial papers ranged, on average, between 26 and 29.8 years of age. See "Zui Nianqing de Jizhequn Peihangbang" (Ranking of the Youngest Journalist Staff), http://press.gapp.gov.cn/tongji/reporter_youngest.php, accessed October 16, 2006. Thanks to Jonathan Hassid for this reference.

[59] *Baoshou* is often translated as "conservative" in the sense of its Latin root (*conservare*), meaning preserving and backward-looking. *Kaifang* is not "liberal" in the Western sense, but carries the meaning of "open." Politically, it is associated with the open door policy. Therefore, some reporters corrected me that the term *kaifang* carried "too much political flavor" and preferred the term *fangkai*, referring to less control and more autonomy.

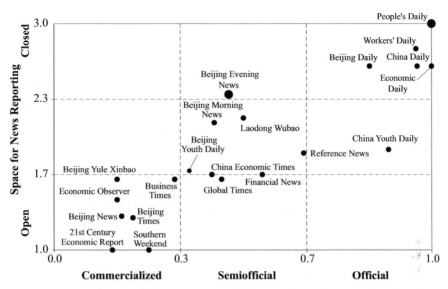

FIGURE 3.2 Newspapers in Beijing as Perceived by Local Media Practitioners. *Source:* Interviews by the Author, 2005.[a]

[a] Titles of newspapers are listed in English, Pinyin, and Chinese characters at the beginning of the book.

later assigned numbers to each response and averaged across them. As shown in these figures, media practitioners associated official papers as being more tightly controlled by the state, whereas nonofficial papers are perceived to be more loosely controlled and face fewer constraints in reporting. Chapters 4 and 5 further investigate whether these perceptions of greater autonomy of newspapers translate into differences in the selection and tone of news stories. Papers that I selected for content analysis are highlighted with larger dots in both figures.

Of course, media practitioners did not always agree on their placement of individual papers. Because of the rapid growth and reform of Chinese media, it is difficult – even for media practitioners – to keep up with rapid changes in a highly complex media environment.[60] There is much agreement among experts to categorize, for example, the *People's Daily* as an official paper because it constitutes the mouthpiece of the CCP at the central level. By comparison, experts disagreed more often regarding, for example, papers registered with the China Youth League. According to conversations with senior editors at *China Youth Daily* and *Beijing Youth Daily*, these newspapers do not function

---

[60] For readability, Figures 3.2 and 3.3 do not display standard deviations of the data points. Newspapers with the highest standard deviations were *Jiankangbao* in Chongqing (s.d. = 0.66), *Global Times* (s.d. = 0.41), *Beijing Morning News (Beijing Zaobao)* (s.d. = 0.4), and *Reference News (Cankao Xiaoxi)* (s.d. = 0.39).

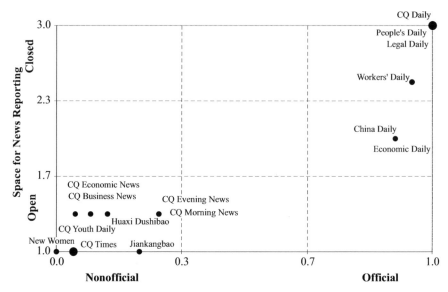

FIGURE 3.3 Newspapers in Chongqing as Perceived by Local Media Practitioners.
Source: Interviews by the Author, 2005.[a]

[a] Titles of newspapers are listed in English, Pinyin, and Chinese characters at the beginning of the book.

as mouthpieces and enjoy greater autonomy than other papers under direct supervision of a state or party unit. As a result, *China Youth Daily* enjoys greater space for news reporting as compared with other official papers, and *Beijing Youth Daily* falls at the boundaries between being semiofficial and commercialized. Individual papers may not always fit neatly into the typology of official, semiofficial, and commercialized papers, and media practitioners may disagree with the placement of some papers. Nonetheless, media practitioners make sense of a highly complex media environment by distinguishing between different types, and they agree, on average, with respect to the key dimensions on which these types differ from one another.[61] Figures 3.2 and 3.3 describe these general tendencies, illustrating media practitioners' own perceptions of local newspaper markets.

Apart from a common relationship between media marketization and space for news reporting, there are also differences between Chongqing and Beijing. Along with Guangzhou and Shanghai, Beijing is leading in terms of its regional advertising revenue, whereas Chongqing's advertising income is closer to average. According to the *Chinese Advertising Yearbook*, the advertising income

[61] Chapter 7 shows that ordinary citizens' assessments of newspapers, on average, match those of media practitioners.

of the advertising industry when I conducted the interviews in 2005 was Chinese Renminbi (RMB) 25,155,760,000 in Beijing and RMB 2,710,220,000 in Chongqing, below the national average of RMB 4,568,870,000. Because the Chongqing newspaper market is smaller and lags behind Beijing in terms of marketization, newspapers only fit into two categories, not three. Because Chongqing is less marketized, the structure of the newspaper market in Chongqing is more similar to that of an average Chinese city, such as Wuxi and Shenyang. Beijing, on the other hand, is on the cutting edge in terms of media reform and is possibly similar to Shanghai. Foshan in Guangdong does not always follow the same patterns as other Chinese cities, thus pointing to an exceptional situation of Guangdong in the Chinese media landscape (see Chapter 9 and Appendix B for details).

* * *

Media practitioners use the terms *official*, *semiofficial*, and *commercialized* papers to simplify the complicated relationship between newspapers and the state in Chinese cities. The CCP has established infrastructures, most importantly, the PD and GAPP, through which it exerts political control over the organization, personnel, and editorial process of newspapers, and newspapers vary in terms of their autonomy from the state. To media practitioners, official papers tend to be less marketized compared with nonofficial papers, corresponding to perceptions of space for news reporting. As we will see, the emergence of such newspaper types allows media outlets to assume different functions in China's media environment.

Conclusion

Since the late 1970s, China has deregulated, commercialized, and partially privatized newspapers, leading to a decrease in control over the business and finances of media outlets. Although newspapers remain embedded in an institutional structure that ties them to the state, this structure has also been adjusted to maintain the state's capacity to exert political control over the organization, personnel, and editorial process of newspapers through the GAPP and most importantly the PD. The result is a peculiar structure of newspapers in Chinese cities in which individual newspapers differ in terms of autonomy from the state, while institutions effectively establish boundaries for news reporting.

Under these circumstances, how does media marketization influence the production of news? To be better able to compare news reporting in different newspaper types, we must turn to specific issue areas that are relevant for Chinese politics. The next chapter lays out the rules for news reporting in the area of labor law and the United States that lead to self-censorship among reporters. Chapter 5 then examines how these rules translate into news content.

PART I

THE PRODUCTION OF NEWS

4

Boundaries for News Reporting on Labor Law and the United States

How do considerations regarding the political sensitivity of news stories figure into the production of news? This chapter explores media practitioners' intuition about politically sensitive stories related to labor law and the United States, revealing where topics within each of these issue areas fit into the open or the closed spectrum. As we will see, political sensitivity serves as a shortcut that guides journalistic behavior, carrying features of the institutional structure in which newspapers remain embedded. Reporters develop norms and routines that guide when and how they cover the news as they experience the mechanisms of political control laid out in Chapter 3. In order to place PD instructions into the broader context, this chapter starts out with a summary of the key changes in the scope and style of editorial control during the reform era.

Scope and Style of Directives by the PD

According to the policy rationale behind Chinese media reform laid out in Chapter 3, changes in newspapers are supposed to be confined to the economic realm. The editorial supervision by the PD is supposed to remain untouched, and the Party continues to be able to exert political control over the production of news. Although the editorial process continues to be monitored by the PD, officials have over time adjusted the scope and style of restrictions to the changing circumstances in the media sector as well as in Chinese society more broadly.

Most importantly, the PD has significantly reduced the scope of its supervision to support the marketization of newspapers. Media outlets are allowed to compete freely in reporting on open topics while the propaganda authorities continue to watch closely over topics for which audience demands potentially may undermine the policies and goals of political leaders. Although official and nonofficial papers are supposed to compete against each other to a certain extent, they are also supposed to divide up work such that official papers focus on politically sensitive topics, whereas nonofficial papers primarily publish nonsensitive ones.[1] For example, a central-level propaganda official explained that the PD gives nonofficial papers more freedom to report, while it pays more attention to official papers due to their focus on political content.[2] Similarly, an editor of a nonofficial paper in Chongqing commented: "we have more societal news, the *Chongqing Daily* has more political news."[3] By maintaining a division of labor between official and nonofficial papers, the PD is trying to keep a tighter grip on politically sensitive topics, thus constraining competition on some topics, while allowing competition on others.

In this context, "political news" is a synonym for politically sensitive stories. A Beijing editor of a weekly nonofficial paper specializing in international news explained that most topics could be covered, but some were "sensitive, for instance, when they give rise to political problems."[4] The editor-in-chief of a nonofficial tabloid in Chongqing explained: "Political news is different [from social news], it is more sensitive."[5] When journalists use the term *political news*, they are not referring to all topics containing political information, but in fact to sensitive stories. Later in this chapter, we will see that many politically relevant topics related to labor law and the United States are in fact considered to be open. Therefore, open topics still contain much political information.

Censorship has also become more "passive" and less comprehensive. Instructions now tend to be more about what *not* to report on, whereas before instructions emphasized more strongly which issues should be covered and how to report on them.[6] A propaganda official and editor-in-chief also noted that they focus on the "big issues" (*da shi*).[7] Over time, journalists and editors gained more freedom to choose topics by themselves as opposed to receiving directions from officials (Wu 1994). Media marketization requires some flexibility

[1] Chapter 5 tests whether and how this division of labor plays out in practice.
[2] Interview with male central-level official in the propaganda *xitong* in Beijing (#30). Similar statements were made by male editor of official and semiofficial paper in Beijing (#8). See also Chengju Huang, "The Development of a Semi-Independent Press in Post-Mao China: An Overview and a Case Study of Chengdu Business News," *Journalism Studies* 1, no. 4 (2000). See also comments by Si Qing, the editor-in-chief of *Renda Xinwen Chuanbo Luntan*, entitled "(Shilun Dangbao Yu Dushibao de Juese Fengong) (The Role and Division of Labor between Party and Metro Papers)," June 12, 2005, http://www.zijin.net/blog/user1/137/archives/2005/942.shtml, accessed November 18, 2011.
[3] Interview with male editor of nonofficial paper in Chongqing (#42).
[4] Interview with male editor of semiofficial paper in Beijing (#13).
[5] Interview with male editor of nonofficial paper in Chongqing (#42). Similar statements were made by male editor of semiofficial and official paper in Beijing and male editor of nonofficial paper in Chongqing (#8, 40).
[6] Interviews with male journalist assisting foreign journalists in Beijing, male editor of semiofficial paper in Beijing, male editor of nonofficial paper in Chongqing, and male journalist of nonofficial paper in Chongqing (#7, 22, 37, 39). See also Yuezhi Zhao, *Communication in China: Political Economy, Power, and Conflict* (Lanham: Rowman & Littlefield, 2008).
[7] Interview with male central-level official in the propaganda *xitong* and male editor-in-chief of official paper in Beijing (#7, 30).

among media outlets as journalists are under pressure to cater to the market. An editor writing for an official and a nonofficial paper in the *People's Daily* group commented: "China is in a transition period from a planned toward a market economy. Previously, under the planned economy you wrote what your superior wanted you to write; this is now not OK, or at least in part not OK. What can you do? Media need to adapt, need to understand what ordinary people like to read, and that's what I write about. Simultaneously, I now also need to consider the opinions of superiors. It's the same for those leaders in charge of media management (propaganda officials); they cannot manage the media using the same methods as before."[8]

In addition to scope, the style and content of documents and instructions from the propaganda authorities have been modified. Internet and mobile phones increasingly exert pressure on media to publish the news in a more timely fashion. As a result, the propaganda authorities have switched from a system that relied primarily on hard copy documents to submitting instructions mainly in oral fashion – either on the phone or at meetings with editors.[9] Conversations with officials at the PD can provide editors with the opportunity to argue that certain issues should not be restricted.[10]

Propaganda authorities for the most part have also retreated from must-carry news. With some exceptions, newspapers can formulate their own news reports. And even when the PD requests to reprint reports by Xinhua, its news reporting has been greatly modified, particularly during the 1990s. Financial limitations provided incentives to take into consideration complaints by subscribers and clients who missed detail, background events, speed of news release, and more investigative news reporting. Additional pressure arose from the spread of the Internet, which challenged the monopoly of Xinhua as the main news agency. Chat rooms and more recently Weibo – the Chinese version of Twitter – have served as alternative information sources. Some commercialized media outlets have initiated online networks since 1996 through which members can retrieve cross-regional news quickly and cheaply. For example, a network initiated by *Chengdu Business News* (*Chengdu Shangbao*) in 1998 covered almost all provinces around the country, although these networks were not allowed to become Associated Press–style newspaper cooperatives or agencies (Xin 2006). Even if newspapers are asked to rely on Xinhua reports or choose to do so to be "on the safe side," the content of these reports has been adapted to the needs of commercialized media outlets that are competing for media audiences.

[8] Interview in Beijing (#8).
[9] Editors-in-chief of major newspapers meet at least once a week with their respective PD. See interviews with male editor of semiofficial paper in Beijing and male editor of nonofficial paper in Chongqing (#13, 38). See also Zhao, *Communication in China: Political Economy, Power, and Conflict*. There is also an internal website system for directives by the Central PD. Thanks to Jonathan Hassid for sharing this information.
[10] Interview with male editor of official paper in Beijing (#7).

On a final note, several journalists mentioned to me that pressure they experienced did not always come from the propaganda authorities. When reporting labor disputes, many companies attempted to influence news content in their favor. Journalists felt hesitant to write critical articles about enterprises they had connections to or had received monetary gifts from.[11] One direct way to influence newspaper content is through monetary gifts (*hongbao*) given to journalists when visiting the company for an interview or a press conference. Journalists face social pressure from other journalists to take the bribe. Some journalists' salaries depend on these additional sources of income because of low salaries. An indirect way is bribery of the PD by enterprises. The bribed official then gets in touch with media institutions to stop negative reporting about a company. As a consequence, some commercialized newspapers have started to abolish the practice of assigning specific journalists to individual governmental institutions or have begun to change these assignments frequently.[12]

Individual officials have also sued newspapers for news reporting, tried to block publication of articles, and even resorted to violence to threaten journalists.[13] Businesses are also engaged in such activities.[14] These incidents have been associated with the growth of corruption and the weakened influence of the central government over local leaders, but the government is also moving toward greater control of media by the courts. Newspapers often need to employ lawyers to give legal advice to reporters and to represent them in court.[15]

Political Sensitivity and the Creation of Norms for the Production of News

Most censorship in the Chinese media takes place before publication. When journalists and editors make conscious or unconscious decisions about censorship, they use their conception of what is political and the accompanying feeling of sensitivity as a shortcut to decide whether to cover a topic and about how to present the issue.

---

[11] Interviews with male journalist of weekly magazine, female journalist of official paper, and male editor of commercialized paper in Beijing (#31, 9, 27). See also Yuezhi Zhao, *Media, Market, and Democracy in China: Between the Party Line and the Bottom Line* (Urbana: University of Illinois Press, 1998).

[12] Interview with male editor of commercialized paper in Beijing (#10).

[13] See Qinglian He, *Zhongguo Zhengfu Ruhe Kongzhi Meiti: Zhongguo Renquan Yanjiu Baogao* (*Media Control in China: A Report by Human Rights in China*) (New York: Human Rights in China, 2003).

[14] Interview with male editor of commercialized paper and male editor of semiofficial paper in Beijing (#10, 13).

[15] The All-China Federation of Journalists has created a committee for the protection of journalists, but it lacks resources and qualified personnel. Interview with male lawyer specializing in media-related cases and male editor of commercialized paper in Beijing (#26, 27). See also Benjamin J. Liebman, "The Media and the Courts: Towards Competitive Supervision?," *China Quarterly* 208 (2011b).

One journalist in Beijing described these boundaries as "glass walls" of news reporting. Speeches by political leaders and other political documents are often vague and leave some room for interpretation, and instructions by the propaganda authorities are situationally constructed as they are constantly adapted to China's rapidly changing political, societal, and economic circumstances. What may be considered a small issue today may become a big issue tomorrow, and propaganda authorities may open up reporting about an event in some instances but not in others. Because there is pressure to cover the news in a timely manner and prepublication censorship slows down the coverage of current events, media staff cannot acquire permission for all news coverage, so they learn where boundaries lie primarily in retrospect. There is a certain degree of uncertainty regarding how the PD will deal with the publication of an individual story.[16]

To overcome this uncertainty, journalists rely on shortcuts or heuristics that aid in estimating the likelihood that a story will get the reporter or media outlet into trouble. Heuristics are "strategies of simplification that reduce the complexity of judgment tasks, to make them tractable for the kind of mind that people happen to have" (Kahneman et al. 1982: xii). Human beings are constrained in their ability to process information due to the fallibility of memory and limitations of the human mind (Lodge et al. 1995). Simplifying heuristics help to overcome this uncertainty by allowing people to estimate the true nature of their more complex environment. Heuristics are often useful in helping citizens to end up at the "right" place, such as in the case of a 1988 referendum in California, when less informed voters took cues from better informed sources (Lupia 1994). However, sometimes heuristics can lead to "severe and systematic" bias in judgment (Kahneman et al. 1982: 3). The second part of this book describes such a situation whereby reliance on media labels leads to erroneous conclusions about political messages in the news. This chapter focuses on a sense of heuristic political sensitivity that reporters develop to estimate the probability that they will have unpleasant encounters with propaganda authorities.

Media practitioners use their conception of what is political and the accompanying feeling of sensitivity as a shortcut to make decisions about self-censorship. Political sensitivity serves as an intuition that allows media practitioners to make an educated guess about which issues and topics are restricted rather than relying on a set of clear-cut rules. This intuition about political sensitivity guides the practice of journalism in Chinese newspapers, encouraging journalists to behave in a specific way and discouraging them from behaving in another way, here referred to as journalistic norms and routines.[17]

[16] Interviews with female and male press officers at the US embassy, male head of press group, male journalist of official paper, and male editor of semiofficial paper in Beijing (#16, 17, 22, 25). See also Rachel E. Stern and Jonathan Hassid, "Amplifying Silence: Uncertainty and Control Parables in Contemporary China," *Comparative Political Studies* 45, no. 10 (2012).

[17] Constructivists in international relations define norms as "shared expectations about appropriate behavior held by a community of actors." See Martha Finnemore, *National Interest in International Security*, Cornell Studies in Political Economy (Ithaca: Cornell University Press,

These routines of journalistic practice can be revealed when asking media practitioners whether they had ever experienced any trouble (*pengdao mafan*) with the PD or by asking specifically about certain issues and topics. Most editors and journalists seemed eager to share their experiences and responded spontaneously without pausing to think much about their answers. Because of their profession, they valued interviews as a source of information and trusted me, as far as I can tell, enough to give me honest responses. However, there is the possibility that media practitioners will not give information to an "outsider." To check, I also analyzed handbooks for journalistic training. These are published by newspapers or communication scholars and distributed to entering journalists. In addition, I could observe many insights I learned through my conversations and in handbooks empirically, as explained in more detail in Chapter 5. Relying on these three different sources, a number of common patterns emerged.

Media practitioners think about political sensitivity as a dimension tied to three norms that guide decisions about news coverage. First, a topic could be so sensitive that it cannot be reported about. The PD phrases such prohibited areas as "stop reporting" (*tingzhi baodao*) or "do not report" (*bu bao*) an issue (IFJ 2010). Officials encourage media to submit internal reports (*neican*) to relevant institutions on such taboo topics, which many journalists do.[18] Second, there are topics that the media are generally free to report about, but there remained constraints about how, when, or how much the media can report about them. If this is the case, the PD demands that media "should orient themselves on official information" (*yao yi guanfang xinxi wei zhu*), "report positively" (*zhengmian baodao*), or reprint "news reports by Xinhua" (*yong Xinhuashe tonggao*) (IFJ 2010). On all remaining topics, editors and journalists feel free to report in any way they wish. This constitutes the third and final norm of journalistic news reporting.[19]

I refer to the first highly sensitive category as *taboo* topics. Topics associated with the second and third norm are both comparatively less sensitive and therefore reportable. However, *closed* topics require self-censorship to accommodate PD instructions, whereas *open* topics do not.[20] Media practitioners in Beijing

---

1996), Peter Katzenstein, *The Culture of National Security: Norms and Identity in World Politics* (New York: Columbia University Press, 1996).

[18] Interview with female official at the All-China Federation of Journalists (#33). On the effects of internal reports on courts, see Benjamin J. Liebman, "Changing Media, Changing Courts," in *Changing Media, Changing China*, ed. Susan Shirk (Oxford: Oxford University Press, 2011a).

[19] Forty-three percent of journalists in Guangzhou report to have a lot of autonomy on content, whereby rules set by the PD, professional ethics, and readers' preferences constituted their main limitations. See Fen Lin, "A Survey Report on Chinese Journalists in China," *China Quarterly* 202 (2010). Chapter 6 discusses different interpretations of professional ethics in relation to demands by the state and audiences.

[20] The expression "new stories, old stories, no stories" (*xinwen, jiuwen, wuwen*), meaning that some stories can immediately be published, some need to wait until they can be published, and some cannot be published at all, further illustrates these norms. See Lidan Chen, *Makesi Zhuyi*

and Chongqiang shared expectations about appropriate behavior depending on a topic's degree of political sensitivity, and they described the majority of topics as completely open, using such words as "social," "apolitical," "soft news," and "not sensitive." Closed topics, on the other hand, were "political," "hard news," and "somewhat sensitive."[21]

This sense of political sensitivity and the accompanying journalistic routines are learned over time through practice. A China Central Television (CCTV) reporter and editor learned by trial and error: political sensitivity was one of many factors why editors criticized her reports during the final inspection before broadcasting.[22] A reporter at a Party paper in Beijing complained about the style of a new editor who put up detailed instructions about "correct" reporting on a message board.[23] A journalist working for Xinhua read previous Xinhua articles on related topics to sharpen his instinct about how to report on issues.[24] Because a journalist's personal assessment is learned over time, it is in many ways subjective, depending on when and how long the person has practiced journalism, where and for which institution, which topics she reported about, and the person's personality: some people are greater risk takers than others.

However, despite these differences, I was surprised to find similar patterns in news coverage on issues as different as labor law and the United States. Such cohesion is facilitated through the institutional structure within which newspapers remain embedded as well as the social networks among media practitioners.

Most importantly, the Central PD and its local equivalents issue detailed materials that are given out at regular update meetings with senior media personnel and other leaders in the propaganda *xitong*. As explained previously, these rules mainly place restrictions on news content and are mostly issued after publication as they are adapted to the ever-changing news environment. Senior media staff, in turn, communicate these regulations within their media outlet. This can take the form of announcements on bulletin boards, oral communication, or training of staff members. Benefits linked to the number of articles published in newspapers in the form of monetary rewards or promotion provide positive incentives for journalists to learn these visions of journalistic professionalism communicated by the propaganda authorities.[25] Of course,

Xinwen Sixiang Gailun (Introduction to Marxist News Thought) (Shanghai: Fudan Daxue Chubanshe, 2003b).

[21] Chinese conceptualizations of hard news and soft news therefore differ from American definitions, as discussed in Chapter 2. Chapter 6 further examines the conceptual realm between the social and the political.

[22] Interview in Beijing (#20).

[23] Conversation in Beijing, June 2005.

[24] Interview in Beijing (#22).

[25] See also Chapter 3 and Ashley Esarey, "Cornering the Market: State Strategies for Controlling China's Commercial Media," *Asian Perspective* 29, no. 4 (2005).

journalistic ethics and routines are completely controlled by propaganda officials and constantly negotiated with media practitioners, as discussed in Chapter 6. Still, over time, reporters develop a general intuition that guides their selection of stories for publication and news coverage once precedence is set. Regarding newly emerging issues that lack such precedence, such an intuition has not yet developed, leading to less self-censorship.

Journalists also learn from each other. They build social networks with other reporters working in the same city or in other regions. They also frequently travel all over China and meet colleagues on their trips. Thus they know how journalism is practiced at different institutions, in other regions, and on topics in which they don't necessarily specialize. There are also websites where media practitioners anonymously discuss the latest news about an editor's sacking or the closure of a newspaper. Stories about other reporters "making mistakes" (*fan cuo*) quickly spread among the media community and subsequently serve as negative examples of what happens if you do not comply with norms of expected behavior.[26] For example, when I asked what kinds of instructions the PD gave regarding American presidential elections, an editor at the *People's Daily* group immediately associated the issue with the story about how the *China Daily* committed a mistake in 2004, explained in more detail in Chapter 5. Without having primed him to think about this particular incident, he told me: "You may know that *China Daily* published the speech by Qian Qichen.[27] Their editor didn't know what he was thinking – that is not what the Chinese government is thinking, that's their (*China Daily*'s) mistake in drafting."[28] Subsequently, he laid out in detail for me the rationale behind the restriction imposed by the PD. Stern and Hassid (2012) call such stories "control parables" that serve as a means to interpret the intention of political leaders to counsel caution and restrict political possibilities.

State instructions communicated to top personnel "do not have an expiration date," as noted by Esarey (2006: 5). They develop into guidelines for news reporting widely known among professionals. Because these are heuristics, these are greatly simplified versions of the more specific instructions given by propaganda authorities. I purposefully do not examine these documents in depth because my focus is on gaining insight into shortcuts that guide journalistic behavior socialized over time through the institutional structures (or infrastructures) in which the CCP exerts political control over the organization, personnel, and editorial process of newspapers, as outlined in Chapter 3. The remainder of this chapter attempts to make these glass walls of journalistic reporting visible. The goal is to take a "snapshot" of the situation in early 2005 – shortly before the LLM and BAS surveys were conducted – to match

[26] "*Fan cuo*" in this context means that the action was criticized by higher ranking officials than the person or organization that committed the mistake.
[27] Qian Qichen served as minister of foreign affairs between 1988 and 1998 under the leadership of Deng Xiaoping and Jiang Zemin.
[28] Interview in Beijing (#8).

my findings regarding the production of news with media credibility, and to then complement these data with more recent examples. I start with a comparison of political sensitivity across topics within each issue area, followed by a comparison across issues in relation to demands by the state and audiences. My main goal is to show that the Chinese state opens up topics when audience and state converge, but closes topics when audience demands challenge the policies and goals of political leaders.

Rules Relevant to News Reporting about Labor Law

In the spring of 2007, an investigative news report swept across China. Fu Zhenzhong, a Henan television reporter, uncovered longstanding practices of exploitation and "slave-like" labor conditions in the brick-making industry in Shanxi Province. Following up on Fu's story, a vast number of news reports appeared in the Chinese mass media informing citizens about labor law and their rights as workers.

The "black brick kilns" scandal is only one of many incidents that Chinese news reporters have used to inform citizens about China's labor laws. Editors and journalists categorize such stories as open "social news." An editor in charge of social and legal news at a popular nonofficial paper in Chongqing explained: "The PD will have some guiding opinions toward the direction of media propaganda. Some are of strong nature, those are the ones you cannot say, and there are some that are of guidance nature. I think the coverage of labor law is of guidance nature."[29] A former Xinhua reporter explained: "Labor disputes belong to social news, not political news, but legal news can be both, political and social news," meaning that announcements of the law itself would be more sensitive compared with labor disputes that do not involve political leaders.[30] In Beijing, a reporter working for a nonofficial paper in the Beijing Youth Daily Group noted: "Regarding labor law issues, expression is not sensitive. Because the greatest fear for the government is that media may not choose the appropriate moment, may sensationalize an issue, or may choose a situation which give rise to social panic. When I worked in the media during the past 10 years – whatever regulations the PD had regarding labor law – I didn't come across them. At least when I wrote news on labor disputes, it was very smooth, I never came into a situation where the PD gave me pressure."[31] Journalists at official papers in both cities made similar comments.

More specifically, in Chonqging, all twelve editors and journalists working for official and nonofficial papers agreed that the local PD then under the leadership of Party Secretary Huang Zhendong, generally did not intervene much in newspaper content on labor issues, but it primarily cared about economic

---

[29] Interview in Chongqing (#41).
[30] Interview with male journalist of semiofficial paper and Xinhua in Beijing (#22).
[31] Interview in Beijing (#27).

development.[32] Topics became more sensitive as they were related to keeping discipline, critiques of superiors, and social stability.

"Keeping Discipline"

News reporting about issues related to labor disputes has not always been open. Coverage was allowed from 1994 onward when the National Labor Law was passed. Asked for an explanation, media specialists say that they have to "keep discipline." Discussing a problem and its possible solutions freely in the press before the government announced an official policy would make the government look "as if it doesn't have a good grasp of the issue."[33] Brady's (2008: 96) study of the PD also found that media are warned off reporting on problems that "can't be easily resolved."

Keeping discipline is still relevant for news reporting about labor law today. For example, a journalistic handbook used in Beijing states: "When [the case has] already entered legal procedures, but the court has not made a decision yet, usually don't report." The informal rule to abstain from reporting on a pending case is supposed to ensure the independence of judges who feel under pressure from media outlets. Judges need to take media accounts into consideration because party-state superiors, who oversee the courts and interfere with individual cases, treat media reports – published or internally submitted – as facts. Such media pressure leads to rapid trials and harsh punishments that sometimes benefit the defendants as the courts act in line with popular demands, but it also undermines the courts' autonomy and does not necessarily result in fairer trials (Liebman 2011a).

The PD may therefore issue instructions to ban all independent reports on trials, such as during the trial of the murder of toddlers in Jiangsu; the trial of Zhu Cainian, one of eight suspects in the killing of a Uyghur in Hubei; or during the Sun Zhigang trials.[34] Violating this rule can have consequences for journalists. In July 2003, the Guangdong Provincial High Court convicted six journalists for reporting about a case before the respective court had made a judgment.[35] However, the general rule to abstain from reporting before a verdict has been made is only loosely enforced. In Chongqing, courts employ a lenient policy toward media reporting. An editor of a nonofficial paper in

---

[32] The Chongqing model of economic growth is based on domestic demand rather than export-oriented development. It emerged after Huang Qifan was appointed vice mayor in 2001. Wang Yang replaced Huang Zhendong as Party secretary in December 2005. After Wang's appointment to the Politburo, Bo Xilai was appointed Party secretary in December 2007. See Zhiyue Bo and Gang Chen, "Bo Xilai and the Chongqing Model," *East Asian Policy* 1, no. 3 (2009).

[33] Interviews with male news assistant of foreign newspaper and female and male press officers at the US embassy in Beijing (#4, 16, 17).

[34] IFJ, "Zhongguo Xinwen Ziyou 2010 (Press Freedom in China in 2010)." On instructions for the Sun Zhigang trials, see Liebman, "Changing Media, Changing Courts," 163.

[35] Interview with male legal scholar in Beijing (#24).

Chongqing pointed out: "We can follow the proceedings over the whole course, no problem. There are many examples of this. For instance, there was a university student who sued his work unit. . . . Before he sued, during the trial and during the final judgment we could report."[36] Enforcement of the rule depends largely on the specific court involved in the case. If the court demands it, newspapers are supposed to keep discipline until the verdict has been announced. Such norms for journalistic practice are in line with the 1999 Regulations by the Supreme People's Court stating that most cases should be open to the public and the media, but also requiring reporters to obtain advance permission from the court hearing the case (Liebman 2011a).

This system of "controlled transparency" of the legal system, as Liebman (2011a) noted, has its roots in long-established political practices. Chinese media are supposed to keep discipline just like politicians. According to the principle of democratic centralism, Party members can freely discuss policies *internally* before a final decision is made. After a policy has been adopted, all Party members are supposed to jointly go along with the decision.[37] Consequently, Party members cannot publicize speech contrary to decisions at the national level in the media, especially not before an official policy has been adopted. Although they do not always obey when trying to sell their stories, media outlets often mimic political leaders' behavior.[38] On potentially controversial decisions, they often abstain from reporting before a final decision is publicly announced by officials within Party and state units or judges in the courtroom. Keeping discipline is a direct result of newspapers' integration into the political structure and the norm of democratic centralism practiced in the Party.

"Don't Criticize the Boss"

National leaders have encouraged investigative news reporting to improve monitoring of rampant corruption among local officials, as explained in more detail in Chapter 6. Corruption of officials, excessive exploitation of peasants, fraud and smuggling, mismanagement of state enterprises, violation of citizen and consumer rights by local officials and businesses, problems in education, housing, and healthcare issues have become topics that are frequently covered by newspapers. Nevertheless, there exist restrictions about the number of corruption stories that newspapers are allowed to feature, as they constitute "negative news," which creates a negative impression of the government.[39]

---

[36] Interview in Chongqing (#37). See also interview with male legal scholar in Beijing (#24).

[37] On the relationship between democratic centralism and deliberation, see Kenneth Lieberthal, *Governing China: From Revolution through Reform*, 2nd ed. (New York: W. W. Norton, 2004), 193.

[38] See also Xupei Sun, *Zhongguo Chuanmei De Huodong Kongjian (China's Space for Media Activity)* (Beijing: Renmin Chubanshe, 2004).

[39] Interview with male journalist assisting foreign journalists in Beijing (#4). See also, "The Press and Its Market after the Fourth Plenum," *China News Analysis* 1531 (1995). For a discussion of

In the area of labor law, journalists point out that much reporting on labor disputes becomes investigative because it ties labor abuse to government officials and enterprises that maintain close ties to each other. However, how much far-reaching criticism does the state tolerate in legal news reporting?

For journalists, news reporting that involves political leaders always requires special consideration. Political leaders are on top of the list of so-called "land-mine topics" in journalistic handbooks: when covering news involving officials, policies, and law, especially speeches by national leaders and major policies, it is recommended to reprint Xinhua and *People's Daily* reports. This is also relevant to news about labor law when supplementary law to the National Labor Law is passed and when officials mention current regulations in their speeches at meetings.

However, certain kinds of officials are more sensitive than others. Which officials can be criticized depends largely on the newspaper's rank within the political structure. Because of the set-up of the Chinese political system, local media generally restrain themselves from criticizing leaders in their own locality and at higher levels. If journalists nevertheless want to expose local leaders, they might pass the story on to colleagues in other provinces or at media outlets higher up in the hierarchy.[40] Newspapers registered with a central-level institution have more flexibility to publish critical news at the provincial level, but even central-level newspapers abstain from criticizing the highest ranks of political leaders. As a result, the news media usually "hit flies, not tigers" (Zhao 2004; Liebman 2005).

The same dynamics affect news reporting about legal disputes. Reporters usually investigate cases that are relevant to their local audience. These cases are first handled by local institutions and are passed on to higher levels if one of the parties appeals the judgment. In part because of their hesitation to criticize agents of the state in their own locality and at higher levels, and in part because of their lack of legal expertise, journalists tend to abstain from exposing incorrect implementation of the law by arbitrators and judges. For example, a journalistic handbook gives detailed instructions about how the news media are supposed to portray verdicts: "After the final judgment is made, unless there is a regulation that you cannot report about it, you can objectively report [about the issue], but you cannot express your opinion about the verdict. If you think that the court's judgment is unfair, or the masses don't agree with the judgment, you can write up your opinion in a document which is kept secret from other departments [and submit it] to the relevant departments." Journalists in Chongqing confirmed that the media are

additional limits to investigative journalism, see Hugo De Burgh, "Kings without Crowns? The Re-Emergence of Investigative Journalism in China," *Media, Culture, and Society* 25 (2003), Yuezhi Zhao, "The State, the Market, and Media Control in China," in *Who Owns the Media: Global Trends and Local Resistance*, ed. Pradip Thomas and Zaharom Nain (Penang, Malaysia: Southbound, 2005).

[40] Interview with male journalist of weekly magazine in Beijing (#31). See also Brady, *Marketing Dictatorship: Propaganda and Thought Work in Contemporary China*.

not supposed to "supervise" arbitrators or judges to ensure the independence of the courts. Unless there is some evident procedural mistake, they only indirectly voice criticism when bringing up one party's dissatisfaction with the outcome. A procedural mistake was, for example, evident in the following case: "Once . . . a judge did not coordinate the respective parties [correctly], . . . [the judge] ruled that both parties had won, both parties triumphed, the plaintiff looked at the verdict and [thought] 'I won,' the defendant looked at the verdict and [thought] 'I won.' We could report this story, in this case the judge made a mistake," a journalist from *Chongqing Evening News* explained.[41] At least in Chongqing, media pressure is tolerated to increase transparency of decision making, although journalists are also discouraged from placing pressure on the verdict itself, as explained earlier.

Overall, the integration of newspapers into the political structure creates a distinct pattern of journalism. In general, journalists are hesitant to criticize their "boss."[42] Who the boss is depends on the administrative rank of the sponsoring institution. Issue sensitivity increases the closer a news story is connected to agents of the state who have the ability to issue binding orders to newspapers through the PD or the institutional sponsor. The possibility of losing one's job if one is repeatedly criticized nurtures this feeling of issue sensitivity. The infrastructures of political control explained in Chapter 3 place structure on the selection and coverage of news stories that involve public officials and civil servants.

Social Stability

The key to understanding restrictions of media reporting in the field of labor is the term *social stability*, primarily associated with mass incidents and collective protest. Apart from the collective interest of the CCP in appeasing potential protesters to maintain its power, individually, local officials also have a strong incentive to avoid discontent among their constituents, as the officials' political reputation and career are at stake if social unrest occurs.

Public outrage or protest is a sign of dissatisfaction with current policies, thus exposing deficiencies in leadership or policies. Since 1993, a cadre responsibility system evaluates officials primarily based on performance to improve government efficiency and monitor lower-level cadres. Although the precise evaluation criteria depend on the specific characteristics of the locality, they largely depend on work achievement related to the economy of the constituency; however, performance contracts are also signed for maintaining public order (Whiting 2001; Edin 2003). Because social unrest can have a negative effect on the local economy by, for example, discouraging foreign direct investment, maintaining social stability is also indirectly tied to economic development, the most important evaluation criterion. Public outrage or protest is a sign of dissatisfaction

---

[41] Interview with male journalist of nonofficial paper in Chongqing (#39).
[42] Interviews with male editor-in-chief of official paper and male editor of commercialized paper in Beijing (#7, 27).

with current policies, thus exposing deficiencies in leadership and policies that can have consequences for an official's political reputation and career.

Not surprisingly, a journalistic handbook states that reporters should be careful when covering issues that can give rise to social instability or can have a negative influence on society. Specifically, worker protests or demonstrations constitute taboo topics. Since about 2008, the PD has allowed media to report on some protests, such as the 2009 unrest in Tibet; other incidents remain restricted, such as a protest by a group of artists against police treatment close to Tiananmen Square in 2010. This selective opening is gradually shifting the topic from a taboo toward a sensitive topic on which coverage is allowed.[43]

* * *

In sum, editors and reporters agreed that most topics related to labor law were not taboo but instead were reportable. At the same time, there is variation among topics within the broader issue area. Topics become more sensitive and closed when related to breaking discipline, criticizing the boss, and social stability.

The glue that holds these limitations together is the institutional structure within which Chinese newspapers remain embedded. If core issues such as political reputation, careers, and continuation of government are at stake, the media either self-censor the article or are prohibited from reporting. Speeches by political leaders, announcements of new laws and policies, and investigative news articles can be published, but with considerations regarding the tone, amount, and timing of the articles. These rules about news coverage are directly related to the institutional structure in which the media are embedded. In the minds of media practitioners, any topic not enforced through the means by which the CCP exerts control over the organization, personnel, and editorial process is open.

Rules Relevant to News Reporting on the United States

"Foreign affairs are no small matter" (*waishi wu xiaoshi*) is a Chinese expression that many reporters use when describing international news reporting before the reform era. Along with Deng's open door policy, guidance of press reporting on international issues loosened up.[44] At the same time, media outlets

---

[43] See also Chapter 6. On directives by the Beijing-level PD, see IFJ, "Zhongguo Xinwen Ziyou 2010 (Press Freedom in China in 2010)."

[44] Interviews with academic, female press officer at the US embassy, male head of press group, and male editor of semiofficial paper in Beijing (#14, 16, 21, 25). For a discussion of whether the relaxation of the principle of *waishi wu xiaoshi* is appropriate, see contributions by Shandong Normal University Professor Yang Wen and a netizen commentator on the news website of the CCP. "Fansi 'waishi wu xiaoshi,' cycnet.com, December 31, 2008, accessed March 9, 2009; "Weiguan, bie wang waishi wu xiaoshi," cpc.people.com.cn, August 8, 2007, accessed March 9, 2009.

underwent marketization and had to think about new ways to attract audiences. One way to show themselves as an original news medium was through the coverage of international news, as a press officer at the US embassy noted: "That's how they really had the ability to take an editorial stand, pick out what kind of story they would cover, all things that a normal newspaper would do. Across the board, a lot of [newspapers] found that it was only true in their international division, but not in their domestic division."[45] Indeed, editors and journalists feel surprisingly unconstrained regarding international news. One editor of *Global Times* commented: "When compared with domestic politics, there is more space for discussing international news."[46] Another editor at *World News Journal* explained: "The Chinese government does not manage Sino-US relations: media can basically report according to their own line of thinking, but some countries where some problems exist are very sensitive, like Japan or North Korea.... In our meetings within China Radio International (Zhongguo Guoji Guangbo Diantai), we mainly discuss news, there are not as many meetings regarding political restrictions as you imagine."[47] Similarly, the head of a press group in Beijing explained: "International news is more open, more diverse (*fengfu*) than domestic news, but some things we cannot report about as we wish, such as when it involves Taiwan, Korea, or Japan."[48] In comparison with domestic news, international news consists of less taboo topics, and few topics require self-censorship. As a CCTV editor specializing in international news reporting told me: "Mostly regarding the US you can report in any way you like. It's like a cake, one slice is sensitive but the rest isn't."[49]

Part of that freedom might be related to the fact that the PD does not have prescribed instructions on how to report about many international events that arise. Consequently, the guidance comes slower than on many domestic issues, and often no guidelines are issued at all.[50] Next I explain the main principle that guides journalistic reporting on stories about the United States.

"Standing Behind China's Foreign Policy"

International news about the United States will cover the most important events related to American domestic and foreign politics, such as presidential elections, mutual leadership visits, or 9/11. Yet apart from covering specific events, there are also many journalists who pick up a story published in foreign media and then repackage it as one considered of interest to Chinese audiences while also supporting the position of China in foreign policy.

Consider, for example, a front-page article in *Global Times* entitled "China's Image Is Better Than America's," published on June 6, 2005. Citing English

[45] Interview in Beijing (#17).
[46] Interview in Beijing (#25).
[47] Interview in Beijing (#13).
[48] Interview in Beijing (#21).
[49] Interview in Beijing (#5).
[50] Interviews with male editor of semiofficial paper and male press officer at the US embassy in Beijing (#13, 17).

magazines, such as *Newsweek*, the article begins with a statement that the war in Iraq has seriously damaged the image of the United States in the world and that Americans themselves have started to discuss how the United States is perceived abroad. Foreign correspondents of the *People's Daily* group in the United States, Germany, and France then explain how public opinion polls conducted by the Pew Foundation show that China is more popular in the world compared with the United States: "11 out of 16 countries – that is more than half – like China, but only 6 out of 16 – less than half – like America." These statistics are not incorrect, but the article omits criticism of China abroad. The only criticism mentioned pertains to negative attitudes voiced in French media regarding Chinese counterfeit products and dumping pricing, but the article quickly raises positive aspects to make up for this criticism: "with respect to China's position regarding the war in Iraq, the French have a just and positive image" of China. The article is superimposed on a picture of happy foreigners standing in front of the Forbidden Palace in Beijing, smiling and waving at the reader.

This story constitutes an illustrative example of how international news supports "the position of China." Media are encouraged to stand behind the position of the government, here voiced in the form of opposition to the war in Iraq. This position is further supported by apparent agreement of other countries with China's more critical stance on US foreign policy and China's popularity compared with that of the US among these countries. When reading the article, a Chinese reader will likely sustain a positive image of herself and also about the Chinese government's position. By equating Chinese people, the state, and the nation as a whole, the government's position is justified and supported.

This is common in Chinese journalism. According to one handbook, a "good journalist" does not openly disagree with China's foreign policy, but instead needs to "uphold the image of China as well as the benefit of the people and should strictly report according to Chinese foreign policy, international law, and international common practice." To support the position of China, journalists must learn about the foreign policy position of the Chinese government. The handbook continues that "these kinds of issues are in principle released by the Xinhua News Agency as the central information provider." In other words, journalists can rely on Xinhua to support the Chinese foreign policy position. Similarly, an editor at *Global Times* explained to me: "The government discourages newspapers from using foreign news as sources of information. That also makes sense, because we want to make sure that our newspapers represent the Chinese point of view."[51] Many reporters made similar statements, arguing that Chinese media should provide their own alternative view on international relations.

The nature of the Chinese position is, in principle, voiced by China's top leadership. One handbook recommends that journalists should know Chinese

---

[51] Interview in Beijing (#25). See also interviews with male editor-in-chief of official paper and male editor of semiofficial paper in Beijing (#7, 8).

foreign policy; only then will they know "what to talk about, what not to talk about, what to emphasize, what not to emphasize, what to advocate, what to oppose, etc." The editor from *Global Times* explained: "You can invite experts, students, ordinary citizens to contribute to a discussion and voice their own opinions, but, of course, those opinions will not undermine the broader political strategy. You cannot voice opinions that advocate the overthrow of the CCP; that goes too far."[52] Brady's study of the PD also found that media are instructed to "bring the thinking of the Chinese people in line with that of the Party center" (Brady 2008: 100).

How do reporters learn about the position of top leaders, given that policies are often vague and leaders may not always be unified on an issue? In 2005, *Global Times* learned about the position of the government by sharing reporters with the international news office of the *People's Daily*. On important events, such as former Secretary of State Condoleezza Rice's visit to China in 2005, the same reporters wrote articles for both papers, putting a different spin on it.[53] Other marketized papers that have less access to the leadership often orient themselves based on reports by *People's Daily* or Xinhua, as suggested in the journalistic handbook mentioned previously.[54]

A central-level propaganda official explained to me: "International news becomes more sensitive when the Chinese state (*guojia*) is involved."[55] Once information threatens to undermine the policies and goals set by the central government either internationally or domestically, it becomes more sensitive.

The number one issue raised by editors and journalists as highly sensitive is Taiwan.[56] Handbooks lay out very specific rules about how to cover Taiwan – to the extent that they even instruct journalists to use the term "my country" (*wo guo*) instead of "mainland" (*dalu*).[57] The Taiwan issue constitutes the main source of tension in the US-China relationship. By restricting news reporting, the Chinese leadership gains greater flexibility in dealing with the Taiwan issue. Because the Chinese government generally aims to foster a stable relationship with the United States, news reporting that causes tension in the US-China relationship can suddenly become sensitive. When some

[52] Interview in Beijing (#25).
[53] Interview with male editor of semiofficial and official paper in Beijing (#8).
[54] Interview with male head of press group in Beijing (#21).
[55] "Guojia" can refer to both country and state. In this context, the official was referring to China as a political entity. Interview in Beijing (#30).
[56] Interviews with female editor at CCTV, male editor-in-chief of official paper, male head of press group, male journalist of official paper, two male editors of semiofficial papers, and two female and male press officers at the US embassy in Beijing (#5, 7, 21, 22, 8, 17, 16, 25).
[57] In addition, the handbook notes that the Office of Taiwan Affairs (Taiban) gives instructions on coverage of Taiwanese people of importance, leadership meetings, and cross-strait relations. Besides, journalists can only report about Taiwan economic issues if they received agreement from the Office of Taiwan Affairs beforehand. Finally, in the case of a crisis, reporters need to rely on announcements by the Office of Taiwan Affairs and the International Communication Office of the CCP Central Committee (*Zhonggong Zhongyang Duiwai Xuanchuan Bangongshi*).

netizens expressed *schadenfreude* related to the 9/11 attacks online, the government quickly requested media to abstain from criticism of the United States (Stockmann 2010b).

During leadership visits, media are often asked to abstain from commentary and report the process in line with official information, such as *People's Daily* or Xinhua.[58] Similarly, in 2010, the State Council Information Office requested that online media positively report on bilateral talks between China and the United States, omitting criticism of China's human rights record and religious freedom, and requested Internet censorship and placement of the stories on pages other than the front page (IFJ 2010). Such comments are omitted both to create the image of a harmonious relationship but also to avoid intensifying social tensions domestically.

Concerns about domestic criticism of the goals and policies of Chinese leaders can sometimes also constrain reports related to American foreign policy that are not explicitly related to China. A central-level propaganda official explained that the government discouraged reporting about terrorist actions in Iraq to not cause conflict with its own Muslim population and inflame the "Xinjiang problem."[59] Similarly, the Central PD requested media to reprint official reports on Secretary of State Hillary Clinton's speech on Internet freedom "since it criticized Chinese censorship of the Internet" (IFJ 2010: 91). Instead of omitting criticism, *People's Daily* explained its own position on some of the criticisms raised in the speech, including Google's (partial) retreat to Hong Kong, and countered with an appeal to the United States to "stop using Internet freedom of speech to accuse China without reason" and instead maintain healthy and stable development of Sino-US relations.[60]

Similar considerations sometimes leak into the otherwise completely unrestricted domain of American domestic politics, as illustrated during President Obama's inauguration speech. Xinhua publicized an uncensored English version, but the Chinese version omitted references to communism and other notes that could be interpreted as a critique of China, such as the sentence "those who cling to power through corruption and deceit and the silencing of dissent, know that you are on the wrong side of history."[61] In 2005, editors raised the 2004 US presidential elections as an issue about which they should report "the process" without commentary, as explained in more detail in Chapter 5.[62]

However, when stories are unrelated to Chinese leaders and thus do not undermine the policies and rule of the CCP, media practitioners consider

---

[58] Interview with male editor of semiofficial and official paper in Beijing (#8).

[59] Interview in Beijing (#30).

[60] *People's Daily*, January 23, 2010. In addition, it published a series of articles and commentaries, including one by the State Council Information Office, presenting extensive factual information to show that "America's so-called freedom of speech in reality completely serves the benefit of the United States and is the American government's freedom to control." *People's Daily*, March 13, 2010.

[61] "Obama Speech Censored in China," BBC News, January 21, 2009.

[62] Interview with male editor of semiofficial and official paper and male editor-in-chief of official paper in Beijing (#7, 8).

stories to be completely open.[63] The article cited previously that compares China's image abroad with that of the United States is not particularly sensitive. Nevertheless, journalists omitted foreign criticism of Chinese policy, as they often equate China with the Chinese leadership.[64] Topics pertaining to China or Chinese politicians are therefore more sensitive than others, but remain, most of the time, reportable – only in rare incidents do such topics become taboo.[65] Therefore, in comparison to management of domestic issues, coverage of international events is less controlled.

* * *

In fact, the rule to "stand behind China's foreign policy" mirrors journalistic norms on domestic news reporting examined earlier in this chapter. First, the media are supposed to go along with China's official policy and to "keep discipline." This is a direct result of newspapers' integration into the political structure and the norm of democratic centralism practiced by the Party. Second, foreign policy is exercised by political leaders at the central level, the highest administrative rank within the system, who have the ability to issue binding orders and to dismiss personnel. Therefore, media practitioners follow the rule not to criticize their "boss" when reporting on China's foreign policy. As before, these guidelines are shaped by the institutional structure in which the media are embedded.

The Official Line and Audience Demands

Because stories on domestic issues are usually more strongly tied to Chinese politicians, international news is often less sensitive in comparison. Despite this important difference across issues, the logic that underlies the guidelines for news reporting within each issue area has been remarkably similar. How does the political sensitivity of a story relate to audience demands? As we will see, stories tend to become more sensitive when audience demands threaten to undermine the official line set by the PD.

Demands by the Government and Readers on Labor Law
Although legal news existed before the reform era, it was not until 1979 that major professional newspapers were founded that specialized in legal news content (Yang and Zhang 2003). In 1986, legal news had become so popular that

---

[63] Conversation with scholar and interviews with female press officer at the US embassy, male head of press group, and male editor of semiofficial paper in Beijing (#14, 16, 21, 25).

[64] Popular nationalism voiced in some nonofficial papers and online challenges this equation by separating China as a nation from the CCP, as it contains criticism of the CCP justified by patriotic sentiment.

[65] For example, in 2010, the Central PD requested that media should abstain from reporting about a lawsuit by the US Department of Justice and Securities and Exchange Commission against Chinese telecommunications company UTStarcom for alleged bribery. IFJ, "Zhongguo Xinwen Ziyou 2010 (Press Freedom in China in 2010)."

an All-China Legal Journalists' Association was established.[66] By 2003, there existed fifty-six newspapers that specialized in law in China, among them, for example, the *China Labor and Social Security News* (*Laodong Baozhangbao*), which is sponsored by the Ministry of Labor and Social Security (Yang and Zhang 2003). In addition, numerous magazines and newspapers, such as, for example, *Legal Evening News*, have sections on legal issues or advisory pages for readers. Starting from the mid-1980s, numerous news shows dealing with legal issues on national and local TV channels have been broadcast; one of the most prominent is CCTV's *Legal Report* (*Jinrishuofa*). Furthermore, in 2004, the national TV Channel for Western China was transformed into the Legal System Channel (*Fazhi Pindao*). Today, Chinese television viewers can watch legal news all over China nonstop.[67]

Although this rise of legal news is part of a broader effort to teach people knowledge and respect for the law in the form of a legal dissemination campaign (*pufa*) (Exner 1995), its success is only partially a result of government support. Stories about the delay of wages for migrant workers have been promoted by government officials such as Premier Wen Jiabao. During his visit to Chongqing in 2003, he engaged in a conversation with the wife of a migrant worker, Neng Deming, who explained that her husband had not received wages for an entire year, totaling RMB 2,240. When Wen Jiabao arranged compensation, the story gave rise to a vivid media discussion about the labor situation of migrant workers, their legal protection, and possible solutions to their problems.[68] High-ranking political leaders also initiated CCTV's Legal System Channel with the concrete aim of educating the population about law content and of building a legal consciousness.[69]

In addition to this support from the central government, media practitioners also believe that their audiences demand more and better information about labor issues, the law, and the legal system. Chinese readers and TV viewers frequently call or e-mail media institutions asking for advice about legal issues, many related to labor.[70] When asked how frequently people in Chongqing, Wuxi, Shenyang, and Foshan watch TV programs related to law, 41.4 percent reported watching such programs frequently, 49.5 percent sometimes, and only 9.1 percent never, according to the LLM survey. When the question refers to social news – journalists also classify labor law as a social issue – 58.3 percent

[66] See website at http://www.legalinfo.gov.cn/gb/moj/zhishudanwei/fazhixinwenxh.htm, accessed on October 4, 2005.
[67] Besides the national legal system channel, there were also two local legal system channels, one in Henan, and one in Heilongjiang. See: http://www.lawbook.com.cn/shopping/shopview_p.asp?id=10273, accessed October 4, 2005.
[68] See, for example, reports by Chongqing local papers, the *People's Daily*, and Xinhua in October 2003.
[69] Interview with male CCTV moderator in Beijing (#23).
[70] See, for example, CCTV's online discussion of "What kind of law programs do we need?" Available at: http://www.cctv.com/law/dsyfz/index.shtml, accessed October 7, 2005.

reported reading newspapers frequently to learn about social news, 32.4 percent sometimes, and only 9.3 percent never.[71]

Bottom-up demand for information about labor issues and the law among the Chinese urban public is caused by a combination of several factors. First, reduced state involvement in people's lives through, for instance, administration and management of labor leaves law as the key institution for providing citizens with basic protections and rights. Citizens demand legal news to learn about what the law says and how to make it work in their favor. Furthermore, obtaining information about the law and the legal system is a way to keep up with China's rapid socioeconomic transformation. The logic of the law, which is based on contract and exchange, is meant to suit the logic of the market. Citizens seek legal information in an effort to lower anxiety about changes in their rapidly transforming environment. Finally, Chinese media audiences seek legal news because of its sensationalist content. These kinds of news stories are often "negative news" – a term describing critical journalism – and the use of specific cases and opportunities for readers and audiences to participate serve to make the media message on law more meaningful and dramatic. The combination of these factors – reduced state involvement in dispute resolution, rapid socioeconomic transformation, and attraction to negative news reporting – has increased demand for more widespread legal information among Chinese urban publics.[72]

This converging interest between demands by the state and audiences comes out very clearly in conversations with editors and journalists. When asked about the guidance of the PD on labor issues and labor law, one Chongqing editor in charge of legal and social news reporting explained: "We can stay in line with the government as far as many propaganda issues are concerned, and this line is also consistent with the demands of ordinary citizens. Why? Because the government after all wants to do things for ordinary people.... Regarding labor law, it is not that strict because the law is linked to the general people and every citizen."[73]

Without exception, editors and journalists who specialized in reports about legal issues believed that the state wants the news media to frame legal issues from the perspective of the weak groups in society. As one editor-in-chief in Beijing explained: "The central government is very clear: Wen Jiabao said that migrant workers should get their salaries on time. Those kinds of problems are labor disputes. If the employer is from a private corporation, he should give the salary on time; if the employer is from a state-owned enterprise, then he should even more do so."[74] The central government has provided the losers

[71] For differences across cities, see Online Appendix to Daniela Stockmann and Mary E. Gallagher, "Remote Control: How the Media Sustains Authoritarian Rule in China," *Comparative Political Studies* 44, no. 4 (2011). Available at www.danielstockmann.net.
[72] For further discussion of these points see Ibid.
[73] Interview with male editor of nonofficial paper in Chongqing (#37).
[74] Interview with male editor-in-chief of official paper in Beijing (#7).

of the reforms with a labor law that ought to protect them against abuse in the workplace. A reporter of the Beijing Youth Daily Group who covered legal news for ten years explained: "Labor law takes the employee as a starting point; its basic principle is to protect the employee's benefit."[75] Another Chongqing editor specializing in social news noted that propaganda officials "want media to stand on the side of the weak, the average ordinary citizen. [They] wish to help them to better understand the law" to solve their hardships.[76] Media practitioners believe that they should depict labor law as an effective weapon of the weak, thus serving demands by readers as well as the central leadership.

Only when it comes to negative news do media practitioners experience tension between market demands and the goals of the state. A comment by a reporter for *Chongqing Evening News* illustrates this point: "Legal news is often stories that are investigative and social, related to ordinary citizens' own issues. For example, if an official is corrupt, of course ordinary citizens will care about it. So if they care, we will cover such news more often; it's decided by the rule of the market.... The PD would like media to only report positively every day to propagate where it did well, which issues the Party managed well. It does not want [us] to report natural disasters or aspects that don't shine, such as corruption. They don't want us to report those issues."[77] Stories become more sensitive if readers' attention provides incentives for media practitioners to publish negative news that conflict with the positive spin demanded by the PD.

For the most part then, perceived audience demand shifts newspaper reporting on labor law in the direction desired by propaganda authorities. Market demands constitute a potential problem when news stories suggest dissatisfaction with the leadership or the rule of the Party. The next section shows that similar dynamics can be observed with respect to news coverage about the United States.

Demands by the Government and Readers Regarding US Foreign Policy

China regards the United States as its most important international partner, and the Chinese government has repeatedly proclaimed its interest in stable relations with the United States. For example, in July 2009, Hu Jintao emphasized that China and the United States should expand common ground, reduce differences, enhance mutual trust, and strengthen cooperation. "This serves the common interests of the two sides and will help advance the positive, cooperative, and comprehensive relationship between our two countries."[78]

To cool down popular nationalist ardor and bring public sentiment in line with China's foreign policy stance, the government under the leadership of Hu Jintao has made efforts to shift public sentiment in a more positive direction. During times of crisis, the government may tolerate the public display of

---

[75] Interview in Beijing (#27).
[76] Interview with male editor of nonofficial paper in Chongqing (#42).
[77] Interview in Chongqing (#39).
[78] Speech at the Strategic and Economic Dialogue, cited by Xinhua, July 27, 2009.

nationalism, but under normal circumstances, there has been an attempt to massage public opinion toward the United States since the early 2000s.[79] The government has changed the way Chinese are educated about the United States – in school and in the media.

In 2003, for the first time since the Cultural Revolution, the chapter on American history in a textbook recommended by the Ministry of Education for teaching world history was revised. The previous version included a story about the Great Depression in which capitalists would rather spill milk on the streets than give it away to starving workers. Years after graduating from high school, people still remembered this story because they had memorized it for exams.[80] The new version discussed Roosevelt's New Deal programs and provided a more complete historical account.

Similarly, propaganda authorities are trying to shift news content on the United States in a positive direction. Without exception, all editors and journalists I interviewed believed that they were supposed to report about the United States in a positive manner. For example, an editor-in-chief of a central-level official newspaper summed up the official stance as follows: "As far as the country is concerned, it wants to devote itself to have very harmonious relations with the United States, quite friendly."[81] An editor working for the *People's Daily* group noted: "Reporting about Sino-US relations will be positive, but newspapers will differ in style. For example, *Global Times* will do more in-depth reporting, not exactly like *People's Daily*, which only discusses the Party itself (*zhi zuo dang lun benshen*)."[82] In recent years, propaganda restrictions have demanded positive and not negative reporting, as has been concluded by observers of government propaganda based on data from the 1990s and earlier (Hollander 1992; Xu 1997; Brady 2008). For example, on May 13, 2010, the State Council Information Office requested that "online media must not post reports on bilateral talks between Chinese and American diplomats on the front page of their websites and reporting should be positive. Reports must not mention issues regarding human rights, religion, and monitoring of the Internet."[83] These instructions aim to portray Sino-US relations in a

---

[79] Content analysis of statements regarding the United States by the Chinese Ministry of Foreign Affairs shows that tone has become more positive over time. See Daniela Stockmann, "Race to the Bottom: Media Marketization and Increasing Negativity toward the United States in China," *Political Communication* 28, no. 3 (2011c). One factor may have been China's anticipated entry into the World Trade Organization. According to a press officer at the US embassy in Beijing, the WTO "became like a firewall . . . , so you didn't want to go too far, be insulting, critical. In fact, it was an extremely important counterbalance a lot of the times." Interview in Beijing (#17).

[80] Conversation with the author in Beijing, May 29, 2006. Chapters related to Japan have not been revised. On content related to Japan in Chinese history textbooks, see James Reilly, "China's History Activists and the War of Resistance against Japan," *Asian Survey* 44, no. 2 (2004).

[81] Interview in Beijing (#7).

[82] Interview in Beijing (#8).

[83] IFJ, "Zhongguo Xinwen Ziyou 2010 (Press Freedom in China in 2010)," 92. The Chinese term *zhengmian baodao* has been incorrectly translated in the English version of the report

positive light by demanding a positive tone and by omitting controversial topics as potential sources of domestic or international tension, thus "harmonizing" bilateral relations between China and the United States.

In addition, these instructions also asked media practitioners to downplay the importance of stories about the United States by abstaining from assigning them to the level of front-page news. Editors specializing in international news reporting and the head of a major press group in Beijing believed that Chinese media focused too much on the United States and that they should instead report more frequently about other countries that had become marginalized in international news.[84] Chinese media practitioners think about international news about the United States in terms of two categories: reports related to China's foreign affairs (*waishi baodao*), which are more sensitive, and news about foreign countries other than China (*guoji baodao*), which are less sensitive.[85] In the *People's Daily*, articles about China's foreign affairs related to the United States have increased over time, whereas stories dealing solely with the United States have declined.[86] As the mouthpiece of the CCP at the central level, these trends ought to give us an indication of support by the government for such news reports. Overall, news reporting about the United States is not "booming" like legal news, but instead has slightly decreased over time, mostly resulting from less coverage of stories solely related to the United States.

When an international event occurs, however, news reporting about the United States can suddenly move to the center of public discourse. Many onetime special programs on international events have been broadcast on television, according to television ratings from AC Nielsen. If these special programs are devoted to a single foreign country, this country is the United States. Special programs dealing with 9/11, the war in Iraq, and the presidential elections in 2004 were watched by a large audience. For instance, in Shenyang, up to 64.9 percent of TV viewers watched "Iraq Special Report" (*Ilake Tebie Baodao*) and "Caring about the War in Iraq" (*Guanzhu Ilake Zhan Shi*).[87] US foreign crises

as "correctly reporting." *Zhengmian baodao* is the antonym of *fumian baodao* (negative reporting).

[84] Although there is no concrete evidence, it is likely that this issue was discussed at a meeting of editors with the PD: all editors mentioned the same argument, referencing a 2005 survey by the Chinese Academy of Social Sciences. Interviews with male head of press group, male editor of semiofficial and official paper, and male editor of semiofficial paper specializing in international news in Beijing (#8, 13, 21).

[85] A third category of international news reporting is aimed at educating foreign audiences about China (*duiwai baodao*). For example, the *China Daily*, English websites of major newspapers, and publications by the State Council Information Office fall into this category. See Mulin Wang and Ming Jing, "Waishi Caifang Baodao (Foreign Affairs Interview Reports)," in *Zhuanye Caifang Baodaoxue (Studies of Professional Interview Reports)*, ed. Hongwen Lan (Beijing: Renmin Chubanshe, 2003).

[86] For empirical results, see Figure OA4.1 in the Online Appendix, available at www.daniestockmann.net.

[87] Many thanks to AC Nielsen for sharing these data. Television ratings were measured by monitoring viewing behavior in randomly selected households, making use of the TNS PeopleMeter,

and issues of domestic significance attract a large Chinese audience and are therefore given special attention in the media. By contrast, media coverage of issues related to labor law is less sensitive to current events and is less common.

Overall, the United States has a strong presence in Chinese media – often triggered by exogenous shocks. At the same time, there is less news coverage today about the United States than in the early 1990s, particularly when unrelated to China. This trend has been associated with efforts by propaganda authorities to tone down news reporting about the United States. In recent years, political leaders have tried to massage public sentiment by shifting news reporting in a more positive (or less negative) direction.

To a certain extent, state demands to tone down news reporting about the United States run counter to audience demands. Chinese audiences are strongly interested in learning about the United States – in part because the United States has become the unspoken comparison point against which China's own backwardness is measured.[88] In the BAS, we asked how much attention Beijingers paid to the news about the United States, and only 35 percent paid no or little attention, whereas 22 percent paid moderate levels of attention, and 44 percent reported to be quite or very attentive. A 2010 survey conducted in Beijing, Shanghai, Guangzhou, Xi'an, Nanning, and Chengdu roughly replicates these results and shows that urban residents in these cities place a strong emphasis on international news reporting about the United States: 80 percent of respondents who read international news pay attention to the United States – more than toward any other country, even Japan.[89]

When reading the international news, readers do not always look for critical stories that run counter to the positive spin on Sino-US relations demanded by the government. American culture, society, education, or other aspects unrelated to American politics are admired by many Chinese, as laid out in Chapter 1.[90] Editors and journalists raised the taste of Chinese audiences for criticism about the American government. Not surprisingly, tension between demands by audiences and the state usually arise when stories about the United States as a political actor become relevant to China.

Consider, for instance, the following comment by the editor-in-chief of a central-level official paper: "Ordinary people, especially netizens and young

---

an electronic device installed inside the TV set in each household. In the case of special programs, TV ratings of each individual program on the war in Iraq were added together. Because some people may have watched several programs, the actual audience size may be smaller.

[88] For a more detailed discussion of this point, see Alastair Iain Johnston and Daniela Stockmann, "Chinese Attitudes toward the United States and Americans," in *Antiamericanisms in World Politics*, ed. Peter Katzenstein and Robert Keohane (Ithaca: Cornell University Press, 2007).

[89] Sampling was done based on probability proportional to size (PPS) random sampling by People's University and the Chinese Academy of Social Sciences. These data are part of a research project on Chinese views of the European Union funded by the 7th Framework Program of the European Commission run by the University of Nottingham in collaboration with the Chinese Academy of Social Sciences, People's University of China, Leiden University, Jakobs University Bremen, and Chatham House.

[90] Why audience demands often coincide with preexisting opinions is explained in Chapter 8.

people, have very strong opinions about foreign policy toward the United States, . . . they criticize the government for being too soft. So the media cannot completely represent the government's opinion and also not the citizens' strong views." Similarly, an editor working for a paper specializing in international news reporting noted the following: "For example, in 1999 ordinary people cared much about the bombing of the Chinese embassy [in Belgrade], why Sino-US relations would take such a shape and give rise to so many problems. At the time, our paper created a new page for discussion and commentary, inviting academics, students, and ordinary citizens to write articles to voice their opinions about international politics. But, of course, these opinions could not divert from the broader political strategy [of the government]."[91]

This last comment also illustrates that there is an upper limit to positive stories about the United States as defined by the position of the Chinese leadership. Editors and journalists considered news reporting on Iraq as an open topic with very little need to self-censor articles, similar to American domestic politics. First, the government had allowed a large number of media outlets, including nonofficial ones, to report live from Iraq. About thirty news organizations sent more than a hundred journalists abroad, including *Global Times*, *Liberation Daily*, and *Guangzhou Daily*, among others.[92] Furthermore, an editor at the *People's Daily* group explained that the Middle East was not closely related to core foreign policy interests of China and was only tangentially related to Sino-US relations, thus giving media more space.[93] Finally, China's position against the US-led invasion of Iraq was backed by audience demands, and there was little need for the PD to issue instructions, according to an editor of a semiofficial paper specializing in international news reporting.[94] As shown in Chapter 5, this overlap between demands by the market and the state resulted in biased coverage opposing the war, while a minority of voices that supported an invasion were marginalized.[95]

Most of the time, however, media practitioners experience PD instructions as attempts to constrain the expression of negativity toward the United States, especially when China or its political representatives are involved. In doing so,

---

[91] Interview with male editor of semiofficial paper in Beijing (#25).

[92] Journalists were recalled after Phoenix reporter Lüqiu Luwei disregarded restrictions and went beyond the frontline for reporting. Interviews with male editor who reported for semiofficial paper in Iraq and female press officer at the US embassy in Beijing (#16, 25). See also Xuebo Zhao, *Zhandi Jizhe Shu Lun (Commentary and Discussion on Journalists on the Battlefield)* (Beijing: Zhongguo Guangbo Dianshi Chubanshe, 2007).

[93] Interview in Beijing #8.

[94] Interview in Beijing #13.

[95] Brady (2008) writes that news coverage on Iraq was strictly controlled, but none of my interviewees, even senior editors, including one who went to Iraq himself, could recall any instructions. Apparently, most media outlets located in Beijing did not have to be reminded of the rule "to stand behind China's foreign policy" because news reporting already supported the Chinese government's views, as in the case of *Beijing Evening News* and *People's Daily* discussed in Chapter 5. See also Brady, *Marketing Dictatorship: Propaganda and Thought Work in Contemporary China*, 100.

they aim to shift newspapers away from the direction that would serve market demands in the eyes of editors and journalists. Officials tighten news reporting when the more lenient stance taken by the Chinese government diverges from audience demands, but open up journalistic space when market mechanisms do not undermine the policies and goals of the CCP.

Conclusion

Not all politically relevant issues are also sensitive in Chinese journalism. Instead, political sensitivity increases as reporting becomes more relevant to political reputation, careers, and continuation of rule by China's political elites. Journalistic norms deter reporters from criticizing public officials and from covering controversial topics that may undermine the goals and policies of Chinese leaders, both domestically and internationally. These rules are socialized and reflect the institutional structure within which newspapers remain embedded.

As we have seen, most topics related to labor law and the United States are reportable and thus do not fall into the most sensitive category of taboo topics. As a rule of thumb, specific topics within each issue area become more sensitive as audience demands shift news reporting away from the position of the government and threaten to undermine political leadership. In the area of labor law, this is a problem primarily with respect to investigative news reporting on labor protests. Generally, however, media practitioners perceive audience demand to converge with the interest of the government, thus providing incentives to depict labor law in a positive light without active promotion of such reporting by the PD. With respect to the United States, media staff perceive readers to demand criticism of American foreign policy rather than to support the more lenient stance of the Chinese government. Therefore, journalists and editors view themselves as positioned in between the government and ordinary citizens, and they perceive restrictions about news reporting by the propaganda authorities as weakening their ability to cater toward their audiences.

This selective opening and closing of space for news reporting illustrates the PD's use of market mechanisms as a tool to manage news content in a way favorable to the authorities. Officials tighten news reporting when issues and specific topics are controversial, but open up journalistic space when market mechanisms work to their advantage or are unrelated to government policies. It is not the absence of restrictions alone that is at work here: without audience pressure, Chinese newspapers would probably more strongly reflect the journalists' own opinions or views encountered through their own social networks.[96] Chapter 5 investigates how the interplay between market and institutional forces influences the content of the news.

---

[96] For statistical data demonstrating that journalists regard audience and state demands as the main factors influencing their reporting, see Chapter 3.

5

Selection and Tone of News Stories

Chapter 4 uncovered the unspoken rules that Chinese journalists follow when reporting news on labor law and the United States. This chapter provides evidence that journalists generally follow these rules, resulting in a distinct pattern of sensitive stories in the Chinese news. First, the division of labor that is intended to limit coverage of closed topics to official newspapers and open topics to nonofficial newspapers is not strictly enforced. Nonofficial papers carry a great deal of political as well as sensitive information if the institutional structure allows them to. Second, nonofficial papers tend to position themselves closer to reader demands than do official papers, but they do not go so far as to voice political positions that are different from those of the central government. This chapter shows how selective enforcement of market and institutional mechanisms synchronizes the news, first in domestic news about labor law and then in international news about the United States.

Open and Closed News Reporting about Labor Law

To test how many stories related to labor law actually fall into open and closed categories, I conducted a quantitative content analysis of all newspaper articles related to labor law in the four months before the survey on labor law mobilization (LLM) was implemented. To analyze 129 articles that mentioned the terms "labor law" (*laodongfa*) or "labor contract" (*laodong hetong*) in three Chongqing newspapers, I used Yoshikoder, a software program that can count keywords in simplified Chinese characters. Apart from facilitating qualitative analysis, the program can also count specific characters or groups of characters, either in the whole text or within a certain distance from a keyword. This allows the quantification of the use of certain concepts or categories of words. Dictionaries for content analysis were carefully pretested and improved based on qualitative reading of the text.[1]

---

[1] See Appendix A and D for further details. Labor Law Computer-Aided Text Analysis (LLCATA) is more limited in scope than United States Computer-Aided Text Analysis (USCATA) because

As examples of official newspapers, I selected *Chongqing Daily* and *People's Daily*, which are both Party papers under direct supervision of the CCP at the local and national level, respectively. For nonofficial newspapers, I investigated articles published in *Chongqing Times*. *Chongqing Times* was founded in August 2004 when it took over the newspaper registration number of the *Chongqing Labor News* (*Chongqing Gongren Bao*). The newspaper's distribution immediately skyrocketed after it received investment from the *Chinese Business Paper*, which belongs to Shanxi China Sage Group, owned by the Association of Returning Overseas Chinese.[2]

First, let us look at political information contained in news to assess the relationship of politics to open and closed topics. To assess an article's relevance to politics, I created a dictionary for names of Chinese politicians at the national and local level in addition to terms representing political institutions, such as, for example, *government* or *administration*.[3] Only three of these reports mentioned an official by name, and all named officials were national politicians. Therefore, at first glance, these articles do not contain much political information. Once we take into account references to political institutions, however, the situation changes: 96.9 percent of the articles referred to political institutions, with little difference in coverage between papers. Party and state units were mentioned about twice as often in official papers, but an average article in *Chongqing Times* still mentioned political institutions about ten times.[4] These results show that news reports contain a large amount of political information, even when published in nonofficial papers.

However, politics in the news does not necessarily mean that news is also sensitive. In line with the journalistic rules outlined in Chapter 4, including few references to politicians already indicates low sensitivity, and all such references to politicians were in official papers. In addition, I assessed each article's sensitivity based on three lists of keywords frequently censored by website administrators.[5] These lists differ in degree of sensitivity and contain terms referring to specific names and events associated with, for example, worker strike, democracy, human rights, freedom, or the advancement of Party members (*dangyuan xianjinxing*). It turns out that only 3 percent of articles

---

of the difficulty to obtain electronic copies of articles. *Chongqing Daily* was only available in hardcopy for the relevant time periods. Search engines for nonofficial papers have changed since 2005 and do not date back to the relevant time periods.

[2] Interviews with male editor of nonofficial paper and male editor-in-chief of nonofficial paper in Chongqing (#37, 38).

[3] Dictionaries for content analysis are available on the author's website at www.daniestockmann. net. For a detailed explanation of the research methods employed in this content analysis, see Daniela Stockmann, "Information Overload? Collecting, Managing, and Analyzing Chinese Media Content," in *Sources and Methods in Chinese Politics*, ed. Allen Carlson, Mary Gallagher, and Melanie Manion (New York: Cambridge University Press, 2010b).

[4] The *People's Daily* mentioned political institutions, on average, 34.4 times; *Chongqing Daily*, 21.2 times.

[5] Many thanks to Xiao Qiang, the head of Berkeley's China Digital Times Project, and Jonathan Hassid for sharing this list.

TABLE 5.1. *Average Sensitivity of Articles on Labor Law.*[a]

		People's Daily Average (s.d.)	Chongqing Daily Average (s.d.)	Chongqing Times Average (s.d.)	Total N
Center only		0.09 (0.3)	–	–	11
Center and local level	Chongqing	0.5 (0.52)	0.44 (0.53)	0 (0)	36
	Other Regions	0.42 (0.5)	0.33 (05.8)	0 (0)	42
Only local level	Chongqing	0 (0)	0.25 (0.44)	0.2 (0.41)	41
	Other Regions	0.21 (0.42)	0 (0)	0.5 (0.71)	24
Total N		72	29	28	129[b]

[a] Sensitivity is measured based on a dummy variable of whether the article mentioned a sensitive keyword or not. As a result, averages are equivalent to the proportion of sensitive articles.

[b] Articles that mention a location outside of Chongqing may also mention Chongqing. Therefore, categories "Chongqing" and "Other Regions" overlap. Results do not change significantly if taking into account overlap between categories.

Source: Labor Law Computer-Aided Text Analysis, 2005.

mentioned keywords that were medium or highly sensitive, whereas another 22.5 percent mentioned terms that were somewhat sensitive. The overwhelming majority of articles (74.4 percent) did not mention any sensitive words.

Were there any differences in terms of the selection of news stories between different newspapers? Because newspapers are integrated into the Chinese political structure, we would expect to find that newspapers registered at different levels of the Chinese administrative hierarchy are more likely to break a sensitive story if the story is tied to a locality that cannot issue binding orders to the paper's sponsoring institution. This assumes, of course, that media practitioners will follow the rule "not to criticize the boss."

Indeed, there is evidence that newspapers follow this rule, as shown in Table 5.1. *People's Daily*, registered at the central level, was more likely to raise sensitive issues when lower levels of government were mentioned than when only dealing with the center.[6] Chongqing papers completely abstained from solely reporting about the center, and *Chongqing Times* left sensitive news reporting on central–local relations to the mouthpiece of the CCP at the Chongqing level. However, there was also evidence that this nonofficial paper tried to reach

---

[6] The low degree of sensitivity among articles in the *People's Daily* on Chongqing was related to the fact that this paper only published six articles mentioning Chongqing compared with nineteen mentioning another locality.

into the sensitive realm by reporting about a locality other than Chongqing. Because Chongqing municipality has the administrative status of a province, localities of the same or lower administrative rank cannot issue binding orders to Chongqing papers. When reporting about other localities, *Chongqing Times* was more likely to raise sensitive issues than *Chongqing Daily*.

These findings help to clarify the relationship between politics and sensitivity in the Chinese news. Chinese media practitioners classify news reporting on labor law as "apolitical," but in fact these articles contain a great deal of political information. Because most articles fall into the nonsensitive realm of news reporting, they equate the absence of sensitivity with the absence of politics. In line with official demands to limit coverage of closed topics to official papers, official papers are indeed more likely to raise sensitive issues than nonofficial papers. Nevertheless, nonofficial papers cover a fair amount of sensitive issues. Ten percent of articles in *Chongqing Times* mentioned sensitive keywords, as compared with 30 percent of reports in *People's Daily* and *Chongqing Daily*. When publishing these articles, newspapers follow the logic "not to criticize the boss," depending on their place within the administrative hierarchy of the Chinese political system. Institutions shape the coverage of sensitive stories in Chinese newspapers.

Does this pattern influence the tone of news stories in official and nonofficial newspapers? The next section examines the tone and selection of news stories about labor law to assess the extent to which papers are in line with the position of the government. As we will see, news stories appearing in *People's Daily*, *Chongqing Daily*, and *Chongqing Times* follow the dual goals of serving the state and the market by portraying labor law as an effective weapon of workers against abuse in the workplace.

Tone and Selection of News Stories about Labor Law

Stories about labor law deal overwhelmingly with problems of concern to workers. In my content analysis, about 60 percent of articles dealt with delays in wages, 35 percent dealt with injury in the workplace, and 27 percent dealt with unemployment. When reporting on labor disputes, all three newspapers predominantly picked cases in which the worker wins or should win the case according to expert opinions.[7] Thus they create an image of the labor dispute-resolution process that is biased in favor of workers. None of the three newspapers examined the problem of implementation or highlighted key structural limitations of the Chinese justice system.

There is a considerable gap between the letter of the National Labor Law and its implementation and enforcement. In theory, the National Labor

---

[7] Among the 17 percent of articles that dealt with a labor dispute, 81.8 percent ended with a favorable judgment for the employee or contained remarks by experts that the worker should be given rights; the remaining articles do not contain a verdict or do not favor either side of the dispute.

Law provides workers with the legal basis and structure to address workers' grievances through legal institutions. In practice, lack of independence of legal administrators – combined with a rising volume of cases, limited resources on the part of labor arbitration staff, and poor legal training – often leads to decisions that favor enterprises over workers and delays in the enforcement of judgments (Ho 2003; Gallagher 2005; Lee 2007). In fact, the dissemination of legal education and mobilization of workers into legal institutions through the means of positive media reporting is part of a strategy to increase pressure on localities to implement the law (Exner 1995; Stockmann and Gallagher 2011).

In reality, a large number of workers who pursue a labor dispute are dissatisfied with the outcome. If they win the case, workers usually are only awarded small sums. Also, because the state's ability to enforce verdicts is weak, workers often do not receive these awarded payments from their employer. According to the LLM survey, if an employer refused to follow a judgment, 76 percent of workers were highly dissatisfied with the outcome. Among a total of fifty-one disputants in Shenyang, Wuxi, Foshan, and Chongqing, 72 percent were only moderately satisfied with the outcome when the verdict was implemented. As a result of lack of implementation, the National Labor Law often does not satisfy workers' grievances.

A typical example is the story of Du Linxiang, an elderly worker who was fired from his company and was not compensated for his thirty-five years of tenure. The media featured him widely after the Intermediate Court issued a decision in Du's favor, awarding him nearly RMB 80,000 (about $10,000) as severance pay. In an interview nearly one year after this decision, Du Linxiang reports that he has yet to receive any compensation or payment from his company. He is disappointed in the legal system: "Filing a lawsuit is too exhausting, I no longer believe in legal channels. Chinese people do not have human rights. Zhu Rongji[8] has really sacrificed our generation, especially since the beginning of the reform period. Justice in China is not real" (Stockmann and Gallagher 2011). Despite his negative experience, media coverage of his case made Du famous, and people sought him out for help and advice on their own legal problems encountered when firms restructured or privatized. Newspapers' focus on the positive aspects of labor disputes is in accordance with the state's desire to improve its support among alienated citizens and to channel worker grievances into legal institutions.

This conclusion is further confirmed when examining the tone of news stories about labor law. This time I used Yoshikoder to isolate positive and negative valence words within a distance of eight words from keywords representing agents of the state (for example, "government" or "administration"), the law (for example, "contract" or "regulation"), the employee (for example, "worker" or "migrant worker"), and the employer (for example, "company"

[8] Zhu Rongji was the premier during the high tide of layoffs and restructuring of state-owned enterprises in the late 1990s.

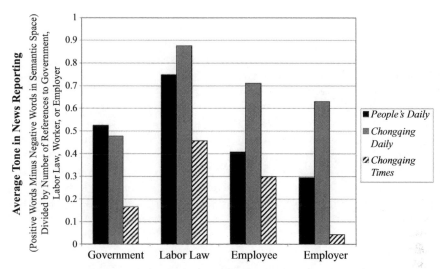

FIGURE 5.1. Average Tone in News Reporting on Labor Law in *Chongqing Times*, *Chongqing Daily*, and *People's Daily*. *Source*: Labor Law Computer-Aided Text Analysis, 2005.[a]

[a] Some legal terms are contained in dictionaries on positive and negative terms. Results do not change significantly when adjusting for dual count of these keywords.

or "boss").[9] According to the logic of computer-aided text analysis, the relative frequency of positive and negative terms within semantic space close to each keyword provides a reasonable indication of positive or negative valuation of the concept. Because the number of matching synonyms for each concept affects the number of negative and positive words found in the text, I normalized this measure by the number of times the concept is mentioned in the text. The resulting measure is negative if the number of words within the semantic space exceeds the number of positive words.[10]

Figure 5.1 summarizes how official and nonofficial newspapers portray each of the key players involved in labor problems: the government, the law itself, the employee, and the employer, displayed on the x-axis. The y-axis shows the average tone in news reporting. Most importantly, we notice that all of these concepts are depicted in a positive light, whereby official papers are consistently more positive – and thus closer to the official line – than nonofficial papers.

[9] Semantic space was chosen based on pretesting. Eight words were broad enough to pick up variation in tone but were narrow enough to ensure that valence words (negative and positive terms) tended to be related to the concept of interest.

[10] Appendix D discusses measurement validity tests. Dictionaries for content analysis are available on the author's website at www.daniestockmann.net. For a detailed explanation of research methods employed in this content analysis, see Stockmann, "Information Overload? Collecting, Managing, and Analyzing Chinese Media Content."

There is a noticeable difference between *Chongqing Times* and official papers, as it tends to use about 30 percent fewer positive words when describing keywords. However, *Chongqing Times* rarely provides a critical view of labor politics and does not go so far as to expose the weaknesses of the legal system.

A typical critical report in *Chongqing Times* is, for example, the article "No Local Residency Permit – You Don't Even Get a First Chance" (March 21, 2005). The article features the story of Tao Meng, a young woman from Shanghai, who was not hired by a Chongqing firm because she did not have a local residency permit. One reason among several for "residency permit discrimination" is explained through the means of an interview with an expert from the city's service center: "Quite a few state organizations and local governments regard nonlocal personnel as competition for local workers. To them, solving the [problems associated with] the local labor force comes first, so they cleverly use the residency permit regulation to constrain nonlocals from entering local work units." In this, the journalist assumes a clear position against job discrimination. He does not go so far, however, as to mention specific politicians or to discuss structural limitations of government policies.

Similarly, *Chongqing Times* emphasized the limits of the law more clearly than the Party papers, thus portraying the law in a more realistic manner. Consider, for example, the story about Ms. Tang, a civil servant who sued the Department of Commercial Affairs because her superior threatened to fire her if she did not have an abortion. Although a professor at Zhongshan University believed that the law was on her side, she was about to lose the case because she did not appear at the first hearing in court. The article conveyed the message that violations of court procedures can result in the loss of a case. Nevertheless, *Chongqing Times* did not go so far as to expose the weaknesses of the legal system. Just like many reports in *People's Daily*, *Chongqing Times* specifically incorporated the governmental slogan "use the law as a weapon!" On the whole, the nonofficial newspaper supported the official line of the state.[11]

On a final note, the more neutral tone regarding employers in *Chongqing Times* only reflects general criticism, but does not raise problems tied to specific cases that are easy to identify. If *Chongqing Times* mentioned companies by name, the name was raised in a positive rather than critical context. Often, these articles brought up a large car company in Chongqing, presenting the firm as a role model for its treatment of workers. Although there is no concrete evidence for surreptitious advertising, it is likely that the newspaper had established connections with the company. Since its founding in 2004, the newspaper reported thirty-one times about the company. Five randomly selected articles were positive or neutral; two of these articles also mentioned the same spokesperson of the company. This could hint at a "friendly relationship" between the journalist and the spokesperson of the company, which is quite common in China. Journalists often feel hesitant to write critical articles about government

---

[11] For examples of reports on labor law in *People's Daily* and *Chengdu Evening News*, a nonofficial paper similar in style to *Chongqing Times*, see Appendix C.

institutions and businesses with which they have developed relations.[12] Reporting in favor of employers did not conflict with being in favor of employees. Being probusiness and proworker can be mutually reinforcing.

In sum, news content of the nonofficial newspapers differs from that of the official newspapers with respect to a more critical evaluation of state policies, a more realistic portrayal of the law, and a positive relationship with companies. However, articles in all newspapers were geared toward providing citizens with information about how to make use of the law effectively. Journalists did not pick cases in which workers lost or investigate deficiencies in the legal system. The observed differences did not vary so much that they differed as far as the core political message was concerned. Readers of *Chongqing Times* would still perceive labor law as a weapon of the weak, a tool for the most vulnerable citizens to protect themselves against abuse by employers.

* * *

How can we explain that Chinese media practitioners feel relatively unconstrained when reporting on labor law while simultaneously reporting in a roughly uniform way? As explained in Chapter 4, in the case of labor law, market demand and government policy converge; there is simply no need for the PD to restrict news reporting if media outlets are pulled in the desired direction by market forces. Yet are marketized media outlets really responding to the demands of their readers when unconstrained by institutions? The next section presents further evidence for this causal mechanism.

Changes in Media Management of Labor over Time

The situation I described thus far was based on interviews and content analysis of data from 2005. I have argued that journalists self-censor news stories on topics for which news content is restricted, while following perceived reader demand on open topics. If this is true, we would expect to find that news content follows readership demand when institutional restrictions are lifted. The case of a taxi driver strike in 2008 provides an opportunity to test this expectation.

In April 2007, the State Council passed the Regulations for the Opening of Government News (*Zhonghua Renmin Gongheguo Zhengfu Xinxi Gongkai Tiaoli*). The central leadership had been working on a strategy to increase transparency since 1999 as part of an effort to address tensions between media and propaganda authorities, as discussed in greater detail in Chapter 6.[13] The

---

[12] Journalists often receive monetary gifts (*hongbao*) from these institutions. See interviews with female journalist of official paper in Beijing and male journalist of nonofficial paper in Chongqing (#9, 39). See Chapter 4 for details.

[13] In 1999, a research project was set up at the Chinese Academy of Social Sciences, which eventually developed into the regulation. See the website of the Henan government at http://www.henan.gov.cn/ztzl/system/2007/04/28/010029374.shtml, accessed April 7, 2009.

anticipation of the Beijing Olympics may have further accelerated its passage as foreign media placed pressure on China to lift restrictions on reporting by foreign journalists during the Olympics. The regulation took effect on May 1, shortly before the Olympics in August 2008.

The regulation required the creation of a public relations system within the administrative structure to make "governmental information" known to the public. Although it confirmed the already familiar rule of keeping "social stability" by stipulating that information should be closed when endangering public order or economic or social stability, it emphasized opening of information more strongly than restrictions. Most importantly from the perspective of media outlets, it specified a series of issue areas as open (*gongkai*) that had often been taboo in the past, including, for example, public health and food product safety, thus moving these topics from being taboo toward being reportable with restrictions.[14] Ordinary citizens, legal entities, and other organizations also obtained the possibility to apply for information from the government when needed for their own production, lives, or scientific research. This provided media outlets with the possibility to inquire about information, although the response period of 15 days poses problems for the timely delivery of the news.

Experts point out the limitations of this administrative regulation, which does not constitute media law.[15] Some local governments also resist implementation of greater information transparency because local officials fear that unfavorable news may inhibit their career opportunities, as happened, for instance, in the case of Liaoning County Secretary Qian Zhenzi. When netizens found out that he was planning to take a leadership position in another unit after his removal from office, they protested online, resulting in merely a temporary position for this "troublemaking" official.[16] As a result of hesitation to implement the regulation at the local level, it initially had little effect on media reporting. However, in November, the Chongqing government decided to open up media reporting and provide extensive governmental information on labor protests, a highly sensitive issue that journalists usually self-censor for the sake of social stability, as shown in Chapter 4.[17]

On November 3 and 4, 2008, taxi drivers went on strike in Chongqing. They protested against a plan to increase an administration fee by the local government and a decline in income caused by unlicensed taxis with lower cab fares. Had this event happened in 2005, the Chongqing media would have abstained from reporting, as indicated by my interviews. None of five large labor protests taking place in Chongqing between 2004 and 2007 recorded by

---

[14] Incidents that the government initially treated as taboo topics include, for example, the severe acute respiratory syndrome (SARS) epidemic in 2003 or the melamine-in-milk scandal in 2008.

[15] Interview with public administration scholar Wang Yukai, *Caijing*, April 26, 2008.

[16] Interview with media scholar Zhan Jiang, *Deutsche Welle*, December 1, 2009, http://www.dw-world.de/dw/article/0,,3839712,00.html, accessed April 7, 2009.

[17] As of early 2010, journalists still face many difficulties when trying to make use of the Regulation on Opening of Government News for investigative news reporting.

the Hong Kong–based *China Labour Bulletin* were mentioned in *Chongqing Evening News.*[18] Yet the 2008 taxi strike broke this pattern.

On the very first day of the strike, the Chongqing government organized a press conference ensuring citizens that immediate action would be taken to restore public transportation. Later, the spokesperson of the Chongqing government stated that this step revealed the progressive (*gongkai*) attitude of the local government aimed at involving the media, netizens, and ordinary people in finding a solution to the problem.[19] To restore public order, the police and the Transportation Bureau persuaded some cabbies to go back to work. This resulted in a "counterattack" by protesting cabbies on the next day, blocking working taxis' paths and even resorting to violent attacks. In response, the government held another press conference apologizing to the public for the strike's occurrence. On November 5, drivers went back to work while the government held yet another press conference to emphasize the government's role in putting the strike to an end and to ensure the public that the government would develop effective policies to deal with this crisis in public transportation. Concluding the events on November 6, Bo Xilai, then Party secretary of Chongqing, met with representatives of taxi drivers and other civilian representatives. He admitted that the administration fee was too high and promised to negotiate with taxi companies to reduce the fee. Bo also suggested the establishment of a workers' union for taxi drivers to allow taxi drivers their own voice. These topics continued to be discussed by government officials and representatives of the All-China Federation of Workers and taxi companies throughout November.[20]

In organizing press conferences as an immediate reaction to the taxi strike, political leaders moved the labor strike from being taboo to being reportable, thus allowing us to observe how newspapers react to a change in the rules. Figure 5.2 compares newspaper reporting in Chongqing with searches for the term "strike" (*bagong*) in Google China during November 2008. Compared with the search engine Baidu, Google is less frequently used by Chinese Internet users, but the development of keyword searches over time gives an indication of searches by netizens during this time. Because readers of nonofficial newspapers share many characteristics with Internet users (see also Chapter 8), Internet searches can give us a rough indication of readership demand targeted especially by nonofficial papers. In both graphs, the x-axis displays the date in November 2008, whereas the y-axis in Figure 5.2a shows the percentage increase of searches for information about a strike in Google and in

---

[18] If strikes were reported, they were not current, but dated back years. The five strikes started in March 2007, August 2005, and September and August 2004. See *China Labour Bulletin*, http://www.clb.org.hk/, accessed December 20, 2011.

[19] See the Chongqing government press conference website from November 5, 2008, at http://www.cq.gov.cn/wszb/DialoguePage.aspx?ID=35, accessed July 22, 2009.

[20] *Sina*, November 7, 2008; *Caijing*, November 8, 2008; *Jingji Caijing Wang*, www.eeo.com.cn, November 10, 2008.

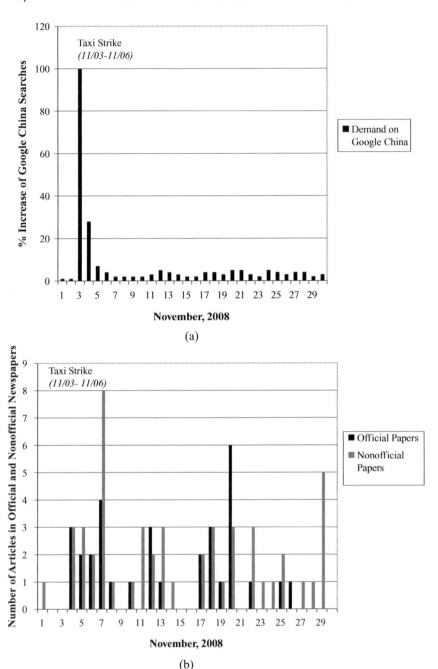

FIGURE 5.2. Comparison between Google China Searches and Newspaper Reporting in Chongqing.[a]

[a] The newspaper report before November 3 is an article in *Chongqing Times*, a nonofficial paper, about problems related to unlicensed taxis.

Figure 5.2b it shows the number of newspaper articles in official and nonofficial papers.

As shown in Figure 5.2a, interest in the term "strike" peaked when the taxi strike began on November 3, but quickly decreased afterward. Figure 5.2b illustrates that *Chongqing Daily*, *Chongqing Evening News*, *Chongqing Times*, *Chongqing Business News*, and even *People's Daily* moved immediately to cover the strikes and responses by government officials with their own articles. There was only a one-day delay, as newspapers publish the news more slowly than the Internet. When the taxi strike moved from being taboo to being reportable, newspapers seized the opportunity to cover the strikes and related political issues to satisfy their readers' interests.

The case of the Chongqing taxi strike shows that rules enforced by political institutions, such as the PD, constrain news reporting. Once the rules change, media outlets are eager to follow readership demand.

* * *

We are now able to formulate a preliminary answer to the puzzle of roughly uniform news content despite claimed freedom in press reporting. Chinese newspapers tend to report about the National Labor Law in a roughly uniform way – despite the fact that media practitioners consider the issue to be open. Because audience demands mostly converge with state policies, market mechanisms synchronize news reporting on labor law. The remainder of this chapter examines these dynamics with respect to news coverage about the United States, starting with selection of open and closed topics.

Open and Closed News Reporting about the United States

As in the case of labor law, I conducted a content analysis using Yoshikoder to assess the relationship between political information and sensitive topics. In contrast to labor law, however, newspapers publish many more articles about the United States, and it was impossible to analyze all reports. To derive a representative sample of news reporting on the United States in one year, I therefore sampled ten constructed weeks in 2003.

In constructed-week sampling, all weeks during a period of time of interest to the researcher are numbered, and subsequently, one Monday, Tuesday, and so on are randomly selected until one (or several) weeks are constructed (Stempel 1952; Lacy et al. 2001). Ten constructed weeks retain representative results for one year of Chinese news reporting about the United States (Stockmann 2010b). The year 2003 is relatively close to the year when the BAS survey was conducted, but also allows for comparison with 1999 for reasons explained in more detail later in this chapter.

I chose *People's Daily* and *Beijing Evening News* (*Beijing Wanbao*) as examples of official and nonofficial newspapers, respectively. Compared with *Chongqing Times*, *Beijing Evening News* is less marketized because it lacks investors.[21] However, *Beijing Evening News* allows us to tap into news stories that more than 50 percent of Beijingers read regularly. Founded in 1958, it was reopened after the end of the Cultural Revolution in 1980 and belongs today to the Beijing Daily Group.[22] Because of the internal hierarchy of the conglomerate, *Beijing Evening News* is subject to the *Beijing Daily* first, and only second to the CCP Party committee at the Beijing level (Song 2004). This feature led most media practitioners to classify *Beijing Evening News* as a semiofficial paper.[23]

Let us first assess the amount of political information in the news about the United States based on references made to politicians and political institutions. Similar to labor law, I created dictionaries for names of Chinese, American, and international leaders as well as political institutions relevant to foreign policy, such as, for example, Hu Jintao, George W. Bush, Kofi Annan, central government, Republican Party, and World Trade Organization (WTO).[24] Politics is a constant theme in international news stories: 37 percent of articles mentioned a politician by name, and 90 percent of articles mentioned a political institution.[25] The average article in *People's Daily* referred about three times to an American, international, or Chinese politician and sixteen times to American, Chinese, or international organizations. Even *Beijing Evening News* referred, on average, once to a politician and seven times to a political institution.

However, political information contained in the news does not necessarily imply that topics are considered sensitive by reporters. As in the case of labor law, I rely on a number of measures to assess sensitivity: one is based on the previously mentioned list of frequently censored keywords by web administrators; the other assesses the texts' relevance to China and its political representatives based on the number of times China or Chinese central-level officials involved in foreign policy making are referenced in the text. In line with media practitioners' claims that news reporting about the United States is largely open, 72 percent of the articles did *not* include any sensitive words, roughly the same as in the case of labor law.[26] Ninety-eight percent of the articles did not mention a

---

[21] On *Chongqing Times'* investors, see Chapter 3.

[22] See "Beijing Wanbao Chuangkan 50 Nian Zhan Shou Du Zhan Chu" (Exhibit "50 Years since the Founding of *Beijing Evening News*" Starts at the Capital Museum), http://media.qianlong.com/38685/2008/03/20/3062@4358623.htm, accessed August 21, 2008. In part, I selected *Beijing Evening News* because its content was available on CD-ROM.

[23] See Chapter 3 for details. Because of the large number of articles required to derive a representative sample of news content per paper, USCATA is limited to two papers only.

[24] Dictionaries for content analysis are available on the author's website at www.daniestockmann.net. For a detailed explanation of the research methods employed in this content analysis, see Stockmann, "Information Overload? Collecting, Managing, and Analyzing Chinese Media Content."

[25] A study by the University of Maryland categorized 50 percent of reports in six newspapers as political in 2001 and 2002. See Maryland Study, "Perspectives Towards the United States in Selected Newspapers of the People's Republic of China," in *Report for the U.S. China Security Review Commission* (2002).

[26] A total of 317 articles mentioned a slightly sensitive term, 20 of 1,202 articles mentioned a moderately sensitive term, and 5 mentioned a highly sensitive term.

Chinese central-level official politician involved in foreign policy making, and 51 percent were, at least not explicitly, related to China.

As in the case of labor law, there is also evidence that official newspapers are somewhat more likely to raise sensitive issues compared with nonofficial newspapers, although differences between papers are even smaller in the case of coverage of the United States. *Beijing Evening News* still covers a substantial amount of sensitive information: 22 percent of articles in *Beijing Evening News* mentioned sensitive keywords, as compared with 37 percent of articles in *People's Daily*. When covering these articles, both papers follow the rule to "stand behind China's foreign policy": both papers publish more sensitive articles when China or Chinese central-level officials involved in foreign policy making are explicitly referenced in the text.[27]

In sum, the division of labor between official and nonofficial newspapers is not as large as is commonly believed. Nonofficial papers place a stronger emphasis on open topics than official papers, but they still cover politics. The correlation between sensitivity and references to politicians or political institutions in the text was only slightly positive (0.19). As we will see next, reporters often purposefully move into open niches for news reporting because this allows them to cater to market demands.

On a final note, my content analysis disputes common claims about the control of international news reporting through Xinhua. Newspapers – especially nonofficial newspapers – publish a large number of articles drafted independently. Even though *Beijing Evening News* does not have foreign correspondents abroad like *People's Daily*, it publishes its own articles. Only about 17.8 percent of its articles about the United States in 2003 were reprints from Xinhua. In comparison, *People's Daily* reprinted Xinhua reports 47.2 percent of the time.[28] In addition, *Beijing Evening News* is not the only nonofficial paper with such a pattern: *Beijing Youth Daily* is also less likely than *People's Daily* to reprint Xinhua articles (Stockmann 2010b). In an effort to attract readers, many nonofficial papers are making an effort to publish their own articles. Reporters make an effort to supplement Xinhua reports with alternative information sources, such as, for example, the Internet or the newsletter of the US embassy. During major events, media institutions may also send reporters abroad. Newspapers remain partially dependent on Xinhua for information, but this dependency is not as strict as is commonly claimed.

---

[27] When China is mentioned, sensitivity is, on average, 0.33, and when articles solely mention the United States, sensitivity is, on average, 0.29 in 2003. When Chinese leaders are mentioned, sensitivity is, on average, 0.66, but only 0.31 when they are not mentioned by name. The first difference in means is statistically significant at the 80% level, the second at the 99% level. Results become more pronounced when adding articles published in 1999. Articles that mentioned at least one highly sensitive term were coded as 3, a moderately sensitive term as 2, and a somewhat sensitive term as 1.

[28] Results are similar when using data from the University of Maryland. See Maryland Study, "Perspectives Towards the United States in Selected Newspapers of the People's Republic of China." Results can be retrieved from the author.

When selecting Xinhua reports, reporters consider the article's relationship to China, but also its relationship to the Chinese central government: newspapers are more likely to reprint Xinhua reports when China is not involved, as it becomes more difficult to obtain information about events abroad. Once Chinese central leaders are explicitly mentioned, reporters prefer the "safe" option of reprinting Xinhua reports.[29]

This distinctive pattern of sensitive news coverage in Chinese newspapers confirms that restrictions on international news reporting only apply to topics that potentially undermine the policies and goals of the Chinese leadership and not to articles that contain political information per se. As shown next, reporters attempt to cater to audience demands when unconstrained by propaganda authorities.

Tone and Selection of News Stories about the United States

Chinese newspaper reporting on the United States is diverse and covers a broad range of topics, ranging from sports and entertainment, science and education, and economics and finance, to US domestic politics and Sino-US relations.[30] A study by the University of Maryland for the US China Security Review Commission found that Chinese newspapers generally covered the United States favorably in 2001, particularly regarding science, education, entertainment, and society. With respect to politics, however, coverage was more mixed: articles were highly positive regarding leadership visits and US-China relations, but were more negative regarding US domestic politics or when there was tension in the US-China relationship, such as during the EP-3 incident[31] or the

---

[29] When China is mentioned, the likelihood to make a reference to Xinhua is 0.2, when articles solely mention the United States, the likelihood to make a reference to Xinhua is 0.4 in 2003. When Chinese leaders are mentioned, the likelihood is 0.38, but only 0.3 when they are not mentioned by name. The first difference in means is statistically significant at the 99% level, the second at the 60% level. The results become more pronounced when adding articles published in 1999.

[30] On the precise distribution of these subtopics, see Maryland Study, "Perspectives Towards the United States in Selected Newspapers of the People's Republic of China" and Zheng Zhai, "Zhongmei Liang Guo Zai Duifang Zhuyao Meiti Zhong De Xiezhao – Dui Renmin Ribao He Niuyue Shibao 1998 Nian Baodao De Duibi Fenxi" (The Mutual Portrayal of China and the US in Important Media – Comparative Analysis of 1998 Reporting in the *People's Daily* and the *New York Times*), http://www.edu.cn/20030728/3088768.shtml, accessed March 29, 2012.

[31] On April 1, 2001, an American EP-3 surveillance plane collided with a Chinese F-8 fighter, which resulted in the loss of the Chinese jet and the death of its pilot. The damaged American plane had to make an emergency landing in Hainan. Beijing blamed the United States for the collision and demanded that the United States end spy flights near its coast and apologize for the loss of its aircraft and pilot. Washington blamed the incident, which occurred in international airspace over the South China Sea, on the Chinese pilot and demanded the return of its plane and crew. After the American crew was released on April 12, negotiations continued until a deal was struck in June 2001 about the specifics of the American aircraft's return to the United States. See, for example, Agence France Presse (April 13, 2001, and June 3, 2001).

Taiwan question[32] (Maryland Study 2002). My content analysis explains how this pattern comes about by distinguishing between reporting on open and closed topics. As we will see, criticism of the United States as a state in the Chinese press usually arises when left unconstrained, whereas reporting is shifted in a more positive (or less negative) direction once topics become more sensitive.

As explained in Chapter 4, international news reporting is quite sensitive to sudden events; in 2003 – the latest year of my content analysis – the events leading up to the war in Iraq and its US-led invasion dominated Chinese media: 386 of 1,202 articles dealt with Iraq, adding up to about 32 percent. By comparison, Taiwan – always a hot topic in the Chinese news – was only the subject of news coverage in thirty-eight articles, adding up to only about 3 percent.

One reason for the high coverage of the war in Iraq was that it constituted a topic for which media practitioners felt relatively unconstrained by the PD. As explained in Chapter 4, reporters described the war in Iraq as largely open, as it was not seen as core to the US-China relationship. Indeed, Chinese leaders and China were about 50 percent less likely to be referenced in reporting on Iraq than on other topics, providing reporters with greater leeway in reporting.[33] Another rationale for the openness of the topic editors brought up was the convergence between market demands and the Chinese government's position, which had announced repeatedly that the Iraq problem should be solved by diplomatic means through the United Nations.[34] As such, newspapers' coverage of the event is illustrative of incidents that are either only tangentially related to China (such as American domestic politics) or crisis situations in which the PD may temporarily allow media to express criticism.[35]

In the weeks leading up to the war, two groups of academics had started online petitions, one opposing and the other supporting a possible invasion of Iraq. The opposing petition, initiated by Han Deqiang, an economist at Beijing University of Aeronautics and Astronautics (Beihang University) on February

---

[32] Chinese officials give a number of reasons why the CCP considers Taiwan's formal independence to be nonnegotiable, indeed an existential threat. One is that independence would be a strategic threat to China (as an independent Taiwan will likely become a formal ally of the United States). Another reason is that independence is a threat to CCP legitimacy – the Chinese population will blame the CCP leadership for selling out the country. This could possibly lead to the collapse of the Party, but most certainly the leadership that "lost Taiwan" would be removed. A third reason is that Taiwan independence will encourage a domestic domino effect, strengthening the determination of Tibetan, Uighur, and Mongolian separatists.

[33] When Iraq is mentioned in 2003, articles mention, on average, China 3 times and Chinese leaders 0.13 times; when Iraq is not mentioned, articles mention China about 6 times and Chinese leaders about 0.8 times. The differences in means of references to China are statistically significant at the 95 percent level; the differences in means regarding references to Chinese leaders are not.

[34] See, for example, comments by the spokesperson of the Chinese Ministry of Foreign Affairs after UN resolution 1441 on November 14, 2002. Available at the Ministry of Foreign Affairs website at http://www.mfa.gov.cn/wjb/adsearch.jsp, accessed January 21, 2011.

[35] During such public opinion crises, the PD sometimes restricts and sometimes opens up news reporting. Chapter 6 explains this point in greater detail.

10, collected more than 1,500 signatures opposing an invasion and appealing to the Security Council of the United Nations (and particularly China, Russia, and France) to "resist pressure" by the Bush administration and assume responsibility to preserve world peace.[36] On February 18, the petition was presented to the American embassy, which, according to *21st Century Economic Report* (21 *Shiji Jingji Baodao*), declared that it would take this important voice of China very seriously. When asked to comment on the scholarly petition on the same day, the spokesperson of the Chinese Ministry of Foreign Affairs, Zhang Qiyue, commented that the Chinese people were peace-loving and that the Chinese government was trying to resolve the conflict through peaceful means.[37] In an interview with Sina.com, Han Deqiang interpreted her comments as supportive of the petition: "The government expressed support. The spokesperson of the Ministry of Foreign Affairs declared that Chinese people are peace-loving. I agree, Chinese people love peace." Wang Xiaodong, a coinitiator of the opposing petition, added: "I like the civilized aspects of the United States, including material civilization (*wuzhi wenming*), political civilization (*zhengzhi wenming*), its culture, its films. But it doesn't play a democratic role when playing the international game, it's playing the role of a hegemon, and that's what I oppose."[38] In Chinese, "hegemonism" (*baquan zhuyi*) refers to tyrannical, bullying, overbearing, often violent, and illegitimate behavior by the powerful, with no regard for the well-being of the less powerful. Thus a reference to the United States as hegemon means the United States is the unjust and overbearing dominant state in the system.[39]

Up until this point, a handful of press reports had discussed the opposing petition and questioned whether it encompassed the view of all Chinese

---

[36] There was a controversy about the accuracy of the signatures on the list after several scholars came forward demanding that their signatures be taken off the petition. It was suspected that netizens with the same name had signed the petition and names were quickly removed from the list if requested. "Zhongguo Xuezhe Fan Zhan Shengming" (A Declaration by Chinese Scholars Opposing the War)," *Economic Observer*, February 24, 2003. The petition, entitled "Fandui Meiguo Zhengfu dui Yilake Zhansheng Jihua de Shengming" (Declaration Opposing the Plan for War on Iraq by the American Government) is available at http://tieba.baidu.com/f?kz=19050125, accessed December 17, 2011.

[37] Transcript of meeting with journalists available at Sina.com, http://news.sina.com.cn/c/2003-02-18/2035913180.shtml#a, accessed December 18, 2011.

[38] Material and political civilization carries the connotation of economic and political development and achievement. "Zhongguo Xuezhe Fanzhan Shengming Faqi Ren Han Deqiang Wang Xiaodong de Liaotian Shilü" (Transcript of a Chat with Han Deqiang and Wang Xiaodong, the Initiators of Chinese Scholars' Declaration Opposing the War), http://news.sina.com.cn/c/2003-02-18/1910913146.shtml, accessed December 18, 2011.

[39] See also Mulin Wang and Ming Jing, "Waishi Caifang Baodao (Foreign Affairs Interview Reports)," in *Zhuanye Caifang Baodaoxue (Studies of Professional Interview Reports)*, ed. Hongwen Lan (Beijing: Renmin Chubanshe, 2003), Alastair Iain Johnston and Daniela Stockmann, "Chinese Attitudes toward the United States and Americans," in *Antiamericanisms in World Politics*, ed. Peter Katzenstein and Robert Keohane (Ithaca: Cornell University Press, 2007).

intellectuals and even the world, as it claimed.[40] On February 20, two researchers of literature at Peking University, Yu Jie and Xu Jinru, initiated an online petition expressing support of an American invasion of Iraq to protect human rights. Its content was highly controversial, as it proclaimed that the opposing petition followed "the world view of Saddam's Chinese colleague and predecessor, Mao Zedong, and proclaimed the justification of dictatorship in the name of people" and explicitly accused the academic opponents, whom they believed represented the new left and nationalists, of hindering democratization of China and "merely flattering their own state authorities rather than standing against the war as the petition soon gained appreciation from the Chinese authorities."[41] Such provocative statements received much criticism online, and the petition was only able to gather about twenty signatures (Wang 2010). Yu Jie claims that some additional signatures were deleted, implying censorship.[42]

Indeed, the few newspapers that reported about the supporting petition omitted Yu Jie and Xu Jinru's criticism of Chinese politics, including the references to Mao, democratization, or the interplay between the opposing petition and statements by the Ministry of Foreign Affairs. *Southern Weekend* and the *Economic Observer* reported on both sides, but only briefly presented Yu Jie's view that limited war can be justified if fought for humanitarian reasons and mostly emphasized his point that Chinese intellectuals did not all share the view of the opposing petition.[43] In comparison, the opposing side received three to four times more coverage.[44]

Other newspapers, including both nonofficial and official papers such as *Beijing Evening News* and *People's Daily*, did not even mention the supporting voices. Both papers featured stories about the US preparation for war and opposing voices against it, whereby *Beijing Evening News* relied on media reactions in the United States and other countries, whereas *People's Daily* included stories by foreign journalists inside Iraq and the United States.[45]

---

[40] See *21st Century Economic Report*, February 17, 2003, and *Southern Metropolitan News*, reprinted on Xinhua Net and Sina.com, February 19, 2003.

[41] New left intellectuals turned to neo-Marxist and postcolonialist literature to develop critical analysis of global capitalism and China's role in it. The petition, entitled "Zhongguo Zhishi Fenzi Guanyu Shengyuan Meiguo Zhengfu Cuihui Sadamu Ducai Zhengquan de Shenming" (Declaration of Chinese Intellectuals Supporting the American Government in Destroying Saddam's Dictatorship), is available at http://news.boxun.com/news/gb/pubvp/2003/02/200302202349.shtml, accessed December 18, 2011.

[42] Based on an interview with Yu Jie, published on a website by Americans of Chinese descent promoting American conservative values at http://www.youpai.org/read.php?%20id=2567, accessed December 17, 2011.

[43] *Economic Observer*, February 24, 2003; *Southern Weekend*, February 27, 2003.

[44] The *Economic Observer* mentioned opponents forty-six times and supporters five times, and the tone surrounding keywords representing the US was −37. *Southern Weekend* referenced opponents twenty-eight times and supporters nine times, and the tone surrounding the United States was −51.

[45] See, for example, *Beijing Evening News* and *People's Daily* on February 9, 13, and 20, 2003. *People's Daily* featured "expert comments" by scholars of international relations who had

In part, supporting voices were marginalized in the Chinese press because media practitioners concluded that ordinary citizens were largely opposed to the war. Sina.com and Xinhua Net (*Xinhua Wang*) printed results of an online poll conducted by *Business Watch Magazine* (*Shangwu Zhoukan*) showing that only 8 of 221 people supported a statement close to the supporting petition. A majority of "voters" supported statements similar to the opposing petition, emphasizing resolution of the conflict through peaceful and diplomatic means and regarding the invasion as a violation of the human rights of the Iraqi people, and claimed that the United Nations had the right to declare war, not the United States.[46]

Although there is reason to question the reliability of these figures, the conclusion many media practitioners drew from them – that audiences were mainly against the war – is probably not false either. Although I am not aware of randomly sampled survey data on the war in Iraq, BAS data show that, at least in Beijing, sentiment toward the United States as a state has increased in negativity over time among cadres and average citizens.[47] The war in Iraq presented an opportunity for reporters to respond to this increase in negativity among readers.

The war in Iraq has become a particularly popular theme – even as of 2012 – in Chinese media because it constitutes an open topic that allows media to satisfy demands among readers for criticism of the United States as a state.[48] When a story combines these features, news about the United States drops to a low point.

We find further evidence for this conclusion when comparing the tone of news reporting on open and closed topics in the *People's Daily* and *Beijing Evening News* in 2003. As before, I measure tone, the dependent variable, based on the relative frequency of positive and negative terms within a semantic space of eight words surrounding terms representing the United States.[49] To

largely not participated in either of the two petitions. See, for example, "Yilake Weiji Yu Xin Yilun Quanqiu Zhengzhi" (The Iraq Crisis and the First Round of Globalization Politics), *People's Daily*, February 20, 2003.

[46] More statements opposed the war than statements that supported the war. In addition, a number of statements represented views not proposed in any of the petitions, such as imposing more economic sanctions or calls for Saddam's resignation. See "Zhongguo Gaoceng Jingli Dui Yilake Wenti Chi He Taidu?" (Which Attitudes Do Chinese High-Level Managers Hold Regarding the Iraq Issue?), http://finance.sina.com.cn/j/20030312/1001319650.shtml, accessed December 18, 2011.

[47] Sentiment toward the United States dropped by about 9 degrees between 1998 and 2002 among cadres as well as "ordinary citizens." For detailed statistics, see Online Appendix to Daniela Stockmann, "Race to the Bottom: Media Marketization and Increasing Negativity toward the United States in China," *Political Communication* 28, no. 3 (2011c). Available at www.daniestockmann.net.

[48] Chapter 8 demonstrates that readers attempt to select newspapers that confirm their preexisting beliefs.

[49] As before, semantic space was chosen based on pretesting. Eight words were broad enough to pick up variation in tone but were narrow enough to ensure that valence words (negative and positive terms) tended to be related to the concept of interest.

TABLE 5.2. *OLS Regression Results for the Tone Surrounding the United States in the* People's Daily *and* Beijing Evening News.

Independent Variables:	Dependent Variable: Tone of US
	Coefficient (s.e.)
People's Daily	1.044*** (0.311)
Politics	-4.948*** (0.864)
Article on China and the US	1.093*** (0.24)
2003[a]	-0.630*** (0.232)
Sensitivity over time	-4.495*** (1.016)
Length	9.811*** (2.606)
Constant	1.008*** (0.305)
N	2,272
R-squared	0.04

* $p<0.1$; ** $p<0.05$; ***$p<0.01$.
[a] Based on a dummy variable, coded zero when article was published in 2003.
Source: United States Computer-Aided Text Analysis, 1999 and 2003.

facilitate interpretation, I do not normalize the measure, but instead control for the article's length in the statistical analysis. The resulting variable runs from -46 to $+43$, indicating that the tone in the article when describing the United States was, for example, 46 words more negative than positive, or 43 words more positive than negative. To simplify, I also measure open and closed reporting by their mentioning of China, but the findings remain robust when using an indicator for the number of times China, Chinese political institutions, or Chinese leaders are referenced in the text. The control variables presented here are reduced to a minimum and only include sensitivity over time and article length, but findings remain robust when adding more controls.[50]

Figure 5.3 and Table 5.1 display the relationship between references to politics and tone in news reports, whereby closed topics related to China in addition to the US are displayed in Figure 5.3a, while open topics solely related to the US are shown in Figure 5.3b. The x-axis shows the number of times a

[50] Robustness test results are discussed in Appendix D. Sensitivity over time was negatively related to tone in news reporting on the United States because the PD tends to restrict stories that depict the United States in a negative light.

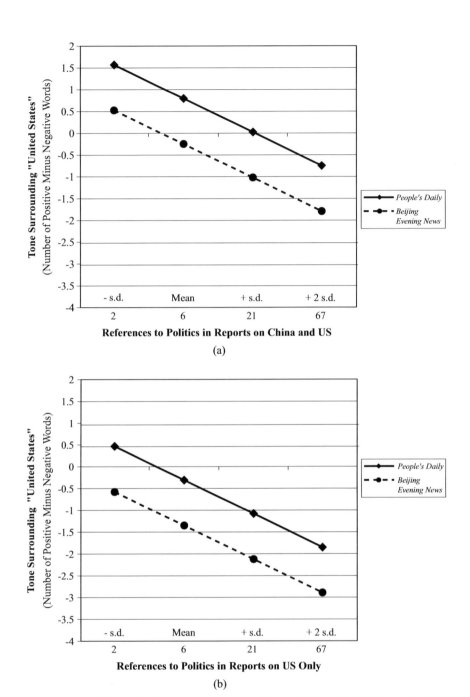

FIGURE 5.3. Relationship between Newspaper Type and Tone of Articles on the United States as Open and Closed Topics Change in 2003. *Source*: United States Computer-Aided Text Analysis, 1999 and 2003.[a]

[a] Results were calculated holding sensitivity over time and length constant at average levels, using Clarify. See Gary King, Michael Tomz, and Jason Wittenberg, "Making the Most of Statistical Analyses: Improving Interpretation and Presentation," *American Journal of Political Science* 44, no. 2 (2000).

reference is made to politics in the article, whereas the y-axis displays the tone of news reporting. The results show that the tone of news reporting changes as articles become more relevant to politics within open and closed topics. The logic for taking into account references to politics is related to the underlying bifurcation of Chinese views of the United States, also expressed by Wang Xiaodong's previously presented comments in which he described the United States as a hegemon internationally, but he admired American culture.

Let us first look at the relationship between politics and the tone of news reporting. As expected, articles tend to increase in negativity as they become more relevant to politics. Figures 5.3a and 5.3b both display a negative relationship, showing a difference of up to five negative words as an article contains more political information. However, when comparing across figures, we also discover that tone differs on open and closed topics: articles were about one word more positive when the articles also dealt with China than solely with the United States. When moving into open topics, such as, for example, the US-led invasion of Iraq, Chinese newspapers reported more negatively about the US than otherwise.[51] In 2003, reporting on the United States that did not mention China was dominated by this theme – about 45 percent of articles also mentioned Iraq – and both newspapers' reporting on the topic was highly negative.[52]

Once an article becomes more relevant to Sino-US relations, and particularly Chinese leaders, reporting becomes more positive. An example illustrative of highly positive reporting about the United States is reporting on leaders' visit. After Premier Wen Jiabao's visit to the United States in December 2003, *Beijing Evening News* quoted newspapers from all over the world, praising the success of the visit as "Sino-US relations have almost never been as stable as both sides become more dependent on each other economically."[53] Similarly, *People's Daily* concluded: "This time's visit by Premier Wen Jiabao promoted the friendship of China and the US, enhanced the companionship and understanding of the two peoples, and pushed forward the further development of a constructive cooperative relationship."[54] At first glance, both papers' positive conclusion about the visit closely mirror each other, but upon closer examination, we discover subtle nuances.

[51] Social identity theory does not explain these results sufficiently. First, the dependent variable is measured by the positivity and negativity of words surrounding an outgroup and not the overall tone of the article. Second, when the number of times Chinese leaders are referenced in the text is used as an indicator for the sensitivity of the article, tone is highly positive, even when controlling for references to China in the text.

[52] For further investigation of the role of Iraq and strategic selection of open topics by individual papers, see Stockmann, "Race to the Bottom: Media Marketization and Increasing Negativity toward the United States in China."

[53] "Quanqiu Meiti Reping Zongli Fangmei" (Global Media Praise Premier's Visit to the United States), *Beijing Evening News*, December 12, 2003.

[54] "Jiaqiang Hezuo, Huli ShuangYing" (Strengthening Cooperation is to Mutual Benefit), *People's Daily*, December 12, 2003.

Whereas the *People's Daily* described Americans as cooperative, welcoming, and understanding, *Beijing Evening News'* account is more restrained and less emotional. The nonofficial newspaper starts with a summary of reactions by the *New York Times*: "Chinese premier Wen Jiabao visited the United States, emphasizing that the Taiwan issue is a major issue. The United States should remind Chen Shuibian that the US side does not support Taiwanese independence or changing its status on its own initiative." Although the American reaction to Wen Jiabao's position on the Taiwan issue was not further discussed, this statement implies some controversy in US-China relations. However, the journalist ends the article with quotes by British, German, and Japanese media that emphasize success and mutual benefit of the Sino-US relationship.

In her study of news reporting on President Clinton's 1998 visit to China, Li (2003) detected similarly subtle differences between *People's Daily* and *Global Times*, a nonofficial newspaper belonging to the *People's Daily* group. Both papers focus on the success of the visit in a way that propagates the viewpoint of China and strengthens the leadership of the CCP. At the same time, the nonofficial paper packages this message in stories that are more interesting to readers, similar to global media coverage in *Beijing Evening News* discussed previously, and also raises some controversial aspects of the US-China relationship. *Global Times* uses more foreign sources to tell the story, ties in different societal voices, and uses a more neutral language. *People's Daily*, on the other hand, uses more emotional language and focuses on political leaders to tell the story. Overall, however, just like *Beijing Evening News*, *Global Times* does not go so far as to have an independent political voice.

We find further confirmation of these differences in Figures 5.3a and 5.3b. *People's Daily* described the United States consistently more positively than *Beijing Evening News*: on average, about one word.[55] This was even the case regarding the war in Iraq. Considering media practitioners' differentiation between official and nonofficial papers presented in Chapter 3, this makes a lot of sense: nonofficial papers tend to be more marketized and therefore more strongly responsive to audience demands, whereas official papers lag behind in terms of media marketization. At the same time, the difference of one positive word in news reporting, although statistically significant, is small and subtle. Overall, news reporting on the United States in the two papers is fairly uniform in tone.[56] Highly negative reporting, as illustrated previously by the events leading up to the invasion of Iraq, is not representative of

---

[55] This is particularly true when it comes to the selection of Xinhua news reports: *Beijing Evening News* is particularly likely to reprint more negative Xinhua reports than the *People's Daily*, because these articles are considered "safe" by journalists. For further discussion, see Online Appendix to Stockmann, "Race to the Bottom: Media Marketization and Increasing Negativity toward the United States in China."

[56] *People's Daily* also tends to use more valence words in its articles, on average, thirty-three positive and twenty-six negative terms. *Beijing Evening News* uses twenty-two positive and eighteen negative terms, on average. The differences between the papers were statistically significant, even if the tone is normalized by article length.

Chinese news coverage. On average, news reporting was slightly positive – even in 2003.[57]

On a final note, it is helpful to consider briefly the role of controversial events in explaining Chinese press reporting about the United States. Because the Chinese government opposed the invasion, how do we know coverage of the war in Iraq was not primarily driven by strong Chinese disagreement with actions undertaken by the US government? A comparison of news reporting in 2003 with reporting in 1999 helps to place the impact of the event itself into perspective. In May 1999, an American aircraft bombed the Chinese embassy in Yugoslavia during a NATO air strike, killing three Chinese journalists and injuring twenty other Chinese citizens. Immediately after the event, the United States declared that multiple errors in several parts of the US administration were responsible for the mistaken bombing and apologized repeatedly through various channels. The Chinese government viewed the 1999 bombing as a deliberate provocation, cut off high-level diplomatic ties, and granted formal approval to mass protests that escalated into violence against US diplomatic facilities. In contrast, the invasion of Iraq did not lead to a crisis situation comparable in scope to that of 1999. Although China opposed the war, Sino-US relations were comparatively more stable in 2003. A content analysis of the tone of statements by the Chinese Ministry of Foreign Affairs confirms that the tone in such statements became more positive between 1999 and 2003.[58]

If controversial events between the United States and China were the main factor influencing Chinese news, we should find that news coverage about the United States tended to be more negative in 1999 than news stories in 2003. However, Table 5.2 shows that this was not the case. Reporting in 2003 was, on average, more negative than in 1999, shown by the negative coefficient of a dummy variable coded as 1 if the article was published in 2003 and as 0 if the article was published in 1999.[59] Reporters used the opportunity to express criticism in the context of the war in Iraq, while they had to restrain themselves in 1999 because of greater sensitivity of the story, despite greater tension with the United States.[60] This pattern further confirms that restrictions imposed on the Chinese press tend to work in favor of the United States rather than against it, whereas a lack of instructions usually results in more negative press coverage.

---

[57] In 2003, tone regarding the United States (normalized by the article's length) was, on average, 0.12 (s.d. = 1.22).

[58] Another advantage of comparing 1999 with 2003 is that 1999 marks the year before the emergence of commercialized papers in the Beijing newspaper market, and 2003 marks the year in which this newspaper type had already established itself. Chapter 6 discusses the underlying reasons for changes in tone over time in greater detail.

[59] *Beijing Evening News* especially becomes more negative when reporting about Iraq in 2003. See Online Appendix to Stockmann, "Race to the Bottom: Media Marketization and Increasing Negativity toward the United States in China." Available at www.daniestockmann.net.

[60] An investigation of Chinese reactions to the American annual human rights reports shows that Chinese reactions do not show any signs of retaliation, not even when confrontation accumulates over time, thus reinforcing the conclusion that confrontation in Sino-US relations does not drive increasing negativity toward the United States in China. See Ibid.

* * *

In sum, content analysis regarding the United States confirms statements by Chinese media practitioners that the propaganda authorities try to shift the media in a positive (or less negative) direction when constraining the news about the United States. The nonofficial papers generally follow the lead of *People's Daily*, which is more positive in tone. We have seen, however, that newspapers switch toward negative reporting on open topics. However, even in areas where journalists and editors feel free to formulate articles in any way they want, political messages conveyed through nonofficial papers do not strongly depart from those presented in official papers. Although nonofficial papers transmit slightly more negative messages, news reporting tends to be roughly uniform in tone.

Are nonofficial newspapers really responding to the demands of their readers when unconstrained by institutions? The next section further explores this causal mechanism.

Changes in Media Management of International News over Time

To observe whether media outlets are indeed following the perceived demands of their readers when reporting negative news, I rely on a case study of Chinese press reporting on the 2004 presidential elections. This event provides us with an opportunity to observe the rationale behind the publication of a news story critical of US domestic politics.

In 2004, Chinese editors and journalists felt free to report on the upcoming elections as they wanted until *China Daily* published a speech by former Chinese Foreign Minister Qian Qichen in which he criticized President George W. Bush's foreign policy.[61] To foreign observers, the content was puzzling, as *China Daily*, a quasi-Party paper,[62] was perceived to represent government opinion. Furthermore, the article also appeared on the English website of *People's Daily*, the official mouthpiece of the CCP.[63] However, the story soon transformed into what Stern and Hassid (2012) have called "control parables," providing a reference point for learning about sensitive news reporting, as discussed in Chapter 4.

In an interview shortly after the incident, a senior editor explained that *China Daily* had been busy going on the market in previous years, which to

---

[61] The speech was given at the CCP Central Party School and translated into English from the Party school's newspaper in the article "US Strategy to Be Blamed" (*China Daily* is published in English). For US reactions, see State Department Briefing, November 1, 2004. Harvey Stockwin. "The Qian Qichen Op-ed: Official Discontent or Just one Man's Opinion?" November 1, 2004. Available at: http://www.asianresearch.org/articles/2462.html, accessed October 17, 2006.

[62] Some papers at the national level are often referred to as Party papers although they are not under direct supervision of the central Party committee: *Guangming Daily*, *China Daily*, and *Economic Daily*. They can be considered "quasi-Party papers."

[63] Online versions of newspapers differ frequently from print versions. Appearing on the Internet, online newspapers have more space for their news reports. See also Chapter 6.

him meant "making readers like the newspaper." Spontaneously raising the 2004 presidential elections as a sensitive issue, he laid out the rationale for publication of the story: "If *China Daily* publishes some things, outsiders often simply conclude that it is the official opinion. But often what *China Daily* publishes represents its own opinion." In his view, the opinion of *China Daily* was defined by its position between the government and ordinary citizens who want to read criticism of American foreign policy. *China Daily* attempted to appeal to popular demands by publishing a critical story about the United States.

Shortly after its publication, the American embassy became involved, and Chinese high-ranking officials criticized *China Daily* for the article. The issue became widely known among journalists and editors as the story about "how *China Daily* committed a mistake" – an expression referring to criticism by propaganda authorities or political leaders. China was supposed to stay out of American internal affairs and to report objectively on the elections. The rationale that many journalists found convincing was that the Chinese government would have to deal with the winner of the elections – no matter which presidential candidate won. Once the presidential elections became an issue in Sino-US relations, the media were asked to not publicly side with either of the candidates until the elections. Not surprisingly, the Chinese media followed suit for the sake of stable relations with the United States. On November 4, *Beijing News* concluded that President Bush's reelection constituted a "hidden opportunity" for China, as his China policy would help to continue the positive development of the US-China relationship.

There are numerous examples of similar attempts by the Chinese media to appeal to audiences with negative news on foreign affairs. In the aftermath of 9/11, for example, many media outlets initially expressed *schadenfreude* when feeling unconstrained, but the state quickly reacted by issuing instructions to media outlets to constrain negativity in the news (Stockmann 2010b). Because appeals to popular demands are predictable in the absence of constraints on news reporting, sometimes the lack of guidance may be to the advantage of the state. However, once the state exerts control over media outlets, reporters are careful not to repeat previous mistakes, as in the case of *China Daily*.

In his inauguration speech, President Barack Obama said: "Recall that earlier generations faced down fascism and communism not just with missiles and tanks, but with sturdy alliances and enduring convictions." Conscious of issue sensitivity, the director of CCTV news quickly turned down the voice of the Chinese translator on hearing the term "communism," leaving an irritated moderator in the studio wondering about how to proceed next.

Freedom without Political Diversity

Media practitioners and handbooks for journalistic training show that PD instructions are limited to a relatively small number of topics related to labor law and the United States. Accordingly, journalists feel free to publicize most topics on these issues in any way they want. Nevertheless, content analyses uncovered that Chinese newspapers generally report about labor law and the United States in a roughly uniform way.

Of course, there are noticeable differences across newspaper types depending on a story's relevance to politics and degree of sensitivity, but these differences are small. Even though nonofficial papers convey much politically relevant information, they usually do not go so far as to critically challenge the policies or goals of political leaders. Newspapers generally convey messages that promote the official line of the government. In the area of labor law, they report from the perspective of the weak and portray legal regulations and the legal system as an effective means to resolve grievances. In the case of the United States, they abstain from criticism to foster stability in US-China relations, although they seize opportunities to cater to audience demands when discovering open niches.

The apparent contradiction between journalistic freedom and rough uniformity in the news can be resolved once we take into account institutional and market mechanisms. Chapter 4 showed that a story increases in sensitivity when it threatens to undermine policies and goals of Chinese leaders, depending on their place within the administrative hierarchy of the Chinese political system. The case of the American presidential elections in 2004 shows that journalists are careful not to get into trouble with propaganda authorities after hearing about "mistakes" by individual media outlets. In many cases, these mistakes happen when editors try to target readers by means of negative news stories. Issue sensitivity is socialized by means of institutions and selectively imposed by propaganda officials when newspapers, if unconstrained publish articles that diverge from the political positions of Chinese officials. The interaction between institutions and the market synchronizes the tone of news reporting in newspapers.

However, many issues do not require the use of coercion through the means of institutions for the media to convey messages that support government policy. In the area of labor problems and legal disputes, newspapers can serve public demands, and the goals of the government converge most of the time. Propaganda authorities can conveniently outsource political control over news content to the market. The adoption of the Regulations for the Opening of Government News in 2007 and their implementation in the case of the Chongqing taxi strike is a sign that Chinese officials have discovered that market mechanisms can work to their advantage: when popular tastes pull the media in the desired direction, there is no need to "guide" the media. Opening up space for news reporting may even strengthen support among media practitioners by lowering coercion, as suggested by the logic of the dictator's dilemma laid out in Chapter 2.

Yet there is a clear limit to the use of market mechanisms as a tool to manage newspapers: market mechanisms only work in a way favorable to the government as long as the public demands information that converges with policy goals and as long as these demands are similar among readership groups.

Therefore, institutions remain key to retaining the state's capacity to enforce press restrictions when necessary.

On the basis of my content analysis, the CCP's institutional capacity is still sufficient to ensure that newspapers generally do not divert much from the position of the government. These findings primarily reflect the situation at the time when we conducted the LLM and BAS surveys in 2005, and they are clearly limited in terms of their applicability to other regions, issues, media outlets, levels of government, and crisis situations. Chapter 6 discusses the implications of my findings presented thus far for the production of news in China more broadly.

6

Discursive Space in Chinese Media

China's top leaders want to be popular. At the 60th anniversary of the People's Republic of China in 2009, participants at the evening gala at Tiananmen Square went up to the Chinese top leaders on the Gate of Heavenly Peace to take them down and make them mingle with ordinary people. This gesture of elevating the leadership with the population was an attempt to improve the image of the government in the eyes of the public, particularly ethnic minorities. Two children who held hands with President Hu Jintao were from Tibet and Xinjiang province, where unrest had taken place in 2008 and 2009. Clearly, the Chinese leadership is concerned about its image among the Chinese public.

Under the Hu-Wen administration, the Chinese leadership emphasized its role of looking after the interests of the vast majority of society for the sake of creating a harmonious society and maintaining social stability. This special emphasis on helping disadvantaged groups is rooted in the Jiang Zemin era, but was revitalized after Hu Jintao consolidated his power (Yang 2006). Economic reforms had brought about rampant corruption among government officials, rising unemployment, growing socioeconomic inequality, and rapid environmental degradation, to name just a few potential sources for social conflict, and political institutions had adapted to these issues only imperfectly, constantly trying to keep up with social pressures by rebuilding and readjusting.

The state responded by delegating responsibilities to economic, legal, and social actors, including the media. These initiatives have opened up interactive space between social actors and political elites, but this relaxation of control has also increased the risk that social forces will press against the structure of the state itself. Public officials therefore live in constant fear that the decrease of control will begin posing a larger threat against them or the broader political system (Oi 2004; Weller 2008; Liebman 2011a). Social spaces have therefore been periodically reduced by repression, carried out more recently by Hu Jintao via his efforts to "construct a harmonious society," which inspired netizens to refer to censoring of online content as "harmonizing" (*hexie*). Thus a number of observers described these dynamics as "carrots-and-sticks" tactics (Oi 2004;

Dickson 2005; Yang 2006) or "cycles of public mobilization" (Reilly 2012). This chapter explores the interaction between institutions and the market in Chinese media.

Tension between Editors and Propaganda Officials

To a certain extent, the introduction of market mechanisms into a planned economy requires relaxation of the control exerted by the Chinese state. As explained in Chapter 3, the government reduced state subsidies and deregulated licensing, personnel management, and business management to support the introduction of market mechanisms into media outlets as a means to address budget deficits. This increase in autonomy was accompanied by greater space for press reporting to allow media to cater to audiences as a means to attract advertising.

This opening of space has led to tensions between media practitioners and propaganda officials. He (2000) even described these dynamics as a "tug of war." Media practitioners see themselves under pressure between the state and the market. As one editor at a semiofficial paper in the *People's Daily* group put it: "You need to fundamentally serve the needs of the government, but also the needs of the market of readers – it's two kinds of pressures. If you lose your readers, don't you die? And if you publish in an unorganized manner (*luan deng*), don't you die as well?"[1] The dependency of newspapers on selling papers provides them with bargaining power when negotiating space with propaganda officials.

Tension between senior media staff and officials primarily arises when the PD gives instructions to abstain from reporting. There are many examples of reporters playing edge ball (*da cabianqiu*), trying to push the boundaries of news reporting. A prominent case the joint editorial by thirteen newspapers, including *Chongqing Times*, that advocated speeding up reform of the household registration system. The editorial was published during the 2010 "two meetings" of the National People's Congress and the National People's Political Consultative Conference, during which the Central Propaganda Department and the Government Bureau of Internet Affairs had issued instructions to not "sensationalize or feature news articles that will create a major impact."[2] The Central Propaganda Department requested that the editorial should "be removed from the Internet" and that media should abstain from sensationalizing or featuring reports on the incident.[3] As the state allows newspapers to

---

[1] Interview with a male editor of semiofficial and official paper in Beijing (#8).

[2] "What Chinese Censors Don't Want You to Know," *New York Times*, March 21, 2010.

[3] Ibid and International Federation of Journalists (IFJ), "Zhongguo Xinwen Ziyou 2010 (Press Freedom in China in 2010)," (2010), 91. Zhang Hong, the editor of the online edition of *Economic Observer* and writer of the editorial, was fired. The editor-in-chief and a vice-editor-in-chief of *Economic Observer* received reprimands that could negatively affect promotion. Editors-in-chief of the other twelve newspapers were admonished by the PD. See also "Shei Jiaomie

cater to the market, some reporters start pushing against the state structure itself.[4]

Arguments in favor of lifting press restrictions often tie the market value of a story to its news value. An editor-in-chief of a central-level official newspaper explained: "Before marketization, people thought media is a form of education. Now we know: first, people have the right to know the facts, we should let people know so-called big issues. Second, we also trust the people. Ordinary people can judge what is right and what is wrong."[5] A comment by a reporter at the *Chongqing Evening News* is an illustrative example: "The PD may not know some issues have happened, so when we reporters learn about them, we publish them very quickly. Once the PD learns about them, they may criticize us, but sometimes they let it go – at last our newspapers' readers have gained their trust!"[6] Interaction between the state and the market have raised a discussion about journalistic ethics among media practitioners, communication scholars, and public officials. Claims that emphasize the necessity to sell papers are often tied to claims about what constitutes "news" and information beneficial for the government.

Let us first consider the position of political leaders emerging from a discussion within the central-level propaganda *xitong*.[7] Like all of his predecessors,[8] Hu Jintao has emphasized that news should be close to reality, such as during his opening speech at the World Media Summit in October 2009, urging media outlets (around the world) to "assume social responsibility and promote truthful, accurate, complete, and objective news and information dissemination."

Often omitted in English reports, the first part of the sentence emphasizes journalistic ethics defined as social responsibility, which, in the context of Chinese media, denotes attitudes and behavior in line with the goals and policies of state and Party units. The vagueness of the goals and policies announced by political leaders allows for leeway in interpretation among media staff, but

---

Jinnian 'Lianghui' Diyi Xinwen Redian" (Who Poured and Killed This Year's "Two Meetings'" Number One News?), http://www.chinainperspective.com/ArtShow.aspx?AID=5727, accessed December 21, 2011.

[4] A similar negotiation takes place in other parts of the cultural sector, as described by Stanley Rosen, "Is the Internet a Positive Force in the Development of Civil Society, a Public Sphere, and Democratization in China?," *International Journal of Communication* 4 (2010).

[5] Interview with a male editor-in-chief of official paper in Beijing (#7).

[6] Interview with a male journalist of nonofficial paper in Chongqing (#39).

[7] When I was interviewing in 2005, PD officials explained that there was a discussion about how to best adopt media management among PD officials, but they could not share its content with me. Some senior editors mentioned that they had been invited by the PD to explain their point of view.

[8] On emphasis and interpretation of truthful information by Mao Zedong, Deng Xiaoping, and Jiang Zemin, see Lidan Chen, *Makesi Zhuyi Xinwen Sixiang Gailun (Introduction to Marxist News Thought)* (Shanghai: Fudan Daxue Chubanshe, 2003b).

interpretation that pleases higher levels opens up opportunities for promotion in media outlets (Stockmann 2011d).

The PD is trying to connect ideas about social responsibility with ideas about truthfulness. In 2011, the Sixth Plenum of the Fifteenth Party Congress issued a decision regarding the deepening of reform of the cultural sector, which asks reporters to "uphold social responsibility and professional ethics, truthfully and accurately disseminate news information, and be aware of committing mistakes." Journalists should "consciously refuse mistaken positions (*cuowu guandian*) and be determined to put an end to fake news."[9] This strategy already became apparent in 2005. A central-level propaganda official explained that journalists' own views about what constituted the interest of "ordinary people" or "vulnerable social groups" were biased, creating a need for propaganda authorities to balance reporting.[10] An editor of the *People's Daily* explained: "Even if the news is factually correct, it needs to be well-written and edited. [If not,] there is no difference from fake news."[11] Young journalists entering the profession in particular lacked professional ethics and needed better training. Another editor-in-chief of a central-level official paper explained: "Media practitioners, on the one hand, need to promote social responsibility, on the other hand, cater to the market."[12] Marketization is associated with fake news and unbalanced news reporting, creating a need for socially responsible reporting.

In addition, social responsibility is tied to social stability and the Party. Propaganda officials often justify instructions regarding social stability, even if they are not obviously related to mass incidents and protests, following such a logic as "if the press breaks discipline, it might give rise to social disorder," or "if the news entails too much criticism, it might result in public outrage."[13] In doing so, they aim to convince editors and journalists that the only alternative to media management is social disorder and chaos in an effort to motivate journalists to voluntarily conform to instructions. A scholar working closely with the *China Women's News Daily* (*Zhongguo Funübao*) stated the following: "Journalists discuss some topics that the state (*guojia*) can resolve, but they won't place too much pressure on the government, because otherwise it

---

[9] "Zhongyang Guanyu Shenhua Wenhua Tizhi Gaige Zhundong Shehui Zhuyi Wenhua Da Fazhan Da Fanrong Ruogan Zhongda Wenti de Jueding" (Central Committee Decision Concerning the Major Issue of Deepening Cultural System Reforms, Promoting the Great Development and Prosperity of Socialist Culture), Xinhua, October 26, 2011.

[10] Interview with male of official paper in Beijing (#30).

[11] Interview with male editor of semiofficial and official paper in Beijing (#8).

[12] Interview with a male editor-in-chief of official paper in Beijing (#7).

[13] Similarly, the Central Committee decision cited previously states that news organizations should strengthen public opinion supervision, promote the emphasis of the Party and the state, reflect the existing problems of the masses, protect the benefit of the people, be close to the relationship between the Party and the masses, and promote social harmony, linking ideas associated with opening of social space to promotion of the Party line, social stability, and positive political outcomes.

will result in chaos (*luan*)."[14] An editor-in-chief of a central-level official paper noted "When you run a newspaper, you can't avoid committing mistakes. You just don't want to give rise to too big problems for the country."[15] An editor in the *People's Daily* group criticized the younger generation of journalists: "They don't understand – it's been only twenty years since the Cultural Revolution, which is quite recent. We have already come to this point and it wasn't easy but actually fast. In fact, I think it was too fast. If it is too fast, contestation (*maobing*) will arise."[16] Fear of social disorder functions as an "empty dignifier," often drawing people with divergent opinions together behind editorial control over media content (Latham 2000).[17]

Although propaganda authorities are eager to convince journalists that socially responsible behavior requires self-censorship, some journalists have their own interpretation of what constitutes truthful and "safe" information. In August 2006, Fujian's Party Secretary Lu Zhangong was quoted in the *Fujian Daily* (*Fujian Ribao*) as accusing reporters from outside the province of writing false reports about the number of dead and injured when Typhoon Saomai hit Fujian province. Lu's position was criticized by the highly marketized *Southern Metropolis Daily* (*Nanfang Dushibao*) and even Xinhua (Qian and Bandurski 2011). Many reporters acknowledged that fake news reporting constituted a problem because some papers invented stories or sensationalized existing stories to attract audiences, such as in the case of a paper that claimed that China had attacked Taiwan since it declared independence or reporting that Indian nuclear warheads were aimed at China.[18] Yet the PD clearly also has some leeway in defining what constitutes truthful information, as in the case of defining the true number of dead and injured by official statistics, as mentioned previously. In other cases, journalists aim to cover important events, such as the mass murder of toddlers in a kindergarten in Jiangsu, which was

[14] Interview with a female professor of communication in Beijing (#19).
[15] Interview with a male editor-in-chief of official paper in Beijing (#7).
[16] Interview with a male editor of semiofficial paper in Beijing (#8).
[17] The CCP did not have to invent such arguments. The Chinese saying "great disorder under heaven" (*tian xia da luan*) refers to the end of dynastic cycles associated with natural disasters, protests, and invasion by foreign tribes. Longji Sun, *Zhongguo Wenhua De Shenceng Jiegou (The Deep Structure of Chinese Culture)* (Guilin: Guangxi Shifan Daxue Chubanshe, 2004), 438–39. By explaining that the only alternative to the current political system is social disorder, the PD aims to improve compliance among media practitioners. See also the definition of regime support in Chapter 2.
[18] See interview with a journalist of a central-level official and a female professor of communication in Beijing (#9, 19). On September 3, 2004, *Global Times* published an article entitled "Bu Yao Kuada Zhongguo Weixie" (Don't Exaggerate the Threat to China), criticizing two newspapers for publishing an article referring to an Indian newspaper as a source that claimed that Indian nuclear warheads were targeting China in the title "Indu Genchu 'Zhongguo Xinbing' Jiang Hedan Tou Miaozhun Zhongguo Bufen Diqu." (The China Problem: India Aims its Nuclear Missiles at Some Chinese Regions). See http://www.people.com.cn/GB/junshi/1078/2766250.html, accessed November 19, 2010.

banned by the Central Propaganda Department in 2010.[19] In such cases, some journalists valued factual coverage more than social responsibility, as defined by the Party.[20]

Hassid (2012) described such reporters as "advocate professionals" who are committed to media independence and see themselves as advocates for the less well-off. When seeking opportunities, advocate journalists – often with the help of broader networks of social activists – engage in contentious politics at the boundaries. From the perspective of propaganda officials, this creates trouble, as journalists are not always doing what they are told or are finding loopholes in the system. Most Chinese journalists, however, do not fall into this category, according to Hassid's interviews.

One strategy in favor of covering such cases is to downplay the political nature of such stories. By arguing that the general population does not care about politics and is interested in affairs close to their personal lives, journalists gain space to cover some topics that are relevant to politics while claiming that such news is social. A reporter at *China Newsweek (Zhongguo Xinwen Zhoukan)*, for example, who traveled throughout China for his work noted that most people want to read social news because "they are uninterested in politics, except in Beijing, where people are more interested compared with, for instance, Shanghai."[21] By trying to negotiate what constitutes a political topic, editors try to move topics into the more open social realm. A reporter at *Chongqing Evening News* noted: "Legal news is often stories that are investigative and social, related to ordinary citizens' own issues. For example, if an official is corrupt, of course ordinary citizens will care about it. So if they care, we will cover such news more often, it's decided by the rule of the market."[22] Thus what constitutes "political" is constantly reinterpreted by the media, as noted by an editor-in-chief of a central-level official paper: "What relates to politics depends on your own assessment of the issue, but if you interpret it incorrectly, that may get you into a lot of trouble."[23]

When media practitioners downplay the political nature of the news, such arguments stand in stark contrast to much empirical evidence demonstrating that Chinese have, in fact, greater interest in issues relevant to politics than is commonly believed. Chapter 4 illustrated that a majority in Chongqing, Wuxi, Shenyang, and Foshan read newspapers frequently to learn about social

[19] On May 15, the Central PD reemphasized instructions to abstain from independent reporting on the incident, IFJ, "Zhongguo Xinwen Ziyou 2010 (Press Freedom in China in 2010)."

[20] For example, *Shanxi Evening News (Shanxi Wanbao)* published a commentary on April 30, 2010. See http://news.sohu.com/20100430/n271858069.shtml, accessed November 25, 2011. Similarly, the magazine *New World (Xin Shijie)* published an article on May 17: http://www.360doc.com/content/10/0521/23/142_28839816.shtml, accessed November 30, 2011.

[21] Interview with a male journalist of magazine in Beijing (#31).

[22] Interview with a male journalist of nonofficial paper in Chongqing (#39).

[23] Interview with a male editor-in-chief of official paper in Beijing (#7).

news; similarly, roughly 35 percent of urban residents in Beijing, Shanghai, Guangzhou, Xi'an, Nanning, and Chengdu are inattentive to news about the United States. These percentages drop to 10 percent when the question is asked more broadly about international news. And even if a question uses the term *politics* – priming people to think about political elites – only 20 percent state that they are not at all interested in politics, according to the China Survey 2008, a nationwide survey that included migrant workers. As we will see in Chapter 7, readers respond to changing political messages in the news by selecting different media sources, and they are eager to learn about the position of the government during official events. Interest in public discourse is, of course, not the only reason for media consumption, but it is an important one.

So why do many media practitioners play down the public's interest in politics? Arguments in favor of greater space for news reporting in China are based on notions that news reporting will not have any negative effects on China's stability and ultimately the survival of the CCP. As shown in Chapters 4 and 5, Chinese understandings of the political are related to the sensitivity of a topic: as stories become more closely linked to political leaders, they develop into "landmine" topics that can cause an explosion when journalists step on the toes of government officials. When media practitioners argue that a topic is "social" and unrelated to politics, in fact, they imply that opening up space for news reporting is safe for the CCP.

Another strategy for downplaying the political sensitivity of an article is to cover cases involving individuals rather than groups, which have greater potential to be considered a mass incident threatening social stability.[24] Even though potentially sensitive, many such individual cases make it through the cracks in the system, as in the case of the much celebrated Sun Zhigang case, discussed in greater detail later in this chapter. One editor at a semiofficial paper in Beijing explained: "Of course, to a large extent, [the previous propaganda] policy still exists, but if you have one incident, you have a second one, a third one, and afterwards you suddenly can report on such a case."[25] Here, journalists are trying to set a precedent that will allow them to cover stories as opposed to abstaining from reporting.

However, stories about marketized media outlets pushing semi-independent space in China are not representative of the regular content of the news that citizens encounter in their daily lives. During the time when the LLM and BAS surveys were conducted, newspapers, on average, complied with the official line demanded by the central government, as shown in Chapter 5. Newspapers are usually in accordance with government policies. Of course, there are many examples of reporters who challenge instructions, as in the case of the joint editorial by the thirteen newspapers discussed previously

---

[24] Interview with a male editor-in-chief of nonofficial paper in Chongqing (#38).
[25] Interview with a male editor of official and semiofficial paper in Beijing (#25).

in this chapter, but resistance is the exception rather than the rule.[26] One editor-in-chief of a central-level official paper explained: The government "will ask all the editors-in-chief and vice editors-in-chief to attend a meeting, inviting someone to explain to us the government's standpoint on an issue. That's the guideline and we follow – very rarely someone ignores it. That's the basic principle that everyone agrees on."[27] When journalists push the boundaries of press reporting, they are not fundamentally changing the dominant message in the news, but taking small steps to be better able to cater to demands.

Yet how do these dynamics play out in domestic and international news reporting more broadly, in regions other than Beijing and Chongqing, other kinds of media crisis situations, and over time? As we will see, the CCP has discovered that proponents of greater space for news reporting are often right when making arguments in favor of lifting restrictions. In fact, there are a lot of topics that are politically relevant, but have been permanently or temporarily opened up because news coverage about these issues does not undermine CCP rule.

Next I explore factors that shape toleration of social space, including variation across issues, among the political elite, crisis situations, and media types.

Toleration of Social Space

At the central level, open space for press reporting depends in large part on the extent to which the central government can find allies among audiences for its policy goals. When there is little potential for conflict, space widens, whereas issues about which the Party suspects or has experienced conflict remain more closed. There are many examples from policy areas other than labor law or Sino-US relations for which the center has employed a similar strategy.

For example, the central government has enacted a wide range of environmental laws and regulations, and it has upgraded the status and strength of the bureaucracy in charge of implementing these policies. Nevertheless, many environmental policies are not being enforced, especially in rural areas (Economy 2004). By allowing environmental nongovernmental organizations (NGOs) to exert pressure on local governments within the policies set by the central government, change in environmental practice was brought about in many cases (Weller 2008). Just like the media, these social organizations are semi-autonomous from the state, and their goals are best achieved if they serve to embolden the state at both the central and local level (Hildebrandt 2013).

---

[26] Hassid's study of Chinese journalists finds that contentious actions are often motivated when the daily routine of journalism is disrupted. Jonathan Hassid, "China's Contentious Journalists: Reconceptualizing the Media," *Problems of Post-Communism* 55, no. 4 (2008).

[27] Interview with a male editor-in-chief of official paper in Beijing (#7). See also interview with a male editor of nonofficial paper in Chongqing (#37).

These NGOs often work together with media to expose industrial pollution of drinking water, problems associated with hydropower, and decimation of endangered species (see, for example, Mertha 2009; Zhan 2011). Not by coincidence, Chinese media practitioners consider environmental protection to be part of the social realm.[28]

Sometimes these stories overlap with other issue areas, such as anticorruption measures that are more politically sensitive. Chinese leaders have been "acutely aware of strongly negative mass public opinion about corruption and regime anticorruption efforts," resulting in a series of anticorruption campaigns (Manion 2004: 198). As part of this attempt to expose corruption and improve implementation of anticorruption efforts, Jiang Zemin actively promoted a watchdog role for the media (*yulun jiandu*) in 1997, which was reemphasized by the Hu-Wen administration (Zhao and Sun 2007; Brady 2008).[29] Top leaders such as former premier Zhu Rongji have been reported to frequently watch investigative programs, such as *Focus Interviews* (*Jiaodian fangtan*) (Zhao and Sun 2007). As explained in Chapter 4, investigative journalism can expose corruption as long as stories remain limited and do not pose a serious threat to the regime. Lorentzen (2010) described these tactics as "deliberate incomplete press censorship."

Opening up policy areas such as labor law, environmental protection, and corruption does not directly affect the central government; even if stories cover negative news, they usually target lower- rather than upper-level officials. As noted by Oi (2004), the center can claim to be the protector rather than the culprit.

Yet with respect to foreign politics, it is not so easy to redirect social pressure to the local level. Nevertheless, even in the area of international politics, the central government opens up space to deal with the pressures and constraints inflicted on the central leadership by popular nationalism.[30] As in the case of the United States, the propaganda authorities actively discouraged negative coverage of Japan when the Hu-Wen administration began pursuing closer diplomatic ties with Japan in late 2002, and these restrictions referred

---

[28] The dynamics here are similar to that of labor law, examined in Chapters 4 and 5. Interview with a male editor of semiofficial paper in Beijing (#10) and conversations with two male journalists at official and nonofficial papers in Chongqing (#35, 36).

[29] For example, Hu Jintao encouraged public opinion supervision during his visit to the *People's Daily* on June 6, 2008, and in the earlier cited address to the World Media Summit in October 2009. On his visit to the *People's Daily* see: http://cpc.people.com.cn/GB/64093/64094/7408960.html, accessed November 19, 2011.

[30] On a discussion of these pressures and constraints, see Kenneth Lieberthal, "Domestic Forces and Sino-U.S. Relations," in *Living with China: U.S./China Relations in the Twenty-First Century*, ed. Ezra Vogel (New York: Norton and Company, 1997), Joseph Fewsmith and Stanley Rosen, "The Domestic Context of Chinese Foreign Policy," in *The Making of Chinese Foreign and Security Policy in the Era of Reform, 1978–2000*, ed. David M. Lampton (Stanford: Stanford University Press, 2001), Susan L. Shirk, *China: Fragile Superpower* (Oxford: Oxford University Press, 2007), James Reilly, *Strong State, Smart State: The Rise of Public Opinion in China's Japan Policy* (New York: Columbia University Press, 2012).

to areas in which audience demands conflicted with the more lenient stance of the government; Japanese culture and society – which Chinese view in a more positive light – were not mentioned (Reilly 2012). Similarly, journalists view news stories regarding many European countries as less restricted, which coincides with positive attitudes toward the European Union member states among Chinese audiences as compared with the United States and Japan (Stockmann In Press).

These findings contrast with common interpretations by scholars, foreign reporters, and pundits that the PD actively promotes antiforeign sentiment. Indeed, Jiang Zemin's patriotic education lay the seeds for popular nationalism in the 1990s and fostered antiforeign sentiment, both indirectly and directly (Y. Zhao 1998; Brady 2008).[31] However, like Reilly (2012), this book finds that the Hu-Wen administration attempted (and succeeded) to limit negative sentiment expressed in Chinese media toward Japan and the United States, except when there was tension, a situation discussed in more detail later.

These examples illustrate that the central state opens up news reporting when there are allies among audiences whose demands coincide with the position of the government. The editor-in-chief of a central-level official newspaper summed up this strategy as follows: "The government also wants to prevent corruption, abolish social drawbacks, and to only depend on governmental strength is not OK. You need the common people to help the government to solve these problems, and the media's help in this is very big."[32] Such a strategy plays out differently across regions, in crisis situations, and across media types.

Factionalism and Fragmented Authoritarianism

Of course, the Chinese party-state is not a unitary actor, but a "hodgepodge of disparate actors" (O'Brien and Li 2006: 66). With respect to the National Labor Law and the United States, media practitioners perceived the center to have developed a coherent official line, but such perceptions may change once issues are subjected to factionalism or policy making within a system of "fragmented authoritarianism." Fragmented authoritarianism asserts that policy made at the center is subject to the organizational and political goals of various vertical agencies and spatial regions charged with enforcing that policy (Lieberthal and Lampton 1992). Both factionalism and fragmented authoritarianism lead to distinct patterns in Chinese journalism.

Intraparty factions continue to be important in the display of support for central-level policies in the media. For example, in the case of Jiang Zemin's

---

[31] All examples covered by Brady (2008: 98–99) to demonstrate instructions by the PD to "demonize the United States" date back to the Jiang Zemin period. Later examples confirm the rule that Chinese media are supposed to stay behind the official position of the government. See Anne-Marie Brady, *Marketing Dictatorship: Propaganda and Thought Work in Contemporary China* (Lanham: Rowman & Littlefield, 2008), 100.

[32] Interview with a male editor-in-chief of official paper in Beijing (#7).

"Three Represents" campaign, provincial Party papers were more likely to publish articles on the campaign if the local Party secretary or governor belonged to Jiang's faction (Shih 2008). Similarly, Chapter 5 revealed that the decision of former CCP Chongqing Committee Secretary Bo Xilai to allow newspaper coverage of the taxi strike covered in Chapter 5 was interpreted as an attempt to please the State Council by expressing support for passage of the Regulations on the Opening of Government News. Similar speculations have been made when Bo's competitor in Guangdong, Wang Yang, decided to suspend some restrictions on news reporting to boost the provincial media's watchdog role in October 2011. Wang seemed to signal his reform-mindedness during the leadership reshuffle.[33]

In addition to factionalism, discursive space differs depending on the media outlet's administrative level. The hierarchical structure of the Chinese political system within which orders from higher-ranking institutions are binding, but orders from units of the same or lower rank are not, leads to systematic opening of space depending on a media outlet's administrative rank. As shown in Chapter 5, *People's Daily* was more likely to cover sensitive topics when lower levels of government were involved, and *Chongqing Times* was more likely to criticize other locales as opposed to its own. Similarly, a careful content analysis by Qian and Bandurski (2011) found that media outside of Fujian "reported higher numbers of dead and injured than did local party media" after a typhoon hit the province.[34] Counterintuitively, media outlets registered with central-level institutions often have more freedom for investigative news reporting compared with lower levels. When Beijing Vice-Mayor Liu Zhihua was stripped of his Party rank in June 2006 on suspicion of corruption, the PD allowed reporting, but only in the form of reprinted reports by Xinhua News Agency. Despite these instructions, the *People's Daily* published its own tiny article placed above the weather report.[35] As a central-level paper, the *People's Daily* did not necessarily seek to protect municipal officials in Beijing. Beijing-level papers stuck to the Xinhua release, but used headlines and placement in the paper to distinguish themselves from each other (Qian and Bandurski 2011).

Within this system of fragmented authoritarianism, journalists have learned how to use the rules of policy making in their favor. Mertha's (2009) study of policy entrepreneurship found that media practitioners join forces with social activists to lobby relevant institutions within the political hierarchy to achieve policy goals. Similarly, local media can play differing interests between the provincial and city-level PDs against each other, giving them more room to

---

[33] "China's Guangdong Reportedly Suspends News Control," BBC Monitoring Research, October 21, 2011.

[34] Information is also less likely to be censored when hosted by a server outside of the locality. See Qiang Xiao, "The Rise of Online Public Opinion and Its Political Impact," in *Changing Media, Changing China*, ed. Susan Shirk (Oxford: Oxford University Press, 2011).

[35] The weather report is one of the most popular pages of newspapers. Thanks to Tak-Wing Ngo for this information based on his personal experience as an editor in Hong Kong.

maneuver compared with municipalities, provided that the provincial-level unit is less restrictive compared with lower levels.[36] In municipalities, guidelines are given by the municipal-level PD only, which may explain why discursive space in municipalities seems to be more tightly controlled as compared within provinces.[37] Guangdong in particular has gained a reputation for its openness in media space; the two other places at the forefront of media reform are Beijing and Shanghai, but reporters view these media markets as more closed compared with Guangdong. Naturally, discursive space varies across China, and factionalism as well as fragmented authoritarianism help to explain some of these differences.

Public Opinion Crisis

In crisis situations, the center's general strategy toward reporting can fundamentally change. Chinese media scholars have referred to these incidents as a "public opinion crisis" (*yulun weiji*). This term refers to a situation in which public opinion and the position of the state on a particular issue are in disagreement, thus endangering social stability and economic growth. Media scholars and propaganda officials claim that nonofficial papers, the Internet, and cell phones serve as catalysts for disagreement between citizens and government, thus stimulating distrust in the government and encouraging people to demand that the government take a stronger stance, as happened during the 2005 anti-Japanese protests.[38]

In this case, the government initially decided to *abstain* from issuing instructions and constraining the expression of popular anger in marketized media and the Internet, as explained in Chapter 8. Only after the first demonstrations had taken place in Beijing did the government issue restrictions, which were quickly followed by market-based and web-based media.[39] Reilly (2012) refers to those situations as cycles of public mobilization, which are sometimes tolerated for a while and sometimes suppressed from the very beginning, as in the case of the 1999 anti-American protests and the 2001 EP-3 incident.[40] Oi

---

[36] Conversation with an academic who gives courses training senior editors across China for the Propaganda Department, August 2009.

[37] Chinese living in municipalities tend to perceive media as less trustworthy compared with people located in provinces or autonomous regions, which could be a result of tighter media control in municipalities. See Chapter 10 for details.

[38] For a review of this literature, see Jie Zhang, "Cong Meijie Fazhan Jiaodu Lun Guojia Yulun Anquan (A Discussion of National Public Opinion Security Based on the Development of the Mass Media)," PhD diss., Peking University, 2006.

[39] Interviews with two male editors of semiofficial and official papers specializing in international news in Beijing (#13, 25).

[40] I have not come across any information that media was encouraged to report negatively about the United States in 1999. The government did support the protests by providing buses for students, but such support does not necessarily imply that the media received instructions to criticize the United States. For a detailed account, see James Reilly, *Strong State, Smart State: The Rise of Public Opinion in China's Japan Policy.*

(2004) also noted that protests by villagers and laid-off workers are sometimes allowed and are sometimes repressed.

The motives of propaganda officials for allowing Chinese media to follow audience demands in the case of nationalist outbursts and to report negatively about the United States, Japan, or other foreign nations are still debated among scholars. They include arguments about fear that outraged nationalists may turn against the regime if not allowed to express their anger, strategic use of protests to increase audience costs in international relations, and division amongst the central leadership (Weiss 2008; Reilly 2012). Independent of the state's intentions, the *absence* of instructions in such incidents and the space for public discourse it creates send signals to potential protesters that the government is at least not against protests and that mobilization is therefore permissible (Stockmann 2011a). Referring to Hirschman (1970), Perry (2007) described such encouragement of "voice" of discontent in forms that also display "loyalty" as "revolutionary authoritarianism." Even if legitimized, protests unravel social forces that do not always act within the framework set by the authorities, leading to attempts by public officials to contain social activism, as in the case of the 2005 anti-Japanese protests or, more recently, the anti-French demonstrations in 2008 (Weiss 2008).

Marketized Media and the Internet

From the preceding discussion about public opinion crisis, it becomes apparent that marketized media are often regarded as working hand in hand with the new communications technology. This is so because these media sources are more autonomous from the Chinese party-state than other media outlets. Numerous observers of Chinese media have noted that television is the most tightly controlled news medium, followed by radio broadcasting, newspapers, magazines, electronic papers delivered to mobile phones, and the Internet. Yet even within the Internet, there remain considerable differences, similar to the distinction between official and nonofficial newspapers.

Political institutions at all level of government have increased their Internet presence, providing new opportunities for citizens to submit letters and petitions online (Hartford 2005). In comparison, online news websites are somewhat less controlled than governmental websites. Chinese netizens can obtain the news from two kinds of websites – those sponsored by traditional media outlets, such as Xinhua Net, and those not directly run by other news entities, such as Sina. The first type is allowed to publish its own independently written articles and is, in fact, managed similar to commercialized papers; the second type is generally not allowed to publish its own reports and tends to republish articles from nonofficial papers (Stockmann (2011a). Apart from these sources, netizens also use BBS chat forums, blogs, chats (such as MSN and QQ), and Weibo, the Chinese version of Twitter, to obtain information about politics.[41]

---

[41] Since its launch in 2009, Weibo has had a strong impact on Chinese journalism, as it allows people to follow reporters, providing new insights into audience attention to stories. It also has

Bloggers are more likely to criticize the state compared with newspaper articles, often republished on online news websites (Esarey and Xiao 2011). However, blogs also have a much smaller audience, percentage wise. According to the randomly sampled national China Survey 2008, more than 60 percent of netizens seek political information from the more tightly controlled official websites and online news websites than from social media.[42] Furthermore, even social media are not completely outside of the reach of the state, where web administrators are in charge of monitoring web content, software is censoring keywords, and Internet commentators, also called fifty-cent Party members (*wu mao dang*), are paid fifty cents for each message posted online that supports the party-state (Bandurski 2008). Still, netizens find ways to circumvent state control, mocking censors by posting homonyms that sound like politically sensitive terms. For example, when the Central PD instructed websites to remove texts and images supporting Google's decision to shift to Hong Kong, netizens referred to "ancient doves" (*guge*) instead of the firm's name.[43] Netizens' usage and reinterpretation of expressions challenge the monopoly of the Party in formalizing language through which it guides public discourse (Schoenhals 1992).

As the most autonomous sources of information, online social media play an even more important role as agenda setters in public discourse (Qian and Bandurski 2011; Xiao 2011). The Chongqing nail house, Deng Yujiao, and Li Qiaoming are just a few examples of "incidents" (*shijian*) that highlighted larger problems within Chinese society.[44] Stories about the fate of these

---

further increased access to information and speed with which information is transmitted, thus placing further pressure on traditional media for greater transparency in reporting.

[42] The survey question primed people to think about sensitive information by asking about "political information" and may underestimate the importance of social media. A total of 21.5% reported to access government websites, 19.4% websites of social organizations, 68.6% online news websites, 20.3% BBS, 14.6% blogs, and 16.6% chats.

[43] On PD instructions, see IFJ, "Zhongguo Xinwen Ziyou 2010 (Press Freedom in China in 2010)."

[44] The Chongqing nail house already existed when I was doing fieldwork in 2005. Yang Wu, a local martial arts hero, and his wife Wu Ping refused to leave their old two-story house after the local government sold the right to use the land to a private developer. The developer dug a more than 10-meter-deep ditch around the house, leaving a small island with a "nail house" on top without water and electricity. Eventually, the dispute was settled, resulting in a new home as compensation for the couple. See also Xiao, "The Rise of Online Public Opinion and Its Political Impact."

Deng Yujiao had been a waitress at the "Fantasy Pleasure City" entertainment complex in Hubei province; she was raped by three men but then stabbed two of them in a struggle. Originally charged with the murder of a local government official, she escaped punishment after the story leaked to the Internet and was published widely in the media. See Benjamin J. Liebman, "Changing Media, Changing Courts," in *Changing Media, Changing China*, ed. Susan Shirk (Oxford: Oxford University Press, 2011a).

Li Qiaoming was arrested for cutting down trees in Yunnan and died while in police custody. Police claimed he received severe brain injuries after running blindfolded into a wall while playing hide-and-seek. In response to online pressure, Yunnan's deputy propaganda chief Wu Hao allowed the creation of an "online investigation committee," allegedly because he had been a Xinhua reporter himself. China Media Project, www.cmp.hku.hk, accessed August 8, 2009.

individuals were communicated in BBS forums, the blogosphere, and QQ discussion groups. Once they were posted online, they were often picked up by nonofficial papers and other marketized media, thus funneled to the center of attention of public discourse. Even though the proportion of netizens is small compared with the whole population, its enormous size – in 2008 it overtook the United States as the largest in the world (Qiu 2009) – facilitates "informational cascades" in which people take informational cues from the aggregate number of people who participate in political action (Lohmann 2002; Xiao 2011). As agenda setters, social media are important players in Chinese public discourse. At the same time, they reach, as of 2011, only a small subset of the population and thus play a much less significant role in guiding public opinion.

* * *

Overall, the strategy of the center to allow media to report freely on issues on which audience demands coincide with its policy interests makes it difficult for outside observers to clearly distinguish between messages that are representative of the state and those that reflect social forces. As one Chinese legal scholar commented: "many phenomena in China are blurred" (*zai Zhongguo hao duo shiqing hen mohu*). I next provide some general tendencies that help to identify the origins of Chinese news coverage.

Once stories are published, more highly sensitive messages can be recognized by the specific mentioning of Chinese officials or institutions by name or when the proportion of Xinhua reports reprinted on a particular topic is unusually high (Chapter 5). Official news items also receive better placement – they are, for example, placed on the first page. Many of my interviewees stated that the really interesting stories were placed in the back of newspapers in the societal news sections as opposed to political news sections (see also He 2000). In this social realm disassociated from the Chinese state, news stories are less likely to be drafted to please propaganda authorities and do, most of the time, reflect both the state and society. Only at the boundaries do Chinese media solely reflect societal voices, such as when journalists act against instructions by propaganda authorities or when an issue is simply not important enough to be placed on the agenda of Chinese politicians.[45]

Because marketized media no longer stick to the division of labor between media types discussed in Chapters 4 and 5, it is *not* good advice to use media labels as a shortcut to distinguish between state and societal voices, as this can lead to profound misunderstandings, as happened in the case of reporting on the US presidential elections by the *China Daily* in 2004 (Chapter 5). My suggestion is therefore to distinguish between open and closed topics rather

---

[45] Examples in which the topic is of less concern to propaganda authorities include American domestic policy or same-sex marriage advocated by lesbian organizations. See Chapters 4 and 5 and Timothy Hildebrandt, *Social Organizations and the Authoritarian State in China* (New York: Cambridge University Press 2013). Similarly, the web is less controlled when the state does not make it a priority. Xiao, "The Rise of Online Public Opinion and Its Political Impact."

than official and nonofficial media outlets when drawing conclusions about state and societal voices.

Political Change without Political Diversification

How do these dynamics develop in the long run? Once we consider how space for news reporting has developed over time, it turns out that China undergoes fairly regular cycles. Major events can disrupt these cycles and lead to public opinion crises that are, of course, dependent on international and domestic events and are less predictable.

Annual Cycles and Leadership Cycles

Each year, China undergoes a cycle of tightening and loosening at around the time of the Spring Festival, followed by the meetings of the National People's Congress and the National People's Political Consultative Conference in Beijing, called the "two meetings" (*liang hui*). During this time (usually between late January and March), reporting is more tightly controlled than toward the end of the year, when there is more room for criticism.[46] The proportion of Xinhua news reports, used as a measure for sensitivity over time in Chapter 5, increased to about 60 percent in the *People's Daily* and about 28 percent in the *Beijing Youth Daily* in 2001 and 2002 (Stockmann 2010b).

In addition, space for news reporting tends to be more tightly restricted when there is a change in the political leadership. Leadership change is always a time of intra-elite competition, which increases the likelihood that leaders will suppress negative news about themselves, as was, for example, the case during the 2003 SARS crisis. Saich (2006: 73) noted, "the fact that China was undergoing a major leadership transition that started formally in November 2002 at the Sixteenth Party Congress and only ended in March 2003 with the Tenth National People's Congress meant that leaders were preoccupied with political jockeying, but also no one wanted to be the bearer of bad tidings." During the same period, "editors had been strictly instructed to report only positive stories in order to maintain political stability" (Brady 2008: 96). To counter potential criticism, leaders attempt to tighten their grip over media during succession.[47]

---

[46] See also Brady, *Marketing Dictatorship: Propaganda and Thought Work in Contemporary China.*

[47] In some instances, the opening of media space may also bolster the position of public officials. Wang Yang's decision to lift some restrictions in Guangdong during the leadership change from Hu Jintao to Xi Jinping was interpreted as a strategic move to increase negative news about his competitor, Bo Xilai. See BBC Monitoring Research, October 21, 2011. When the central government shifted from not allowing reporting toward publicizing restricted information about SARS in 2003, such a change in information management was seen as a political victory by the Hu-Wen administration, which was in favor of more "timely, accurate, and comprehensive" information. See Tony Saich, "Is SARS China's Chernobyl or Much Ado About Nothing?," in

Yet even after the official leadership has formally assumed office, the PD may still try to keep media on a shorter leash. When asked about Hu's management of the media in 2005, one Beijing senior editor commented: "When a new government takes office, everything is new, so it is very concerned about stability. Regarding many issues, it will adopt a conservative attitude and restrain propaganda to allow its administration to get things done. I think if you wait another two years or so you will find that [space] will become more open."[48]

Indeed, content analysis confirms such leadership cycles. China has managed to institutionalize succession, resulting in a fairly regular change in leadership every ten years. Figure 6.1 visualizes these leadership cycles, displaying the word counts of the sensitive term "social stability" (*shehui wending*) in headlines of the *People's Daily*; the x-axis displays time spanning from the final years of the Deng Xiaoping era to Jiang Zemin and Hu Jintao. During Jiang's and Hu's leadership, word counts declined whenever power was in the process of being handed over to a successor. Especially during the succession, public officials are likely to keep media on a shorter leash, lasting for a period of more than a year.[49]

At the same time, succession is also characterized by divided leadership as power is passed on between different generations of leaders. If leaders fail to give clear signals about the center's policy stance because they are distracted by other issues or divided amongst themselves, such periods also provide opportunities for societal forces to mobilize (Fewsmith and Rosen 2001; Reilly 2012). Therefore, leadership successions may be periods of heightened tension between state and societal forces in media as leaders are attempting to control and media are seeking opportunities to cater to audiences.

Trend Toward Greater Openness?

Apart from these regular cycles, does tension between media and the state lead to greater toleration of space for news reporting in the long run? It seems so. Changes in information management during public opinion crises suggest that reporters' ability to cover stories during crises improved during the second half of the Hu-Wen administration.

China's system of crisis communication was established in 1989, when the State Council and the Central Propaganda Department issued the Announcement on Improving Emergency Incident Reporting. During an emergency, news coverage needs to be approved by senior officials in the State Council and should solely be reported by official media outlets at the national level, as well

---

SARS in China: Prelude to Pandemic?, ed. Arthur Kleinman and James L. Watson (Stanford: Stanford University Press, 2006), 101.

[48] Interview with a male editor of semiofficial paper in Beijing (#13).

[49] Dual hits in the *Renmin Ribao* Full-Text Archive were subtracted from the total number of hits. Word counts in headlines in the *People's Liberation Army Daily* (*Jiefangjunbao*) follow the same pattern. See Figure OA6.1 in the Online Appendix available at www.daniestockmann.net.

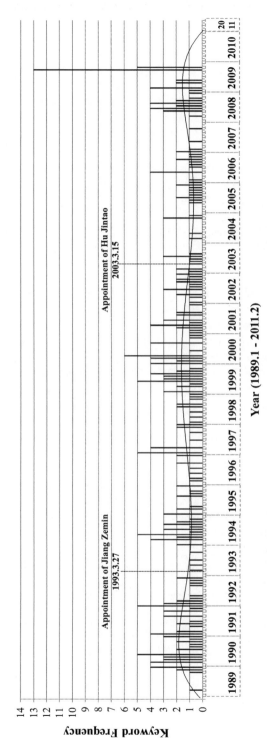

FIGURE 6.1. References to Social Stability in Headlines of the *People's Daily*. *Source: Renmin Ribao* Full-Text Archive.

as released by Xinhua. A later announcement from 1994 confirmed this basic principle, which meant that local media did not have the right to report as events unfolded, and media were often not permitted to cover incidents (Chen 2008).

However, the SARS epidemic in 2003 led to important changes in the rationale for information management among Chinese leaders. As a result of its concurrence with the leadership succession and the "two meetings," the PD initially instructed the Chinese media to provide an identical perspective, followed by instructions to abstain from reporting its outbreak (Brady 2008; Chen 2008). In the absence of information, rumors started to spread, facilitated by new communication technologies such as the Internet and SMS messages. Even after the government decided to release information, many still believed that the government was covering up the real situation.[50]

Worries about the credibility of domestic media led the government to reconsider its management of information during crises. In 2007, an Emergency Response Law was put into effect, which did not contain any explicit restrictions on reactions by the media in the case of an emergency, which were required under the previous system (Chen 2008). The absence of a total information-stop shifted the topic from being taboo to being reportable, requesting positive coverage or "in line with official information" (*yi guanfang xinxi wei zhu*).[51] After the 2008 Wenchuan earthquake, it took the government only two hours to publicly acknowledge the severity of the disaster, and the State Council gave daily press conferences (Chen 2009; Hui 2009). In contrast to the state's initial reaction after the SARS crisis, reporters were allowed to cover relief efforts, later inspiring vivid scholarly discussion among Chinese communication scholars and journalists about how to deal with the new challenges of disaster coverage.

About a week after the earthquake, increased transparency led to tensions as reporters featured stories on the abuse of funds and poor monitoring of construction of school buildings, accusing public officials of corruption.[52] Stories about "tofu" buildings burying thousands of students and teachers had a high

---

[50] In Beijing, about 9 percent of respondents to a survey found rumors more reliable than official media outlets; 25 percent believed neither of the two sources. See Guoming Yu, *Yu Guoming Zixuanji: Bie Wu Xuanze: Yige Chuanmeixueren De Lilun Gaobai (Collection of Self-Selected Works by Yu Guoming: Others Don't Have a Choice: A Report on Theory by an Expert in Communications)* (Shanghai: Fudan Chubanshe, 2004). Yu's survey was conducted among Beijing residents on April 22–23, 2003, by the Public Opinion Research Institute of People's University in collaboration with the *Beijing Youth Daily* (n=396). Unfortunately, we lack information about sampling techniques or response rates.

[51] Handbooks for journalistic training from 2004 still strictly forbid reporting in the case of natural disasters or other cases of national emergency. In contrast, Central PD restrictions regarding the 2010 Yushu earthquake demanded positive coverage on April 15. On August 6, 2010, the Central PD asked that media be in line with official information. IFJ, "Zhongguo Xinwen Ziyou 2010 (Press Freedom in China in 2010)."

[52] *Southern Metropolitan Daily*, May 22, 2008; *Southern Weekend*, May 29, 2008.

potential for social disruption, and propaganda authorities quickly succeeded in repressing controversial stories.

Still, the newly acquired space for reporting set a precedent for what is and what is not allowed under the new rules of crisis communication. Although journalists could increase space for *what* they could report, they could not change *how* to cover what they observed at the grassroots level. Public relations events organized by the government communication team were carefully planned to portray the leadership as responsible, empathetic, effective, and oriented toward the public (Chen 2009). Nevertheless, this shift from a taboo to being reportable constitutes a significant opening in space for news reporting. Similar changes have taken place with respect to reporting about protests: mass incidents such as the unrest in Tibet in 2008, the Congqing taxi strike in 2008, or the 2012 Anti-Japanese protests could be covered by Chinese media.

These observations differ from common accounts that stress the tightening of media control during the Hu-Wen administration. Indeed, the propaganda apparatus has stepped up its efforts to hold advocate journalists and netizens on a short leash by adjusting its institutional mechanisms of control. For example, the central government reacted to an initiative of provincial PD officials and introduced new regulations to deal with the practice of media outlets from one province reporting critically about another.[53] If we consider the rise of protests and mass incidents in China during the Hu-Wen years, Figure 6.1 above also suggests that, compared with the Jiang Zemin era, reporting on social stability has been suppressed in many instances. To keep overall reporting within a roughly similar range as before, the *People's Daily* probably had to abstain from frequently raising social stability as a key issue.

Under responsive authoritarianism, toleration and control are two sides of the same coin. To allow media to become profitable by attracting audiences, the state needs to tolerate a certain degree of autonomy. However, as media outlets compete for audiences, they also have incentives to widen their space. To synchronize media messages, the state reacts by gradually adjusting the institutions in charge of maintaining the balance between toleration and control. As one editor put it: "We should not say that the PD is changing its management of the media. This change is brought about by the media as it forces the state to react."[54]

As the Hu-Wen administration is coming to an end, it remains to be seen whether these changes will last under a new leadership. These advances may also be corroded as a new generation of leaders takes office, but there are also constraints on the Chinese top leadership as China seeks to integrate globally and join the framework for international governance. Since China's entry into

---

[53] According to the "two whenevers," permission must be sought from the PD having jurisdiction over the locality of the news story and from the superior of any involved official. Yuezhi Zhao, *Communication in China: Political Economy, Power, and Conflict* (Lanham: Rowman & Littlefield, 2008), 43.

[54] Interview with a male editor of semiofficial paper in Beijing (#25).

the World Trade Organization (WTO), it has been under pressure to open up
the domestic media market to competition with foreign information services.
In 2008, the European Community requested consultation with China through
the WTO's dispute settlement body, claiming that regulations placed foreign
information providers at a disadvantage compared with Chinese providers, in
particular Xinhua News Agency.[55] An agreement was reached, but there are
plans to bring the dispute back. Meanwhile, the top leadership has been gradually adjusting its management style to make domestic media more competitive
with foreign information sources and to decrease tension between domestic
media and the state.[56] Cadres are now undergoing training in public relations
work to prepare themselves for greater transparency of information, courts
are increasingly supervising media outlets, and the Hu-Wen administration has
placed more emphasis on "socially responsible" journalism as management
shifts away from taboo topics to controlled transparency.[57] To what extent
China's new leadership will continue this trend remains to be seen.

Changes in Content Over Time

Is this trend toward open space politically significant? As a first test, I investigated news content over time, comparing two years in which a local newspaper
market became more competitive. As discussed in Chapter 2, media marketization provides incentives for reporters to overstep boundaries for news reporting
as they cater to audiences. Such efforts should increase as more highly marketized media outlets enter the market.

Chapter 5 mainly focused on news reporting in 2003, after the emergence
of commercialized papers in Chinese newspaper markets. However, Table 5.2
also allowed us to compare the tone of news reporting in 1999 and 2003,
marking the years before and after the rise of the commercialized *Beijing
Times* in Beijing. This allows us to assess the extent to which the emergence
of new competitors in the form of commercialized papers exerted pressure on
established papers to accommodate news content to audience demands.[58] The

[55] See http://www.wto.org/english/tratop_e/dispu_e/cases_e/ds372_e.htm, accessed November 30,
2011. On WTO and Chinese media, see Zhengrong Hu, "The Post-WTO Restructuring of the
Chinese Media Industries and the Consequences of Capitalization," *Javnost/The Public* 20, no.
4 (2003), Yuezhi Zhao, "'Enter the World': Neo-Liberal Globalization, the Dream for a Strong
Nation, and Chinese Press Discourses on the WTO," in *Chinese Media, Global Contexts*,
ed. Chin-Chuan Lee (New York: Routledge, 2003), Baiquan Ding, *Jiaru WTO Yu Zhongguo
Xinwen Chuanboye (Entry into the WTO and China's News and Communication Industry)*
(Beijing: Shehui Kexue Wenxian Chubanshe, 2005).
[56] Based on conversations with central-level officials and media practitioners between 2005 and
2011.
[57] See also Brady, *Marketing Dictatorship: Propaganda and Thought Work in Contemporary
China*, Qian Gang and David Bandurski, "China's Emerging Public Sphere: The Impact of
Media Commercialization, Professionalism, and the Internet in an Era of Transition," in *Changing Media, Changing China*, ed. Susan Shirk (Oxford: Oxford University Press, 2011), Liebman,
"Changing Media, Changing Courts."
[58] I deliberately selected 1999 as a year of tension between the United States and China and
2003 as a year when relations were comparatively stable to account for this important counter-
explanation. Therefore, the rise of negativity toward the United States in the two newspapers

rise of the Internet reinforced the competitive pressure that established papers experienced.[59]

In response to increased competition, even *People's Daily*, arguably the most tightly controlled newspaper in China, adjusted its position over time to take a more critical stance regarding the United States, resulting in an increase of negative news about the United States across papers. The negative tone of reporting increased in the *People's Daily* as well as in the *Beijing Evening News* – despite more positive statements by the Chinese Ministry of Foreign Affairs in 2003 compared with 1999.

This adjustment of the position of the central CCP as publicized by its mouthpiece seems to have been unintended by the state. As explained in Chapter 4, the PD imposes press restrictions situationally, often without empirical knowledge of long-term trends. Furthermore, newspapers are creative about disguising their strategies to circumvent press restrictions. Because propaganda authorities only place emphasis on highly sensitive topics, the *People's Daily* published fewer stories on closed topics to satisfy demands by the state, but increased coverage of open topics to cater to audiences. As a result, even official papers can adjust to audience demands over time, while propaganda officials get positive feedback that press restrictions are implemented effectively (Stockmann 2011c).

This change in news reporting in the *opposite* direction of China's foreign policy position as voiced by the Ministry of Foreign Affairs further illustrates tension between the media and the state brought about by the marketization of the media. However, it also demonstrates that media can continue to play a "main melody," even when there is such tension. As long as official papers *also* accommodate the news to audience demands, nonofficial papers do not provide readers with political messages that differ strongly from those of official papers. Yet arguably, such a diversification of political messages would be required to lay the foundations for a more democratic political culture or public sphere in which different political positions are contested through deliberation.

These findings, though neither representative of the Chinese media as a whole nor of news reporting more generally, help place common expectations about the liberalizing force of media marketization, as discussed in the introduction of this book, into perspective. The introduction of market mechanisms requires a certain degree of autonomy from the state, but such an increase in autonomy does not necessarily bring about greater diversity of political messages in the news. Greater competition can induce changes in political messages that satisfy both requests by the state for a one-sided information flow and demands among audiences for news that is closer to their own positions.

---

is unlikely to result from a direct response to confrontational events between the United States and China.

[59] For a detailed explanation, see Online Appendix to Daniela Stockmann, "Race to the Bottom: Media Marketization and Increasing Negativity toward the United States in China," *Political Communication* 28, no. 3 (2011c).

Media marketization may lead to change in information flows without political diversification.

Media Pressure and Political Decisions

What about effects on political outcomes? Isn't the emerging watchdog role played by market- and web-based media a sign of a movement toward democracy? There are a number of landmark cases that have been celebrated as a showcase for the power of public opinion supervision (*yulun jiandu*), among which the Sun Zhigang case is probably the most famous.

Sun Zhigang was a graduate student from Wuhan who was arrested by police in Guangzhou when he failed to present his temporary residency card, the official permit for migrants to reside in urban areas. He was beaten in a special holding center, where he died of his injuries. When the highly marketized *Southern Metropolitan Daily* disclosed the case in 2003, the story was picked up by other media outlets and received much attention online. Public pressure led to the punishment of the guards and inmates involved in the beating and the introduction of a new system that prohibits local police from detaining migrants or imposing fines on them (Zhao and Sun 2007; Qiu 2009).

In a number of similar cases, officials have shown responsiveness to popular demands voiced by market- and web-based media. After the 2008 Wenchuan earthquake, for example, authorities responded to media pressure by initiating official investigations, eventually acknowledging for the first time that poor construction of "tofu" school buildings may have led to collapses, thus accommodating popular views.[60] Together with various government bodies, the State Council also launched a campaign to ensure that school buildings will be capable of withstanding natural disasters in the future.[61] Heurlin (2011) observed similar policy changes in response to protests by landless farmers and evicted homeowners.

A number of observers have described this tendency of the Chinese leadership to adjust its policies to satisfy popular demands when under social pressure (Yang 2006; Liebman 2011a). Populism considers society to be separated into two homogeneous and antagonistic groups, the people versus the elite, arguing that politics should be an expression of the general will of the people.[62] Public opinion supervision (*yulun jiandu*) of Chinese media over the Chinese bureaucracy and courts can lead to adjustments of decisions to popular demands. Most of the time, these incidents result in the dismissal of officials, not in policy changes, as in the case of Sun Zhigang or the tofu buildings (X. Zhang 2006; Zhao and Sun 2007; Liebman 2011b).

---

[60] Xinhua, May 23, 2008, *New York Times*, September 8, 2008.

[61] *Beijing Youth Daily*, July 8, 2008.

[62] Most scholars agree on this notion of populism, which also has a moral dimension because it glorifies the people and denounces the elite (in the Chinese case, local cadres). Populism is not confined to socialist ideology and is present in other political systems. See Koen Vossen, "Populism in the Netherlands after Fortuyn: Rita Verdonk and Geert Wilders Compared," *Perspectives on European Politics and Society* 11, no. 1 (2010).

These examples make clear that the populist rhetoric in which the center claims to be the protector of the common people is not just some lip service paid to stay in power. Responsive authoritarianism has led to some noticeable changes in policies adopted by public officials. In cases of public opinion supervision, such as the tofu school buildings or Sun Zhigang, the central government (cautiously) improved the safety of school buildings and accommodated popular demands for better treatment of migrants, although this adjustment has been partial and arguably only temporary, as the policy measures employed by the central government fail to address the roots of the problems – inequality, discrimination, and rampant corruption (Manion 2004; Zhao and Sun 2007; Qiu 2009).

Yet are these changes in political outcomes a sign of democratization? Not if we consider the political content of public discourse. Xiaoling Zhang's (2006) careful content analysis of CCTV's investigative program *Focus* (*Jiaodian Fangtan*) detects criticism without giving voice to different political perspectives. Producers involve experts and audiences actively in the discussion but avoid incorporating opposing views on an issue. Hua (2000) noted that such discussions remain trapped in a morality in which the government is supposed to stick to its goal to serve the people, which precludes any questioning of the system structuring the relationship between "ordinary citizens" and the state. Even in the highly celebrated Sun Zhigang case, critics who sought to question the fairness of the trials and to ask whether the defendants were being made scapegoats for more senior officials were not permitted to voice their opinions (Liebman 2011a).

Nevertheless, to many Chinese, greater influence of "ordinary people" on political decision making marks a democratization of the political system. When using the term *minzhu*, most Chinese do not have in mind a liberal democracy characterized by free, fair, and competitive elections, as well as greater protection of civil liberties. According to the randomly sampled Asia Barometer Survey, about 42 percent of Chinese could not explain what democracy was, but among those who had an idea, a large percentage associated the term with statements such as "government takes the people's interest into consideration when making decisions," "government takes care of the people's interest," or "government allows people to tell their opinions" (Shi and Lu 2010). As Chinese public officials accommodate popular views, they may satisfy demands for such interpretations of democracy, focusing on greater influence by certain subgroups within Chinese society. However, they are also careful to avoid political diversification and blame of societal problems on the overall political system that could serve as a catalyst for the breakdown of the current regime and the establishment of a new political system that could – but does not have to – resemble liberal democracy.

Conclusion

Many observers of Chinese media have noted that Chinese media are constrained when discussing politics while having more space for news reporting in the social realm. We now have a better sense of where this conceptualization comes from. Chinese journalists' understanding of the political must be understood in light of a general trend toward state retreat from interference in media reporting as the state allows media outlets to cater to market demands. Over the course of reform, the state also has gradually retreated from many aspects directly relevant to people's lives as the CCP pursued economic and bureaucratic decentralization (Landry 2008a). Given this general trend toward deregulation, it is not surprising that media practitioners describe politically relevant issues that are no longer directly administered by the state as "apolitical."

However, the opening of social space leads to tension between media practitioners and propaganda authorities as societal actors voice opinions that would otherwise be internalized. By depoliticizing topics and focusing on individual rather than systemic stories, societal actors are pushing the limits of reporting, pressing against state structures. It is therefore precisely in the social realm that the boundaries for news reporting are challenged. The negotiation about what constitutes a taboo topic or not is fundamentally about what constitutes "safe" reporting for the CCP, rather than what is relevant for politics. Although the institutional structure has a strong influence on how journalists are socialized in China, rules for journalistic practice are not completely determined top-down, but are constantly negotiated between the media and propaganda authorities.

As the representative of the Party, the PD obviously has a more authoritative position compared with media staff in this discussion. Calls by the PD are carefully prepared as propaganda officials draft texts to ensure that clear instructions are conveyed. They often do not even mention their names or give call-back numbers.[63] Editors do mention opportunities to voice their own positions, but ultimately remain trapped in the overall political structure that ties them to the state: the need to depoliticize political discourse and confine themselves to the social realm prevents reporters from critically interrogating the broader social and political structure. In addition, the need for allegiance between public officials and media practitioners leads to appeals that stay within a morality in which the government is supposed to stick to its claims to serve the people as the center signals support to social allies.

Still, these dynamics between state and society with the media as mediator may produce significant political change under the guise of a Leninist system. First, they may lead to greater autonomy among media outlets as topics shift from being taboo to appearing in public discourse. And second, they may result in adjustments of political messages and even political decisions to satisfy the tastes of media audiences.

However, such changes do not necessarily lead to the foundations for democratization, as media abstain from discussing topics pertaining to various political perspectives, do not analyze systemic causes for social and political

---

[63] Interview with male official in Beijing (#30). See also "Open Letter from Party Elders Calls for Free Speech," *China Media Project*, http://cmp.hku.hk/2010/10/13/8035/, accessed November 25, 2011.

problems, and do not diverge much from the official line publicized in the most authoritative official media outlets. Should the propaganda authorities lose the capacity to enforce such restrictions, however, Chinese media are likely to serve as a catalyst for political diversification of media outlets and disintegration. As media practitioners practice to serve the market within the social realm and test its limits, they are building the infrastructure for autonomous media outlets that could also function within the political realm.

Before turning to a discussion of the broader political implications of this risky strategy, we must first take a closer look at media audiences. Within this social realm that serves both the state and the market, which voices within Chinese society do marketized media reflect? And who is most likely to be influenced by their content? Part two of this book is devoted to these questions.

PART 2

MEDIA CREDIBILITY AND ITS CONSEQUENCES

7

Media Credibility and Media Branding

If nonofficial papers do not diverge much from the position of the government, why do media practitioners distinguish between different kinds of newspapers? This chapter introduces the concept of media labels that readers associate with newspaper types. Media practitioners as well as ordinary citizens perceive official papers as experts on the position of the government, publishing propaganda, and nonofficial papers as experts on public opinion, reporting "real news." Differences in branding strategies across newspaper types aid in creating the label of more and less credible media outlets, whereby nonofficial papers rank higher in terms of credibility than official papers. The result is a peculiar information environment in which media messages vary in terms of credibility, but generally stick to an "official line."

This chapter begins with an overview of the components of media credibility to lay a foundation for differentiating between more and less credible media sources. Next I draw on my qualitative interviews with media practitioners and public opinion surveys to explore labels associated with different newspaper types. After laying out the content of these labels and their relationship with media credibility, I turn to the question of how these labels come about. Marketized media outlets have become engaged in branding, which is a marketing strategy to establish a newspaper as different from existing media types. Content analysis shows how the framing of labor law and the United States aid in the establishment of media labels. After examining branding and framing, I show evidence from a field experiment demonstrating that the label associated with a story is more influential than its framing in establishing the credibility of a news report. Readers use media labels as a shortcut to estimate the source's expertise and trustworthiness.

Expertise and Trustworthiness

When examining the credibility of the mass media, we are interested in the characteristics that make a source credible among media audiences. *Source credibility* has been defined as "the qualities of an information source which cause what it says to be believable beyond any proof of its contentions" (West 1994). Social psychologists found that credibility is composed of two dimensions: perceived source *expertise* (also called "competence," "qualification," or "knowledgeability") and *trustworthiness* (also referred to as "objectivity") (McCroskey 1966).

Expertise refers to a source's "presumed knowledge and ability to provide accurate information" (Petty and Wegener 1998). For example, official newspapers may be seen as experts on the government's policies while also regarded as less knowledgeable about ordinary people's concerns. The second component, trustworthiness, describes the source's motivation to reveal the truth (Petty and Wegener 1998). Works in political communication found that trustworthiness was linked to perceptions of media sources to be unbiased, accurate, fair, and "to tell the whole story" (Iyengar and Kinder 1985; Miller and Krosnick 2000). Together, expertise and trustworthiness create the perception of a reliable source. A source that seems to know the truth, but that nevertheless appears to mislead, is not perceived to be credible. Similarly, a source that appears sincere, but is not knowledgeable enough to provide accurate information, will be perceived as unreliable (Eagly et al. 1978).

There is much evidence that perceptions of objective, unbiased, accurate, and complete reporting play just as much of a role in China as elsewhere. The Beijing Readership Survey 1982, which is, according to my knowledge, the first survey on media credibility in China, investigated why readers distrusted propaganda published in newspapers. When asked "why can you not completely trust newspaper propaganda?" 44.3 percent of Beijingers indicated that propaganda did not reflect reality, 43.7 percent stated that propaganda was one-sided, 29.2 percent explained that propaganda "only propagated the happy things, not unhappy things," and 17 percent were worried about fake news; only 9.3 percent picked the answer category "couldn't tell" (Beijing Academic Association of Journalism 1984). These percentages need to be taken with a grain of salt, because the survey question was formulated as a leading question and may have resulted in overreporting. Nevertheless, these responses implied standards of accuracy, completeness, and unbiasedness when referring to conceptions of reality, fake news, one-sidedness, and bias toward positive reporting. In a more recent survey of rural residents in Hubei province Mingxin Zhang (2006) confirmed that perceptions of accurate content on TV and radio and in newspapers and magazines are related to feelings of trust in the respective media types. These survey data show that objective, unbiased, complete, and accurate reporting are important components of media trustworthiness in China.

Chinese media scholars have thus far paid less attention to expertise as an additional component of media credibility. Existing studies focus solely on trustworthiness or general measures of credibility (Liao et al. 2004; M. Zhang 2006; G. Yu 2009). As we will see, interviews and survey data indicate that expertise also constitutes an important component that makes information sources credible to audiences. If information sources are considered experts by ordinary citizens, readers can more closely identify with them, leading to higher levels of media credibility when combined with trustworthiness.

Media Labels

A brand or label is a name, term, logo, trademark, or any other identity designed to identify a product and distinguish it from other products in the same category (Kotler 1991). The name, term, symbol, and other identifiers are brand identities that together make up the brand. Branding, therefore, describes the process of explaining the meanings and associations of brands to consumers (Oyedeji 2010). Other researchers conceptualize a brand as the added value of brand identities to a product (Farquhar 1990; Aaker 1991). In China, this added value is associated with the credibility of types of media, thus creating media labels.

In my interviews, I asked media practitioners about perceptions of different kinds of newspapers. Editors and journalists believed that official papers were experts on the position of the state organization the paper was registered with, whereas nonofficial papers were especially knowledgeable about the common people. Official papers were described as "representing the government's opinion" and providing "service for the government."[1] Nonofficial papers, however, stressed issues that were "close to ordinary people's lives" and "what ordinary people care about."[2] Official media sources were considered to be experts on information about the state, whereas nonofficial media sources were seen as voicing public opinion.

In addition, media practitioners had opinions about the trustworthiness of different newspaper types. According to editors and journalists, official newspapers published propaganda, which they defined as subjective opinion aimed at guiding the reader in a certain direction. This direction was generally positive, emphasizing issues such as economic development, social development, and people's happiness to keep the public in a positive mood.[3] Propaganda was also characterized by selectively reporting about events or issues. Most of the time this implied *not* being able to report an issue, especially when sensitive.[4] In contrast to propaganda, media practitioners believed that nonofficial papers published what they called "real news." Real news reported the

[1] Interviews with male editor of nonofficial paper and female news assistant of foreign newspaper in Beijing (#27, 2).
[2] Interviews with female staff member in charge of distribution at nonofficial paper in Chongqing and male editor of nonofficial paper in Beijing (#43, 8).
[3] Interviews with male editor-in-chief of nonofficial paper in Chongqing, male editor of nonofficial paper in Beijing, and male news assistant of foreign newspaper in Beijing (#38, 27, 4). See also Yin Kang, *Xinwen Yu Zhengzhi Yaolue (Summary of News and Politics)* (Beijing: Beijing Guangbo Xueyuan Chubanshe, 2001).
[4] See also Chapters 4 and 5.

facts in a balanced fashion, providing the audience with the complete story that also included negative aspects.[5] Nonofficial papers also "played edge ball,"[6] constantly pushing the boundaries set by the state by either quickly reporting to preempt instructions from the propaganda authorities or by disrespecting previously issued instructions. Overall, official papers were regarded as propaganda organs, whereas semiofficial and commercialized papers were perceived to be more complete and accurate in reporting.

In this context, it is important to note that the Chinese term for propaganda, or *xuanchuan*, embodies a different meaning and connotation than the English translation. The Chinese term is used in a nonpejorative way, similar to the English term *persuasion*. For example, Chinese media scholar Chen Lidan defines *xuanchuan* as "using various symbols to communicate a certain concept in order to influence people's thought and their actions" (Chen 2003a). Mao Zedong had an even broader definition of propaganda: "If a person talks to someone else he is conducting propaganda work" (cited in Chen 2003b: 298). As explained in Chapter 2, the CCP reemphasized after the Cultural Revolution that propaganda had to be based on reality. Today, propaganda is supposed to be based on facts while also guiding readers in a certain direction. When contrasting propaganda with real news, editors and journalists therefore do not go so far as to propose to abolish propaganda. As explained in Chapter 6, many editors and journalists have come to believe that the only alternative to the current political system is disorder or chaos, which ought to be avoided. As a result, all of my interviewees accepted the need for propaganda for the collective benefit. However, some emphasized that real news may not always endanger social stability or can even reinforce social stability in some cases.

Let me also point out that the preceding perceptions of differences in credibility between official and nonofficial newspapers primarily reflect views of media practitioners working for nonofficial papers. Media staff working in official media outlets and public officials in the propaganda system had different opinions about which media sources were trustworthy. They believed that the more tightly controlled official media reported about political issues more accurately, because official papers maintained close relationships to government organs and were consequently perceived to be more accurately informed about political developments. In this context, they often brought up the negative consequences of media marketization on news content, most importantly

---

[5] Interviews with male editor-in-chief of nonofficial paper in Chongqing as well as male editor of commercialized paper, male editor of semiofficial paper, and male news assistant of foreign newspaper in Beijing (#38, 27, 10, 4). See also Zonghe Zhao and Fei Cai, "Maohe Er Shenli: Cong Chuanbo Neirong De Jiaodu Kan Xinwen Yu Xuanchuan De Chayi (Apparently Harmonious but Actually Different: Difference between News and Propaganda from the Perspective of Communication Content)," paper presented at the 8th National Conference on Communications Studies, Tsinghua University, Beijing, 2004.

[6] *Da cabianqiu* refers to an excellent shot in ping pong that hits the very edge of the table, making it extremely difficult for the opponent to return it.

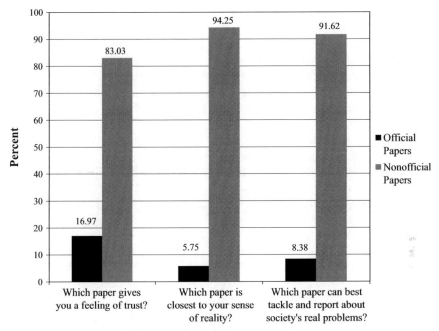

FIGURE 7.1. Trustworthiness of Official and Nonofficial Papers. *Source:* BRS 2002.

surreptitious advertising and fake news.[7] Public opinion surveys demonstrate, however, that average citizens share the beliefs of editors and journalists who work for nonofficial media outlets.

According to the Beijing Readership Survey (BRS) of 2002,[8] Beijingers found nonofficial newspapers to be more trustworthy than official newspapers. When Beijingers were asked to pick one newspaper among several as their favorite, most trustworthy one, their choices revealed a strong preference for nonofficial papers (see Figure 7.1).[9] This was the case when asked about a feeling of trust,

[7] Interviews with female official and female academic in Beijing (#33, 19). Interviews with nine central-level officials engaged in public service advertising conducted in the fall of 2008 and 2009 confirm these results.

[8] The BRS was conducted by the Public Opinion Research Institute of People's University and was administered by a research institute under the supervision of the Bureau of Statistics at the Beijing level. In 2002 the response rate was 97.4% (n=1,290). Sampling was done according to probability proportional to size (PPS), a form of stratified random sampling. Lists of registered Beijing residents (with *hukou*) are issued every year, but exclude migrant workers (because they usually do not have a Beijing *hukou*). The BRS 2002 was partially self-administered, partially based on face-to-face interviews.

[9] To distinguish between official and nonofficial papers, I relied on media practitioners' categorizations laid out in Chapter 3. The survey questionnaire included the following daily and weekly newspapers: *People's Daily, Beijing Daily, Beijing Evening News, Beijing Youth Daily, Beijing Times, Reference News, Beijing Morning News, Beijing Yule Xinbao, Laodong Wubao, China Times, Beijing Shangbao, Global Times, Southern Weekend, Zhongguo Jingyingbao,*

closeness to reality, or the ability of the paper to report about society's real problems, which implies completeness of news reporting. These findings from Beijing were confirmed by a nationwide random survey on Chinese Mass Media Credibility (CMMC), conducted in 2005 at about the same time as when the surveys presented in this book were conducted.[10] When asked to choose the most trustworthy one among a total of eleven papers, local evening papers and metro papers were preferred over local Party papers (G. Yu 2009).[11] These findings confirm that urban residents tend to perceive nonofficial papers as more trustworthy than official papers.[12]

In addition, there is some evidence that Chinese citizens clearly differentiate between newspapers and political institutions. According to the World Values Survey (WVS) 2000, a randomly sampled public opinion survey conducted nationwide, Chinese citizens' level of trust in newspapers was quite distinct from their level of trust in political institutions.[13] Only about 16 percent believed that newspapers could be trusted as much as the Party and the government in Beijing.[14] Clearly, there was something that distinguished

---

21st Century Economic Report, Economic Observer, Lifestyle (Jingpin Gouwu Zhinan), Titan Zhoubao, Soccer News (Zuqiu), Nanfang Sports (Nanfang Tiyu), and *World News Journal*. Respondents were also given the opportunity to add other papers and to pick papers specializing in literature, health, economics, computers, law, sports, and life. The latter were excluded from the analysis (n=169).

[10] CMMC was conducted by the Public Opinion Research Institute of People's University based on probability proportional to size (PPS) random sampling. This method excludes most migrant workers as they usually do not have an urban *hukou*. The total sample size was 4,278, as well as 755 interviews conducted in rural areas. Respondents were given the following choices among newspapers: *People's Daily, 21st Century Economic Report, Economic Observer, Southern Weekend, Reference News, Global Times*, local provincial or city Party paper, local evening paper, local metro paper 1, local metro paper 2, other. In the survey report it remains unclear which papers were selected for answer categories "local metro paper 1 or 2."

[11] According to this study, *People's Daily* constituted an exception, turning out to be the most trustworthy paper. This finding is inconsistent with findings for *People's Daily* in the BRS and the analysis presented in Chapters 7 and 8. Because this paper constituted the first choice among the eleven papers, it may be a result of the order of the answer categories.

[12] When question wording is more general, respondents tend to give more affirmative answers regarding official news and media, possibly due to social desirability bias. See Guoming Yu, *Biange Chuanmei: Jiexi Zhongguo Chuanmei Zhuanxing Wenti (Reforming the Media: Analyzing the Chinese Media's Pattern of Transformation)* (Beijing: Huaxia Chubanshe, 2005), Joseph Fewsmith, "Assessing Social Stability on the Eve of the 17th Party Congress," *China Leadership Monitor* 20 (2007).

[13] The WVS 2000 was conducted by RCCC. Sampling was done according to probability proportional to size (PPS), a form of stratified random sampling. The response rate was 72.2%, resulting in a final sample size of 1,000. The sample frame excluded the migrant population as well as 5% of the population residing in Tibet, Gansu, Qinghai, Ningxia, Xinjiang, and Hainan. Interviews were conducted face to face by trained interviewers. A total of 156 interviews were randomly double-checked by telephone. For more information see: http://www.worldvaluessurvey.org, accessed July 1, 2009.

[14] The WVS asked "What is your degree of confidence in the organizations below?" Newspapers, the government in Beijing, and the Party (among others). Based on the last two items, I created a scale for the level of political trust (Cronbach's alpha = 0.79). To compare evaluations,

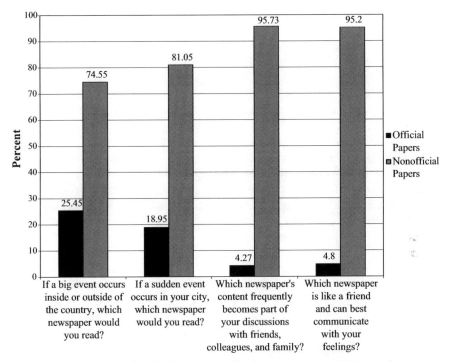

FIGURE 7.2. Expertise of Official and Nonofficial Papers. *Source:* BRS 2002.

newspapers from government institutions. Most people (43 percent) found the press more trustworthy than political institutions, although a sizable number (41 percent) placed the government and the Party higher than newspapers in terms of trustworthiness. In Chapter 10, we will see that these differences can be explained by the degree of media marketization of the local media environment: people perceive the press to be more trustworthy than political institutions as their regional media become more commercialized. Media marketization and trustworthiness of newspapers are strongly correlated with one another.

What expertise, if any, did readers attribute to newspapers? The BRS 2002 cited earlier can give us some clues about the answer to this question. Because Beijingers only had two choices for official papers – the *People's Daily* and *Beijing Daily* – when answering these questions, these results are skewed toward nonofficial papers. Nevertheless, responses point to a general tendency among readers to perceive official papers as experts on the government and nonofficial papers as experts on ordinary citizens.

First, when asked to pick one paper to read about an important national or local event, about 25 percent selected an official paper (see Figure 7.2). Note that a greater percentage of people selected official papers to learn about events

I subtracted political trust from trust in newspapers. One hundred thirty nonresponses were excluded from the analysis.

than chose an official paper as the most trustworthy one in Figure 7.1. During national or local events, Beijingers are motivated to learn about the political reaction by the local and the national government. Thus they are more likely than under regular circumstances to read official papers, despite their lack of trustworthiness.

Furthermore, a very small minority selected official papers when asked to choose one paper that is raised in discussions among citizens and that feels close to the reader (see Figure 7.2). This percentage was even smaller than those who chose an official paper as the most trustworthy in Figure 7.1. Official papers may be regarded as more trustworthy by some, but even those individuals are unlikely to closely identify with the paper. Overall, official papers may be regarded as experts on the policies and goals of the government, but nonofficial papers are clearly regarded as being more knowledgeable about ordinary people's concerns.

* * *

In sum, qualitative interviews with media practitioners and public opinion surveys show that newspapers in China carry different labels associated with the credibility of the media outlets. Official papers are considered to be experts on the position of the state aimed at manipulating public opinion. Nonofficial papers are seen as reporting from the perspective of ordinary people in a less biased way. Together, expertise on ordinary citizens and trustworthiness create the perception of a credible source. Official papers generally ranked lower in terms of both of these factors. They may be perceived as knowledgeable regarding political decisions, personnel changes, and other information about governance, but such perceptions of expertise do not necessarily make information more persuasive. In addition to the survey data provided thus far, this chapter will provide further evidence that ordinary citizens choose official papers when trying to learn about the position of the government without being persuaded by these papers. Yet before turning to media consumption, it is helpful to explore the origins of these media labels.

Marketization and Media Branding

Where do these different labels for official and nonofficial papers come from? As we saw in previous chapters, market influences newspapers' responsiveness to demands of their readers, thus creating systematic but limited variation in terms of the tone of news reporting. In the American context, Peffley et al. (2001) argued that modest departures from balanced news reporting are capable of prompting strong perceptions of bias in favor of the opposing side of an issue among media audiences. Similarly, media labels in China are rooted in small differences in tone across newspaper types as official papers. In Chapter 5, we saw that official papers, such as *People's Daily*, tend to use more emotional language compared with nonofficial papers. Greater balance in positive and negative expressions creates distance from overly positive reports in official papers, associated with "real news" and propaganda. However, their ability to build a reputation based on tone or other forms of political statements is limited. Because Chinese newspapers are constrained by the state in differentiating themselves in terms of political messages in the news, they have to resort to branding strategies to distinguish themselves from other papers.

Media branding refers to the marketing strategies of media outlets to establish themselves as distinctive players in the media market. Here I am particularly interested in the creation of media labels for newspaper types (*shu-xing*). I am only aware of two studies that discuss media branding strategies, one conducted by Chinese public administration scholars Xue Ke and Yu Mingyang and the other by Chinese media historians Fang Hanqi and Chen Changfeng.

Both of these studies describe the emergence of branding strategies as a result of fierce competition between marketized media outlets. When the GAPP relaxed licensing policies in the 1990s, competition increased, and with it pressure increased on newspapers to differentiate themselves from other products in the market. Because official papers still received indirect state subsidies, competitive pressure hit the more highly marketized papers the hardest. Commercialized papers therefore invented a specific "look" or wrapping that readers associate with its degree of marketization.

Chinese newspapers use various techniques to brand their news product. Most importantly, newspapers began engaging in promotion of their services and placing advertising both in their own papers and in other media outlets. China's first metro paper, *Huaxi Dushibao* in Sichuan province, invented a new delivery system whereby the newspaper would be delivered to each household for one month for free, with the option of subscribing to the newspaper afterwards (Fang and Chen 2002). This system has been employed by many other newspapers. Similarly, when I visited the *Chongqing Business News* in 2005, the paper had just started to deliver milk along with the newspaper in the morning to increase its subscription rates. Moreover, newspapers began engaging in advertising. *China Youth Daily* approached local media outlets all over China by means of its delivery service to establish an "advertising exchange" (Xue and Yu 2008). Slogans used for advertising almost always relate to the credibility of the paper, both in terms of its trustworthiness and expertise among ordinary citizens. For example, *Beijing News* advertises itself as "The Paper That Talks Responsibly about Everything!"; *Beijing Youth Daily* as "Where There Is News, There Is Us!"; *Legal Evening News* as "We Make a Paper That Is Close to YOU!" The first slogan hints at completeness of information; the second at timeliness; and the third at expertise about ordinary people's concerns.

Newspapers may also use publicity of a big event or investigative news reporting to promote their name and attract readers (Fang and Chen 2002; Xue and Yu 2008). Consider, for example, the case of *Southern Weekend*'s interview with President Obama during his first visit to China in November 2009. On the day before its publication, the Central PD issued a directive for all media outlets not to reprint the interview. The story leaked immediately into the Chinese blogosphere, where netizens could see pictures of the official PD document and speculated that the President's first interview with a Chinese media outlet may be censored.[15] On November 19th the interview was published as planned, but half of its cover page and the lower half of page 2 just below the interview was left blank. On these blank spaces, *Southern Weekend* printed the text: "Not every issue has an exclusive interview, but each week you can read and understand China. Subscribe to the 2010 *Southern Weekend.*"

As the first incident of such kind of "blank advertising," it immediately provoked a discussion within the broader media community. Although some believed the blank space to imply censorship, others were convinced that the ad was deliberately placed as a marketing strategy. A reporter at an official newspaper commented: "it is impossible to spend that much space on a fifteen-minute interview [and censor two half-pages of text]; the *Southern Weekend* seized the moment to advertise itself." Another blogger commented "the PD gave *Southern Weekend* a gift." Although the paper's true intentions remain unclear,[16] its blank advertising underlined the paper's commitment to overstep boundaries and creativity in finding new ways to do so. The placement of the ad directly attached to the interview helped to further promote the paper's name and its reputation for investigative news reporting.

Another example of how playing edge ball can be an effective means of branding is *Global Times*, which has gained a reputation for its nationalist slant and affirmative stance on Chinese foreign policy. When one editor of *Global Times* analyzed the content of the paper's own reporting regarding Japan in 2003 and 2004, he found, to his own surprise, that most reporting regarding Japan was positive rather than negative. "What attracts people most is aggressive reporting and such aggressive reporting will give people an impression [of the paper],"[17] he explained to me. Sensationalist news reporting attracts readers, and it also aids in establishing a media label as people henceforth associate these stories with the newspaper. Such stories often coincide with stories that are politically sensitive, as those attract much attention. Precisely because the PD restricts news reporting on controversial issues, these issues are particularly attractive to media audiences.[18]

---

[15] See, for example, blogs at www.hetaolin.com, accessed November 22, 2009.

[16] Media staff at *Southern Weekend* were hesitant to talk about the true intentions of the paper. Officially, to not provoke a negative reaction from the PD, the blank page was just intended as a regular commercial without implying censorship. However, media staff admitted that pictures – not text – were supposed to be printed where space was left blank in the final publication. Such pictures may have included President Obama's autograph, cited in Chapter 1. According to my conversations, the change in the appointment of editor-in-chief Xiang Xi in December 2009 was unrelated to the paper's "blank advertising."

[17] Interview in Beijing (#10).

[18] I do not intend to downplay the importance of an emerging professionalism and investigative journalism in China (see also Chapter 6). My point here is that politically sensitive stories *also* serve the goal to increase profit by establishing themselves as a credible source of information that will attract Chinese audiences. On the relationship between sensitive information and the

Second, media outlets create specific corporate identities that define their position in the market. For example, *21st Century Economic Report*, a paper belonging to the *Nanfang Daily* group, wants to produce "news that creates value" (*Xinwen chuangzao jiazhi*) by growing with China after its entry into the WTO. That is, it sees its role as witnessing China's economic development and serving as a gateway for readers into this process. To keep readers engaged, it has adopted a specific style of "fun financial news" (*caijing xinwen yulehua*), which is supposed to be objective and balanced while also keeping the reader interested by using such writing techniques as turning points, original combinations of facts, and transitions (Xue and Yu 2008).

The framing of a story is an integral part of the establishment of a paper's style and corporate identity. *Framing* is the way in which journalists package a story, expressed in the presence or absence of certain words, phrases, images, and sources (Vreese 2003). *People's Daily* and *Global Times* are an interesting case in point because the same journalists often write up the same story twice, using different frames for each newspaper. Editors of the *People's Daily* group explain that *People's Daily* only discusses the Party itself, whereas *Global Times* publishes more in-depth reporting and commentary by academic experts and students and letters by ordinary citizens.[19] The style of a newspaper constitutes the secret to success in the Chinese media market.[20]

A third way in which newspapers market themselves is by expressing their uniqueness and specialization through special columns and famous reporters. For example, the *People's Daily* has a brief discussion column called "Talk of Today" (*jinri tan*), which deals with traditional customs in modern society. *China Youth Daily* has a well-known column called "Freezing Point" (*bing dian*), which devotes space to the average person's opinions and experiences. The *Big River Paper* (*Da he bao*) publishes "Reporters in Odd Jobs" (*jizhe dagong*), which describes the difficulties people encounter at work whereby the reporter puts himself in the shoes of workers. By means of these columns, newspapers convey their service orientation as they emphasize their closeness and usefulness to their readers (Fang and Chen 2002).

In addition, newspapers also build a reputation by appointing well-known reporters. Some papers, such as the *Economic Observer*, established an "Important Writer System" (*zhubizhi*) according to which famous writers are invited to write the main article on each issue's front page. Others give to journalists and editors whom they consider to set positive examples as journalists the title of "chief reporter," "chief commentator," or "chief editor" (*shouxi jizhe, shouxi pinglunyuan, shouxi bianji*). According to Xue and Yu (2008), such

---

attention of netizens, see Ashley Esarey and Qiang Xiao, "Digital Communication and Political Change in China," *International Journal of Communication* 5 (2011).
[19] Interviews in Beijing (#8, 25).
[20] Interviews with male editor of nonofficial paper in Chongqing and male editor of official and nonofficial paper in Beijing (#37, 8).

titles draw attention to the professionalism of reporters, helping to build a paper's reputation.

A fourth technique is to distinguish a newspaper from others by layout. Shanxi's *Chinese Business Paper*, also the investor in the *Chongqing Times*, uses a blue frame on the front page. *Beijing News* concentrates on one large picture on the front page, using a grey font to frame the text. Many newspapers, such as the *New Woman Paper*, part of the *Chongqing Daily* group, print an index on their front page to facilitate readers' search for information (Xue and Yu 2008). A reporter at a nonofficial paper in Guangdong explained that newspapers use these indices to communicate to readers the important news of the day. Apparently, this system was invented by *Guangzhou Daily* to attract readers. As the Guangzhou Party committee's mouthpiece, *Guangzhou Daily* still printed information considered important for local officials on its first few pages, but the index allowed it to point readers to the more exciting news stories printed in the second half of the paper (Xue and Yu 2008). Over time, readers grow familiar with such organization and design of a paper, thus facilitating recognition of the paper at a newsstand.

As these examples show, media branding is not confined to nonofficial papers, but it is associated with a distinct commercialized style. From a branding perspective, in the beginning of the reforms, official papers initially faced an advantage in terms of their image, as it was well known that they represented Party and state units. At the same time, these labels constituted a disadvantage, as they were considered to be traditional (*baoshou*) and associated with the propaganda system in full gear during the Cultural Revolution. If they intended to establish themselves as experts by people, as in the case of *Guangzhou Daily*, official papers had to make an extra effort to replace their image with a more "modern" one in the eyes of readers. However, official papers were more strongly protected by the state and had less of an incentive to engage in branding a new product. As a result, most official papers lagged behind nonofficial papers in branding strategies. Many inventions to improve the service function of newspapers for readers originate from metro papers (Fang and Chen 2002). For example, as the first Party paper, *Southern Daily* (*Nanfang Ribao*) changed in 2002 from a traditional to a six-column format similar to international standards, which is now used by many nonofficial papers (Xue and Yu 2008). Media branding is associated with marketization.

Those official papers that successfully engaged in branding, such as *China Youth Daily*, *Beijing Youth Daily*, *Southern Daily*, and *Guangzhou Daily*, are almost always described as exceptions to the rules of thumbs people use to categorize papers laid out in Chapter 3. Media practitioners were eager to point out that these papers were "doing better" than other official papers. Therefore, it is possible for official papers to establish themselves as highly commercialized and quasi-nonofficial, but this seems to depend on the agenda of senior personnel, as well as support for "behaving" like nonofficial papers by the sponsoring organization. For example, when I asked senior personnel at *Beijing Youth Daily* about their role as a mouthpiece of the Communist Youth

League at the Beijing level, they were eager to point out that their sponsor had given them leeway in the management of the paper since its very early years. Media staff at the paper did not see themselves as a mouthpiece, and the Beijing Youth League equally supported this disengagement from propaganda works.

In sum, marketized newspapers rely on marketing techniques to distinguish themselves from other players in the market, and nonofficial newspapers have faced fewer obstacles in building a reputation as expert on the concerns of ordinary citizens. Branding strategies that built nonofficial papers' reputation as experts on ordinary citizens' concerns and trustworthiness in news reporting include advertising, reporting on big events and controversial topics to push the boundaries for news reporting set by the state, corporate identity, special columns and writers, and layout. Because the style of the newspaper is one important means by which the paper establishes its image in the eyes of readers, it is difficult to determine which of these two – style or label – has greater influence on the credibility of the paper. To test whether the brand of the newspaper or the style of the news report is more influential in persuading readers, I conducted a field experiment with ordinary citizens in Beijing.

Style or Label?

To be able to separate the effect of a newspaper's style from its label, I conducted an experiment with ordinary citizens in Beijing relying on experimental vignettes. A *vignette* is a short story about a political event, in this case a story about migrant workers who successfully went to court to retrieve compensation for unpaid wages. The power of vignettes derives from their experimental nature and their ability to test causal effects. If respondents make different choices, and if all differences among respondents have been randomized, then the most likely causal source of the choices is the attribute that is manipulated by the vignette (Gibson and Gows 2003).

Treatments and Experimental Design
In my experiment, there was a total of four vignettes (or treatments), all of them telling a typical news story about the successful use of the National Labor Law as a weapon of the weak, as explained in Chapter 5. These stories differed, however, in terms of framing and media labels. In total, the experiment was based on a 2×2 factorial design, including four treatment groups and one control group.

To explain the treatments, it is helpful to first introduce the concepts of episodic, thematic, and human interest framing. The framing of the story is typical for the style of official and nonofficial papers. Episodic frames report on a case or an event without placing it into the broader context. Journalists pick one theme or individual case and depict public issues in terms of these concrete instances. Journalists often aim to make situations more easily understandable when using this frame. Thematic frames often use abstract information to discuss general outcomes or conditions (Iyengar 1991). A human interest frame "brings human face or emotional angle to the presentation of an event, issue or problem" (Semetko and Valkenburg 2000). It is aimed at capturing and retaining audience interest. Stories focus on how persons or groups are affected by events, issues, or problems and they are written in such a way as to generate emotions among their readers. Because of the focus of episodic frames on individuals, they often coincide with human interest frames.

Official and nonofficial newspapers differ significantly with respect to the way in which they frame stories. When comparing articles similar in tone in the content analysis of news stories on both labor law and the United States, it turns out that nonofficial papers often rely on episodic and human interest frames, whereas official papers tend to publish thematic frames.

For example, stories on labor law in nonofficial papers usually pick specific workers as examples and personalize the events. A typical example is the story of the wife and relatives of 37-year-old migrant worker Zhang Youren, who died because of exhaustion at the workplace. When his wife, Su Lan, demanded compensation from the factory, the company claimed that the reason for Zhang's death was unclear and it refused to compensate the family for its loss. From behind the scenes, the journalist observes how a policeman arrives at the scene and is unsuccessful in solving the conflict. The journalist ends with an interview with a lawyer citing the legal regulation for the official Chinese eight-hour work day, contrasting sharply with Zhang's working hours of more than twelve hours a day (*Chongqing Times*, March 29, 2005). The tragedy of the story immediately catches the reader's attention, and its focus on Zhang and his family personalizes the story. The language of this article is colloquial and easy to understand. Episodic and human interest frames in the *Chongqing Times* contrast sharply with official papers.

In contrast, the *Chongqing Daily* and *People's Daily* rarely mention ordinary citizens by name. They prefer terms such as "the masses" or generalize to the whole group of migrant workers. Even if stories focus on individual cases, ordinary citizens rarely become the main actors in a story. "Since we can watch television, you can well imagine how happy we are. Thanks to the cadres of Zhu village who arranged this great thing for us!" reads, for example, the beginning of a *People's Daily* report on the achievements of cadres in Guangdong before the Spring Festival (*People's Daily*, February 22, 2005). The hero of the story is not, however, the villager cited in the introduction. The journalist examines in detail how training courses for cadres strengthened the relationship between cadres and the masses and the organizational capabilities of the Party. In addition to bringing television to villagers, cadre training in Guangdong also resulted in compensation for 168 migrant workers worth more than RMB 200,000 in salary that had been delayed by enterprises. Both the *Chongqing Daily* and *People's Daily* provide much abstract information and use formal language to explain official rules and regulations as well as government statistics. They both employ a macro-level perspective, the *People's Daily* for the nation and the *Chongqing Daily* for Chongqing municipality.

This generic frame in official papers contrasts sharply with the gritty stories of the hardships of urban life in China provided by nonofficial papers.

Similar differences in style can be observed with respect to news about the United States. When comparing reports with an average tone about the war in Iraq, *Beijing Evening News* turns out to rely more often on an episodic and human interest frame, whereas reports by the *People's Daily* are more generic. For example, *Beijing Evening News* published a story about the reaction of Iraqi people to the war, featuring an 11-year-old as the only student sitting in an empty classroom during the end of the war. "Not only students," writes the journalist, "but Iraqi people are all very annoyed (*fan*)!" Daily life without electricity and public transportation is chaotic. The article ends with a reference to an American magazine that reported: "after the takeover by the new Iraqi government the United States one more time plans to carry out 'cultural change'" (*Beijing Evening News*, April 23, 2003). In contrast when the *People's Daily* publishes its own reports, it relies on its foreign correspondent located in the United States. When reporting about people's initial reactions to the invasion of Iraq, the reporter primarily cites a public opinion survey among New Yorkers. Only to illustrate these statistics does the reporter quote a young protester in front of the White House: "Bush just hit Iraq, who knows which country he is going to hit next!" These differences in framing also show in the selection of Xinhua news reports, whereby *Beijing Evening News* prefers to print articles with quotes by individuals, whereas the *People's Daily* chooses stories that analyze events in a more abstract and general manner.

It now becomes clear why media practitioners often claim that nonofficial papers deliver "soft news," whereas official papers provide "hard news." In China, statistics and legal documents originate in Party and state units and thus constitute official forms of political information. Discussion of generic political problems is reserved for government officials who are legitimated to discuss, analyze, and solve political issues by means of their status as a vanguard within the Leninist political system.[21] Soft news, on the other hand, draws attention away from the general toward the individual. This feature makes the story vivid and interesting as readers can personally identify with the main players in the plot of these stories.

This contrast between nonofficial and official papers contributes to perceptions of newspaper types as representatives of ordinary citizens and the state. Greater focus on individuals, sensationalism, and colloquial language helps nonofficial papers to establish themselves as being close to people. More

---

[21] Vladimir Lenin was an impatient Marxist. Karl Marx believed that countries would naturally progress from feudalism to socialism, followed by communism, which was an ideal state in which government was unnecessary as the people would rule themselves. Yet when workers did not organize to overthrow the Russian Empire at the beginning of the 20th century, Lenin called for the formation of a party to bring about political and socioeconomic transformation. The party was composed of an elite with a strong revolutionary consciousness. This vanguard was supposed to guide society into communism. On the structure of Leninist systems, see Chapter 3.

generic discussion, abstract information, and formal language in official papers underline the closeness of official papers to the position of the government.

To test the impact of official and nonofficial frames on media credibility, I selected two news stories that were similar in terms of length and tone, but different in terms of their frame. The official frame was published by the *People's Daily*, whereas the nonofficial frame was published by the *Chengdu Evening News* (Chengdu Wanbao). Both stories are similar in that they describe the case of a group of migrant workers whose wages were delayed by their employer. After going through the legal system, both cases have a happy ending, as the court rules in favor of workers who receive compensation for their work. The stories differ, however, in terms of the frames used to tell the story.

First, the nonofficial frame is personalized by using the names of the employer and employees, whereas the official frame relies on generic names, such as "the migrants." Second, the official frame provides abstract statistical information to portray the work of the courts in a positive light, whereas the nonofficial frame focuses on the relationship between the workers and their lawyers at the legal aid center to tell the story from the perspective of ordinary citizens. As shown in this section, these frames are not distinct to either the *People's Daily* or the *Chengdu Evening News*. Rather, they are quite common among official and nonofficial papers more generally, including in both Chongqing and Beijing, as well as across issue areas.

In addition to the impact of the framing of a news story, the experiment also tests the impact of the media label. At the beginning of each story, a reference is made to one of two sources: either *Beijing Daily*, the local Party paper, or *Beijing Evening News*, a local semiofficial paper. Both of these papers belong to the same press group, but differ in terms of their degree of marketization.

By cross-referencing official and nonofficial frames with each of the two media labels, we can test which of the two factors – framing or media label – has a stronger persuasive influence on a person's evaluation of labor law. If people are randomly assigned into treatment and control groups and make systematically different choices based on the treatment, the vignette is the most likely causal explanation for these choices. The next section explains the experimental procedure and the main results of the experiment. Further details, including the text of the vignettes, are included in Appendix C.

Experimental Procedure and Results
For the experiment, the interviewers (a group of Chinese students) and I went to a popular park in the center of Beijing. I chose this site because typical Beijingers gather in this park to exercise and relax in the mornings, and I expected that people had time to answer a few questions.

People in the control group were simply asked two questions: First, interviewers asked: "Have you heard about the [National] Labor Law?" If the response was affirmative, they asked: "In general, is the implementation of the [National] Labor Law very effective, somewhat effective, not so effective, or not at all effective in protecting workers' rights?" The wording of this question was exactly the same as that in the LLM survey to allow for comparison with the survey data.

In each of the four treatment groups, interviewers gave participants one of four cards with a different vignette before asking the question. Interviewers were instructed to let respondents hold the card until the questions were asked to give them an opportunity to reread the text. Because people in the park tend to be older than the average Beijinger, interviewers were also instructed to approach those closer to age 38–40 years.

To place respondents into treatment and control groups, each of the five students conducting the interviews received a coder sheet that randomly assigned every six participants into treatment and control groups; two of six participants were placed into the control group.[22] As a result, assignment into control and treatment conditions was random, even though selection of participants for the experiment was nonrandom, as in most experiments. If there are systematic differences between respondents in their perceptions of the effectiveness of labor law depending on their exposure to the vignette, then the most likely causal explanation is the attribute that is manipulated by the treatment.[23]

What kinds of differences did we detect based on this experiment? To analyze the results, let us first look at the control group, displayed in the middle of Figure 7.3. Just as in the four cities of the LLM, the average person in the control group was 68 percent more likely to regard the law as effective in protecting workers' rights. On the left side of Figure 7.3, we see averages among participants grouped by exposure to official or nonofficial frames; on the right side, we see averages grouped by exposure to official or nonofficial media labels.

Let us first look at the impact of framing. Compared with the control group, participants perceived the National Labor Law as slightly more effective when exposed to any frame, but the nature of the frame was insignificant. In contrast, the media label attached to the frame had a strong effect on the persuasiveness of the news story. When reading any of the two frames referenced to a nonofficial paper, in this case *Beijing Evening News*, people were

---

[22] The size of the control group was increased to ensure a sizable number of respondents to the question on perceptions of the National Labor Law's effectiveness, which depended on an affirmative response to the question of whether respondents had ever heard about the National Labor Law. Only four of forty-six people in the control group turned out not to have heard about the law before. For more details, see Appendix C.

[23] Due to the lack of sociodemographic characteristics of respondents, I could not conduct balancing tests for treatment and control groups. Yet in this case, balancing tests may not be necessary. We had control over assignment to experimental conditions, respondents did not undergo attrition differently as a result of assignment to a given treatment, and we assured that those assigned to a given treatment were, in fact, exposed to the treatment. This strengthens our confidence that the results reflect the impact of treatments rather than systematic differences between participants of experimental groups. See Diana C. Mutz and Robin Pemantle, "The Perils of Randomization Checks in the Analysis of Experiments," University of Pennsylvania, 2011.

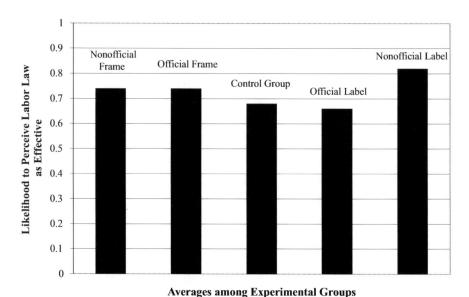

Averages among Experimental Groups

FIGURE 7.3. Perceived Effectiveness of Labor Law among Control and Treatment Groups. *Source:* Labor Law Experiment, 2009.

about 14 percent more likely to have a positive view of the National Labor Law compared with the control group. Yet when reading the same text references to an official paper, in this case *Beijing Daily*, they perceived the National Labor Law as less effective compared with the control group. People exposed to the official and nonofficial media label had significantly different opinions from one another, both substantially and statistically.

These findings demonstrate that the brand name of a newspaper affects media credibility more strongly than the framing of the news story. This makes a lot of sense because the media label is the overall product of a media outlet's combined branding strategies, not only one aspect of it, such as, for example, framing. Furthermore, the experiment shows that a positive tone in news reporting influences a person's attitude toward labor law, but only in combination with reference to a nonofficial paper.

Of course, we cannot conclude with absolute certainty that these causal relationships are common among all Chinese citizens and all Chinese newspapers.[24] However, the relationships detected here are remarkably similar to the results from the LLM and BAS survey data presented in Chapter 9, thus strengthening the conclusion that media credibility is closely associated with the label of the paper.

---

[24] Results may differ across social groups. Findings could not be replicated in a major shopping area in Beijing (*Xidan*). The reason may be that pedestrians in this area differ from those spending their free time at the park. Interviewers also reported that pedestrians expected them to be conducting market research, which may also distort the results.

These findings have implications for the ability of official papers to transform themselves into nonofficial papers. Even though it may be possible for official papers to market themselves as papers that publish "real news" and represent ordinary people, the results from the experiment suggest that it is rather difficult to overcome the stereotype of an official media outlet. It is not as simple as changing the style of news reporting; instead the paper would have to undergo a "total makeover," including the techniques of media branding outlined earlier. As we have seen in Chapter 6, the dynamics between official and nonofficial papers lead to an adjustment of news content among both types of newspapers parallel to each other, whereby nonofficial papers tend to stay closer to their readers than official papers. The state's tighter grip on official papers makes it extremely difficult for official papers to establish themselves as nonofficial papers, although in fact they are also over time adapting to the taste of readers.

Conclusion

This chapter revealed that Chinese citizens rank nonofficial papers higher than official ones in terms of credibility. Official media outlets tend to be perceived as mouthpieces of government and Party units publishing propaganda, whereas nonofficial media outlets have a reputation to represent public opinion and to publish the real news of the day. These media labels are associated with differences in media credibility. The source of these different levels of credibility has less to do with the tone and style of news reporting than with the ability of the newspaper to "brand" itself as a nonofficial paper. The commercial wrapping of the newspaper is a combination of the corporate social identity of the paper aimed at attracting a particular social group, its advertising, design, employment of famous reporters, and its ability to gain a reputation for its coverage of big and/or sensitive news. Although it is not impossible for official media outlets to establish themselves as nonofficial media outlets, it is more difficult than just adopting a new style in reporting. Even though official papers have over time adjusted their reporting to the demands of Chinese readers, most are nevertheless constrained in their ability to brand themselves as a nonofficial media outlet. As a result, official and nonofficial papers systematically vary in terms of their level of credibility in the eyes of ordinary citizens. The remaining chapters deal with the consequences of media credibility for the selection of newspapers and their effects on public opinion.

8

Newspaper Consumption

Many scholarly and media writings on propaganda in authoritarian states assume that people are passive absorbers of information. However, much research in communications has shown that people selectively seek, choose, and screen the information they use. This is true for China just as much as for other places in the world. Most Chinese are aware that the government attempts to actively change their views by means of propaganda. Therefore, it is all the more puzzling that most citizens do not turn away from the state media unless they strongly disagree with its content. As we saw in Chapter 5, the Chinese media environment is characterized by a roughly uniform information flow. This chapter shows that the absence of diverse political messages in the news creates a certain degree of dependency of citizens on the information sources available to them. For most people, getting some information is better than getting no information. Therefore, people often choose to use media outlets that are inconsistent with the beliefs they hold.

However, lack of alternative choices can only partially explain media selection in China. Among the choices available to them, citizens prefer to read credible information sources, and media credibility is not only a function of autonomy from state control that influences perceptions of trustworthiness but also is strongly influenced by a person's identification with the media outlet that is related to perceptions of its expertise. Relying on theories of selective exposure, this chapter examines which newspapers citizens read and when and why citizens select official or nonofficial papers. Because little is known about the behavior of media audiences in China, the chapter starts with a short overview of Chinese patterns of media consumption.

Patterns of Media Consumption

Most Chinese obtain information about the news of the day through mass media. Newspapers are one of the most important media sources in urban areas. In recent years, newspapers have continuously been ranked the second favorite news media source after television.[1] In rural areas, regular readership of newspapers had declined to about 20 percent in the early 1990s. In Zhejiang, villagers preferred television and radio over newspapers in 1991. In 2005, villagers in Hubei spent, on average, about sixteen hours watching TV, but only three hours reading newspapers and two hours listening to the radio.[2]

According to the BAS and LLM, in Beijing about 80 percent of urban residents read newspapers, and in Chongqing, Shenyang, Wuxi, and Foshan, about 92 percent of urban residents read newspapers. In these cities, migrants read newspapers less frequently than do urban residents, but still, about 77 percent read newspapers. Because reading requires literacy, those who don't read any newspapers tend to have lower education levels.[3] Many also indicate that they don't have the time to read newspapers and that they already feel sufficiently informed by the electronic media, such as, for example, television or radio broadcasting.[4]

Most of the time people read newspapers in the late afternoon or evening, skimming the headlines first and reading the article in more detail if interested.[5]

---

[1] In 2000, 95.3 percent of Beijingers watched television, 72.5 percent read newspapers, and 26 percent listened to the radio. See Huixin Ke, *Meijie Yu Aoyün: Yige Chuanbo Xiaoguo De Shizheng Yanjiu (The Media and the Olympics: A Quantitative Study of Media Effects)* (Beijing: Zhongguo Chuanmei Daxue Chubanshe, 2004). The BAS 2004 confirmed this pattern. According to the LLM 2005, in Foshan, Chongqing, Wuxi, and Shenyang, 97–98 percent watched the news on TV, about 89–92 percent read newspapers, 56–69 percent read magazines, 29–54 percent listened to the radio, and 36–48 percent surfed the Internet to learn about the news.

[2] In the Chinese communication literature, studies of media use in the countryside are extremely rare. The above data are based on surveys conducted in Beijing, Zhejiang, Jiangsu, and Hubei. See Xuehong Zhang, "Wo Guo Nongcun Xinwen Chuanbo Xiantai Yanjiu (A Study of Media Communication in China's Rural Region)," in *Zhongguo Chuanbo Xiaoguo Toushi (A Perspective on Media Effects in China)*, ed. Chongshan Chen and Xiuling Mi (Shenyang: Shenyang Chubanshe, 1989), Chongshan Chen and Wusan Sun, *Meijie – Ren – Xiandaihua (The Media – People – Modernization)* (Beijing: Zhongguo Shehui Kexue Chubanshe, 1995), Xiaohong Fang, *Dazhong Chuanmei Yu Nongcun (Mass Media and the Countryside)* (Beijing: Zhonghua Shuju, 2002), Mingxin Zhang, "The Present Situation and Analysis of Mass Media Use & Media Credibility in Countryside of Mid-China: The Case of Hubei Province," *China Media Research* 2, no. 4 (2006).

[3] According to the LLM 2005, those who don't read newspapers at all have, on average, about two years less education than those who read newspapers in Chongqing, Wuxi, Foshan, and Shenyang. See also Ke, *Meijie Yu Aoyün: Yige Chuanbo Xiaoguo De Shizheng Yanjiu (The Media and the Olympics: A Quantitative Study of Media Effects)*.

[4] For details, see Beijing Academic Association of Journalism, *Beijing Duzhe, Tingzhong, Guanzhong Diaocha (Survey of Beijing Newspaper, Radio, and Television Audiences)* (Beijing: Gongren Chubanshe, 1984), Guoming Yu, *Meijie De Shichang Dingwei: Yige Chuanboxuezhe De Shizheng Yanjiu (The Position of the Media Market: A Quantitative Approach to the Study of Communications)* (Beijing: Beijing Guangbo Xueyuan Chubanshe, 2000), Yu Guoming Zixuanji Bie Wu Xuanze: Yige Chuanmeixueren De Lilun Gaobai (Collection of Self-Selected Works by Yu Guoming: Others Don't Have a Choice: A Report on Theory by an Expert in Communications) (Shanghai: Fudan Chubanshe, 2004).

[5] Beijing Academic Association of Journalism, *Beijing Duzhe, Tingzhong, Guanzhong Diaocha (Survey of Beijing Newspaper, Radio, and Television Audiences)*, C Chen and X Mi, *Zhongguo Chuanbo Xiaoguo Toushi (A Perspective on Media Effects in China)*, Guoming Yu, *Biange*

In 2003, Beijingers and Chongqingers spent less than one hour reading newspapers (Huang et al. 2004).[6] In contrast to readers in Europe or the United States, only a minority of Chinese readers subscribe to newspapers. In 1996, about 30 percent of Beijing residents subscribed to newspapers using their personal as opposed to public funds (Yu 2000). People usually read the newspaper at their work unit or purchase it at a newspaper stand (Yu 2002). As a consequence, Chinese readers switch frequently between newspapers and read a great variety of newspapers. In Beijing, for example, people read, on average, two newspapers, and some read up to ten different papers.[7] This also means that people are not necessarily only using one newspaper type.

In Beijing and Chongqing, readers generally favor nonofficial newspapers. In Beijing, about 36 percent of readers choose to read official papers, but only 7 percent exclusively read official papers. Similarly, in Chongqing, about 15 percent read official papers, but among those only 4 percent solely read official papers (see Figure 8A.1 in Appendix E). In cities with a more complicated structure of newspapers, such as, for example, Beijing, most readers seek semiofficial papers. The situation of commercialized papers is similar to the one of official papers: a relatively small percentage of readers solely reads commercialized papers (see Table 8A.1 in Appendix E).[8]

Disregarding differences between commercialized and semiofficial papers for a moment, we can generally identify three groups of readers in urban China. These groups differ with respect to their consumption habits of newspaper types: those who exclusively read official papers (3 to 9 percent of readers), those who solely read nonofficial papers (52 to 84 percent of readers), and those who read both kinds (12 to 39 percent of readers).[9] To understand when and

Chuanmei: Jiexi Zhongguo Chuanmei Zhuanxing Wenti (Reforming the Media: Analyzing the Chinese Media's Pattern of Transformation) (Beijing: Huaxia Chubanshe, 2005).

[6] Somewhat counterintuitively, the amount of time spent reading the news seems to have increased over time. In 1986, the average reader of the *Beijing Evening News* spent only 22 minutes reading. See Chen and Mi, *Zhongguo Chuanbo Xiaoguo Toushi (A Perspective on Media Effects in China)*. In 1996, readers in Beijing spent, on average, 42 minutes a day reading newspapers. See Yu, *Meijie De Shichang Dingwei: Yige Chuanboxuezhe De Shizheng Yanjiu (The Position of the Media Market: A Quantitative Approach to the Study of Communications)*. In 1999, Yu found that the average reader in Beijing spent 65 minutes reading newspapers. See Guoming Yu, *Jiegou Minyi: Yige Yulunxuezhe De Shizheng Yanjiu (Public Opinion Analysis: A Quantitative Approach to the Study of Public Opinion)* (Beijing: Huaxia Chubanshe, 2001).

[7] Based on BAS 2004 data. Similar patterns have been reported by Beijing Academic Association of Journalism, *Beijing Duzhe, Tingzhong, Guanzhong Diaocha (Survey of Beijing Newspaper, Radio, and Television Audience)*, Yu, *Meijie De Shichang Dingwei: Yige Chuanboxuezhe De Shizheng Yanjiu (The Position of the Media Market: A Quantitative Approach to the Study of Communications)*.

[8] Because these measures are based on self-reported media use, these percentages are likely to be inflated. For a discussion, see Daniela Stockmann, "One Size Doesn't Fit All: Measuring News Reception East and West," *The Chinese Journal of Communication* 2, no. 2 (2009).

[9] See Figure 8A.1 in Appendix E. Foshan is an exception to the rule, most likely due to the unusually high level of marketization of official papers in Guangdong.

why readers select these different newspapers, it is helpful to examine theories of "selective exposure" in social psychology and communications.

Selective Exposure to Information

The study of selective exposure can be traced back to cognitive dissonance theory, first developed by Festinger (1957). *Cognitive dissonance* exists when two cognitions (attitudes, beliefs, or knowledge) have opposing implications for behavior. Consider, for example, a worker who won compensation in court but never received payment because of problems associated with the implementation of the legal system. He would experience cognitive dissonance when being exposed to media messages that encourage people like him to use the legal system as a means to solve labor problems.[10] Because dissonance is considered to be a negative state, an individual will be driven to reduce it whenever it arises. Reduction of cognitive dissonance can be attained by selectively looking for decision-consonant information and by avoiding contradictory information, also called *selective exposure*. For example, the previously mentioned worker could reduce cognitive dissonance by abstaining from using the media.

A person's drive for selective exposure depends on the intensity of the dissonance, which is defined by the relative proportion of inconsistent and consistent cognitions in the person's cognitive system as well as on the cognitions' relative importance. Selective exposure is most pronounced at moderate levels of dissonance. Festinger (1957) argued that there is a ceiling effect where, at a given point, the person considers it to be more effective to revise rather than retain her original belief and therefore prefers information that argues against the original belief.

Early studies aimed at testing dissonance theory did not find much empirical support for Festinger's hypothesis. Therefore, Sears and Freedman (1971) concluded in a highly influential article that experimental studies had not detected much evidence for selective exposure. However, later empirical studies demonstrated that the preconditions for selective exposure explained the lack of selective exposure effects in these early studies (Frey 1986b). People seek information that conflicts with their preheld beliefs under particular circumstances. Next I explain how the Chinese media environment creates incentives for people to seek information that contradicts their beliefs.

A first factor figuring into selective exposure is related to freedom of choice and the number of choices available to individuals. One consistent finding in social psychology is that people are more likely to engage in selective exposure if they feel free to seek information as they wish (see, for example, Brehm and Cohen 1962; Frey and Wicklund 1978). Chinese generally feel free to seek information sources as they wish, but their choice is limited. Readers may choose between a wide range of newspapers, which, as we have seen in Chapters 5 and 7, differ in terms of framing, style, and language used, but not much

---

[10] This example is taken from the Du Linxiang case in Chapter 5.

when it comes to the central political message embodied in newspaper articles. Therefore, if a person's beliefs conflict with the official government line, she cannot selectively seek newspapers with political messages that are consonant with her preheld beliefs. She can only abstain from reading newspapers or seek nonofficial papers, which tend to slightly diverge from the official line.

Under these circumstances – when there is not much alternative information available to individuals – selective exposure effects tend to be smaller. For example, Frey (1986a) demonstrated that people were less likely to seek consonant information when they only had two choices (one supporting and one contrary to the person's belief) and were more likely to selectively expose themselves to consonant information when they had ten choices (five supporting and five contrary to the person's belief). Because the Chinese media environment does not offer positions that strongly diverge from the official government line, we would expect that the likelihood of avoiding newspapers entirely is low even if the overall information environment conflicts with a person's belief (*absence of choice hypothesis*).

Although we would generally expect that average citizens do not avoid the news media in China, previous research can give us insights into who is more likely to engage in selective exposure. Much evidence has been provided for the fact that a person needs to be highly committed to a certain position for selective exposure to occur (see, for example, Brehm and Cohen 1962; Schwarz et al. 1980). Similarly, in China, we would expect that those who hold attitudes that strongly contradict the official line of the state are more likely to be selective in the information they seek (*commitment hypothesis*). I refer to those who hold more extremely dissonant attitudes as *strongly committed citizens*.[11] In the American context, Gunther (1988) found that those who hold extreme attitudes also tend to distrust the media.

Apart from commitment, people's perceptions of media credibility should play into selective exposure. Consistent information and perceptions of its bias, trustworthiness, and quality often "travel" together: in social psychology, researchers have found that people tend to test inconsistent information more critically than consistent information and expect consistent information to be of higher quality than inconsistent information (Sears 1969; Ditto and Lopez 1992; Miller et al. 1993; Ditto et al. 1998). In addition, people seek supporting information in their attempt to select the best information, particularly when dissonance increases (Lowin 1969; Frey 1986b; Fischer et al. 2005). In communications, this phenomenon has been called "hostile media effect" (see, for example, Vallone et al. 1985; Dalton et al. 1998). Simply put, an observer's own involvement in a group or issue is likely to determine her own views of media coverage as biased despite unbiasedness in news content (Dalton et al.

---

[11] My assumption here is that those who hold extreme attitudes also feel intensely about these attitudes. Unfortunately, the BAS survey does not allow me to test this assumption. However, it is reasonable to assume that Chinese who report attitudes in public opinion surveys that extremely contradict the position of the state also care deeply about these attitudes. Therefore, commitment is likely to be related to conviction and intensity, as discussed in Chapter 2.

1998), and anticipated agreement influences the selection of news (Iyengar and Hahn 2009).

These works suggest that citizens in China will seek the news product that they find most credible, that is, will be most likely to report "the truth" as defined by the subjective position of the individual, when experiencing cognitive dissonance. This should be true even if the actual content of the message does not reduce their cognitive dissonance much. Chapter 7 has already provided some evidence that ordinary citizens find nonofficial newspapers to be more credible than official newspapers. Therefore, we should find that Chinese citizens prefer more credible nonofficial papers when experiencing cognitive dissonance (*credibility hypothesis*).

I have outlined thus far how the Chinese media environment creates a context that is generally not favorable for selective exposure to occur, which individuals we would expect to be most likely to nevertheless engage in selective exposure, and which papers would be preferred. In addition, existing research has provided us with insights about the conditions that motivate people to seek information that conflicts with their beliefs.

Most importantly, Festinger (1964) argued that people would be more likely to expose themselves to inconsistent information if they anticipated that this information would be useful to them in the future. Later works have provided evidence based on experimental studies (see, for example, Knobloch-Westerwick et al. 2005). Chaffee et al. (2001) found that Americans exposed themselves to inconsistent information during a state election campaign, especially when they were highly attentive to politics and likely to vote. In China, official papers are perceived as mouthpieces of government units, and their content tends to be closer to the official line. We would therefore expect that those who have close ties to the government are particularly likely to seek information that contradicts their beliefs, as this information will be particularly useful to them (*utility hypothesis*).

This group of people encompasses more than just those who work in Party or state organizations. Because the government continues to be closely involved in the economy, some work units not associated with the state or Party subscribe to official papers to supply employees with information about the government position on important issues. According to the Beijing Readership Study 2002, a randomly sampled survey according to probability proportional to size, about 30 percent of managers in enterprises in Beijing indicated that their work unit planned to subscribe to either the *Beijing Daily* or the *People's Daily* during the following year. In total, about 18 percent of respondents stated that their work unit would subscribe to an official paper. As a result, the cost of information is particularly low for individuals to whom the information provided in the official papers will be particularly useful. Because official papers are not always available for sale at Chinese newspaper stands,[12] the cost of obtaining official papers for average citizens is higher. Studies in social

---

[12] It used to be the case that official newspapers were not sold at newspaper stands. This changed in late 2004, but not every newspaper stand might offer official papers. Interviews with male

psychology have shown that individuals are more likely to seek inconsistent information if the cost of obtaining the inconsistent information is low (Frey 1981b; Frey 1981c). Therefore, we would expect that Chinese citizens will be more likely to read inconsistent messages if the cost of obtaining this information is low (*availability hypothesis*).

Utility of information can also provide citizens with incentives to seek information that they do not find credible. Experimental findings suggest that individuals seek inconsistent information if (1) the source is believed to be of low quality and can therefore easily be refuted (Lowin 1969), and (2) inconsistent information is believed to be useful in the future (Frey 1981a). Together, these two propositions lead us to expect that Chinese citizens are likely to expose themselves to opposing news messages provided in official papers despite low levels of credibility if they seek information about the position of the government, such as, for example, during an official event (*official event hypothesis*).

In this section, I have explained how findings in social psychology can help us to understand why individuals seek different newspaper types. In the preceding paragraphs, I specified the expectations regarding Chinese citizens' use of newspaper. These expectations are not mutually exclusive – they together explain when and why media citizens selectively choose newspapers that conform to their attitudes or are opposed to them. The absence of choice and commitment hypotheses explain how the interaction between the overall information environment and characteristics of the individual contributes to selection or avoidance of newspapers more generally. The remaining hypotheses clarify the mechanisms that lead to different patterns of newspaper use among readers of official and nonofficial papers.

A Quasi-Experimental Study of Source Selection

The BAS was originally planned for late 2004 (and thus named BAS 2004), but was delayed until the spring of 2005.[13] About half way through conducting the survey, Beijingers took to the streets to protest against the Japanese Ministry of Education's approval of history textbooks that were interpreted to whitewash war crimes committed during the Second World War. During the protests, ordinary citizens demanded a strong reaction from the state, whereas the Foreign Ministry took a more lenient stance. To diminish public anger toward Japan, the PD changed its management of the news media from relatively loose to strict control over news content, and the resulting changes in media messages created cognitive dissonance. By chance, the BAS was conducted before and after these press restrictions, thus providing a unique opportunity to examine how citizens reacted to changes in media management based on a quasi-experiment.

---

editor of a semiofficial paper and female market researcher on newspaper distribution in Beijing (#8, 34).

[13] Interviews in one district were delayed for reasons unrelated to the protests. The results remain stable when the interviews in this district are controlled for.

A *quasi-experiment* draws an analogy between a situation observed in real life and an experiment. Its main advantage is that we can observe how people behave naturally without imposing artificially created treatments and settings upon them. I employ a time-series experimental design, whereby the behavior of similar but different people are observed over time throughout the course of conducting a survey. At some point, a treatment is introduced, which is compared with the (control) group of respondents interviewed before the treatment. Because this method relies on nonrandom assignment to treatment and control groups, the assumption that members of treatment and control groups are indeed similar to each other must be tested (Cook and Campbell 1979; Shadish et al. 2002). The treatment group was only slightly more educated, affluent, male, and younger than the control group; these features were controlled for in the statistical analysis.[14] Therefore, it is plausible to interpret changes between those interviewed before and after the protests as media selection effects.

Timeline of the Anti-Japanese Protests
In the months before the 2005 anti-Japanese protests, relations between China and Japan became increasingly tense. In February 2005, Japan and the United States for the first time explicitly stated that the Taiwan Strait issue was of concern to their security alliance, which provoked a sharp response by the Chinese government about Japanese intervention in China's domestic affairs.[15] The Diaoyu Islands in the East China Sea, where China and Japan had both taken steps to exploit reserves of natural gas, became a point of contention in early April, when the Japanese government initiated procedures to grant Japanese firms the right to conduct test drilling. At about the same time, the United Nations was reviewing the possible promotion of Japan and other countries to permanent membership in the Security Council. When on April 5, the Japanese Ministry of Education approved new junior high school history textbooks that appeared to sanitize Japanese war crimes during its occupation of China and South Korea in the 1930s and 1940s, violent attacks on Japanese businesses and protests erupted in China, South Korea, Vietnam, Canada, and Europe.[16]

The first protest in Beijing took place on April 9.[17] After a peaceful demonstration in Zhongguancun district, several hundred protesters tried to storm the residence of the Japanese ambassador, throwing stones and bottles into the walled compound before riot police officers broke up the confrontation.

[14] Table 8A.2 in Appendix E displays differences between the control and treatment groups. Tables 8A.3 to 8A.5 show that the results remain stable when holding the control variables constant.

[15] The issue was brought up at a meeting between Koizumi and Hu at the Asian-African summit in May. See *People's Daily Online*, May 2, 2005.

[16] *New York Times*, April 9, 10, and 20, 2005; Agence France-Presse April 14, 2005; TASS, March 6, 2005.

[17] In other cities, protests took place the first week of April. See *China Daily*, April 1, 2005, Deutsche Presse Agentur, April 7, 2005.

Meanwhile, protests continued in Shanghai and other cities until the government made it clear that it would not tolerate any additional protests. In Beijing, a further protest march was effectively prevented on April 17 when police presence at a meeting point intimidated protesters.[18] This protest would have coincided with a meeting between Chinese foreign minister Li Zhaoxing and his Japanese counterpart Nobutaka Machimura as part of the Seventh Asia-Europe Meeting.

Before the first demonstration, editors and journalists in Beijing reported feeling unconstrained in their coverage of Japan.[19] After the first demonstration in Beijing took place on April 9, however, space for news reporting closed. The PD issued instructions not to report about protest marches and to keep news reporting close to the government line.[20] The media were asked to publicize calls by the Foreign Ministry for people to express feelings in a "calm, rational, and orderly manner in accordance with the law"[21] and to let the government handle the crisis through diplomatic ties.

Newspaper reporting during these weeks was roughly one-sided, both before and after press restrictions were imposed. Before the imposition of press restrictions on April 10, the *People's Daily* and the *Beijing Youth Daily* reported highly negatively about Japan when covering Japanese history textbooks, and as the nonofficial paper, *Beijing Youth Daily* was even more critical than the official paper, the *People's Daily*. In an effort to attract readers by presenting themselves as an outlet of enraged citizens, nonofficial papers, such as *Beijing News*, detailed how the newly approved textbooks by the Japanese Ministry of Education downplayed Japan's imperialist past. *Beijing Youth Daily* featured the story of Saburo Ienaga, a Japanese historian who refused to let the authorities censor his textbooks, went to court about it, and eventually won after thirty-two years. By contrast, official papers, such as the *People's Daily*, established themselves as representative of the government by contrasting the reactions by the Chinese and Japanese Foreign Ministry spokespersons. In its coverage, the *People's Daily* omitted explanations by the Japanese spokesperson why the controversial textbooks did not reflect government opinion.

Starting on April 10, nonofficial and official newspapers continued to present themselves as representatives of citizens and government, but Japan disappeared from the main headline, and individual news reports were toned down. Using Yoshikoder to assess tone in news reporting, I found that the *People's*

---

[18] Personal observation by the author.

[19] None of my interviewees asked about issue sensitivity in international news reporting before April 9 mentioned Japan. In handbooks used at newspapers in Beijing to train journalists, Japan was not mentioned as a sensitive issue.

[20] Interviews with two male editors of semiofficial paper, female academic, and male editor-in-chief of semiofficial paper and director of media group in Beijing, April and June 2005 (#13, 20, 21, 25). See also Deutsche Presse Agentur, April 11, 2005; Agence France-Presse, April 10, 2005; *Herald Tribune*, April 20, 2005; *New York Times*, April 20 and 25, 2005.

[21] According to the demonstration law of October 31, 1989, Chinese citizens have the right to demonstrate, but have to apply for permission at the Public Security Bureau first. See www. gjxfj.com/2005–01/13/content_3560962.htm, accessed July 23, 2008.

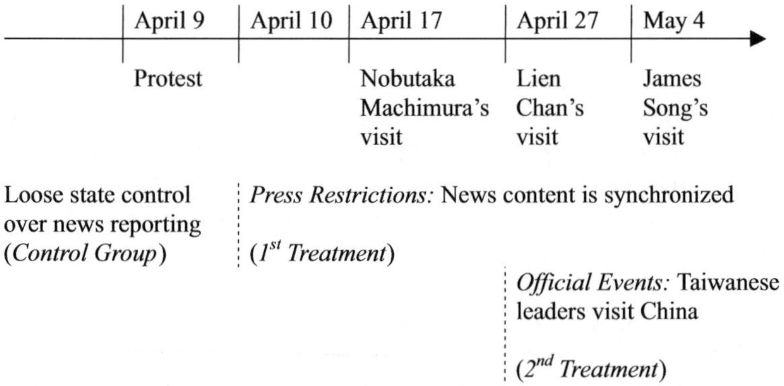

April 9	April 10	April 17	April 27	May 4
Protest		Nobutaka Machimura's visit	Lien Chan's visit	James Song's visit

Loose state control
over news reporting
(*Control Group*)

Press Restrictions: News content is synchronized

(*1ˢᵗ Treatment*)

Official Events: Taiwanese
leaders visit China

(*2ⁿᵈ Treatment*)

FIGURE 8.1. Timeline of Events in Beijing.

Daily and *Beijing Youth Daily* became, on average, about eight words less negative after press restrictions had been imposed by the PD. Although *Beijing Youth Daily* had been about two words more negative beforehand, the difference between the newspapers decreased after April 9 (Stockmann 2010a). Similar changes can be observed on the online news website Sina.com (Stockmann 2011a).

During this time, official and nonofficial newspapers continued to present themselves as representatives of the government and people. *Beijing Youth Daily* publicized a collection of quotations from Internet websites, quoting netizen views calling on others not to cause trouble to the Party and the government. Meanwhile, the *People's Daily* printed an article by "Zhong Xuanli," a pen name for the Central Propaganda Department, which warned not to cause public disorder. Despite the different packaging of the articles, the basic political messages did not vary significantly between different newspaper types (Stockmann 2010a).

Self-censorship of news content related to Japan continued throughout April and May for two main reasons. First, spring has traditionally been a time when students have organized protest marches, such as on the anniversary of the May 4th movement. Second, the government hosted two important visitors from Taiwan in late April and early May: Lien Chan, the leader of the Kuomintang Party, visited the mainland for about a week in late April. This was the first time a Nationalist leader had paid an official visit since the Nationalists retreated to Taiwan in 1949. Immediately afterward, James Song, the leader of the People's First Party in Taiwan, arrived for a nine-day visit. Reporting on Japan continued to be tightly restricted during the two politicians' visits.[22]

Figure 8.1 summarizes these events. The change in media management from loose to tightened state control as well as the official leadership visits constitute the two treatments of the quasi-experiment. The BAS was conducted between mid-March and mid-May, thus allowing us to compare three groups of people,

[22] Interviews with female academic, male editor-in-chief of a semiofficial paper and director of media group, and male editor of semiofficial paper in Beijing, June 2005 (#20, 21, 25).

as follows: before the first anti-Japanese demonstration in Beijing, the state had loosened control over the news media. I therefore assign respondents who were interviewed during this first period to the control group that allows us to observe people's attitudes and behavior during periods of relatively unconstrained news media reporting. When space for news reporting closed after April 9, Beijingers received a *press restrictions treatment*: news content became more uniform and less negative. This created cognitive dissonance between public negativity toward Japan and the predominant message in newspapers. This first treatment allows us to observe citizens' selection of newspapers as cognitive dissonance increases.

In addition to receiving the press restrictions treatment, BAS respondents received an *official events treatment*. This second treatment was induced in two different "doses." Visits by Lien Chan and James Song were big media events that were continuously reported about even after the two had returned to Taiwan. After both leaders had left the mainland, official papers continued to feature articles related to their visits throughout May. For example, the *People's Daily* published 12 percent of all articles on Song and 17 percent of all articles on Lien after their respective visits. Because it was the first time that Taiwanese leaders visited the mainland in fifty years, both events encouraged Beijingers to find out how the central government dealt with the two representatives from Taiwan. Official events therefore provided a strong incentive for readers to use official papers despite experiencing cognitive dissonance.

The assumption for this second treatment is that readers who were interested in Japan were also interested in the outcome of Lien's and Song's visits. Indeed, according to the BAS sample, Beijingers who worried about Japanese imperialism tended to also feel threatened by Taiwanese independence (correlation was 0.6). Those who held extremely negative views toward Japan also cared strongly about the Taiwan issue. The same kinds of people should therefore experience some opposing incentives: on the one hand, the change toward less negative news reporting about Japan should draw them away from official papers. On the other hand, Lien's and Song's visits to the mainland should provide incentives for them to read official papers to learn about leadership politics.

Next I provide more detailed information about statistical models and measurement of the dependent and explanatory variables. Detailed information on question wording and coding of the variables can be found in Appendix D.

Measuring Media Use

The BAS devoted some space to the measurement of mass media exposure, including a series of questions asking respondents whether they often read newspapers, watched the news on TV, or read the news on the Internet, and what kinds of newspapers, TV news programs, and websites they read and watched. To identify which papers respondents read, they were presented with a list of newspapers available in Beijing and they had the option to add additional ones to the list; multiple choices were possible. Based on these items, I created a series of dummy variables for being a frequent user of individual papers, newspapers more generally, and any of the three media types. Based on media practitioners' categorization of newspapers in Chapter 3, I then created dummy variables for using official, nonofficial, semiofficial, and commercialized papers. Because these dependent variables were dummy variables, I employed multivariate probit regression analysis.

It is important to keep in mind that respondents are likely to inflate their response when employing self-reported measures for media use (Prior 2007). In addition, the BAS questions were asked in a leading way and referred to typical rather than recent behavior, which also induced over-reporting (Price 1993). Thus the true percentages of media use may be lower. Even with this caveat in mind, the relationship between consumption of different sources and explanatory variables should not be affected by over-reporting.[23]

Measuring Treatments

Because I am employing a time-series experimental design, I assessed treatments based on the date during which the interview was conducted. To test the credibility, absence of choice, and commitment hypotheses, I rely on a dummy variable for receiving the press restrictions treatment. Respondents who were interviewed after April 9 were coded as receiving the press restrictions treatment. To test the official events hypothesis I assessed to what extent respondents received the official events treatment. Respondents who were interviewed during Lien's visit (April 27 to May 3) were coded as receiving the first "dose" of the official events treatment (and coded 0.5). Respondents interviewed during Song's visit (May 4 to May 15) were coded as receiving the second "dose" (and coded 1). Overall, 40 percent of the sample received the press restrictions treatment and 15 percent the official events treatment.

Measuring Commitment

To test the commitment hypotheses I allow the press restrictions treatment to interact with a person's commitment. Commitment was measured by a "feeling thermometer," asking Beijingers how warmly they felt toward the country on a scale from 1 to 100, whereby 100 represented the warmest feeling. On average, Beijingers felt only 30 degrees warmly toward Japan.

Measuring Utility

To probe the utility hypothesis, I rely on demographic indicators. Because of the close linkage between political and economic elites in China, we would expect that cadres and those with higher levels of education and income are more likely to find information about the position of the government useful. Although the

---

[23] Surveys that employed different question wording revealed similar patterns, thus restoring our confidence in the validity and reliability of the BAS questions. For results of tests exploring measurement error, see Appendix D. For an in-depth discussion of the validity of self-reported measures, see Stockmann, "One Size Doesn't Fit All: Measuring News Reception East and West."

term *cadre* seems to suggest that cadres are part of the government, Beijingers who identify themselves as cadres do not necessarily work in a Party or state unit in Beijing. In fact, most cadres in the BAS held leadership positions in local state-owned enterprises.

Measuring Availability

The availability hypothesis was also tested based on demographic indicators. I included dummy variables for working at a Party or government unit and working in residential services. In China, neighborhood committees receive funding from the government to subscribe to official newspapers. In urban areas, every subdistrict of a district of a city is divided into many communities (*shequ*) or neighborhoods (*juminqu*). Each of them have a neighborhood committee (or community committee or residents' committee). These social service workers, predominantly older women with relatively low income, often organize collective readings of these newspapers for senior citizens in their neighborhood.[24]

Control Variables

Treatments, commitment, utility, and availability provide a list of the most important factors that influence media use in China. Therefore, we do not necessarily need to add further control variables to the statistical analysis. An investigation of the demographic characteristics of commercialized newspaper readers revealed, however, that the extent to which someone takes advantage of the increased mobility and internationalization entailed in globalization plays a role when selecting semiofficial versus commercialized papers for reasons that are specific to Beijing. I will return to this point later in this chapter. To assess a person's mobility and international orientation, I relied on questions concerning the number of years a person had lived in Beijing, whether and where a person had traveled abroad, whether a person had studied some English, and whether a person read the news online. Additional demographic controls, such as age and gender, as well as control variables for views of the United States and attention to news about the United States, were included in robustness tests, laid out in detail in Appendix D.

Profiles of Readers in Beijing

Before we examine the results of the quasi-experiment, it is helpful to first examine the demographic characteristics of different kinds of readers in Beijing. Earlier in this chapter, I reported that there is a considerable amount of overlap among readers of different kinds of newspapers. For example, some people read all three newspaper types. This overlap constitutes a challenge for the empirical analysis, as we cannot rely on one dependent variable to distinguish between preferences for different newspaper types. To address

---

[24] Based on conversations with Benjamin Read, Chen Juan, and Wang Yuhua in Ann Arbor, 2006.

this problem, I conducted the analysis in two steps, first distinguishing simply between using official and nonofficial papers among readers and second differentiating between consuming semiofficial and commercialized papers among those who reported reading at least one nonofficial paper.

In the first step, the statistical analysis indicated that income, education, and profession played a key role in the selection of official newspapers. The estimated relationships between income, education, identifying as a cadre, working for a government or state unit, and working as a neighborhood committee worker were positive for reading official papers. In the second step, the statistical results revealed that the extent to which a person took advantage of the increased mobility and internationalization entailed in globalization plays a role in the selection of commercialized papers among readers of nonofficial papers. Percentage of life spent away from Beijing, travel abroad, having studied some English, and surfing the Internet increased the likelihood of reading commercialized papers. Similar results were obtained regardless of what control variables were included or excluded.[25]

To illustrate differences between readers in Beijing, I developed profiles for four types of readers, henceforth called "Old Wang," "Comrade Shu," "Mrs. Li," and "Little Zhao." These profiles are empirically drawn based on predicted probabilities to read different kinds of newspapers in the statistical models among BAS respondents described previously.

Old Wang represents the average reader in Beijing in 2005. He earned about RMB 2,338 per month and had received about eleven years of education, which was equivalent to a Chinese high school degree. He preferred to read semiofficial papers, particularly the *Beijing Evening News*. Therefore, Old Wang was only 37 percent likely to read official papers.[26]

Comrade Shu, Mrs. Li, and Little Zhao differ from Old Wang in ways that made them more likely to read other newspaper types. Official newspapers are read by two kinds of readers, denoted here as Comrade Shu and Mrs. Li. Comrade Shu identified himself as a regular official who worked for a Party or government unit and who received about three more years of education and had a monthly salary about four times higher than that of Old Wang (about RMB 9,464). Party and government units usually subscribe to official papers to make sure that officials are informed about political decisions made by state units at higher and lower levels of government. Because Comrade Shu was conveniently supplied with newspapers at work, he was 71 percent likely to read official newspapers,[27] about 34 percent more likely than Old Wang.

Mrs. Li also favors official newspapers, but in contrast to Comrade Shu, who also bought commercialized newspapers, she exclusively read official papers. Mrs. Li was a neighborhood committee worker. Such workers often organize collective newspaper readings for senior citizens in the neighborhood and are

[25] For robustness tests, see Appendix D.
[26] Ninety-five percent confidence interval ranged between 31 and 42 percent.
[27] Ninety-five percent confidence interval ranged between 53 and 85 percent.

therefore supplied with newspapers at work. Her low salary (about RMB 936) may explain her reluctance to purchase nonofficial papers at newspaper stands. Overall, she was 63 percent likely to read official papers.[28]

Finally, Little Zhao is part of a group of residents who tend to be more mobile and internationally oriented than the average Beijinger. In contrast to Old Wang, Little Zhao had spent most of his life in places other than Beijing, had traveled to North America or Europe, had studied some English, and read the news online. These characteristics made him 75 percent likely to read commercialized papers, which was about 42 percent more likely than Old Wang.[29]

Together, Old Wang, Comrade Shu, Mrs. Li, and Little Zhao illustrate the demographic characteristics of different readers of official, semiofficial, and commercialized papers in Beijing. These different readership patterns especially the profiles of Comrade Shu and Mrs. Li, also confirm the utility and availability hypotheses. Keeping these profiles in mind will facilitate the interpretation of the quasi-experimental findings presented next.

Changes in Newspaper Use over Time

Because newspaper content was synchronized after April 9, we first must investigate general newspaper use to detect avoidance of newspapers. When experiencing cognitive dissonance, some Beijingers, especially those with the most negative view of Japan, would try to avoid reading newspapers entirely. Because of the absence of media outlets with more negative reporting than newspapers, however, these effects would be relatively small, as predicted by the absence of choice and commitment hypotheses.

It is helpful to first take a look at the raw data. Figure 8.2 displays patterns of newspaper use among Beijingers between late March and mid-May. The x-axis displays weekly changes over time, and the y-axis displays percentage of readership. The results show that the percentage of newspaper readers remained relatively stable over time, although there seems to be a slight movement toward increased newspaper use at around the time of Lien's and Song's visits.

This basic finding became more pronounced when modeling the relationship. Once we allow the dummy variable for the press restrictions treatment to interact with commitment we find substantively and statistically significant selection effects. The solid sloping line in Figures 8.3a and 8.3b indicates how the likelihood of reading newspapers changed for the average Beijinger, Old Wang, as his feelings toward Japan became colder. The dashed line displays the 95 percent confidence interval for the estimated selection effects. By comparing the situation before and after the PD restricted space for news reporting

---

[28] Ninety-five percent confidence interval ranged between 36 and 86 percent.
[29] Ninety-five percent confidence interval ranged between 55 and 90 percent. Old Wang is only 33 percent likely to read commercialized papers (95 percent confidence interval ranged between 24 and 42 percent).

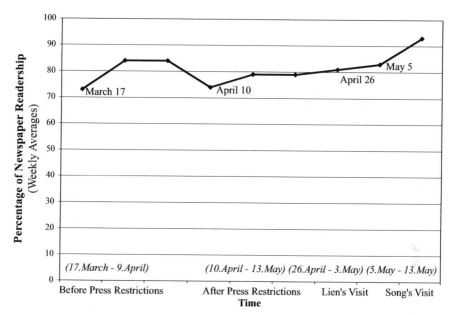

FIGURE 8.2. Development of Readership in Beijing (Raw Data). *Source:* BAS 2004.[a]
[a] Weekly averages included groups of about fifty people.

we can assess the changes that occurred as a result of the press restrictions treatment.[30]

Let us first examine the situation before press restrictions were issued, as shown in Figure 8.3a. As Old Wang's feelings toward Japan became more negative, he appeared more likely to read newspapers. The trend lines for reading newspapers show a positive relationship between more negative sentiment toward Japan and reading newspapers. As the Chinese news media reported about Japan in a highly negative way during this period, this does make a lot of sense: when Old Wang had warmer feelings toward Japan, he tended to abstain from reading newspapers that contradicted his beliefs. However, the colder his feelings toward Japan became, the more likely he was to also read negative articles.

When press restrictions "pulled" news media reporting in a more positive (or less negative) direction, however, Old Wang's choice to read newspapers changed. This change is displayed in Figure 8.3b. As Old Wang's feelings became colder, he was less likely to read newspapers. Negativity toward Japan and newspaper use became negatively related. At high levels of negativity, press

[30] See Table 8A.3 in Appendix E. For a detailed comparison between use of online news websites and newspapers, see Daniela Stockmann, "What Information Does the Public Demand? Getting the News During the 2005 Anti-Japanese Protests," in *Changing Media, Changing China*, ed. Susan Shirk (Oxford: Oxford University Press, 2011a).

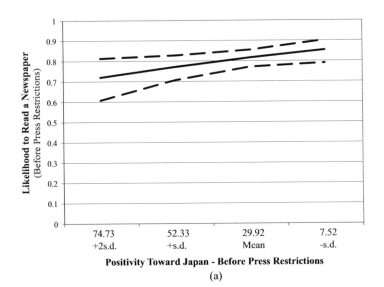

Positivity Toward Japan - Before Press Restrictions

(a)

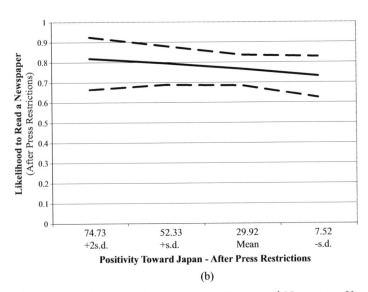

Positivity Toward Japan - After Press Restrictions

(b)

FIGURE 8.3. Relationship between Commitment and Newspaper Use among Average Beijingers Before and After Press Restrictions. *Source:* BAS 2004.

restrictions made Old Wang 12 percent less likely to read newspapers while he held just as negative feelings toward Japan.

The other three readers mentioned earlier, Comrade Shu, Mrs. Li, and Little Zhao, are not much different from Old Wang with respect to the relationship between sentiment toward Japan and newspapers and online news consumption. They share the same basic pattern, moving parallel to each other. Comrade

Shu always remained more likely than the others to read newspapers, followed by Mrs. Li and Little Zhao.[31]

In the documentary *In Search of China*, directed by Adam Zhu (2000), an unemployed worker tells the reporter: "We rather not listen to the radio anymore. They are not reporting the truth. They only report the positive news and that's why people won't listen." The results from this section confirm that similar dynamics can be at work with respect to newspapers. Those who are strongly committed about an issue are especially likely to move away from media sources when media reporting contradicts their beliefs. At average levels of negativity toward Japan, however, these effects made up only about 8 percentage points. Selective exposure effects are relatively small, confirming the absence of choice hypothesis.

Changes in Use of Newspaper Types Over Time

How did patterns of newspaper readership change among those who continued reading newspapers? We would expect that those who stayed with newspapers after April 9 searched for the most credible news product in their attempt to expose themselves to messages consistent with their own negative sentiment toward Japan. However, official events should have provided an incentive to learn about the position of the government and thus draw readers back to official papers, even though news reporting on Japan remained more positive than public sentiment toward Japan.

As previously mentioned, raw data already confirm these expectations. Figure 8.4 displays use of newspaper types among readers in Beijing between late March and mid-May. The x-axis displays weekly changes over time, and the y-axis displays percentage of readership. When comparing the use of official papers with that of nonofficial papers, we can see that readers move away from official papers when greater dissonance was produced between comparatively more positive newspaper reporting about Japan and public sentiments. During Lien's and Song's visits, however, readers were drawn back to official papers.

As before, these effects became more pronounced when modeling the relationship. Figure 8.5 illustrates the estimated effects of the press restrictions and official events treatment on newspaper use of the average Beijinger, Old Wang. The x-axis displays time (control and treatment groups), and the y-axis indicates the likelihood to read official papers for the average reader in Beijing.[32] The dashed line represents the likelihood to read commercialized papers, and the continuous line represents the likelihood to read official papers.

As expected, Old Wang reacted to press restrictions and the official visits by Taiwanese leaders. Once press restrictions were imposed on the news media and newspaper content became more positive than public opinion, readers

[31] See Table 8A.3 in Appendix E.
[32] See Tables 8A.4 and 8A.5 in Appendix E.

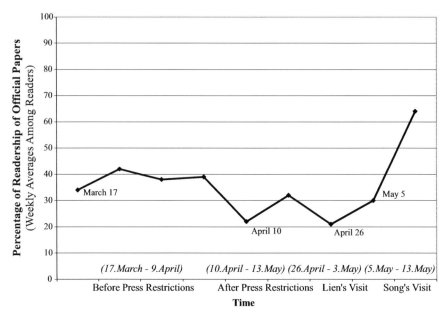

FIGURE 8.4. Development of Readership of Official Papers among Readers in Beijing (Raw Data). *Source:* BAS 2004.[a]

[a] Weekly averages included groups of about fifty people.

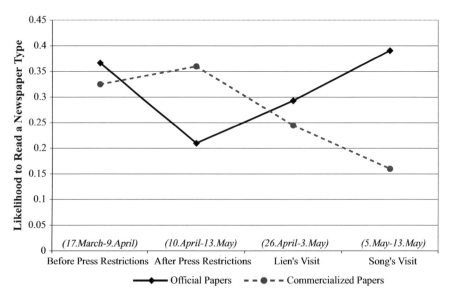

FIGURE 8.5. The Average Beijinger's Use of Newspaper Types Over Time (Among Readers). *Source:* BAS 2004.

searched for the news product that they expected to diverge from the official line and to report from the perspective of ordinary citizens. Accordingly, Old Wang was 16 percent likely to move away from official papers and toward nonofficial papers. When comparing use of commercialized papers with that of semiofficial papers, Old Wang was slightly more likely to select commercialized papers, but these findings were not statistically significant. This is consistent with our expectations that nonofficial papers are more credible than official papers. However, official events provided an incentive for him to move back to official papers and away from commercialized papers. Old Wang was 18 percent more likely to select official papers and 20 percent more likely to prefer semiofficial papers over commercialized papers.

Again, the other three readers mentioned earlier, Comrade Shu, Mrs. Li, and Little Zhao, were not much different from Old Wang with respect to their reactions to the treatments. They share the same basic pattern, moving parallel to each other. Comrade Shu always remained more likely than the others to read official papers, followed by Mrs. Li and Little Zhao.[33]

These findings confirm the credibility and official event hypotheses. When news content was synchronized, Beijingers searched for the most credible news product and selected nonofficial papers. Once incentives were given for citizens to acquire information about how the government dealt with the first official visit of Taiwanese politicians since 1949, they again became more likely to read official papers – while remaining sceptical about news content on Japan.

* * *

Overall, the findings of the quasi-experiment strongly support the hypotheses outlined at the beginning of this chapter. Readers normally do not avoid newspapers when dissonance is created between the news product and a persons' stance on an issue. Yet as their commitment increases, they become more likely to avoid newspapers. At average levels, however, these effects are small. People are likely to continue to read newspapers, but patterns of newspaper selection change. When dissonance increases but news content stays uniform, citizens reach for newspapers that they believe to be more credible. Nonofficial papers have this credibility bonus, because they are believed to report from the perspective of ordinary citizens and therefore are more likely to diverge from the official line. However, readers can be drawn back to official papers as experts on the position of the government, despite official papers' low credibility. Furthermore, people for whom the information provided in official papers is particularly useful and available are always more likely to read official papers.

Thus far, I have explained the main argument. The remainder of this chapter presents results from some variations and tests of these basic findings. In the

---

[33] See Tables 8A.4 and 8A.5 in Appendix E.

next section, I provide additional confirmation that it is indeed low credibility that leads readers to avoid official papers. At the end of the chapter, I show evidence that these basic findings hold across regions.

Are Official Newspapers Really Less Credible?

Of course, official newspapers may be regarded as accurate information sources about the policies and goals of the government. However, do such perceptions also promote their persuasiveness among citizens? Chapter 7 explained that credibility is a function of trustworthiness and expertise among ordinary citizens, and official papers lack both, leading to lower levels of credibility. Such an interpretation is consistent with the preceding analysis, leading readers to seek nonofficial papers and to avoid official papers, when cognitive dissonance is created.

In addition, the BAS data allow us to conduct some additional tests. BAS respondents were asked about their level of confidence regarding the national and local government's implementation of pension reform. I entered an inter-action term between low levels of political trust and the dummy variable for the official events treatment when estimating use of official papers among readers. The results show that lack of political trust *increased* the likelihood of reading official papers.[34] Official events had an even stronger positive effect on the average reader in Beijing when having no political trust. These results reinforce the conclusion that low levels of credibility travel together with low levels of political trust – a message diverging from the official line. This appears to be the case even when readers have incentives to learn about the position of the government.

Is Beijing Different from Other Cities?

Most of the analysis in this chapter has been limited to Beijing. Yet Beijing is not necessarily representative of other cities in China. Beijing is China's capital and its political center. The stereotype of Beijingers in China is that they are particularly interested in and more savvy about politics than those elsewhere. Furthermore, many foreigners come to Beijing for work, study, or travel. Earlier we saw that this international environment creates a particular kind of news-paper audience for commercialized papers. In this section, I therefore explore the extent to which findings from Beijing can be generalized to other cities.

First, urban residents more generally demand information that represents public opinion but that also provides information about the position of the state. According to Guoming Yu's (2009) survey conducted in 2005, 67.5 per-cent of Chinese citizens indicated that the media should supervise both the government and society, 61.1 percent indicated that the media should serve as a platform for competing free-floating diverse opinions, and 54.9 percent

---

[34] See Table 8A.4 in Appendix E.

indicated that the media should serve as the mouthpiece of the Party and government. Only about 15 percent indicated that the media should serve as either an entertainment instrument or an instrument of the Party and government to manipulate public opinion.[35] These nationwide survey results confirm public demand for information that represents both society and the state. It also hints at a general resistance toward propaganda: the expression "manipulating public opinion" (*zhidao shehui yulun*) is generally associated with the main task of the PD.

Indeed, LLM survey data conducted in Chongqing, Foshan, Wuxi, and Shenyang confirm that citizens primarily read official newspapers when they are useful and easily available to them. Just like in Beijing, cadres and people working at Party or state units are particularly likely to read official papers in other cities in China. In addition, higher levels of education among readers of official papers point to the particular usefulness of these papers to the Chinese elite (see Table 8A.6 in Appendix E). These basic patterns are shared by all cities and remain significant even after adding more control variables.[36]

Cities differ, however, in terms of the popularity of official newspapers, whereby official papers were most popular in Foshan in Guangdong, followed by Wuxi in Jiangsu, Shenyang in Liaoning, and finally Chongqing city in Chongqing municipality. This pattern is related to the level of media commercialization of the province, whereby citizens become more likely to read official papers as their information environment becomes more marketized. According to the *China Advertising Yearbook*, Guangdong was ranked second, Jiangsu fourth, Shenyang eighth, and Chongqing eleventh in terms of income of its local advertising industry in 2003. This pattern conforms to an increasing likelihood of reading official papers as local advertising income increases.[37] Level of economic development, population size, administrative rank, and region do not align with this pattern.[38] This strengthens our previous conclusion that Chinese urban citizens are attracted by the commercial look of newspapers.

Although the survey data from these four cities do not provide us with the opportunity to conduct a quasi-experiment as in the case of Beijing, these findings indicate that utility and availability of official newspapers are the main determinants that motivate urban citizens to seek official papers. However, when official papers commercialize, they are able to attract a larger readership and can even partially make up for their lack of credibility.

---

[35] Respondents could select several answer categories.

[36] For robustness test results, see Appendix D.

[37] See Table 8A.6, in Appendix E.

[38] As provincial capital and municipality, Shenyang and Chongqing share equal rank; Wuxi and Foshan are both cities at the township level. Chongqing city and Shenyang have about equal population size, followed by Wuxi and Foshan. According to official statistics, gross domestic product per capita was about equal in Foshan and Wuxi, followed by Chongqing and Shenyang in 2002; Wuxi and Foshan are both located in Southern China, Chongqing in the mid-West, and Shenyang in the North-East.

Conclusion

Chinese urban readers seek newspapers that they perceive as credible. Readers are conscious of the fact that official papers publish propaganda. Although Chinese citizens generally tend to accept the idea that propaganda is necessary, such acceptance of citizen education does not necessarily entail that people find propaganda persuasive. A person may support education of others while not believing propaganda published in official papers herself. Instead, readers decide to read newspapers that they perceive to be closer to their own position and report about the news of the day in a way that they can relate to. As we have seen in Chapter 7, differences in the reputation of newspapers are achieved by means of branding and overstepping of boundaries for news reporting, thus boosting nonofficial papers' credibility in the eyes of readers.

Despite a general preference for nonofficial newspapers, however, under certain circumstances, such as during official events, citizens selectively choose to read official papers to learn about the position of the government. For the same reason, political and economic elites in China consistently read official papers, but elites tend to expose themselves to both newspaper types. Readers who exclusively read official papers do so because the cost of obtaining these newspapers is low. Citizens with low levels of income whose work units subscribe to official papers prefer not to spend money on purchasing nonofficial papers.

Overall, the absence of diverse political messages in the news creates a dependence of citizens on the information sources available to them, even if their opinions diverge from the official line. Most people stay with media sources, unless political control over news content tightens and news reporting strongly conflicts with their beliefs. However, there is also some evidence that avoidance of the news media is only temporary. During big national or local events, the utility of information in the news media provides a strong incentive to return to previous readership habits. Because of the absence of a diverse news product when it comes to political issues, even when they are perceived to be remote from politics, avoidance of the news media is limited to the highly committed and is only short-lived.

Given this dependency on information sources that are roughly similar in terms of political content, how does media credibility figure into the ability of the state to influence public opinion by means of newspapers? The next chapter takes up this question by analyzing media effects.

9

Media Effects on Public Opinion

Chinese propaganda officials often assume that the media affect people's attitudes and behavior. Most of their knowledge about the effectiveness of propaganda is based on conversations with friends and relatives, letters, and reading about ordinary people's opinions on the Internet. To determine the effectiveness of propaganda, they primarily look at the nature and number of messages that are published in the media, but they hardly ever base their policies on evidence from systematic research, because in China even academics rarely conduct studies on media effects.[1] As pointed out in Chapter 7, the predominant view among propaganda officials is that official newspapers maintain higher credibility in the eyes of the Chinese public, although they are aware that nonofficial newspapers are better at reaching the Chinese public as a result of their higher circulation rates. These arguments justify constraints imposed on further media marketization and government support for official papers.

In Chapters 7 and 8, we saw that propaganda officials' conclusions about how Chinese citizens perceive newspapers are flawed. Despite these misperceptions, this chapter reveals that, on the whole, the propaganda system is working in favor of the government. Next I examine the extent to which media credibility influences whether or not citizens are persuaded by what they read in newspapers about labor law and the United States. By comparing media effects across issue areas and cities, we can learn about how novelty with an issue and greater choice of newspaper types affect media influence, and we can draw inferences about how these relationships may play out when citizens read about other issues in the news and in different regions of China. Before

---

[1] Most studies on media effects in Chinese communication studies are based on bivariate relationships between exposure and attitudes, thus uncovering correlation but not causation. See, for example Guoming Yu, *Zhongguo Dazhong Meijie De Chuanbo Xiaoguo Yu Gongxingli Yanjiu (Study on Communication Effects and Credibility of Chinese Mass Media)* (Beijing: Jingji Kexue Chubanshe, 2009).

taking up the empirical analysis, it is useful to first learn more about how media credibility figures into persuasion of media audiences.

Media Credibility and Media Influence

Mere exposure to the media alone does not change people's attitudes. Instead, the extent to which a person is influenced by the mass media depends on the level of attention a person pays to a particular issue. Counterintuitively, moderately informed citizens tend to be most easily persuaded by new information, as has been found in numerous studies in American public opinion research.

In 1962, Converse was concerned that the majority of the American electorate was not only uninformed, but also had unstable attitudes, thus being more easily manipulated during electoral campaigns. However, in a careful empirical analysis, Converse (1962) found that the moderately informed were the most likely to be persuaded by election campaigns. The poorly informed were difficult to convert because they rarely came into contact with the campaign message. By contrast, well-informed citizens were heavily exposed to the political campaign, but at the same time, they were the hardest to persuade because they were less willing to accept a message that ran counter to their preexisting beliefs. To put it differently, well-informed individuals tended to have stable attitudes and were therefore more difficult to convert.

This basic nonlinear relationship between a person's level of political information and attitude change has been confirmed by numerous studies – even in authoritarian regimes (Geddes and Zaller 1989). In contrast to Converse (1962), however, contemporary works interpret the relationship in a somewhat different way. Starting with Zaller (1992), scholars of political communication commonly use a person's level of political knowledge as a proxy for political awareness, defined as the extent to which a person pays attention to politics and understands political information. In this chapter, I use the term *attention* rather than *awareness* because I do not always use a knowledge scale to assess the concept.[2]

According to Zaller's exposure-acceptance model, a person's likelihood to be persuaded by a piece of information depends on two factors: first, her likelihood to be exposed to and to comprehend the message (reception), and second, her likelihood to accept the message (acceptance). Zaller found evidence for a complex, nonlinear, empirical relationship between a person's level of political information and her political beliefs, as first described by Converse. However, when interpreting the relationship, Zaller argued that poorly informed citizens are less likely to receive news media messages because they are little aware of

---

[2] BAS results are based on self-reported levels of attention rather than a knowledge scale. This measure is a valid measure for news reception in China. See Daniela Stockmann, "One Size Doesn't Fit All: Measuring News Reception East and West," *The Chinese Journal of Communication* 2, no. 2 (2009).

politics. Highly informed citizens are more aware and are thus very likely to receive political information conveyed through the mass media. At the same time, however, they also scrutinize the information in light of their predispositions and therefore tend to be more resistant to changing their political views.[3] As a result, the moderately informed are the most likely to be influenced by media messages.

Zaller also asserted that a person's opinion is composed of considerations that happen to be most accessible when asked for an opinion. These considerations are broadly defined as justifications for favoring or opposing an issue or policy. For Zaller, most people hold opposing considerations at the same time and form their opinions by averaging across the considerations that are accessible to their short-term memory at any given moment.[4] Those who are highly aware (the highly informed) hold more considerations than those who are less aware (the less informed). They are better able to think critically about an issue and are predisposed against the message by their party identification or values. One more piece of information is unlikely to induce much attitude change.

Apart from the characteristics of the recipient, such as a person's level of sophistication or awareness, and of the message itself, such as, for example, news media content, a person's response to new information depends on his perceptions of the source. Previous studies have shown that source characteristics such as a speaker's public approval, insider status, accuracy and objectivity, expert status and knowledgeability, likeability, reputation, and ideology can matter for persuasion.[5] Recently, scholars of American politics have become interested in how these perceptions are created and they have started to investigate media labels and the ideological reputations their brand names carry. These labels serve as important judgmental shortcuts, which media audiences employ to interpret the meaning and implications of messages in the media.

[3] Zaller defines predispositions as "stable, individual-traits that regulate the acceptance or non-acceptance of the political communication a person receives." See John Zaller, *The Nature and Origins of Mass Opinion* (New York: Cambridge University Press, 1992), 22. The most important predisposition in Zaller's model is political ideology.

[4] According to memory-based models of opinion formation, more recent considerations are more accessible in short-term memory. The main alternative model of opinion formation is the online processing model, whereby people continuously update their beliefs when new information becomes available to them. Any new piece of information is immediately stored as an affective component along with the object of the attitude. As a result, people are more likely to recall, for example, whether they liked or disliked a candidate than the specific information associated with her. The two models are generally regarded as being more applicable under certain circumstances rather than one model being more accurate than the other. See Stanley Feldman, "Answering Survey Questions: The Measurement and Meaning of Public Opinion," in *Political Judgment: Structure and Process*, ed. Milton Lodge and Kathleen McGraw (Ann Arbor: University of Michigan Press, 1995), Milton Lodge, Marco Steenbergen, and Shawn Brau, "The Responsive Voter: Campaign Information and the Dynamics of Candidate Evaluation," *American Political Science Review* 89 (1995).

[5] For a review of this literature, see James N. Druckman and Arthur Lupia, "Preference Formation," *Annual Review of Poitical Science* 3, no. 1 (2000).

Shortcuts help people manage the flood of information by allowing them to make political judgments based on cues they receive about a message's content (Popkin 1991; Lupia 1994).

Prior research on media labels has primarily focused on their sources and less on their effects. A noticeable exception is research by Baum and Groeling (2009) that demonstrates the importance of media labels in persuasion of American television audiences based on experiments and survey data. Ascriptions of partisanship on part of CNN and Fox strongly influenced which messages citizens found credible in terms of their messages about President George W. Bush's handling of national security during the war in Iraq. Media labels were particularly influential when conveying the message through a certain media outlet imposed some cost on the speaker. Viewers found, for example, Democratic criticism of a Republican president more persuasive if it appeared on a network considered as conservative. Conversely, they tended to be more critical of the same statement if broadcast by a liberal media outlet because in this case the network and the criticism had shared political interest.

As we have seen in Chapters 7 and 8, media labels in China are not associated with different parties aligning on a left–right ideological continuum as is the case in liberal democracies. Instead, people make sense of a complicated news media environment by dividing media sources into categories that differ with respect to their level of trustworthiness and their expertise on the government and the public. Because most readers identify with the public, previous chapters have shown that Chinese citizens tend to find nonofficial newspapers to be more credible. In line with Baum and Groeling's (2009) findings, we would therefore expect that readers find messages conveyed in nonofficial papers more persuasive than when published in official papers, particularly if they confirm the government's message.[6] In line with previous findings of roughly uniform positive messages across different newspaper types, we would therefore expect that people's attitudes move in a positive direction when being susceptible to media messages and in a negative direction when being resistant. Because readers perceive nonofficial papers as more credible, they tend to perceive labor law as a more effective weapon of the weak and have a warmer feeling toward the United States when reading nonofficial papers than when reading official papers (*susceptibility hypothesis*).

Because the more highly aware are more likely to notice ideological valence in information and ascribe bias to media outlets (Zaller 1992; Baum and Gussin 2007), this relationship should become more prevalent as a person becomes more attentive to the issue. As readers pay more attention, media labels should matter more. The effect of media labels should be strongest at high levels of attention (*attention hypothesis*).

---

[6] Conversely, official papers should be perceived as more credible when voicing criticism of the government. I do not explore this point further here due to lack of suitable data.

To test these expectations, I examined the interaction between reading a newspaper type and attention among readers in Chongqing and Beijing. Because labor law is a new issue to most citizens, they tend to be more susceptible to media messages than when reading news about the United States. Even the highly attentive are easily persuaded by media messages (Stockmann and Gallagher 2011). Labor law is thus a special case in Zaller's exposure and acceptance model, whereby attentiveness and attitudes are linearly related. Given the rapid pace in which China is undergoing transition, the government frequently introduces novel issues when making decisions about the direction of ongoing reform. By contrast, Chinese citizens have had more time to make up their minds about how they feel toward the United States. To account for this difference, I modeled the relationship between attention and attitudes linearly in the case of labor law and nonlinearly with respect to the United States. A mathematical description of the statistical models can be found in Appendix D.

As is well known, relying on statistics to detect media effects can be problematic because coefficients only represent correlation, but not causation. Results could indicate that citizens selectively expose themselves to information that is consistent with their preheld beliefs. However, for reasons explained in more detail later in this chapter, I will interpret the findings of the statistical analysis in this chapter as media effects.

Labor Law

To assess the validity of the empirical results presented later in this section, it is important to first lay out in detail how I measured the key concepts playing into the way in which official and nonofficial newspapers affect people's evaluations of labor law.

Measuring Perceived Effectiveness of the National Labor Law

Attitudes toward the National Labor Law were captured by a question that asked respondents whether they thought the National Labor Law was very effective, somewhat effective, not so effective, or not at all effective in protecting workers' rights (coded from 4 to 1, respectively). In the four cities, roughly 4 percent perceived the National Labor Law as highly ineffective, 32 percent perceived it as ineffective, 55 percent perceived it as effective, and 10 percent perceived it as highly effective (coded from 1 to 4, following the same order). Because the dependent variable was a categorical variable, I employed ordinal probit regression analysis. A total of 726 of 4,112 respondents who had never heard about the National Labor Law and could therefore not hold an opinion about it were not asked to give their opinions and were thus excluded from the analysis.

Measuring Exposure to Newspaper Types

To assess exposure to newspaper types, I created multiple measures based on the interviewees' self-reported newspaper use. In the LLM, respondents first were asked to indicate whether they frequently, sometimes, or never read newspapers. If they reported to be frequent readers, they were asked which two papers they read. Apart from a series of dummy variables for reading specific papers, I also created dummy variables for reading official or nonofficial papers. Coding of these variables was based on local media practitioners' assessments and the rationales.[7] On average, 25 percent of the respondents read official papers, with significant variation between cities.

Measuring Attention
In line with common practice in research on political communication, attention was measured based on six items that tapped into the respondents' level of knowledge about the National Labor Law and labor dispute resolution.[8] On average, people in the four cities were moderately attentive to this issue.

Measuring Control Variables
Apart from the media, personal experience with labor disputes, alternative sources of information, social standing, and socialization could affect how people perceived the National Labor Law. Regression analysis allows us to control for these alternative factors that could influence the perceived effectiveness of the National Labor Law. I therefore added variables indicating years of education and whether a person had experienced a labor dispute, had received information provided at a work unit, held an urban residence permit, or was a worker.

Additional control variables were included when I tested for omitted variable bias. To allow interpretation of the intercept, all independent and control variables were recoded from 0 to 1. More details on question wording, coding, and robustness tests can be found in Appendix D.

Media Effects on Readers' Perceptions of the National Labor Law
In line with the expectations of this chapter, we can observe a systematic relationship between exposure to different newspaper types, attention, and perceived effectiveness of the National Labor Law. Figures 9.1a and 9.1b illustrate the results of the basic model, displayed in Table 9.1. The figures show results for two possible outcomes of the dependent variable as somewhat effective (Figure 9.1a) or not so effective (Figure 9.1b). The y-axis displays how likely respondents were to perceive the National Labor Law as either more or less effective.[9] The x-axis indicates levels of attention, ranging from low

---

[7] See Appendix D for further details.

[8] See Appendix D for details. For a detailed review of measurement of news reception and concept validity tests in the Chinese context, see Stockmann, "One Size Doesn't Fit All: Measuring News Reception East and West." Concept validity results of the knowledge scale used in this analysis are included in Stockmann (2009), endnote 11, page 154.

[9] Equivalent to the coefficients of the probit regression analysis after transformation into the cumulative normal distribution.

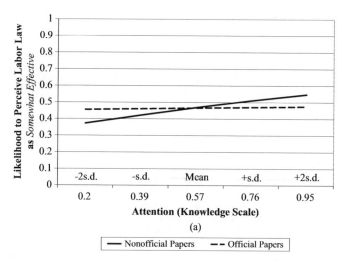

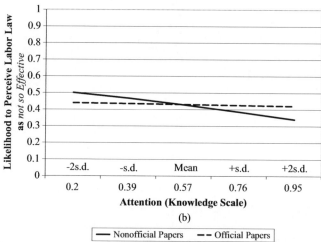

FIGURE 9.1. Effect of Exposure to Official and Nonofficial Papers on Perceptions of Labor Law as Attention Changes. *Source:* LLM 2005.

levels (minus two standard deviations from the mean), to the mean at approximately 0.6, to high levels (plus two standard deviations from the mean). The dashed line presents statistically significant results for reading official papers, and the solid line presents statistically significant results for reading nonofficial papers. Readers of nonofficial papers are more likely to perceive the National Labor Law as effective than readers of official papers as their level of attention increases. Similarly, they are less likely to view the National Labor Law as ineffective. As shown by the cut points in Table 9.1, the relationships are similar

TABLE 9.1. *Ordinal Probit Results for Perceived Effectiveness of Labor Law among Frequent Readers.*[a]

Independent Variables:	Dependent Variable: Effectiveness of Labor Law Coefficient (s.e.)
Official papers	0.393**
	(0.19)
Attention	0.784***
	(0.196)
Official papers * attention	−0.704**
	(0.299)
Foshan	0.103
	(0.085)
Wuxi	0.390***
	(0.07)
Shenyang	0.181**
	(0.071)
Cut 1	−1.812***
	(0.296)
Cut 2	−0.278
	(0.293)
Cut 3	1.464***
	(0.294)
N	2,049
Pseudo R-squared	0.02

* $z < 0.1$; ** $z < 0.05$; *** $z < 0.01$.
[a] Table 9A.1 in Appendix E presents the full results, including the control variables.
Source: LLM 2005.

with respect to perceiving the National Labor Law as highly effective or highly ineffective.[10]

To interpret these results, it is helpful to return to the profile of an average reader, as in Chapter 8. Because we are interested in perceptions of labor law, this time the average reader has somewhat different characteristics, and I will refer to him as "Mr. Chen." Mr. Chen has received about ten years of education, which is equivalent to some high school education. He is also a worker and an urban resident. He has not experienced a labor dispute himself; neither has he received information about the National Labor Law at his work unit. Based on these characteristics, I calculated the predicted probabilities for the average reader, or Mr. Chen, in Chongqing, as shown in Figure 9.1.

First, let us assume that Mr. Chen reads official newspapers. When Mr. Chen paid little attention to the news about labor law, he was about 45 percent likely to regard it as effective. His attitude changed little, even

[10] A Wald test revealed that the parallel regression assumption holds. Results can be retrieved from the author upon request.

when he became more attentive to this issue. However, when reading nonofficial papers, Mr. Chen's attitudes changed. When paying little attention to this issue, he was about 37 percent likely to have a positive view about labor law; as he became more attentive, however, this likelihood increased to about 55 percent. When reading nonofficial papers, he was more easily persuaded by favorable reporting on labor law in the news.

People living in Chongqing, Shenyang, Wuxi, and Shenyang were similar to each other in this respect. There is also evidence, however, that the degree of media marketization increases the persuasiveness of media messages. As indicated by the dummy variables for the cities in Table 9.1, people in Wuxi tend to have more positive views than those living in Shenyang, followed by Chongqing. This corresponds to differences between the cities in terms of local advertising revenue.[11] Foshan constitutes an exception to this rule, not differing much from Chongqing.

These basic results were similar when conducting a statistical analysis of the relationship between reading individual papers on the perceived effectiveness of the National Labor Law as attention changes. Just as in the basic model, explained previously, readers of official papers, such as, for example, the *Chongqing Daily*, did not change their opinions or were more likely to view the National Labor Law as ineffective as their level of attention increased. For readers of nonofficial papers, such as, for example, the *Chongqing Times*, the situation was reversed: as they became more attentive to the labor law, they also were more likely to perceive it as effective. Similar results were obtained when relying on different measures for the dependent variable and when including additional control variables.[12]

In this section, I have concentrated on the main results. The next two sections are dedicated to variations of the model that provide further evidence of the mechanisms that link exposure to different newspaper types and perceived effectiveness of the National Labor Law.

Does Reading a Second Newspaper Matter?

Chapter 8 has shown that people rarely read only one newspaper, especially in a rapidly emerging newspaper market such as that in China. What happens when we take into account that people read more than one newspaper?

Reading more newspapers reinforces persuasion and scepticism among readers. When comparing readers of only one versus two papers in Chongqing, readers of two papers showed stronger signs of resistance than those who only read one paper. When reading nonofficial papers, the situation was reversed. The results in the other cities were inconclusive,[13] but we can be fairly confident that,

---

[11] See also Chapters 8 and 10.

[12] See Appendix D for details on robustness test results.

[13] The relationship was reversed in Foshan, consistent with an interpretation of Guangdong as an exceptional media environment in China (see also Appendix B). For results, see Online Appendix available at www.daniestockmann.net.

at least in Chongqing, reading additional papers reinforces the credibility of nonofficial papers, whereas it increases scepticism about nonofficial papers.[14]

Is Media Credibility Really the Causal Mechanism?

We can further test whether the labels of newspapers increase susceptibility and resistance by examining how readers respond to media messages when they are exposed to different newspaper types.

In Baum and Groeling's (2009) study mentioned previously, Americans were more easily persuaded by criticism when it originated in a source that was perceived as noncritical on the issue. For example, criticism of a conservative president was more credible when it appeared in news outlets that were perceived as conservative. Similarly, messages favorable to a conservative president were more credible when published in liberal media outlets.

Applying the same logic to the Chinese context, messages consistent with the official line should be more credible when they originate in nonofficial newspapers. This relationship should be particularly strong when readers are exposed to official as well as nonofficial papers, because then papers that are regarded as representatives of the public *confirm* news messages appearing in the official papers. Indeed, I found that readers who read both types of newspapers, official and nonofficial, were more likely to perceive the National Labor Law as effective than those who only read official papers.[15] Due to the small number of readers in each of these groups, these results were not statistically significant, but the coefficients do move in the anticipated direction. The findings therefore strengthen the conclusion that media messages are particularly effective if they are confirmed by nonofficial media outlets.

* * *

Overall, the empirical findings confirmed the expectations laid out at the beginning of this chapter. Because of the novelty of labor law, Chinese citizens were easily persuaded by the mass media – even the highly attentive, who are more likely to notice and ascribe bias. When reading nonofficial papers, they were particularly likely to believe media messages. As attentiveness increased, they also were more likely to perceive labor law as an effective weapon of workers against abuse in the workplace. However, when reading official papers, their views of labor law were likely to remain relatively stable.

Does this relationship hold when an issue is more controversial and people show greater resistance? In the next section, I repeat the analysis with respect to sentiment toward the United States in Beijing, this time accounting for the nonlinear relationship between attention and attitudes as predicted by the exposure-acceptance model.

---

[14] See Table 9A.2 in Appendix E.
[15] See Table 9A.3 in Appendix E.

United States

Similar to the preceding analysis of labor law, this section first lays out how I measured the key concepts figuring into official and nonofficial papers' influence on sentiment toward the United States.

Measuring Positivity toward the United States

To ensure consistency with the content analysis, attitudes toward the United States were measured based on a "feeling thermometer," asking Beijingers how warmly they felt toward the United States as a nation on a scale from 1 to 100, whereby 100 represented the warmest feeling. On average, Beijingers felt about thirty-nine degrees toward the United States, which was about ten degrees warmer than they felt toward Japan. Because the dependent variable was continuous, I employed ordinary-least-square regression analysis.

Measuring Exposure

To assess exposure to newspaper types, I created multiple measures based on interviewees' self-reported frequent newspaper use. Similar to the LLM, I created a series of dummy variables for frequently reading individual newspapers and specific newspaper types. On average, 29 percent of Beijingers read official papers.

Because the newspaper market in Beijing is characterized by three as opposed to two types of newspapers, I also created a variable that measured the extent to which a reader was, on average, exposed to official messages. The BAS contained information about which and how many newspapers respondents reported to read. Based on how media practitioners had assessed each paper in terms of their level of marketization, as indicated in Figure 3.2 in Chapter 3, I assigned weights to each newspaper and calculated the average score among all newspapers a person indicated reading. The resulting variable ran from 0 to 1, whereby low numbers reflect being, on average, exposed to commercialized messages and high numbers being, on average, exposed to official messages. On average, Beijingers received semiofficial messages through the means of newspapers.

Measuring Attention

When we conducted the BAS, we did not have enough space in the survey to ask a series of knowledge questions about the United States. Instead, I developed an alternative indicator that was based on a person's self-reported level of attention to the news about the United States. This measure turns out to be a highly valid indicator for news reception in Beijing.[16] Beijingers were, on

---

[16] For a detailed review of measurement of news reception in the Chinese context and concept validity tests of self-reported levels of attention, see Stockmann, "One Size Doesn't Fit All: Measuring News Reception East and West."

TABLE 9.2. *OLS Regression of Attention on Positivity toward the United States as Exposure to Official Messages Changes (Among Readers).*[a]

Independent Variables:	Dependent Variable: Positivity Toward the United States Coefficient (s.e.)
Attention	−92.676**
	(38.978)
Attention squared	106.965***
	(38.31)
Exposure to official messages	−10.54
	(15.992)
Exposure to official messages * attention	127.604*
	(71.822)
Exposure to official messages * attention squared	−153.769**
	(72.429)
Constant	47.394***
	(14.866)
N	482
R-squared	0.12

* p<0.1; ** p<0.05; *** p<0.01.
[a] Table 9A.4 in Appendix E presents full results, including control variables.
Source: BAS 2004.

average, moderately attentive to news about the United States.[17] To account for the nonlinear relationship between attention and sentiment toward the United States, I squared attention in the statistical model.

Control Variables

Apart from the media, the strength of a person's national identity, personal contact with foreigners, socialization, and education are said to affect how she perceives foreign countries. Therefore, I included measures for national identity, personal contact with Americans, being socialized during rapprochement between China and the United States between 1972 and 1989, and education.

Additional control variables were included when I tested for omitted variable bias. As before, all independent and control variables were recoded to run from 0 to 1 to allow for interpretation of the intercept. More details on question wording, coding, and robustness tests can be found in Appendix D.

Media Effects on Readers' Sentiment toward the United States

As in the case of labor law, statistical analysis detected a systematic relationship between exposure to different newspaper types, attention, and attitudes. First, note that there is strong evidence of a highly nonlinear relationship, as shown in Table 9.2 and Figure 9.2. In the figure, the x-axis reflects attention to the

[17] For detailed statistics, see Chapter 4.

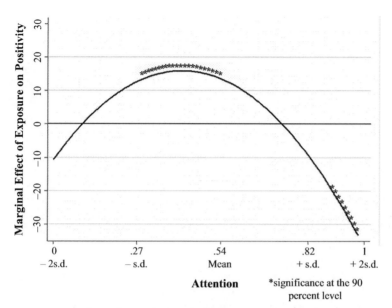

FIGURE 9.2. Effect of Exposure to Official Messages on Positivity toward the United States as Attention Changes. *Source:* BAS 2004.

news about the United States, ranging from low (minus two standard deviations from the mean), to moderate, to high levels (plus two standard deviations from the mean). The y-axis indicates the effect of exposure to official messages on positivity toward the United States.[18] The results show that exposure to official messages affected Beijingers differently, depending on how attentive they were to the news about the United States.

To substantively interpret this relationship, it is helpful to consider where the readership profiles introduced in Chapter 8 end up on the scale of exposure to official messages. Mrs. Li (the neighborhood committee worker) ended up at the higher end of the scale, and Little Zhao (the "globalized" Beijinger) ended up at the lower end of the scale; Comrade Shu (the official) and Old Wang (the average Beijinger) fell between these two extremes. Note that this variable only reflects the readership habits of these readers and not their other characteristics.[19]

Because Mrs. Li and Little Zhao were located at the two extremes of exposure to official messages, let us compare how their views changed in relation to each other as they became more attentive. In Figure 9.2 the slope line is roughly representative of Mrs. Li's situation and the zero line of Little Zhao's situation.

---

[18] Equivalent to the coefficients of the OLS regression analysis.
[19] This is a result of the statistical analysis being based on OLS regression rather than probit used in Chapter 8 or ordinal probit regression relied on in the analysis of labor law.

Let us follow their relative behavior as their level of attention changed from low to high values on the x-axis.

When unattentive to the news about the United States, Mrs. Li felt about ten degrees colder toward the United States than Little Zhao. As she became moderately attentive, however, being exposed to official messages moved her attitudes in a positive direction and she felt about sixteen degrees warmer about the United States than Little Zhao. Being exposed to official messages changed her attitude by about twenty-six degrees. However, as attention increased further, Mrs. Li became more resistant to positive messages about the United States originating in official papers, whereas Little Zhao became more susceptible to messages publicized in commercialized papers. Reading official papers moved Mrs. Li's attitudes in a negative direction from feeling about sixteen degrees more positive toward feeling about thirty-three degrees more negative than Little Zhao. Between moderate and high levels of attention exposure to official messages made a difference of about forty-nine degrees.

Due to averaging across sources when measuring exposure to official messages, not all estimates are statistically significant, but the key relationships at moderate and high levels of attention remain significant at the 90 percent level. These results were reinforced when relying on different measures and when including more control variables.[20] Therefore, we can be confident that we would receive similar results when relying on different samples.

As in the case of labor law, these findings confirm the expectations outlined at the beginning of this chapter. Statistical results indicate that readers of official newspapers, such as, for example, the *People's Daily*, tend to hold more negative views of the United States than readers of nonofficial papers, such as, for example, the *Beijing Youth Daily*. These differences were strongest when people paid much attention to the news about the United States because the more highly attentive are more likely to ascribe bias to media outlets.

In contrast to labor law, however, we detect strong evidence of a nonlinear relationship. Beijingers hold more negative views of the United States than conveyed in newspapers. Because they pay little attention to the news about the United States, readers' sentiments are not much affected at low levels of attention. At high levels of attention, they remain skeptical of positive news content, except when conveyed by more credible nonofficial papers. When readers are only moderately attentive, however, media labels are less influential. Therefore, readers are more easily persuaded by media messages and adjust their opinions to slightly more positive content on the United States published in official papers as compared with somewhat more negative messages originating in nonofficial papers. This difference in the relationship between exposure, attention, and attitudes results from the contrast between a novel issue for which reader demands and the position converge and a familiar issue that is more controversial.

---

[20] See Online Appendix available at www.daniestockmann.net.

In this section, I have concentrated on the main results. The next two sections are dedicated to variations of the model that will provide further evidence of the mechanisms that link exposure to different newspaper types and sentiment toward the United States.

Does Reading a Second Newspaper Matter?

When taking into account that people read more than one newspaper, the results demonstrated that reading additional papers reinforced persuasion and scepticism among readers. When comparing readers of only one with those of two papers in Beijing, the nonlinear relationship between attention and positivity toward the United States increased among readers of two papers.[21] When allowing the number of newspapers a person read to interact with attention and exposure to official messages, this relationship remained consistent. This procedure of adding additional interaction terms to the model increased multicollinearity and therefore led to unbiased coefficients but large standard errors (Brambor et al. 2006). Despite statistical insignificance, the unbiased coefficients strengthen our confidence that reading additional papers reinforces credibility of nonofficial papers while increasing scepticism about nonofficial papers, as in the case of labor law.

Is Media Credibility Really the Causal Mechanism?

With respect to labor law, we have tested whether exposure to official newspapers on top of exposure to nonofficial newspapers is particularly effective in persuading readers. The rationale behind this claim was that nonofficial papers *confirm* news messages appearing in the official papers, thus boosting the credibility of media messages. When repeating this analysis with respect to the United States, I retrieved similar results. Readers who read both types of newspapers, official and nonofficial, tended to have more positive views toward the United States than those who only read official papers, provided that a person paid at least some attention to the news about the United States.[22] Positive news media messages were particularly effective if they were confirmed by media outlets that were associated with the people rather than the state.

* * *

Overall, regression results from the issue area of sentiment toward the United States confirmed findings related to evaluations of labor law. Readers in Beijing had a more positive view of the United States when reading commercialized papers than when reading official papers; readers of semiofficial papers fell between these extremes. This relationship was the strongest among the highly attentive. As they became more attentive to the news on the United States, they became more susceptible or resistant, depending on the kind of newspaper

---

[21] See Table 9A.5 in Appendix E for details. The results can be replicated based on LLM, as shown in Table 9A.2 in Appendix E.

[22] See Table 9A.6 in Appendix E.

types they read. As expected, media labels played a strong role in the ability of newspapers to influence the attitudes of their readers.

At the same time, the relationship between attention and attitudes also differed between the two issue areas. As expected, Chinese citizens were more easily persuaded by media outlets with respect to novel issues, such as labor law. When the issue was more controversial, as in the case of sentiment toward the United States, citizens showed more signs of resistance, especially when reading official newspapers.

Thus far, when interpreting the empirical results, I implied that the coefficients in the statistical analysis can be interpreted as media effects. The next section explains why such an interpretation is reasonable and provides further evidence for the causal direction of the relationship.

Media Effects or Selection Effects?

All evidence presented thus far in this chapter has come from statistical analysis, which detects mutual relationships between variables, or correlation. However, when interpreting the empirical results, I implied that the media influence people's views about labor law and the United States rather than selecting media sources based on their preheld beliefs. This requires further explanation.

Chapter 8 showed that Chinese citizens do indeed make an attempt to selectively choose media sources that they expect to report in a way consistent with their own views. However, because the Chinese state is able to homogenize the messages in the mass media through the means of the PD, they lack the choice that would allow them to pick information that is truly reflective of their opinions. Only when the core political message in newspapers strongly conflicts with their preheld beliefs do citizens temporarily abstain from reading newspapers. Therefore, most citizens generally continue to read newspapers, even though they do not fully reflect their own views.

In addition, Chapter 5 has demonstrated that news reporting also tends to be roughly uniform in terms of the tone. Features associated with the core message conveyed in official and nonofficial papers can therefore not fully explain why people select newspapers. Instead, Chapter 7 has shown that nonofficial papers have been able to establish themselves as media sources that are perceived to report the real news of the day from the perspective of ordinary citizens. Most importantly, different branding of nonofficial papers creates the perception of a more credible news product that is preferable to ordinary citizens. In fact, however, the actual content of the message in nonofficial papers differs only slightly from the one in official papers. The commercial outlook of newspapers boosts the credibility of newspapers, which in turn influences the selection of nonofficial papers. However, because of the absence of diverse messages in the news, readers' opinions are pulled in a direction that is closer to the official line when reading these papers.

Evidence for the causal direction of the relationships presented in this chapter comes from experiments. With respect to labor law, the experimental findings presented in Chapter 7 revealed that a nonofficial label *caused* readers to be more easily influenced by a newspaper article. Readers found those articles that originated in a nonofficial newspaper more convincing than those originating in an official newspaper. The framing of the report did not influence persuasion. These findings add internal validity to the statistical analysis.

In addition, it is highly unlikely that the coefficients detect selection rather than media effects due to the lack of familiarity with the issue among the Chinese public. The National Labor Law is new to most Chinese. It was only passed in 1995 and has been subject to changes since then. Also, few people relative to the large population have experienced the labor dispute resolution system and have had a chance to form their opinions based on firsthand experience. Only 51 of 4,112 citizens in the four cities of the LLM had completed a labor dispute. Therefore, most people do not have access to information about the legal system despite what they read, watch, and hear from the mass media. Citizens seek information about the law primarily out of curiosity about issues related to labor law – to learn about what the law says and how to make it work in their favor. In other words, they seek to form an opinion rather than confirm previously held beliefs.

With respect to the United States, sorting out selection from media effects requires further testing. As explained in the introduction, perceptions of foreign countries, particularly the United States and Japan, are closely linked to Chinese nationalism. Therefore, I took advantage of the quasi-experimental research design explained in Chapter 8 to provide additional evidence for the causal direction of the relationships. The results show that it is reasonable to interpret the coefficients in the statistical analysis presented in this chapter as media effects.

Media Effects during the Anti-Japanese Protests

In this version of the quasi-experiment, I examined how reading official and nonofficial newspapers affected Beijingers' sentiment toward Japan before and after newspaper content switched from being highly negative to only slightly negative on April 9, 2005 (referred to as the *press restrictions treatment* in Chapter 8). If the results presented earlier in this chapter are correct and people are indeed more easily persuaded by nonofficial than official papers, we should find that readers of nonofficial papers will have more positive feelings toward Japan after April 9. Readers of official papers should, however, be moved in a more negative direction, as they tended to be more resistant to news stories in official papers.

We need to take into account that some individuals avoided reading newspapers after news content became tightly controlled. The analysis of readership habits in Chapter 8 revealed that newspaper use decreased slightly when media reporting contradicted people's preheld beliefs, but complete avoidance of newspapers was rare. Therefore, changes in attitudes among average readers are unlikely to be caused by abstaining from reading newspapers. To further strengthen our confidence that changes in attitudes after the press restrictions treatment indeed constitute media and not selection effects, I limited the analysis only to readers and also included control variables for having a strong Chinese identity and perceiving Japan as a threat. When holding these variables constant in the empirical analysis, we should be able to detect the media effects.

The empirical results provided strong support that the media effects differed systematically, depending on which newspaper type readers were, on average, exposed to. News reporting about Japan became more positive in official as well as nonofficial papers after April 9, as discussed in Chapter 8. However, readers of different types of newspapers reacted very differently to a similar tone in news content.

Those exposed to official newspapers, such as Mrs. Li, felt about 9 degrees colder toward Japan than before the protests, which contradicted the shift toward a (comparatively) more positive tone toward Japan in such papers. The lower credibility of official papers made readers more resistant to changes in the tone of news reporting. By contrast, exposure to nonofficial papers shifted readers' views of Japan in a positive direction of up to 6.33 degrees.[23] Little Zhao, for example, only felt about 3 degrees colder toward Japan after April 9 than beforehand. In this case, the commercial wrapping of newspapers made readers more susceptible to the tone toward Japan in the news.

Overall, everyone felt more negatively toward Japan after the demonstrations, but being exposed to nonofficial newspapers mitigated the effect of the event. Taking into account that Beijingers read more than one newspaper strengthens these results. For example, readers of official papers, such as Mrs. Li, became more resistant to news reporting as they read more newspapers.[24]

These results demonstrate that Beijingers' attitudes toward foreign countries are influenced by what they read in the news. Furthermore, media influence was more effective when messages originated in nonofficial papers. Less media marketization was associated with greater skepticism, whereas more media marketization boosted the credibility of media sources.

Conclusion

This chapter examined the relationship between marketization of media outlets and their ability to influence people's opinions. When issues are novel to

---

[23] The coefficient of this interaction term was not statistically significant because of the small number in the treatment group. As a result, we cannot be 95 percent certain that we would retrieve similar results over repeated samples. However, the dynamics are remarkably similar when comparing Beijingers' use of the Internet and newspapers, revealing that "new" media are more effective than "old" media in appeasing citizens. See Daniela Stockmann, "What Information Does the Public Demand? Getting the News During the 2005 Anti-Japanese Protests," in *Changing Media, Changing China*, ed. Susan Shirk (Oxford: Oxford University Press, 2011a).

[24] The statistical results are displayed in Table 9A.7 in Appendix E. For more detailed interpretation of the results, see Daniela Stockmann, "Who Believes Propaganda? Media Effects During the Anti-Japanese Protests in Beijing," *China Quarterly* 202 (2010a).

citizens, as in the case of labor law, they tend to be generally more receptive to media messages. Nevertheless, we have detected a significant difference between readers of official and nonofficial papers. Readers in Chongqing, Shenyang, Wuxi, and Foshan were more easily persuaded by news about labor law and labor problems when the papers they read had a commercial look. Susceptibility and resistance increased as people became more attentive.

This relationship was even more pronounced in an issue area about which the state is actively trying to change deeply held beliefs. In the case of sentiment toward the United States in Beijing, we found strong evidence that varying degrees of credibility among more and less marketized newspapers played a key role in media influence. As a result of the higher controversy of the issue, readers of official papers showed much stronger resistance to positive media messages when reading news about the United States than when being attentive to labor law.

Despite this key difference between issue areas, the findings consistently support the expectations laid out at the beginning of this chapter: higher levels of media marketization of nonofficial newspapers promoted the ability of the state to influence public opinion through the means of the news media. The conclusion of this book will place these findings into the broader context of Chinese state–society relations and authoritarian resilience.

Media Citizenship in China

"So," says Liu, the head of a major newspaper group in Beijing, "you want to talk about media commercialization in China? We used to be managed by government departments, but this is no longer the case. And the trend goes toward more and more commercialization. Why? Because otherwise you don't have any influence, and if you don't have influence, you can't attract advertising. Media commercialization and influence among audiences mutually reinforce each other."

At the time of this interview, I did not know how much truth there was to Liu's statement.[1] Media marketization provides incentives for newspapers to find ways to circumvent boundaries for news reporting, and if they cannot, media practitioners revert to marketing strategies to brand themselves as a credible news product. From the perspective of readers, this is a positive development, as consumers are more satisfied with the news, leading to preferences for market-based papers and greater susceptibility to media messages. From the perspective of advertisers, the greater reach and persuasiveness is desirable for their placement of commercial advertising.

Haiqing Yu (2009) referred to such active involvement of the audience with media as *media citizenship*. Different social groups, such as political elites, intellectuals, entrepreneurs, and social activists, may reveal different patterns of engagement with media.[2] My focus in this book has been on general media

---

[1] To ensure anonymity of my interviewee, I am using a pseudonym here.

[2] For studies on these social groups' engagement with media, see Victor Shih, "'Nauseating' Displays of Loyalty: Monitoring the Factional Bargain through Ideological Campaigns in China," *Journal of Politics* 70, no. 4 (2008), Yuezhi Zhao, *Communication in China: Political Economy, Power, and Conflict* (Lanham: Rowman & Littlefield, 2008), Fanxu Zeng, "Gujia Kongzhi Xia De NGO Yiti Jiangou: Yi Zhongguo Yiti Wei Li (NGOs' Media Agenda Building under State Control: The Case of China)," *Chuanbo Yu Shehui Xuekan (Chinese Journal of Communication and Society)* 8 (2009), Daniela Stockmann, "Media Influence on Ethnocentrism Towards Europeans in China," in *Chinese Views the ELL: Public Support for a Strong Relation*, eds. Lisheng Dong, Zhengxu Wang, and Henk Dekker (London: Routledge, In Press).

audiences in China, referred to as "ordinary citizens" and "primary audiences" by media practitioners. Ordinary citizens have a variety of means to engage with the media; they may discuss politics online or contact the media to place a story. However, the two most widespread forms of media citizenship in China involve the selection of news and information processing. As we have seen, media credibility plays a key role in both forms of engagement.

This chapter places these findings within the Chinese media environment more broadly. I examine variation between regional media markets and their respective levels of media credibility, uncovering a credibility gap in Chinese media between regions. Subsequently, I explore in more detail the characteristics of the most active media citizens. In contrast to common claims about audiences of market-based media, I do not find much evidence that they belong to a middle class. Rather than thinking about media citizens in terms of social class, audiences in China are best understood when taking into account people's identification with the media outlet and their membership in issue publics.

Media Marketization and Access to Media Types across Regions

When I conducted fieldwork in 2005, I learned that revenue reported by the advertising industry provided a more accurate estimate of commercialization of local media markets than figures reported by media outlets.[3] Figure 10.1 displays these more accurate statistics for regions managed by the CCP through the infrastructure laid out in Chapter 3. Using statistics from the advertising industry as a basis, we can compare regional media environments in terms of their level of commercialization. Compared with 2005, advertising income has grown in most regions over time, but regional differences in advertising income have remained roughly constant over time.[4]

Among the five cities covered in this book, Chongqing ranks lowest, followed by Shenyang in Liaoning province and Wuxi in Jiangsu province; Foshan in Guangdong province and Beijing fare best. As a rule of thumb, those located in more developed coastal provinces tend to be surrounded by more commercialized media outlets than those in the less developed inland, but there are also exceptions to this rule. For example, Tianjin has a much lower advertising income than its gross regional product per capita level would predict. Similarly, the media in Sichuan, Anhui, and Hunan are more commercialized than other regions at similar levels of economic development, such as Shanxi, Guangxi, or Xinjiang province.[5] This distribution also roughly coincides with access to the Internet, China's most open source of information. Provinces that are more commercialized also tend to have higher percentages of

[3] See also Appendix A.
[4] See Table 8OA.1 in the Online Appendix available at www.daniestockmann.net.
[5] The correlation between advertising income in 2008 and gross regional product in 2007 was 0.86. I chose these years in order to allow for comparison with the WVS survey data from 2007.

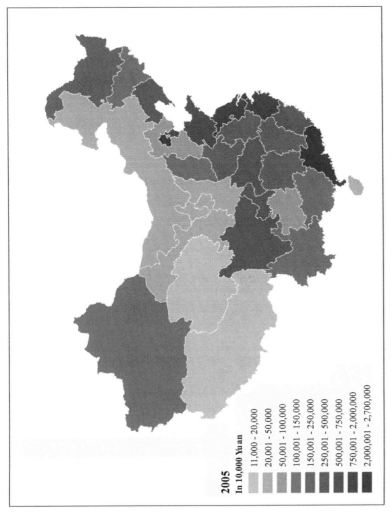

2005

In 10,000 Yuan

11,000 - 20,000
20,001 - 50,000
50,001 - 100,000
100,001 - 150,000
150,001 - 250,000
250,001 - 500,000
500,001 - 750,000
750,001 - 2,000,000
2,000,001 - 2,700,000

FIGURE 10.1. Regional Advertising Income in China, 2005. *Source: China Advertising Yearbook.[a]*

[a] Regional advertising income in China, 2005. RMB 10 million. Source data: (1) Stocmann, 2009; *China Advertising Yearbook.* (2) Boundary Files from China 2000 Province Population Census Data (Shapefile). Version III. Shanghai: All China Marketing Research Co., Ltd., 2000. Map Created by Megan Reif, 2010.

Internet users.[6] Media commercialization tends to go along with the growth of the Internet in China.

The uneven spread of market-based and online media affects urban and rural China differently, as people living in the cities and the countryside do not have access to the same media. In the cities, 81.3 percent watch television, 38.2 percent read newspapers, and 21.3 percent surf the Internet, according to the China Survey 2008.[7] These national percentages are based on the most reliable data regarding Chinese national media consumption as of 2012, but they also hide significant differences between regional media markets in urban China. As shown in Chapter 3, the more marketized newspaper market in Beijing is characterized by a greater number of newspaper types than the less marketized newspaper market in Chongqing. Besides Beijing, there are two other cities that lead in terms of local advertising income – Shanghai and Guangzhou. Just like Beijing, these places are also characterized by more Internet users than most other cities in China. They also share a sizable group of people who benefit from globalization, which, at least in Beijing, corresponds to a sizable readership for commercialized papers that do not seem to be common in most Chinese cities. Media markets in Beijing, Shanghai, and Guangzhou are quite different from those in the rest of China and are neither representative of Chinese media as a whole nor indicative of its future. Guangdong may even constitute an exception altogether, as official papers apparently managed to brand themselves as marketized media outlets.[8]

In the countryside, the situation is much different. Because most newspapers do not deliver to rural areas and Internet access is uncommon, villagers primarily consume broadcasting media. According to the China Survey 2008, only 5.2 percent of villagers surf the Internet and only 11.8 read newspapers; villagers' television programming consumption was comparatively high at 77 percent, reaching almost the same level as that in the cities. Because villagers are more dependent on broadcasting media compared with people living in the cities, they interact with market-based media primarily through television and less through newspapers and the Internet.[9]

---

[6] For example, Shanghai and Beijing had about 45 percent of Internet users in 2007, whereas only about 6 percent of people in Guizhou and Yunnan used the Internet, according to statistics from the China Internet Network Information Center. The correlation between advertising income in 2008 and the percentage of Internet users in 2007 per province was 0.92.

[7] The China Survey was based on a national sample using GPS random sampling, which includes migrants. Self-reported levels of media use are often exaggerated, but in this case respondents were asked about media use on the day before the interview. Therefore, actual media consumption rates may be higher. Chapter 8 demonstrates that consumption rates for newspapers increase as the survey question refers to a longer period of time. Unfortunately, the China Survey did not include a comparable question on radio use, but studies of radio consumption in China suggest that Internet use may have overtaken radio use in urban China. For further discussion of measurement, see Daniela Stockmann, "One Size Doesn't Fit All: Measuring News Reception East and West," *The Chinese Journal of Communication* 2, no. 2 (2009).

[8] See Chapters 7 and 9 and Appendix B.

[9] Most studies on Chinese media consumption focus on cities. Noticeable exceptions include Xuehong Zhang, "Wo Guo Nongcun Xinwen Chuanbo Xianzhuang Yanjiu (A Study of Media

These differences between the cities and the countryside, and the more developed east coast and the less developed western inland, have important implications for the ability of media to satisfy the demand for credible information across China. In Chapter 8, readers in Wuxi were more susceptible to news than those in Shenyang and Chongqing. Do people located in other regions also perceive market-based media as more credible? And does the credibility boost entailed in marketization apply to types of media other than newspapers? To answer these questions, I explored the credibility of newspapers and television across twenty-four provinces, autonomous regions, and municipalities.

China's Regional Credibility Gap

To assess media credibility, I return to the comparison between trustworthiness of political institutions and media based on the World Values Survey 2007, introduced in Chapter 7. Here, I subtracted the average level of political trust among respondents within a province, municipality, or autonomous region from their average level of trust in the press or television. The resulting measure is a continuous variable that ranges from -1 to $+1$. Negative values indicate that people found the media less trustworthy than political institutions, and positive values indicate higher credibility of the media compared with political institutions.

Media marketization is measured by an index that combines advertising income and percentage of Internet users, ranging from 0 to 1. The logic behind combining these indicators is that Internet users share characteristics of the more mobile and internationally oriented media users who prefer the most marketized media outlets, dubbed "Little Zhao" in Chapter 8. The results do not change if you use each of these indicators separately or if you normalize advertising income by gross regional product. More details regarding coding and robustness tests are discussed in Appendix D.

Figure 10.2 shows the partial regression plot of the OLS regression analysis of media marketization on media credibility. The control variables include the ratio of the rural population, the level of economic development, the ratio of Han Chinese, and the administrative level of a municipality or autonomous region, displayed in Table 10.1.

There is a strong positive correlation between media marketization and media credibility. Media marketization alone made up the difference between not perceiving any difference at all and perceiving the media as somewhat more trustworthy compared with political institutions. Chinese media lack credibility in regions where media are less marketized and gain credibility when regional media environments are more marketized. This relationship also applies to perceptions of television across Chinese regions.

Communication in China's Rural Regions)," in *Zhongguo Chuanbo Xiaoguo Toushi (A Perspective on Media Effects in China)*, ed. Chongshan Chen and Xiuling Mi (Shenyang: Shenyang Chubanshe, 1989), Xiaohong Fang, *Dazhong Chuanmei Yu Nongcun (Mass Media and the Countryside)* (Beijing: Zhonghua Shuju, 2002).

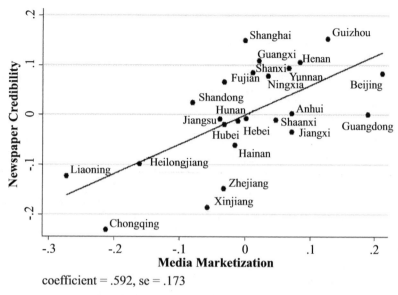

coefficient = .592, se = .173

FIGURE 10.2. Media Marketization and Media Credibility Across Regions, Residuals. *Source:* China Regional Media Data, 2007.[a]

[a] Partial regression plots permit evaluation of the role of individual variables within multiple regression models by allowing examination of the marginal role of the main independent variable given the control variables in the model. It plots the residuals of the main independent variable (media marketization) on the control variables (the x-axis) against the residuals of the dependent variable (media credibility) on the control variables (the y-axis). The slope is equivalent to the estimated regression coefficient.

However, once we start comparing people's perceptions of different types of media with one another, we find that media credibility is not only influenced by the employment of market mechanisms in the production of news. There are also features associated with the nature of the news medium that lend the media credibility.

The Internet may emerge as a more credible information source compared with traditional media. During the 2005 anti-Japanese demonstrations, highly committed Beijingers moved to the Internet and away from newspapers, just as they preferred nonofficial to official papers (Stockmann 2011a). At least in Beijing, the discontented found the Internet more credible compared with newspapers, possibly because the Internet is considered to be more representative of public opinion and more trustworthy than traditional media.

However, the same logic does not necessarily apply to other media types. Broadcasting media remain powerful propaganda instruments in China. Television does not require its audience to be literate nor even to expend the effort of reading; whether because of its authenticity, intimacy, or the combination of two sensory channels (image and sound), many suggest that television has

TABLE 10.1. *OLS Regression Results for Media Marketization on Media Credibility Across Chinese Regions.*

Independent Variables:	Dependent Variable:	
	Newspaper Credibility Coefficient (s.e.)	Television Credibility Coefficient (s.e.)
Media marketization	0.592***	0.605***
	(0.173)	(0.178)
Ratio of rural population	0.626*	0.601*
	(0.321)	(0.331)
Economic development (logged)	0.106	−0.344
	(0.887)	(0.915)
Ratio of Han Chinese	0.16	0.197
	(0.214)	(0.221)
Municipality	−0.194**	−0.230**
	(0.088)	(0.091)
Autonomous region	−0.015	−0.022
	(0.089)	(0.092)
Constant	−0.618	−0.185
	(0.814)	(0.841)
N	24	24
R-squared	0.53	0.52

* $p<0.1$; ** $p<0.05$; *** $p<0.01$.

Source: China Regional Media Data, 2007.

greater emotional power than other media sources.[10] These features lend television and possibly radio the potential for considerable influence.

Indeed, television and radio broadcasting, especially legal television and radio shows, were more effective than print media and the Internet in creating the impression that labor law protects workers among media users in the four cities of the LLM (Stockmann and Gallagher 2011). Landry's (2008b) study of Chinese courts also finds the strong effects of television in mobilizing people to participate in the legal system. Therefore, broadcasting media may be more credible compared with newspapers and the Internet – even though viewers are aware that television and radio are more strictly controlled by the state.

Greater dependence on broadcasting media in villages compared with cities may explain why villagers find media slightly more credible compared with urban citizens. Regions with a higher ratio of rural population tend to perceive media as slightly more credible, as illustrated by the positive coefficient in Table 10.1.[11] Differing education levels may also play into somewhat higher

[10] For references, see Daniela Stockmann and Mary E. Gallagher, "Remote Control: How the Media Sustains Authoritarian Rule in China," *Comparative Political Studies* 44, no. 4 (2011).

[11] Another alternative explanation may be lack of alternative choices, creating dependency on television. Chapter 8 suggests that such an explanation is unlikely. When people had less choice between newspaper types, consumers relied more heavily on official papers, but still perceived nonofficial papers as more credible.

levels of credibility.[12] Compared with the regional credibility gap, however, the differences are not large.

Interestingly, media credibility also varies based on the region's administrative status. People living in a municipality – a city with provincial-level status – tend to find media more trustworthy. In Table 10.1, municipal status is about one-third as influential as media marketization and works in the opposite direction. As discussed in Chapter 6, in provinces the media may have slightly more space to satisfy media consumers than in municipalities. Surprisingly, the status of an autonomous region does not seem to matter, although the central government may focus more strongly on certain kinds of autonomous regions, such as Tibet or Xinjiang, due to the potential for unrest.

* * *

Overall, China's media environment is fragmented and differs in terms of access and credibility. As we move from the cities to the countryside, people become more dependent on broadcasting as opposed to print and online sources of information. As we move away from the more developed eastern provinces toward the less developed western interior, people are surrounded by less marketized media to get the news. Together, these patterns lead to a sizable credibility gap across regions, with important implications for China's stability. In less marketized regions, such as Jilin, Shaanxi, Qinghai, or Heilongjiang, political elites have a much more difficult time disseminating information and manipulating public opinion, especially in cities. In those regions, people probably rely more strongly on other sources of information to form opinions than in regions where people are surrounded by thriving advertising markets, as in Jiangsu or Zhejiang. The credibility gap makes it easier for the state to guide public opinion on the east coast than in the western inland.

Paradoxically, the credibility gap also leads to uneven influences on public discourse among Chinese. As media consumers, citizens have a stronger impact on media content in more marketized media environments. The enormous regional variation in China among media markets empowers consumers on the east coast, and overproportionally in Beijing, Shanghai, and Guangdong, whereas voices in other regions are more easily not heard.

However, who are those consumers of highly marketized media? Who is particularly likely to exert an influence on public discourse, while also being more easily persuaded by its content? The remainder of this chapter explores the characteristics of these audiences.

Middle Class or Bourgeois Bohemians?

Many researchers of Chinese media have argued that the expansion of the media market has overly benefited some social groups, but disadvantaged others.

---

[12] According to the *China Statistical Yearbook*, the correlation between the percentage of people living in townships and villages and the percentage of people who obtained education above high school was −0.86 in 2007.

For example, Zhao (2008) argued that the urban middle class was overly represented in media discourse, whereas women, farmers, and migrant workers became marginalized. In her examinations of middle-class culture in Chinese newspapers, He (2006) also found that lifestyle magazines construct a biased image of urban middle-class life, with possible negative consequences for disadvantaged groups.

The underlying assumption in these studies is that the target audience of marketized media is the rising urban middle class and that market mechanisms therefore substantially contribute to its overrepresentation in media content. Yet once we turn our attention to the characteristics of Chinese media audiences, both from the perspective of advertising companies and of habits of media use, we discover that audiences are actually much more inclusive than these studies of media content and lobbying of the media would suggest.

Advertising companies in China obviously have different strategies as a result of the vast cultural and economic differences across the country. In Wang's (2008) in-depth study of the Chinese advertising industry, he describes mainstream consumers as blue-collar workers; luxury-good consumers have yet to come into being; and white-collar workers save their income for the education of their children and housing rather than consumer spending. Wang estimates this consumer group to be five times larger than the "middle class." Other main consumer groups include young women, the single-child generation, and, to a lesser extent, rural China.

One particularly interesting consumer segment is the "bourgeois bohemians." These people are attracted to the lifestyle of "exquisite taste and quality, but more important, products that display character and the essence of a free spirit" (Wang 2008: 183). Rather than already belonging to a middle class that could afford living such a lifestyle on a daily basis, so-called "bobos" differentiated themselves from mainstream consumers by displaying a middle-class lifestyle while in fact living a less well-off social reality.

Rather than attracting an existing middle class, advertising in China is often directed at awakening in people the aspiration to belong to a middle class. Multinational, foreign-owned, and Chinese state-owned firms, and private and joint ventures, have actively promoted a middle-class lifestyle to increase private consumption (Li 2010).

In the previous chapters, I have not been able to detect evidence that a middle class, defined by objective indicators such as income, education, or occupation, is more attracted by a highly marketized news product. To the contrary, the more affluent, the more educated, and officials – who arguably belong to China's upper-middle class (Wang and Davis 2010) – like to read official papers to stay informed about the policies and goals of the government. Official papers may not be their sole information source – officials also read nonofficial papers and go online to read the news – but income or education does not induce people to turn to highly marketized papers.

Instead, readers of commercialized newspapers in Beijing, similar to Little Zhao in Chapter 8, may be attracted to a middle-class lifestyle. Despite average income and education levels, those readers take advantage of globalization: they tend to be more mobile, surf the Internet, and to be oriented toward Europe and the United States. In their analysis of the construction of the middle class in China, Zhou and Chen (2010) argued that globalization promoted the construction of middle-class identities via consumption. Indeed, the preceding profile of commercialized readers shares similarities with consumers in Shanghai, Guangzhou, and Beijing that emphasize quality and innovation (Paek and Pan 2004). It is possible that Little Zhao, like bobos, aspires to live a middle-class lifestyle, although social reality does not allow for practicing it (yet).

Bourgeois bohemians may explain a bias toward a middle-class lifestyle across newspapers, but this bias also leaves room for responsiveness to demands about the political content of news that differ from those of China's political and economic elite. If income, education, or working as an official does not lead to consumption of market-based media, there is room among audiences for the less well-off.

In contrast to common claims, I have not found evidence that disenfranchised social groups are excluded or alienated from public discourse due to media marketization. For example, women and the retired in Chongqing, Shenyang, Wuxi, and Foshan are active media citizens, with a slight preference for more rather than less marketized papers. Migrants without an urban *hukou* do not differ significantly from those who hold an urban *hukou*.[13] Here, my findings mirror Qiu's (2009) study of Internet and mobile phone users in which he found that China's information have-less, which include migrants and laid-off workers, males and females, retirees and students, actively use communication technologies to obtain information and, to a certain extent, also shape public discourse.

My point here is that media users in China do not fall into social categories that are frequently used to describe dynamics in state–society relations, such as middle class or weak groups (*ruoshi qunti*). Clearly, there is great value in understanding how these "imagined communities," to use the words of Anderson (1983), are formed by and through the media. Yet these categories do not help to explain media credibility, consumption, or persuasion, as media citizens of the old and new media cut across social strata. Media citizenship is better understood when exploring factors other than sociodemographic characteristics, including a person's identification with the media outlet and issue publics.

Implications for Media and Identity

In addition to trustworthiness, we have seen that expertise shapes perceptions of the media as credible information sources. If newspapers are perceived as representatives of society, readers turn to such a source and regard it as convincing, because they identify more strongly with the source. In light of the

---

[13] The LLM survey was based on GPS random sampling that includes migrants. The relationships are presented in Table 8A.6 in Appendix E.

preceding findings, people's identification with the media constitutes a promising area for future research.

For simplicity, previous chapters have mainly focused on the distinction between state versus "ordinary citizens" that is so much a part of the language that Chinese media practitioners use to describe the dynamics of state–society relations in media. Yet clearly Chinese state and society are more diverse, as Perry (1994) reminds us. To obtain a more differentiated picture, distinctions may be drawn between media outlets that represent central versus local governments, Han Chinese versus minorities, and professional papers and broader tabloids, to name just a few examples.

When exploring people's perceptions of these media outlets and how those relate to their own identities, it is important to keep in mind that people have multiple identities. Earlier, I suggested that the more mobile and internationally oriented identify more closely with commercialized papers, but this aspect of their identity may not always be most salient in the selection of newspapers. Which identity influences attitudes and behavior depends on the social context (see, for example, Wong 2010).

Greater emphasis should also be placed on the interaction between identity and access to media, especially those originating outside the infrastructures that China built to control information flows. Even when Chinese had access to information originating in Taiwan, Hong Kong, and foreign media, only about 14 percent of people in Xiamen and Chengdu accessed those media through satellite television or the Internet (Shi et al. 2011). In the BAS 2005, only 2 of a total of 617 residents surfed news websites in English, and only one surfed websites based in Hong Kong, Macao, or Taiwan.[14] Although the total number of those "free media users" is not negligible, media citizens prefer to stay inside the Great Chinese Firewall and domestic media when getting the news. Free media may still have an indirect influence, for example, when translated and posted on blogs or published in *Reference News*. However, people do not directly obtain news from nonmainland media, because they may not identify with them.

Media access does matter, but it is not the only factor that matters. In fact, the Chinese government could probably be more tolerant in granting Chinese access to foreign sources without facing significant challenges to regime stability. Having access to outside information does not necessarily entail consumption, and consumption does not necessarily lead to persuasion. Mainland Chinese perceive mainland media as credible – in part because they can more closely identify with them. News that cannot establish this

---

[14] This was true even though Internet users in Beijing had studied, on average, 5.7 years of English. Exposure to "Western" media among undergraduate students in Shenzhen was much higher (29.8 percent) in 1994, but these data were based on a nonrandom sample of volunteers. See Lars Willnat, Zhou He, and Xiaoming Hao, "Foreign Media Exposure and Perceptions of Americans in Hong Kong, Shenzhen, and Singapore," *Journalism and Mass Communication Quarterly* 74, no. 4 (1997).

connection is unlikely to succeed in disseminating information or persuading citizens.

Implications for Media and Issue Publics

Chinese *xitongs* are similar, but not equivalent, to issue publics. *Xitongs* are groupings within the bureaucracy that together deal with the same policy area. Similarly, an issue public is composed of those who are highly informed and aware of an issue, but rather than being members of an elite, issue publics may include ordinary citizens (Converse 1964). People who belong to these issue publics tend to have more stable opinions that are interconnected with each other in a systematic manner, forming constraints. Such issue publics shape engagement with media outlets.

During the 2005 anti-Japanese protests, Beijingers who were highly attentive to international news and whose beliefs conflicted with the official line in the news searched for alternative information sources closer to their preexisting beliefs, which were perceived as more trustworthy (see Chapter 8 and Stockmann 2011a). This issue public was not composed of the angry youth (*fenqing*), as commonly claimed, but of people who had strong anti-Japanese sentiments and cared strongly about China's relationship with Japan. Indeed, public officials often rely on web- and market-based media as indicators of extreme opinions (Shirk 2007). These opinions may not always be highly ethnocentric, as in the case of the anti-Japanese protests, but can also include people who are less ethnocentric than average Chinese (Stockmann In Press).[15] The most autonomous information sources in China serve as a "collecting pit" for people whose opinions differ from the dominant political message in public discourse. The Chinese Academy of Social Sciences refers to such issue publics as a "new opinion class" that is able to induce action and bring about societal change within a very short time frame (Xiao 2011: 221).

In addition to moving into the most autonomous media, Chinese issue publics are also the most likely to filter information. With respect to both issues examined here, people who were highly attentive toward an issue were also more likely to filter information based on their perceptions of media credibility. Again, people who were concerned about labor law and China's relationship with the United States cut across a wide range of social strata, but their respective issue publics were more susceptible to nonofficial papers due to their higher credibility.

---

[15] Here, my findings differ from those of Jack Linchuan Qiu, *Working-Class Network Society: Communication Technology and the Information Have-Less in Urban China* (Cambridge: MIT Press, 2009), 169, in that I did not find strong relationships between dissatisfaction with the media and social groups; instead, disagreement with the official line cut across social groups and motivated people to use more autonomous sources of information, which included commercialized papers but also the Internet.

As discussed in Chapter 2, Chinese officials have a preference to influence issue publics based on their proclivity to protest. Therefore, media marketization (and to a certain extent, also the Internet) aids the state in reaching and persuading potential activists. At the same time, the responsiveness of these media to such audiences also allows the state to learn about the preferences of potential troublemakers.

What are the issues with the greatest explosive potential for political activism? According to a 1999 national public opinion survey, about 32 percent cared strongly about China's status in the world. By comparison, urban residents cared much more strongly about issues related to their personal livelihoods: 100 percent considered health important, 59 percent considered wealth important, 59 percent considered housing important, 46 percent considered family life important, and 41 percent considered income and job opportunities important (Tang 2005). Not surprisingly, a major health-oriented disaster similar to the 2003 SARS crisis or an economic crisis affecting housing, income, and job opportunities carries greater explosive potential than the 2005 anti-Japanese protests, which already affected more than forty cities (Weiss 2008).

We do not know much about how these issue publics evolve in China. Most research on public opinion suggests that such change will rarely occur outside of elite influence (see, for example, Carmines and Stimson 1989). Change can be driven from the grass roots, when social movement activists are able to mobilize oppositional counterpublics and find collaborators among the political elite (Lee 2002). In China, there have been cases in which officials, intellectuals, journalists, netizens, and mobile-phone users have placed new issues on the public agenda and reframed public discourse (Zhao 2008; Mertha 2009; Qiu 2009). These cases help us to understand social activism, but we have little understanding of how much concern there is about these issues among the broader population, who belongs to these issue publics, and how they evolve – despite the fact that even single news reports "can instantly nationalize and legitimize a focus for popular action" (Li and O'Brien 1996: 48).[16]

There is a greater potential for people to become actively engaged when issues are close to their personal livelihood, but the evolution of issue publics also seems to be biased toward issues of concern to urban and more developed regions, and particularly the "globalized" citizens located in Beijing, Shanghai, and Guangzhou. These individuals are not always primarily concerned about their own well-being and may feel passionate about helping the less well-off, but the extent to which they succeed in speaking up for the disadvantaged still remains to be seen.

---

[16] Such research could make use of a number of existing public opinion surveys, for example, cases that highlight social injustice, such as Sun Zhigang, could be linked with survey data on perceptions of income inequality. See, for example, Martin King Whyte, *Myth of the Social Volcano: Perceptions of Inequality and Distributive Injustice in Contemporary China* (Stanford: Stanford University Press, 2010).

Conclusion

Chinese media outlets often claim to attract the urban middle class. However, this target audience does not conform to actual readers in practice. Although it is true that uneven geographical locations place the countryside and the western inland at a disadvantage, those who actively use the most marketized media in China come from various social backgrounds and differ in terms of their identification with the media outlet and depending on the issue at stake.

This group of people exerts considerably more influence on the development of Chinese media and public opinion than other media citizens. Urban issue publics located in more marketized regions of China have a stronger voice in public discourse, while their beliefs are also more susceptible to media content.

With respect to the United States, for example, readers have a taste for negative news expressed via consumer preferences, and marketized media seek opportunities to satisfy these demands when competing for audiences in local media markets. As explained in Chapter 6, these dynamics result in an increase in negative tone regarding the United States over time. At the same time, readers are also more easily persuaded by nonofficial newspapers due to their higher credibility. When journalists write critical stories about the United States, they may be responsive to growing assertiveness among the Chinese public and simultaneously feed into popular nationalism and antiforeign sentiment.

Over time, these dynamics may lead to a broader change in public discourse and public opinion that is driven by audience demands of urban issue publics. Those having access to China's more marketized media markets may especially emerge as opinion leaders whose voices are more likely to be taken into account and influenced by each other.

Considering the significantly lower levels of media credibility in the rest of China, it remains much more challenging for Chinese leaders to obtain feedback about and guide public opinion in rural and less developed regions. If China's regional credibility gap is growing, such an increase may lead to a polarization of public opinion across China, whereby the rulers' ability to obtain feedback through media is biased toward one pole.

Chinese leaders are attempting to overcome fragmentation of Chinese public opinion by synchronizing information flows. It is true that the CCP's control over information flows remains essential in using media marketization to the advantage of the Party because the combination of the two promotes public opinion guidance. However, there are also certain limits to manipulating public opinion.

Chinese public opinion is not endlessly malleable. Media citizens identify with marketized media outlets in part because they consider them to be closer to their own lives. If media messages do not align with personal experiences, their credibility suffers. With respect to labor law, for example, we have seen that disputants tended to be more resistant to positive media messages. Severe problems in the Chinese state's ability to regulate the workplace and enforce judicial decisions are likely to reduce confidence that rights on paper have significance to people's lives. As a result, people might become more resistant over time to messages that do not accord with what they hear firsthand from friends, colleagues, and neighbors. Mass media raise people's expectations for a more effectively functioning legal system and thus create pressure on legal administrators to improve implementation. However, if these demands are not met by changes in legal institutions, public opinion guidance is likely to become a less effective means to induce change over the long run.

This is a challenging endeavor on the part of the Chinese state. The remaining chapters discuss the origins and prospects of the CCP's capacity to use responsive authoritarianism to its own benefit.

11

China and Other Authoritarian States

The Jasmine revolution in China was a complete failure. Following the example of Twitter- and Facebook-planned protests in Tunisia, Egypt, and many other Arab countries, an anonymous posting on Twitter called for peaceful protests in a dozen Chinese cities on February 20, 2011. Yet in contrast to the protests in the Arab world, turnout in China remained low.

Why were people inspired to take to the streets and demand change in the Arab world but not in China? One possible explanation relates to the regime's ability to monopolize information in a way perceived as credible by citizens.[1] Just like many of its Arab counterparts, the CCP attempted to disconnect Chinese from global information flows by blocking and filtering information. Unlike many Arab countries, however, the Chinese propaganda apparatus soon managed to put its own spin on media messages, including the Internet and marketized media that enjoy higher levels of credibility among the populace.

Online opponents of protests, supported by fifty-cent Party members,[2] portrayed the outcome of revolution as an undesirable alternative to the current situation, as it would lead to chaos rather than stability. Newspapers, such as *Global Times* and *Beijing Daily*, portrayed organizers as a minority of dissidents who, supported by foreign media, used the Arab Spring as a means to destabilize China but instead met with the overwhelming support of the masses for the Party (Bondes 2011). In contrast, social media networks and

---

[1] The literature on social movements points toward opportunity structures, injustice frames, and mobilizing structures. Information flows can influence grievances and perceptions of opportunity structures among potential protesters. For a detailed discussion on the role of digital media in the Arab Spring movements, see Philip N. Howard and Muzammil M. Hussain, "The Role of Digital Media," *Journal of Democracy* 22, no. 3 (2011), Marc Lynch, "After Egypt: The Limits and Promise of Online Challenges to the Authoritarian Arab State," *Perspectives on Politics* 9, no. 2 (2011).

[2] Internet commentators who are paid fifty cents for each message supportive of the party-state. See also Chapter 6.

marketized satellite television in the Middle East and North Africa continued to diffuse information that disrupted the one-sided information flow in favor of the regime. Although Mubarak and his information minister called Al Jazeera's television anchors personally to berate them for unflattering stories, Al Jazeera continued to give voice to protesters, working closely with social media networks. Cairo's attempt to shut down the Internet and the mobile phone network had only limited success (Howard and Hussain 2011).

Why are some authoritarian regimes better than others at synchronizing information flows and persuading citizens? The previous chapters have focused on the effects of newspaper marketization on the production of news and media credibility in China. The empirical evidence indicates that media marketization provides incentives for media practitioners to diversify political messages in the news, but the Chinese state is able to mitigate diversification by means of institutions, most importantly the PD. At the same time, media marketization boosts the credibility of the media, leading to greater selection and persuasiveness of marketized media outlets. In China, the combination of roughly uniform information flows and credibility of market-based media has created support for the policies and goals of the central government, thus stabilizing authoritarian rule.

These benefits of media marketization for the Chinese party-state are ultimately dependent on its capacity to enforce a roughly uniform information flow, when necessary. This chapter places China in a comparative context to further explore the nature of this capacity, drawing on scholarly discussion of the function of parties and their formation in authoritarian regimes. In contrast to common portrayals of China's propaganda system as exceptional, I find that other one-party regimes are also better able to synchronize media messages. States that monopolize power in one ruling party are more likely to coopt elites and build infrastructures that mitigate the diversifying power of media marketization. Personalist and military regimes are less capable of monopolizing information, and media marketization undermines their rule more easily.

China as a One-Party Regime

One-party regimes are the most common type of authoritarian rule. Among the 192 countries in the world, about half are authoritarian, and about 57 percent among those are ruled by one party (Diamond 2002; Magaloni and Kricheli 2010). These states can be further divided into two kinds, often referred to as single-party and dominant-party regimes, with the difference being that single-party regimes, such as China, proscribe opposition parties' participation in elections, whereas dominant-party states, such as in Zimbabwe or Mexico before its democratization in 2000, permit opposition parties to compete in multiparty elections in which the dominant party tends to win. During the Cold War, single-party states, and particularly Leninist states, outnumbered dominant-party states, but since the fall of communism in 1989, their numbers have been declining. Besides China, only four Leninist states survived the breakdown of the Soviet Bloc: Vietnam, Cuba, North Korea, and Laos. Instead, there has been a growing trend toward dominant-party states that are often described as "electoral authoritarian" or "competitive authoritarian." Because of their tendency to adopt seemingly democratic institutions, dominant-party states are also sometimes called "hybrid regimes."

In these states, the party monopolizes political power. In a groundbreaking article, Geddes (1999) differentiated authoritarian regimes based on the interests and power bases of rulers, originating in the country's military, a party, or a personal clique.[3] In contrast to military and personalist regimes, cadres within a party have incentives to cooperate, as all members are better off when the party holds power. Without the party, the opposition has fewer opportunities to influence policies or obtain material benefits. Geddes argued that this incentive structure stabilized authoritarian rule.

Authors of later works felt hesitant to designate personalist rule, a situation in which one personality dominates the state and military apparatus, as a regime type and preferred to refer to the rule of kinship networks as monarchies (see, for example, Gandhi 2008). Here my emphasis is less on different classifications of authoritarian states. My main goal is to illustrate that the dynamics observed in the previous chapters within a single-party regime also apply to other authoritarian states that are dominated by one ruling party. Therefore, this chapter primarily draws a distinction between one-party regimes, including single-party and dominant-party states, and other forms of authoritarian rule.

The Durability of One-Party Regimes

Compared with other authoritarian states, one-party regimes tend to last longer.[4] This has sparked a great deal of curiosity to learn about the functions ruling parties serve in these states and their relationship to regime stability.

To ensure their survival, authoritarian rulers have to make sure that members of the ruling elite as well as ordinary citizens comply with their rule. Threats to their political survival originate either within the ruling coalition or from below, the citizenry. Between the two, the loss of support by elites poses a greater danger. More than two-thirds of the time, dictators are removed by government insiders; only about 20 percent of the time a leader has to step down when facing popular uprisings or public pressure to democratize (Svolik 2009). One-party regimes are better able to withstand these dangers because of their ability to coopt opposition and to create support.

Cooptation allows rulers to bring into the regime unruly elements of civil society, such as business entrepreneurs, interest groups, or other recalcitrant

---

[3] Geddes' typology of authoritarian regimes predates the literature on competitive authoritarianism. Thus many states she originally termed as single-party regimes are equivalent to the states scholars now describe as one-party regimes.

[4] For a summary of the discussion, see Beatriz Magaloni and Ruth Kricheli, "Political Order and One-Party Rule," *Annual Review of Political Science* 13 (2010).

societal forces. Membership in the ruling governing party promises access to privileges and perks as well as a certain degree of policy influence denied without membership (Gandhi and Przeworski 2007). By means of party membership, rulers can more credibly guarantee a share of these benefits in the long run. This credible commitment is established by the party's ability to build coalitions among elites by mediating conflict and facilitating cooperation. As an institution, the party provides a structure for career advancement and access to power positions, which make individual policy disputes less threatening. Short-term concessions aid in bargaining with competing factions in the long run. When competing factions mutually benefit from cooperation, elites will be less likely to conspire against the regime (see, for example, Geddes 1999; Brownlee 2007; Magaloni 2008). Parties therefore not only coopt potential opposition lurking outside the regime but also within the regime itself.

In addition to cooptation, the Party also aids in creating support among the citizenry. One-party regimes have denser organizational networks to monitor and sanction the disloyal. The party machine also monopolizes access to scarce resources and distributes them to loyal supporters relying on patronage networks (Magaloni 2006). The greater capacity of the Party to create compliance among citizens by means of coercion and the distribution of economic resources stabilizes authoritarian rule.

In Chapter 2 I argued that the marketization of media reduces the need to rely on coercion and economic means to reach compliance. However, in order for media marketization to work in favor the authoritarian regime, the state needs to retain a certain degree of control over the production of news. Here, I specify the specific circumstances under which authoritarian rulers can enforce press restrictions despite market liberalization: One-party regimes have greater capacity to synchronize information flows, allowing them to use media marketization to their advantage.

State Capacity under One-Party Rule

Students of authoritarian politics and revolutions have long emphasized the importance of state capacity for regime stability and further development of authoritarian states. Two key elements of state capacity, sometimes referred to as "incumbent capacity" (Way 2005) or "infrastructural power" (Mann 2008), constitute the ability to implement policies and to reach into society, both facilitated by means of infrastructures.[5] Such infrastructures do not always have to take the form of a state bureaucracy, but may include other formal and informal channels through which information and commands are transmitted within a state in a routinized manner (Mann 2008).

---

[5] Way (2005) referred to these elements as the scope of the state and its ability to control, which define authoritarian state power along with the size of the state. Lucan A. Way, "Authoritarian State Building and the Sources of Regime Competitiveness in the Fourth Wave: The Cases of Belarus, Moldova, Russia, and Ukraine," *World Politics* 57, no. 2 (2005).

Formal practices and structures consist of "the official, written-down rules, contract enforcement, extraction and redistribution, and the designated organizations that serve and enforce these rules" (Grzymala-Busse and Luong 2002: 534). For example, Russian President Vladimir Putin issued a series of decrees to strengthen the central state and to curb growing regional independence (Stoner-Weiss 2002).

Informal practices and structures occur outside of these formal channels, but are widely recognized and taught as informal rules. They consist of "shared understandings, personal agreements, or organizations without legal recognition or legitimate power that nonetheless serve as the basis for extracting and allocating resources" (Grzymala-Busse and Luong 2002: 534). For example, the Japanese Liberal Democratic Party relies on local support groups, the *koenkai*, to disburse donations and organize activities during election campaigning. These social networks usually include important local figures, such as owners of local businesses, heads of religious organizations, and officials of the local agrarian cooperatives (Curtis 1988).

Apart from relying on the party to rule the country, one-party regimes are particularly likely to build additional formal institutions. The literature on competitive authoritarianism explores how dominant parties create and shape electoral rules and other electoral institutions to win elections. In Mexico, the constitution was modified to the PRI's advantage 400 times to change electoral laws and to weaken the power of judicial institutions (Magaloni 2006). Countries ruled by rulers with a civilian title (a category into which most single-party regimes fall) also tend to allow the creation of multiple parties and legislatures (Gandhi 2008).

Of course, this does not mean that informal institutions are less important under one-party rule. On the contrary, one-party regimes tend to build extensive patronage networks to redistribute resources to secure support (Wright 2009). However, such informal institutions are often tied to the party, strengthening its organizational capacity. For example, the Peruvian American Popular Revolutionary Alliance and the Mexican PRI built extensive organizational networks without stable bureaucratic structures that relied on informal, activist-led neighborhood networks to deliver particularist provisions (Levitsky 2003). In comparison, in personalist regimes in Kyrgyzstan, Uzbekistan, and Kazakhstan, patronage networks came to define the political system itself, whereby parties played only a secondary role. To implement policies and allocate resources, competing elites primarily relied on patron–client relationships between tribal chiefs and clan leaders that had been transformed into a relationship between regional leaders and administrative units under Soviet rule. Where formal structures were more developed, such as in East-Central Europe and Russia, elites relied more strongly on formal structures, supplemented by informal practices (Grzymala-Busse and Luong 2002).

The scholarly discussion is unsettled about the origins of such differences in reliance on informal and formal structures as well as infrastructural capacity in authoritarian contexts. Still, research suggests that economic and political

context plays a key role. One-party regimes tend to emerge in countries dependent on the productive resources of the economy as opposed to "unearned"
income from natural resource rents, such as oil reserves, and foreign aid. When
dependent on productive resources, rules are motivated to build legislatures
to solicit cooperation from citizens and to form a credible constraint on the
regime's confiscatory behavior, which fosters economic growth (Gandhi 2008;
Wright 2008).

In addition to the economic situation, a strong opposition provides incentives to build formal institutions. Huntington (1968: 425) located the origins
of strong parties in the struggles that brought them to power, noting that the
"more intense and prolonged the struggle and the deeper its ideological commitment, the greater the political stability of the one-party system." Indeed,
one-party rule is most likely to emerge during periods of civil war, anarchy, or
military dictatorship – circumstances under which leaders confront a strong
opposition (Magaloni and Kricheli 2010). One-party regimes also share greater
organizational strength to inhibit protest and repress opposition (Slater 2008;
Way 2009).

The infrastructures that these regimes create aid the ruling elite to secure its
authority over the political apparatus or to coopt potential opponents. Faced
with substantive competition, political elites try to close formal loopholes and
substitute informal with formal rules to undermine the ability of the opposition
to take advantage of informal access to state assets. In Poland and Hungary,
where political parties faced enormous electoral pressures during transition to
democracy in the 1990s, formal institutions were built more rapidly than in
the Czech Republic and Slovakia (Grzymala-Busse 2010).

Furthermore, political elites may need to make policy concessions to foster
cooperation with the regime and create institutionalized channels for potential
oppositions to articulate their interests (Brownlee 2007; Gandhi 2008). Under
the leadership of the Arab Socialist Union in Egypt, trade unions were tied to
the party through corporatism. Once the party split into several political parties
in the 1970s, newly formed clubs and business organizations could advance
their interest through specialized committees of the legislature (Ehteshami and
Murphy 1996).

Overall, the specific circumstances of one-party rule, including economic and
political factors, create needs to build infrastructures to govern the country.
Political elites construct formal and informal structures around the party that
facilitate communication and organization to implement policies. The intersec-
tion between the party and society enables the elite to manipulate formal and
informal institutions to their advantage. Of course, one-party regimes also vary
in terms of the scope of the state and their ability to control (Slater 2008), but
compared with other authoritarian regimes, one-party regimes tend to be characterized by greater infrastructural capacity to address economic and political
challenges. The mere presence of such infrastructures does not necessarily lead
to successful implementation of policies. As an overly bureaucratized state, the
Soviet Union lacked the capacity to provide effective governance and adjust to
changing societal needs. As convincingly argued by Stoner-Weiss (2002: 130),

infrastructures per se do not necessarily enhance state capacity, but it is "certain kinds of institutions, particularly ones that capture, restrain, and incorporate emerging societal interests into the policy process" that make a positive difference in integrating states and in effective governance. The next section specifies infrastructures that link the party with media, allowing media to operate at the nexus between state and society.

One-Party Rule and Media Control

Students of authoritarian resilience sometimes mention media as one factor stabilizing regimes, but it remains unclear why some authoritarian states are better able to use media to their advantage than others. To answer this question I first turn to the production of news, followed by the role of media credibility in authoritarian regimes.

There is a significant amount of variation among authoritarian states to restrict press freedom and impose barriers on access to information (Egorov et al. 2009; Norris and Inglehart 2009). This variation can be explained in part by the economic situation of the country. Resource-rich countries are more likely to censor media, because they are less likely to use media as a tool to obtain feedback about policy performance and have more to lose from protests stimulated by more autonomous media (Egorov et al. 2009). However, as we will see, the presence of oil reserves is only part of the story. Media marketization also has a strong effect on information flows, depending on the institutional design of the regime. To understand why institutional design matters, it is helpful to summarize the key conditions that enable the CCP to effectively impose restrictions on news production.

A first key condition emerges out of the analysis of the role of factionalism in Chapter 6. Internal Party politics continues to significantly shape public discourse in China. Local media are tied to local leaders through a number of infrastructures, and power struggles between factions are reflected in media content. Therefore, the ability of the Party to coopt elites and sustain a political coalition remains crucial. As Brownlee (2007: 208) noted in the context of elections in authoritarian regimes: "Elections do not cripple regimes; regimes that have fragmented coalitions cripple themselves." Similarly, the ability of elites to manipulate media marketization to their advantage depends on cooperation among political elites, which is enhanced by the party.

Yet why are media responsive to elite division? According to most studies on one-party rule, the ability of the party to monopolize and distribute scarce resources, relying on patronage networks, would be crucial in achieving compliance among media staff. The Party has loosened its grip over senior personnel and decentralized personnel management, and along with commercialization and partial privatization, the CCP has lost its monopoly over economic resources. Performance bonuses provide financial incentives for self-censorship, but this distribution of economic benefits in exchange for loyalty does not substitute for the infrastructures the CCP has created to monitor and control media content. As the key infrastructure for communicating and disseminating press restrictions, the PD gives these incentives a common direction.

Distribution of rents and patronage networks seems to constitute only one source of state capacity to synchronize information flows. According to country reports by the African Media Barometer, authoritarian rulers attempt to place party members or those with financial interests in the broadcasting industry on the board of public broadcasters in personalist regimes, such as in Chad or Uganda, just as much as in one-party regimes, such as in Kenya, Tanzania, Zambia, or Zimbabwe. Although all authoritarian rulers attempt to influence personnel decisions, in one-party regimes, patronage networks reaching into the media may be more cohesive, thus leading to greater discipline among media staff.

A second, potentially more important, source of state capacity constitutes the institutional framework within which newspapers are embedded. In China, infrastructures that enhance the capacity of the Party to exert control over the production of news take the form of formal institutions, most importantly the PD and GAPP. Through these institutions, the CCP is able to monitor media content and personnel and can issue administrative reprimands, that lead at its worst to discharge from employment. The absence of a rule of law that protects freedom of press further bolsters the influence of these institutions, making them more influential in day-to-day journalism than the threat of violence against journalists or fear of imprisonment.

China is not the only country in the world that has built such infrastructures, although the Party's involvement in editorial control is rarely as evident as in the case of the Chinese PD. Under the leadership of Ben Ali, the Tunisian Ministry of Communications had a department in charge of publishing and distributing official releases related to public and international affairs to the media.[6] The Kibaki government in Kenya created the Office of Public Communication, which addresses media on critical policy issues weekly to "enlighten citizens on their rights and responsibilities, at the same time encouraging them to be proud of their country."[7] In Zimbabwe, President Mugabe established a Media and Information Commission in 2002, which obliges newspapers to be registered and journalists to be accredited annually.[8] All of these states are examples of one-party regimes that allow a certain degree of contestation between political parties during elections. Although these infrastructures are less obviously involved in synchronizing information flows than the Chinese PD, they

[6] In 2010, the Ministry of Communications launched a new portal. Information is based on a previous portal, at the time available at http://www.tunisie.gov.tn/index.php?option=com_ministeres&Itemid=382&tadsk=view&id=18, accessed October 10, 2009.

[7] Office of Public Communication, http://www.communication.go.ke/pcu.asp?id=3, accessed January 20, 2012. In 2007, the Kibaki administration created the Media Council of Kenya, aimed at fostering self-regulation.

[8] See Country Report Zimbabwe, African Media Development Initiative, http://www.bbc.co.uk/worldservice/trust/researchlearning/story/2006/12/061208_amdi_zimbabwe.shtml, accessed January 26, 2012.

nevertheless fulfill similar functions and increase the capacity to exert control over political information.

Because of the lack of suitable data, we are unable to evaluate which of these key features of one-party rule – party patronage networks or formal institutions – enable authoritarian rulers to effectively impose restrictions on media content. However, we can explore whether regime type influences information flows. If the rule of governance in one-party regimes mitigates the liberalizing effect of media marketization, we should observe that media marketization is negatively related to diverse information in one-party regimes, as authoritarian rulers are better able to use market mechanisms to their advantage. In other forms of authoritarian rule, however, media marketization should be positively correlated with diversity of information, as political leaders have less capacity to enforce press restrictions (*diversity of information hypothesis*).

In addition, one-party rule should have consequences for media credibility. Chapter 10 has shown that Chinese have different perceptions of media when they live in a municipality. Because of their administrative rank, media in some regions seem to be more tightly controlled than others, and citizens are more skeptical of media in such regions.

Similarly, we would expect that media marketization increases the credibility of the media in all authoritarian regimes, but people living in one-party regimes should perceive media as somewhat less credible due to the party's synchronization of information flows (*skepticism hypothesis*). As media outlets adopt market mechanisms, they face increasing pressure to adjust to popular tastes. In an authoritarian media environment in which citizens are aware of state restrictions on media content, the commercial wrapping of media creates the image of a more credible information outlet that represents people rather than political leaders. In one-party regimes in which rulers have greater infrastructural capacity to restrict media content, journalists cannot differentiate themselves by means of political messages in the news. Instead, they turn to branding strategies that aid in creating the label of nonofficial media despite roughly uniform political information in the news. This contrast may induce a certain degree of skepticism on the part of audiences in one-party regimes, but because it is difficult to decipher when the state issues instructions and when not, people use media labels as shortcuts for media credibility. Among the media available to them, market-based media have established a reputation for disseminating information that is more trustworthy and representative of society. Media marketization increases media credibility in one-party regimes, just as in other kinds of authoritarian states, but citizens tend to be somewhat more skeptical.

A Cross-Country Study of Media Marketization and Authoritarian Rule

To test the above expectations, I collected data from thirty-eight authoritarian countries between 2001 and 2009, summing up to a total of 130 cases. All of these countries are located in the Middle East and North Africa, Sub-Saharan

Africa, or the post-Soviet region. Cases were included if classified as partially free or not free by Freedom House. Because of lack of comparable data, China and other countries in Asia are not included in the data set. Appendix D includes more details on case selection, measurement, and coding of variables.

Let us first take a closer look at the interactive effect of media marketization on the diversity of information as regime type changes. Because of the lack of reliable data in many authoritarian systems, it has been difficult to locate measures that are consistent across a large number of cases. To assess diversity of information and media marketization, I rely on the Media Sustainability Index (IREX). IREX is based on a panel of experts drawn from representatives of local media, nongovernmental organizations, professional associations, and media-development implementers. Among other aspects, country experts assess how strongly a country has met the criteria that "state or public media reflect the views of the entire political spectrum, are nonpartisan, and serve the public interest," which I relied on to assess the diversity of information. Countries were, on average, characterized by low to medium levels of diverse political messages, with an average of 1.7 (s.d.=0.61), whereby 0 represents completely uniform information and 4 completely diverse information.

To assess media marketization, I rely on IREX's assessment of business management, constructed based on evaluations of management style, source of media income, and availability of market research, among others. Given that many authoritarian states have undergone marketization of the media, it is not surprising that these countries had, on average, begun to operate as profit-making businesses and received advertising revenue.[9] At the lowest end of the scale, the advertising industry in Uzbekistan, Tajikistan, and Belarus is in its initial stages of development, and most media receive direct or indirect state subsidies; private media may be allowed but rarely manage to sustain themselves as a result of the small size of the advertising market. At the highest end of the scale, in Russia, Kuwait, and Qatar, the advertising industry is thriving, and advertising revenue as a percentage of the entire profits corresponds to or slightly exceeds general standards in commercial media. Media outlets are run as profit-making enterprises and are supported by marketing research to develop strategies to tailor news production to audiences. Private ownership is allowed.

One-party rule was measured based on two existing data sets coded by Geddes (1999) and Brownlee (2007).[10] Among the thirty-eight countries, there were ten one-party regimes varying within regions: Tunisia, Armenia, Ethiopia, Georgia, Kenya, Mozambique, Tanzania, Ukraine, Zambia, and Zimbabwe. These one-party regimes or hybrids between one-party regimes and military or personalist regimes were coded as 1; otherwise countries received a score of 0.

To address alternative explanations of variation in political information in the news, I added control variables for oil reserves, Freedom House rankings,

[9] The mean on a recoded scale from 0 to 1 was 0.4 (s.d.=0.14).
[10] I am grateful to Barbara Geddes and Jason Brownlee for sharing these data.

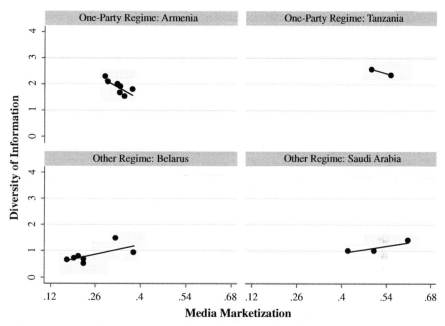

FIGURE 11.1. Media Marketization and Diversity of Information in One-Party and Other Authoritarian Regimes, Bivariate Scatter Plots. *Source:* Media and Authoritarianism Data, 2001–2009.

population size, region, and regime length. The coefficients remain consistent in direction and size when using different measures and when adding control variables, as discussed in Appendix D.

Media Marketization and Diversity of Information

The statistical results demonstrate that one-party regimes can, on average, retain uniform information flows, even as they liberalize media markets. Figure 11.1 displays bivariate scatter regression plots of media marketization on the political diversity of information, selecting four of the thirty-eight countries as examples. In Armenia and Tanzania, both one-party regimes, we observe a negative relationship: as the media become more profit-oriented and more dependent on advertising revenue as opposed to state subsidies, the media tend to reflect fewer views in the political spectrum. The opposite is the case in Belarus and Saudi Arabia, both of which are personalist regimes: as marketization increased, the media became more politically diverse. Adding control variables in multivariate statistical analysis further strengthens the conclusion that the relationship between media marketization and information flows in authoritarian regimes depends on the type of regime.

Table 11.1 presents the results of fixed effects and random effects models. There is an ongoing debate about the appropriateness of various methods to cope with panel data. These methods – put simply – differ in the assumptions

TABLE 11.1. *Fixed and Random Effects Regression Results for Media Marketization on Diversity of Information as Regime Type Changes.*[a]

Independent Variables:	Dependent Variable: Diversity of Information		
	Fixed Effects		*Random Effects*
	Among One-Party Regimes Coefficient (s.e.)	Among Other Regimes Coefficient (s.e.)	Coefficient (s.e.)
Media marketization	−2.089* (1.116)	0.515 (0.42)	1.478*** (0.323)
One-party rule	–	–	0.294 (0.356)
Media marketization * one-party rule	–	–	−1.937** (0.833)
Freedom House ranking	−2.337** (0.89)	−2.44** (0.972)	−2.041*** (0.361)
Oil reserves (logged)	–	−2.24 (2.155)	−0.368 (0.823)
Freedom House ranking * oil reserves	–	2.564 (2.448)	0.571 (1.039)
Regime length	3.047 (1.83)	−0.553 (0.971)	0.246 (0.325)
Population (logged)	−120.05* (58.575)	5.171 (7.996)	−1.226 (0.831)
Middle East/North Africa	–	–	−0.246 (0.325)
Sub-Saharan Africa	–	–	0.349** (0.144)
Constant	105.305** (50.025)	−0.836 (6.794)	3.58*** (0.766)
Number of countries	10	28	38
Total N	32	98	130
Adjusted R-squared	0.79	0.87	–

* $p/z < 0.1$; ** $p/z < 0.05$; *** $p/z < 0.01$.

[a] The results for dummy variables for year and country are not presented in Table 11.1. The differences between models and robustness test results are discussed in Appendix D. Wooldrige tests show no significant first-order autocorrelation in the data, but Wald tests reveal significant group-wise heteroscedasticity for the fixed-effects model in other regime types and the random effects model. Bootstrapped or cluster-robust standard errors do not significantly change the results presented here.

Source: Media and Authoritarianism Data, 2001–2009.

they make about the independence of observations and their ability to estimate the effects of variables that rarely change over time, as in the case of our main variable of interest: regime type. It is therefore reasonable to employ various methods.[11]

Although specific estimates differ across the methods employed here, they consistently point in the same direction: the relationship between media marketization changes depending on regime type. The dummy variable for one-party rule in the random effects model signifies that one-party regimes differ only slightly from other authoritarian regimes when media markets are not liberalized. As market forces are introduced into media, their relationship with diversity of information depends on regime type. In personalist and military regimes, media marketization is positively associated with greater diversity of information. In one-party regimes, governments may face similar pressures, but the negative coefficient of the interaction term demonstrates that one-party regimes are better able to resist diversification of information as media markets liberalize, turning into a slightly negative relationship.[12]

Two examples of countries in Sub-Saharan Africa illustrate this point. Ethiopia and Uganda are both similar in terms of their population size, level of political liberalization, lack of oil reserves, and regime length in the region. The two countries differ, however, in terms of regime type and level of media marketization. Ethiopian politics is dominated by the Ethiopian People's Revolutionary Democratic Front. In 2008, Ethiopia's private media drew revenue from subscriptions and advertisements, whereas government-run media depended on subsidies. In comparison, Uganda's public and private media operated as profit-generating businesses independent of the government in the same year. According to Geddes' coding, Uganda constitutes a personalist regime.

The preceding random effects model predicts that liberalizing the media market in these two countries would have opposite effects. In both countries, the media markets became more liberalized by about 0.2 on the IREX five-point scale between 2008 and 2009. The estimated increase of political diversity in the news in Uganda is about 0.04 points in a positive direction, whereas Ethiopia's media should remain roughly at similar levels, decreasing by only 0.01 points, thus widening the difference in political information between the two countries. Indeed, Uganda's diversity of information increased from 2.25 to 2.35, whereas Ethiopia's decreased from 1.38 to 1.15 on the IREX five-point scale between 2008 and 2009.[13] Obviously, larger changes in the level of media marketization correspond to more impressive changes in information environments.

---

[11] Appendix D discusses these differences in detail in the section on robustness tests.
[12] The estimated relationship between media marketization in single-party regimes is $1.478 - 1.937 = -0.459$.
[13] The predictions do not fully match these numbers because the values of the control variables also changed in this period. Partial residual plots show that the residuals scatter around the regression line.

Overall, these findings show that media marketization has a much greater potential to disseminate opposition voices in regimes that are not dominated by one party. However, this does not mean that market-based media cannot serve as a catalyst for the breakdown of authoritarian regimes when governed by one party, as illustrated by the case of Mexico, examined in Chapter 12. Clearly, media marketization can contribute to the decomposition of the one-party system, but the preceding findings suggest that this potential is much stronger in other political contexts. The fact that protests play a stronger role in the collapse of authoritarian rule of personalist leaders, according to Geddes (2007), is consistent with such an interpretation, although we need to keep in mind that media influence does not constitute the only factor affecting protests. These findings strengthen our confidence that the circumstances that facilitate political control over the media in China apply to other authoritarian contexts.

In addition, once we consider the impact of media marketization on media credibility observed in this book, one-party regimes are not only better able to marginalize alternative political views and opposing voices in the media – they also profit from the credibility boost entailed in marketization.

Media Marketization and Media Credibility

As a result of the lack of reliable public opinion surveys in authoritarian states that allow for a systematic comparison across countries, my analysis of media marketization and media credibility is much more limited. To assess media credibility, I rely on country averages for a question on the trustworthiness of the media in the 2000 and 2005 waves of the World Values Survey.

One problem when comparing people's responses to public opinion surveys across countries is that people use different scales when answering the question. For example, Chinese report that they tend to have more say in getting the government to address issues they care about than Mexicans despite living in an authoritarian state, because they tend to give more positive answers to the same question (King et al. 2004). To address potential problems associated with the comparability of survey data across countries, I placed people's evaluations of newspapers and television in relation to their evaluations of political institutions, using the same measure as in Chapter 10 when comparing across regions in China. As before, negative values indicate that citizens found media less trustworthy than political institutions, whereas positive values reveal higher levels of media trustworthiness compared with political institutions. Among the six countries for which these data and IREX data were available, the average level of media credibility was 0.164 (s.d.=0.05). In these authoritarian states, media tend to be regarded as slightly more trustworthy than political institutions.

Does media marketization really boost the credibility of the media in authoritarian states? Figure 11.2 shows the partial regression plot of the OLS regression analysis of media marketization on media credibility, after controlling for one-party rule, level of economic development, and regime length.

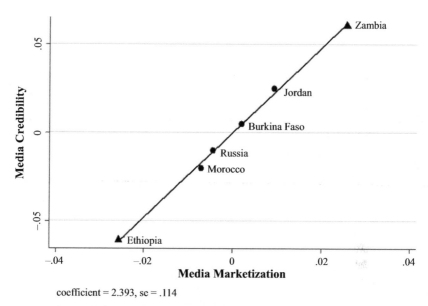

coefficient = 2.393, se = .114

FIGURE 11.2. Media Marketization and Media Credibility, Residuals. *Source:* Media and Authoritarianism Data, 2001–2009.

Despite the small number of cases, the statistical analysis demonstrates a strong positive relationship between media marketization and media credibility. In Figure 11.2, individual countries line up nicely on the regression line. Citizens in authoritarian states perceived media as less trustworthy than political institutions when marketized. Once states allowed media to impose market forces, citizens perceived media as even more trustworthy than the party, the government, and legislatures.

As expected, this relationship can be observed in all authoritarian states, despite regime type. However, Ethiopians and Zambians, who live under one-party rule, were more skeptical of newspapers and television than Russians, Moroccans, Burkinabes, and Jordanians, as exemplified by the negative coefficient for one-party rule in Table 11.2.

Citizens living under authoritarian rule are no fools. They are aware of media control by the government. Africans and Russians recognize biases of more authoritarian-dominated media and decipher political messages (Mickiewicz 2008; Moehler and Singh 2009). At the same time, more strongly controlled media still benefit from media marketization, possibly disguising media's inability to cater to demands for political diversity among audiences by branding strategies, as we have seen in China.

Considering the greater capacity of one-party regimes to synchronize media content compared with other forms of authoritarian rule, these findings suggest that party cadres in highly marketized media environments may also be more effective in disseminating information and convincing citizens as people seek

TABLE 11.2. *OLS Regression Results for Media Marketization on Media Credibility.*

Independent Variables:	Dependent Variables: Media Credibility Coefficient (s.e.)
Media marketization	2.393**
	(0.114)
One-party rule	−0.406**
	(0.017)
Level of economic development (logged)	−2.325**
	(0.103)
Regime length	−0.007
	(0.007)
Constant	0.953**
	(0.036)
N	6
R-squared	1

* $p < 0.1$; ** $p < 0.05$; *** $p < 0.01$.
Source: Media and Authoritarianism Data, 2001–2009.

and believe market-based media to learn about politics. In personalist and military regimes media marketization does not necessarily lead to collapse. However, credible and politically diverse media pose pressure on the stability of the regime and raise the costs of maintaining rule through other means than media.

Conclusion

In light of these findings, it is perhaps less surprising that the media apparently served as a catalyst of the Jasmine revolutions in the Middle East but not in China. Most countries in the Middle East and North Africa, with the exception of Tunisia, were not ruled by one party, but by monarchs or personalist leaders. Clearly, these were motivated to clamp down on media reporting, but had less capacity to enforce control, as in the case of President Mubarak's call to Al Jazeera mentioned earlier. Most regimes did not build infrastructures that could manage media in times of crisis, and the exceptions, such as Iran, were better able to withstand public pressure. As Lynch (2006: 25) noted, "the Arab public sphere remains almost completely detached from any formal political institution." Put simply, Mubarak could neither give binding orders to a Qatari television station that emphasized politics and open debate, nor cut out satellite television from public discourse in Egypt. In the absence of suitable infrastructures, political protest movements used Al Jazeera to spread messages and to protect themselves from the worst of regime repression (Lynch 2011).

State capacity plays a strikingly similar role with respect to the Internet. As Diamond (2010) observed, the impact of new communication technology depends on the state's political organization and strategy. Online publications, blogs, discussion forums, social media, and cellphones have the potential to offer space for commentary and debate, give voice to political opposition, empower individuals, and facilitate independent communication and mobilization. However, if states maintain a greater capacity to filter and control Internet content, and to identify and punish dissenters, they are more resistant to these impacts. Morozov (2011) noted that such states not only resist such changes, but actively use the new communication technology to their own advantage. Political context matters: it promotes regime stability in some cases, while diluting it in others.

The findings of this chapter indicate that the distinction between authoritarianism and democracy does not capture the characteristics of this political context adequately. Without taking into account the institutions that govern authoritarian states, we are unable to sufficiently explain the role of media in these environments. The final chapter and conclusion of the book explores in more depth the role of political strategy and skill in maintaining responsive authoritarianism in the media.

12

Responsive Authoritarianism in Chinese Media

> "Before economic reforms, there were few media at all in China, and all were
> restrained by both ideological controls and by the system of the planned economy.
> Today, Chinese media are as numerous as stars in the sky, and many media now
> operate commercially. So even as political controls on the media remain relatively
> strong, the amount of free space has increased."
>
> Qian Gang, "Letter from Home," July 30, 2011, RHTK Radio

In July 2011, two high-speed trains collided near the city of Wenzhou,
Zhejiang province. As passengers escaped the train, they took pictures with
their mobile phones and posted them on the Internet. Once the pictures
appeared online, they were quickly picked up by market-based media, thus fun-
neling the information about the train accident to the center of public discourse.
As Vice-premier Zhang Dejiang rushed to investigate the scene, propaganda
authorities attempted to control the message, initially instructing the media to
use official information released by Xinhua but soon asking the media to cool
down reporting, leading to censorship of numerous stories.[1] Nevertheless, the
central government publicly responded to the incident. In December, the State
Council under the leadership of Wen Jiabao issued a report concluding that
mismanagement had caused the incident. Fifty-four officials were punished,
and the Railway Ministry was ordered to improve its management.

Such incidents have happened frequently in recent years, sparking a discussion about the effects of market- and web-based media in China. Scholars
and media activists interpret these dynamics in two ways, one side stressing
liberalization and prospects for democratization, and the other emphasizing
control and authoritarian resilience (see, for example, Gang and Bandurski
2011; Esarey and Xiao 2011; Zhao 2008; Brady 2008). How can we make
sense of these two assessments of the political consequences of Chinese media?

---

[1] See "Chinese Media Muzzled After Day of Glory," Hong Kong Media Project, July 31, 2011,
http://cmp.hku.hk, accessed March 24, 2012.

The answer I have offered in this book is that both interpretations are right in part, but not as different as they seem at first glance. Responsive authoritarianism in Chinese media requires a certain degree of toleration for societal space in order for market-based media to become profitable. Marketization has reduced government spending on a highly expensive media industry that was fully owned and financed by the state, as well as the exercise of coercive instruments to achieve compliance with state policies among journalists and editors. This increase in autonomy of media outlets associated with media marketization opened up space for societal forces to influence the production of news, leading to tensions between reporters and officials when audience demands diverge from the official line promoted by the state. If only a small percentage of reporters test the boundaries of news reporting in a country with a media industry the size of China, such incidents can take place frequently, creating the impression that China "is like a pressure-cooker" on the verge of explosion (Reilly 2012: 34–35). As social forces start pressing against the state, officials become concerned about social instability and feel pressured to accommodate societal feedback, showing responsiveness to popular demands.

In this struggle between media and the state, neither of the two sides emerge as the winner, although a balance between tolerance and control has a stabilizing effect on the overall system. From the perspective of media practitioners, media marketization is associated with greater space for news reporting, which allows them to cater to audience demands. By constantly pushing the boundaries set by the state, market-based media can also brand themselves as a credible news product, which attracts media audiences.

From the perspective of public officials, market-based media function as a source of public opinion that allows the state to obtain societal feedback about its policies and political goals. Constant negotiation between media practitioners and propaganda officials for societal space constitutes one mechanism through which the Chinese leadership learns about when public opinion diverges from the official line of the state.

In addition, the credibility boost entailed in media marketization allows Chinese media to be more effective in disseminating information and guiding public opinion, particularly among potential troublemakers. Issue publics are particularly susceptible to market-based media and can be successfully appeased by political messages in those sources, as we have observed in the case of the 2005 anti-Japanese protests. However, there are also clear limitations to the malleability of public opinion as media messages become detached from people's personal experiences. And, more broadly, Chinese audiences in the more developed east coast tend to have access to more highly marketized media than those living in the less developed western inland; there is enormous variation within China in terms of marketized media environments, leading to a large credibility gap across regions. Therefore, marketization of media primarily benefits the state in urban issue publics located in coastal regions, whereas audiences in other regions are probably less easily reached and more resistant to media messages.

Public opinion guidance does not always operate how it is supposed to and does not always follow the rationale of propaganda officials. Nevertheless, market liberalization works, on the whole, to the advantage of the Chinese leadership. Responsive authoritarianism in Chinese media requires the Chinese state to strike a balance between communicating information from society to the state while simultaneously maintaining the capacity to disseminate the goals and policies of the government and to guide public opinion. If propaganda officials can walk the fine line between toleration and control, market mechanisms can be beneficial to the state. A certain degree of social space and pressure aids the state in creating support among a wide range of media citizens who differ considerably in terms of their socioeconomic backgrounds but who are united by their policy concerns, here termed as issue publics.

Yet just how much tolerance can responsive authoritarianism in media endure? In other words, where is the tipping point at which China may start to lose the capacity to synchronize information flows? The precise moment is unpredictable and is usually explained in retrospective (Kuran 1991; Przeworski 1991). Nevertheless, comparison of China with other authoritarian regimes suggests that Chinese media are unlikely to serve as catalyst for the breakdown of CCP rule in the near future.

The Tipping Point

Responsive authoritarianism is a risky endeavor on the side of the Chinese state as it is planting the seeds of its own collapse. Losing control is much more costly today than it was in 1978 before the introduction of market mechanisms. Since then, media practitioners have become used to greater autonomy and alternative sources of funding that could allow media to function independently from the state. New information technology has placed additional pressure on China's propaganda apparatus, as it has increased the speed of information diffusion. Today, leaders have only hours to regain control over the message. This potential threat to regime stability may explain why top leaders have held a much tighter grip over media compared with other industries.

However, China is not the only state building infrastructures that contain the seeds of subversion. Many authoritarian rulers establish representative institutions, including legislatures, multiparty elections, and judiciaries. To stabilize the regime, these need to be granted at least minimal autonomy, which opens up the potential to turn against the regime itself. As Schedler (2010: 77) notes: "rulers cannot have one without the other. They cannot establish institutions that will effectively secure their rule without accepting the structural risks that these involve." The institutional ambiguity observed in Chinese media signifies a broader dilemma that authoritarian rulers face.

And still, some authoritarian rulers are better able to manage these institutions than others. As we have seen, one-party regimes can prevent diversification of political information in the news as a result of media marketization. In those countries, the party enhances cooperation among elites, and patronage networks as well as formal institutions tie the media to the party, allowing the leadership to retain roughly one-sided information flows in the news.

Elite cohesion is also a crucial factor to observe in China's further development of media and politics. Even when Chinese elites are fairly cohesive, factionalism influences the content of political messages in Chinese newspapers, as discussed in Chapter 6. Yet should the political leadership be unable to reach a consensus or become engaged in a power struggle between factions, as was the case during the 1989 Tiananmen demonstrations, marketized media will seek opportunities to cater to market demands on topics where no clear guidance is given. Audiences do not necessarily favor regime change – in fact, most public opinion surveys suggest that the vast majority of Chinese do not – but market-based media would likely serve as the voice of criticism that is currently underrepresented, placing pressures on the government. In addition, in the absence of unified leadership, media are likely to become caught up in a power struggle between factions. Still being subject to local PDs, media in different regions are likely to function as mouthpieces of local leaders, thus possibly accelerating political divisions across regions. Such a situation does not necessarily have to lead to breakdown and chaos, as proclaimed by the central leadership, but the media could serve as a catalyst for political change in the form of adjustment to popular demands, as discussed in Chapter 6.

A second important factor to watch the institutional infrastructure that establishes boundaries for news reporting. Most scholarship on transition of authoritarian regimes treats media as a secondary factor compared with political elites, lacking the power to "craft" new political systems. Although this book confirms that elite dynamics remain important as factionalism and internal power struggles loosen the regime's capacity to synchronize information flows, it also draws attention to the structures that link political elites to media outlets. Cooperation among elites and attempts to clamp down on the media are probably less effective in the absence of patronage networks or formal institutions that enhance the capacity of the regime to achieve compliance among reporters.

Mexico's transition to democracy provides an illustrative example. Under the rule of the PRI, the media were owned by private individuals who had favorable relations with the ruling party. The government also relied on indirect state subsidies in the form of advertising, bribes to underpaid journalists, and manipulation of access to broadcasting concessions. As a result, the media systematically favored the PRI during electoral campaigns and was silent on topics that were potentially damaging to the regime. However, as competition between media outlets increased and became marketized, journalists discovered the financial success of critical news reporting, thus promoting pluralism in the press and independent-minded journalism. The PRI did not tie the media to the Party through institutional infrastructures similar to China's PD, the Tunisian Ministry of Communications under the leadership of Ben Ali, or the Media and Information Commission in Zimbabwe, discussed in Chapters 3 and 11, and Party patronage became less effective as alternative sources of funding became available to the media. Therefore, market liberalization in the media promoted political liberalization in Mexico despite official attempts to restrict press freedom: an independent media emerged "not because ruling elites encouraged its emergence, but rather because official response proved inadequate to prevent it" (Lawson 2002: 183).

This example from Mexico illustrates that media can play a role in regime transition independent of elites, but suggests that the extent to which they emerge as a factor separate from elite dynamics depends on the capacity of the party to exert political control. In comparison to other dominant-party regimes explored in Chapter 11, Mexico may be exceptional in that the PRI had not built formal institutions to restrict press freedom, which could provide a more stable structure compared with patronage networks. Many studies on regime transition of one-party regimes stress the importance of party strength and institutional capacities for regime change (see, for example, Solnick 1996; Way 2009).

In China, the institutional framework within which the media remain embedded is being adjusted to a changing media environment, but the media are unlikely to reach the same level of autonomy from the state as Mexican media did. In many ways, the emphasis on fostering social responsibility among media practitioners and the shift toward competitive supervision by the courts under the Hu-Wen administration mirror developments in dominant-party regimes. Tanzania's media, for example, are self-financed and run primarily for profit with a range of public and private media, although private ownership is concentrated in a few hands. According to IREX, most topics can be freely covered by the media unless they are considered "negative." Negative news is either withheld altogether or reported with an angle favorable to the government. Why do journalists self-censor many stories critical of the government?

One important factor figuring into the considerations of journalists are legal defamation cases. According to the African Media Development Initiative, constitutional provisions to promote freedom of speech are undermined by libel laws that leave wide room for interpretation and high penalties in cases of defamation. Many defamation disputes are handled by self-regulatory bodies such as the Media Council of Tanzania (MCT), but cases touching on government matters or personalities usually find their way to the Information Services Department (MAELEZO) under the Prime Minister's Office, or to the Tanzania Communications Regulatory Authority (TCRA). There have been instances in which MAELEZO has fined or banned reporting for certain periods for alleged defamation and insult of public figures. The government under the leadership of the Revolutionary State Party (CCM) strengthened the authority of these institutions in the early 2000s. The TCRA, for example, was established in 2003 to increase the efficiency of licensing and regulating broadcasting and electronic media, previously handled by two separate commissions. Board members are appointed by the minister of information, and the board chairman and director general are presidential appointees, according to the African Media Barometer.

There has also been an increasing emphasis on fostering self-regulation of the media by means of training journalists in professionalism and ethics. Many of these activities are carried out by the MCT, a consultative body that functions as a mediator between state, media, and society. According to the African Media Development Initiative, the MCT is facing increased government influence on its activities.

Should the new government continue the trend that the Hu-Wen administration has put in place, China's management of the media may resemble more closely that in Tanzania under the Kikwete government. Such a system would be considered considerably more free – in 2011, Freedom House ranked Tanzania's media partly free, scoring 48 of 100, whereby 100 represents lack of freedom of press; in the same year, China's media, however, was ranked as not free, with a score of 85 of 100. Despite much greater freedom of press, the Kikwete government still managed to exert a considerable amount of control over news content, resulting in biased reporting similar to the other highly marketized media environments in one-party regimes explored in Chapter 11. According to IREX, in 2009, Tanzania's media ranked above average in levels of diversity of information among one-party regimes. These findings suggest that there is considerable leeway for the Chinese government until infrastructures start to crumble, as happened in Mexico.

In addition to elite cohesion and state capacity, keeping a balance between toleration and control also requires a fair amount of skill. Heilmann and Perry (2011) argued that China's adaptive capacity derives from a guerrilla policy style that allows political leaders to embrace uncertainty and flexibility to adjust to changing circumstances in ways that promote political power and strategic goals. This world view stresses continuous flux driven by ceaseless interaction of opposing elements and may also facilitate striking a balance between toleration and control under responsive authoritarianism. Institutions, such as the PD, do, however, greatly enhance the ability of political leaders to successfully exercise control over information flows, should they decide that control is necessary.

A final challenge to the capacity of the Chinese leadership to keep the delicate balance between tolerance and control in the media is any unexpected change in audience demands that strongly conflicts with the official line of the government. The most likely scenario for such an unanticipated change in public opinion is a public opinion crisis induced by an exogenous shock, such as the Wenchuan earthquake or the SARS epidemic. Issues can suddenly move to the center of public discourse when highlighted by external disruptions to the established order (Carmines and Stimson 1989).

As we have seen, the Chinese leadership has made considerable improvement in information transparency to address the lack of media credibility during crisis situations. Instead of treating topics as taboo, the government is now adopting a public relations strategy to shape information flows, as in the case of the Wenchuan earthquake. Potential activists have in the past interpreted such an opening of news reporting as a signal that public mobilization and political protest were permissible (Stockmann 2011a). To deter more widespread political activism, tolerance of media responsiveness to audience demands during crisis situations is likely to be followed by tightening of control, resulting in roughly one-sided messages in the media. As a result of their higher credibility, market-based media are better able to appease protesters, even when press restrictions are enforced (Stockmann 2010a). Again, infrastructures remain key in allowing the Chinese state to strike this delicate balance; the institutional capacity to control information flows when necessary remains at the core of responsive authoritarianism in Chinese media.

The combination of these factors, some of them deriving from China's one-party rule and some of them perhaps credited to the skills of Party officials to adjust and pragmatically adapt to changing circumstances, suggest that market-based media are likely to continue to serve as an instrument for stabilizing CCP rule in the near future. The media will continue to put pressure on Chinese rulers to show responsiveness to popular pressures and possibly induce political change without political diversification.

Implications for Liberal Democracy

Since the end of the Qing dynasty, Chinese intellectuals and politicians have been engaged in a discussion about the extent to which "Western" ideas and theories apply and should be applied to the Chinese context. Throughout this book, I have shown that many theories and methods developed in different regions of the world help to understand Chinese media and public opinion. Here, I would like to shift my focus and raise the question of what lessons we can draw from China for liberal democracy.

Authoritarianism is not completely incompatible with liberal democracy. Gibson (2005) reminded us that authoritarian elements exist or have existed at the subnational level in many democracies. In federalist countries, some states have been dominated by one party, such as in the Free State of Bavaria in Germany or in the American South up until the middle of the 20th century. Other leading parties, such as the Liberal Democratic Party in Japan or the Nationalist Party in Taiwan before the 2000 presidential elections, have managed to govern the country for an extensive period of time. This book suggests that the political context matters for the relationship between citizens and the state in these countries and regions.

Nongovernmental organizations that monitor press freedom, such as Freedom House, Reporters without Borders, IREX, or the African Media Barometer, only provide limited insight into party patronage networks or formal institutions that may tie media to hegemonic parties. Clearly, under rule of law, the hands of political actors in liberal democracies are more strongly restricted than in most authoritarian countries. Nevertheless, there is some initial evidence that hegemonic parties may resort to similar means in their attempt to control information flows.

In Japan, a press club system promotes the ability of the Liberal Democratic Party and bureaucrats under its leadership to influence what and how the media report about politics. In these information cartels, journalists do not blindly follow the dictates or wishes of state sources, but the system for gathering and reporting the news frequently leads them to support state goals, according to Freeman (2000). Of course nonmainstream media as well as books and magazines contribute great diversity to Japanese media, but Japan scholars have noted a relationship between infrastructures and limits on diversity of information flows. As noted by Krauss (1996: 358), "What may be distinctive about Japan is not that nonpluralist and controlled elements exist, but rather that in Japan the institutions of newspaper and broadcast journalism, business, and the state connect in such a way that their information processes have often wound up limiting the pluralism and autonomy that the formal structures should provide."

In Italy, former prime minister Silvio Berlusconi and his coalition allies broke with previous practices in which each of the major parties had a share in appointments of directors and overseers of the main public broadcaster Radiotelevisione Italiana. Already a powerful player in commercial broadcasting when elected, Berlusconi managed to dominate both public and private television broadcasting by adopting majoritarian winner-takes-all policies (Marletti and Roncarolo 2000). As news content on public television shifted to the right after the 2001 elections, Italian viewers responded by modifying their choice of news programs, similarly to Chinese reactions to press restrictions imposed during the 2005 anti-Japanese protests. Right-leaning viewers increased their propensity to watch public channels, and left-wing viewers switched to another public channel that was controlled by the left. In line with these shifts in media consumption, Durante and Knight (2009) also found evidence of an increase in trust in public television among right-wing viewers and a corresponding decrease among left-wing viewers.

These examples bare striking similarities with the relationship between the state, media, and citizens in China. Even in liberal democracy, politicians can and do rely on formal and informal infrastructures to mange media content to their advantage. If one political player dominates these infrastructures, such a situation shapes information flows and reactions among media citizens. If so, may an understanding of China also teach us insights about liberal democracy?

Appendix A

Notes on Data and Research Design

To study the consequences of media marketization in China, I used diverse research methods to capture the degree of media marketization, the production of news, and media credibility. A focused study of newspapers in Beijing and Chongqing based on open-ended interviews with media practitioners and content analysis uncovered patterns of political control over newspaper content. Survey questions were added to the Beijing Area Studies of Beijing Residents (BAS 2004) survey and the survey of Labor Law Mobilization (LLM 2005). Analyses of these survey data reveal the relationship between media exposure and attitudes and provide opportunity for cross-regional comparisons. Experiments provide further insights into causal relationships. Additional information on the collection of these data and the broader research design follow.

In-Depth Interviews

During fieldwork, I spent extensive time in Beijing and Chongqing, conducting in-depth semi-structured interviews with forty-six editors, journalists, media researchers, and officials within the propaganda *xitong*.[1] Originally, my goal was to rely on both subjective and objective measures to assess media marketization, but soon I discovered that the objective data available on advertising income provided by newspapers were unreliable. Newspapers reported higher advertising income to official state units to create an image of being successful. I therefore decided to primarily rely on subjective indicators, which also led to the discovery of media practitioners' categorizations of newspapers into different types. Because media practitioners collapse deregulation, commercialization, and partial privatization into one dimension when discussing newspaper types, this places limitations on my ability to distinguish the influence of these three elements separate from one another. When using official data to compare across cities and regions, I rely on advertising income reported by advertising

---

[1] *Xitongs* are groupings within the bureaucracy that together deal with a policy area.

companies as these have less incentives to overreport their income due to tax policies.[2]

My conversations took place between August 2004 and August 2005; they were updated during annual fieldwork trips. To reduce selection bias, I relied on a total of eighteen initial contacts, including one Internet website that reporters use to chat about work-related issues. The response rate was 96 percent. Interviews were conducted in Mandarin at a location of the person's own choice to make sure that he or she felt comfortable to talk to me openly. Locations included restaurants, cafes, offices, and the person's own living rooms. Interview questions are included in the Online Appendix at www.daniestockmann.net.

Content Analysis

In addition, I also systematically sampled and analyzed newspaper content that corresponded to the issues covered in the two public opinion surveys. To improve reliablity and comparability of newspaper content, I used Yoshikoder, which is, to my knowledge, the only content analysis software that can handle Chinese characters. Because news reporting about the United States in 2005 was about ten times more frequent than that about the National Labor Law, I sampled the whole population of news reports on labor law, but used constructed-week random sampling to derive at a representative content analysis data set for news reporting on the United States. According to this technique, all weeks during a period of time of interest to the researcher are numbered, and subsequently one Monday, Tuesday, and so on is randomly selected until one or several weeks are constructed (Stempel 1952; Lacy et al. 2001). Because the number of sampled constructed weeks depends on the variance in the variable of interest, I relied on the Maryland Study, an existing oversampled content analysis data set on Chinese newspaper reporting on the United States, to learn that ten constructed weeks retrieve representative and efficient results for about one year of news reporting about the United States. Detailed findings have been published in Stockmann (2010b), along with a discussion of the strength and weaknesses of using electronic sources to collect Chinese media sources, constructed week sampling, and computer-aided text analysis for improving our understanding of Chinese politics.

In this book, I address potential selection bias due to sampling from newspaper websites by transforming print articles in the *Chongqing Daily* into electronic format and using electronic CD collections of newspaper reporting published by the *Beijing Daily* News Group. Measurement of the dictionaries used in computer-aided text analysis was developed based on extensive qualitative reading of the texts and repeated pretesting. The resulting data sets covered more than 2,000 articles and are available at www.daniestockmann.net for

---

[2] Media are classified as public institutions (*shiye danwei*) and are therefore often eligible for tax exemptions according to Chinese tax law.

further investigation, along with a detailed memo on problems and solutions during data collection.

Although the preceding procedures improved the representativeness or *external validity* of the data, one potential problem of relying on statistical analysis is that it demonstrates correlation but not causation between independent and dependent variables. The technique is thus low in terms of *internal validity*.

One way to reveal causal relationships between variables of interest is to examine their development over time: any change in the independent variable (degree of media marketization) should result in a corresponding change in the dependent variable (tone in news reporting). Because commercialized newspapers emerged in Chinese newspaper markets in approximately 2001, I decided to compare news reporting two years before and after this date. The more recent year, 2003, was relatively close to the carrying out of the surveys. This comparison between two points in time is limited to content analysis of the United States because of the availability of public opinion survey data to detect audience demands.

Because the resulting data set only includes two years, our ability to draw definite conclusions about changes in the production over time is limited, but the most important alternative explanations, the impact of events and instructions by propaganda officials, do *not* apply (Stockmann 2011c). Therefore, it is reasonable to conclude that the drop in the tone of news reporting on the United States in Chinese newspapers is primarily driven by media marketization and competition between newspapers.

To further separate the effects of media marketization from PD instructions, I also observed how news reporting changes once instructions change. Case studies show that newspapers cater to demands of readers when restrictions are lifted, but impose self-censorship once receiving instructions. A cross-country comparison of thirty-eight authoritarian states at different stages of media marketization between 2001 and 2009 demonstrates that these findings are not specific to China or specific cities within China. Depending on the political context of China's regional media environments and of one-party rule, media marketization affects regime stability differently.

Surveys and Experiments

A major hurdle for studying communication and public opinion in nondemocratic contexts has been that survey data are considered to be biased and of poor quality, as citizens may be afraid to report their true opinions, state institutions exert restrictions on public opinion polling, and researchers lack the funding and adequate training to conduct surveys. In China, the government has become more tolerant of survey work over time. Today, the state itself finances public opinion polls to get ideas about the content of people's opinions. Market research has become a lucrative business. This supposedly lowered response rates among urban citizens who are frequently contacted to give their opinion on consumer products. However, despite the frequent carrying out of surveys, there still remain major problems for surveys in China.

Survey research in China has been subject to official sensibilities about what constitutes politically sensitive questions. In addition, any survey research in an authoritarian context ought to take into account the possibility of social desirability bias, whereby respondents may either give incorrect responses or choose the nonresponse category when a question is politically sensitive. To address these problems, I explicitly decided to focus on nonsensitive but politically relevant issues for this study.[3] This does not negatively affect the research design of this study. Any changes that occurred as a result of media marketization should become most evident in the open realm. If political messages are relatively uniform even if journalists feel unconstrained, this constitutes a "most difficult" test of the hypothesis that media marketization brings about diversity in news content.

Another key issue is survey sampling. Although most polling institutes claim to randomly select participants, critical follow-up questions often reveal that randomness is interpreted loosely, ranging from coincidental selection of pedestrians in the street to knocking at the neighbor's door if the sampled interviewee is not at home. The conductors of the two surveys used in this study, the Research Center for Contemporary China (RCCC), employ high standards for rigorous social science research in their work. The BAS was modeled after the Detroit Area Studies and strictly sampled according to probability proportional to size (PPS), a form of stratified random sampling. The LLM employed the global positioning system (GPS) sampling technique and was one of the first surveys conducted in China that included migrant workers, a large social group normally excluded when sampling is done based on lists of registered households, as in the BAS. Interviews were conducted face-to-face by trained interviewers and resulted in data that are representative of their sampling population. The LLM response rate in the city of Chongqing was 73 percent (n=1,019), in Foshan 72 percent (n=1,029), in Wuxi 73 percent (n=1,029), and in Shenyang 72 percent (n=1,035). The BAS response rate was 56.1 (n=617).

Statistical testing of these survey data is an appropriate method to examine the relationship between readers and media outlets at the individual level. If sampling techniques and statistical analysis are properly employed, the results of the statistical analysis are representative of the sampling population. This external validity of the survey method allows for a general assessment of the link between media marketization of newspapers, readership habits, and opinions.

However, as explained earlier, a problem of relying on statistical analysis is that it demonstrates correlation but not causation between independent and dependent variables. To increase internal validity, I followed two paths. First, I combined the survey method with a quasi-experimental study. A quasi-experiment is a research design that uses natural treatment groups

[3] Public opinion polls are also conducted on evaluations of political leaders and governmental institutions, but these surveys are conducted and analyzed for internal review of Party and state units only.

without random assignment (see, for example, Cook and Campbell 1979). In this research, I employ a time-series experimental design, whereby similar but different participants are observed over time. At some point in the series of observations, a treatment is introduced. One advantage of a natural experiment is that the setting and treatment are not artificially imposed on participants. Chapters 8 and 9 apply this quasi-experimental design to increase internal validity.

Second, I rely on a field experiment with ordinary Beijingers to disentangle the effect of a news story's frame from its label. Originally, I intended to include the experimental vignettes laid out in Appendix C in one of the surveys. Because experimental vignettes had not been used in survey research in China, this original plan was not realized during my fieldwork in 2004/5. Instead, I decided to conduct the experiment with visitors at a popular park during another trip to Beijing in 2009. As explained in more detail in Appendix C, I trained Chinese students in approaching potential participants and asking them to respond to only two questions, either directly (the control group) or after first reading one of four possible vignettes (the treatments). Participation in control and treatment groups was randomly assigned among every sixth person, whereby two of the six participants were assigned to the control group. As a result, the people participating in the experiment were nonrandomly selected, but differences among respondents in the treatment and control groups were randomized. If respondents make different choices under these conditions, the most likely causal source of the choices is the attribute that is manipulated by the vignette (Gibson and Gows 2003). In addition to providing us with an opportunity to draw conclusions about the importance of framing versus the newspaper's label, results from this experiment also increase the internal validity of the investigation of media effects on attitudes toward labor law.

On a final note, most evidence of the relationship between audiences and media outlets is based on cross-sectional data. Because of the absence of suitable time-series survey data, I could not observe how changes in media marketization affected media credibility, consumption, and persuasion over time. Instead, I draw conclusions about these relationships by investigating differences in types of newspapers at one point in time. However, media practitioners regard official papers as relics of previous stages of media marketization. Therefore, it is reasonable to assume that the relationship between citizens and official papers used to be similar before the rise of nonofficial papers. Furthermore, a comparison between Chinese regions and across authoritarian states shows that media marketization is positively correlated with media credibility, thus further supporting this assumption. These data also provided the opportunity to further test the generalizability of my research findings, as explained in more detail in Appendix B in this book.

Appendix B

Notes on Case Selection and Generalizability

This book compares newspaper reporting on two issues in five Chinese cities. Its focus on newspapers allows me to hold other features of the medium constant. Audiences interact differently when reading print versus electronic media. These different relationships can explain why a person selects a media source, how it is selected, and why he or she is influenced by it. We can control for these alternative explanations by comparing newspapers with each other.

Because the Chinese newspaper market remains strongly fragmented and localized by cities, I started out with an in-depth study of newspaper markets in two cities, Beijing and Chongqing. To address problems associated with the correlation between issues and cities in terms of the survey data – survey questions on labor law were only asked in Chongqing, and survey questions related to the United States were only asked in Beijing – I complemented my research findings with additional data from Wuxi in Jiangsu, Foshan in Guangdong, and Shenyang in Liaoning province after I returned from my fieldwork. The results strengthen the conclusion that differences observed concerning media effects based on LLM and BAS data in Chapters 8 and 9 are driven by characteristics associated with the issue rather than differences in the level of media marketization between Beijing and Chongqing. Next I explain in more detail the rationale for choosing these two cities as the main sites for the fieldwork and for drawing general conclusions about China as a whole.

When I headed to China to conduct fieldwork, my choice of research sites was limited to the cities in which the LLM and BAS were going to be conducted, as I had opportunities to collaborate with these ongoing projects. Among the cities in the LLM, I selected Chongqing as the second site because this municipality has province-level status, just like Beijing. Administrative status is important because the central government must go through the administrative hierarchy when it tries to influence news content at the local level. Because Beijing and Chongqing both have the same administrative rank, their status within the state bureaucracy can be excluded as an alternative explanation of the research findings.

At the same time, a key difference between Beijing and Chongqing turned out to be an advantage for the purpose of this study. According to the *China Advertising Yearbook*, Beijing's advertising industry came in second (after Shanghai) and Chongqing's came in eleventh in terms of its advertising income in 2005, with Beijing earning about 9.3 times more than Chongqing.[1] With advertising income being closer to average levels, Chongqing's structure of the newspaper market is similar to an average Chinese city. In contrast, Beijing is on the frontline of media marketization, with structures similar to Shanghai and Guangdong, although Foshan is exceptional in terms of people's susceptibility to newspapers, a point I will return to later.

One potential problem of the research design laid out so far is the correlation between issues and cities: survey data from the LLM and BAS do not allow for comparison of the relationship between newspapers and audiences on both of these issues in Chongqing as well as Beijing. To address this problem, I extended the statistical analysis on media consumption and persuasion to all four cities contained in the LLM after I returned from my fieldwork. I was able to replicate key results in Wuxi, Shenyang, and Foshan after I discovered that the categorization of newspaper types by media practitioners in Beijing and Chongqing was strongly correlated with the year in which a newspaper was founded. I also checked my coding based on categorization of newspapers types with the help of Chinese students from these cities at the University of Michigan. This enabled me to differentiate between official and nonofficial papers in three more cities. Comparison across cities based on the LLM data allowed me to disentangle the effects of the issue from those of media marketization.

The problem of correlation between issues and cities is most worrisome with respect to the analysis of media effects in Chapter 9. The results of content analysis in Chapters 4 and 5 are consistent across issue areas and cities: official papers tend to report about both issues in a slightly more positive way than nonofficial papers, but political content tends to be relatively uniform across newspapers. The PD opens up space for news reporting when market mechanisms pull newspapers in the desired direction and it imposes restrictions when reader demands potentially undermine the goals of the central government. This is true when comparing across issue areas and topics within individual issue areas. Similarly, analysis of media consumption in Chapter 8 shows that the same factors that drive the selection of official papers in Beijing also play a key role in Chongqing, Shenyang, Wuxi, and Foshan, where citizens were asked about labor law. Only Chapter 9 detects significant differences between LLM and BAS data in terms of readers' susceptibility to nonofficial papers.

To decide whether the nature of the issue or the characteristics associated with the city is driving these differences, I replicated the relationships observed in Chongqing in the other cities contained in the LLM. Statistical results presented in Chapter 9 confirm that the linear relationship between attention and attitudes observed in Chongqing also apply to Wuxi, Shenyang, and Foshan.

---

[1] Detailed advertising income per region is shown in Table 8OA.1 in the Online Appendix.

Evidence for a nonlinear relationship between attention and attitudes is only found in Beijing. These results strengthen the conclusion that the comparatively higher resistance at high levels of attention observed in Beijing is driven by the nature of the issue.

In addition to helping to address the problem of correlation between issues and cities, complementing the findings from Chongqing and Beijing with data from Foshan, Shenyang, and Wuxi also facilitated generalizability. Readership and susceptibility to newspapers increase as advertising income of local newspapers increases. In Chapter 8, respondents are more likely to read official papers as the city's advertising income increases. The level of economic development, administrative rank, population size, and region do not align with this pattern. Similarly, in Chapter 9, readers in Wuxi tend to be more susceptible to positive news stories about labor law, followed by Shenyang and Chongqing. Only Foshan does not follow this pattern. Readers in Foshan tend to be as susceptible as readers in Chongqing, pointing to Guangdong's exceptional situation in the Chinese media landscape. However, a cross-regional comparison in Chapter 10 further confirmed that higher levels of advertising income are usually associated with greater media credibility.

This interpretation is further supported by the media and authoritarianism data set I collected to test whether China is significantly different from other authoritarian states. As a result of the lack of suitable data on media and public opinion in authoritarian states, my choice of cases was limited by the availability of existing data. The final data set included a total of 130 cases in 38 countries observed at different stages of media marketization between 2001 and 2009. The results replicate key findings from China. They reinforce the conclusion that China's management of media is more typical of one-party rule than commonly assumed and that political context is key in promoting regime stability by means of marketized media.

Appendix C

Experimental Treatments

The National Labor Law experiment presented in Chapter 7 was conducted in December 2009. Interviewers approached a total of 231 people, and among those, 138 people volunteered to participate. Participants were asked to answer two questions related to Beijingers' opinions. Assignment into treatment and control groups was random among every six participants, whereby two of the six were assigned to the control group. Table AC.1. indicates the distribution of the different experimental conditions among the interviewers. Interviews were conducted by five female Chinese university students.

Survey Question (asked in all conditions):

Source: LLM, 2005.

您有没有听说过《劳动法》?

总的看来, 您认为《劳动法》的贯彻执行对劳动者权利的保护是非常、比较、不太还是完全无效?

"Have you heard about the [National] Labor Law?" If yes, respondent was asked: "In general, is the implementation of the [National] Labor Law very effective, somewhat effective, not so effective, or not at all effective in protecting workers' rights?" The variable was coded 1 if the respondent had heard about the National Labor Law and thought it was somewhat or very effective; otherwise it was coded 0. Thirteen of the 138 participants had never heard about the National Labor Law and were therefore not asked the second question. Among those, four were sampled in the control group and nine in treatment groups.

Official frame:

"据(北京晚报/北京日报), 王村煤矿欠郑平均等20人劳动报酬3万多元。眼看春节将至, 民工们想回家过节, 多次向煤矿索要所欠工资, 煤矿以无钱为由拒绝给付, 民工们万般无奈之下诉至北京市门头沟法院, 要求王村煤矿给付所欠劳动报酬。

TABLE AC.1. *Distribution of Control and Treatment Conditions among Interviewers.*

Interviewer	Control	Treatment 1	Treatment 2	Treatment 3	Treatment 4	n
1	14	7	7	7	7	42
2	8	4	4	4	4	24
3	8	4	4	4	4	24
4	8	4	4	4	4	24
5	8	4	4	4	4	24
n	46	23	23	23	23	138

事关民工的切身利益, 门头沟法院对此案非常重视, 迅速立案, 并根据原告的申请, 缓收了案件受理费。在法官们的努力下, 此案得以调解结案, 民工们在结案当天便领到了部分劳动报酬, 有了回家过年的路费。

据统计, 自1995年我国劳动法实施以来, 全国法院共受理各类劳动纠纷案件425726件。这些纠纷的合法、及时和妥善处理, 有力地保护了广大员工的合法权益, 各级法院依法引导和规范了改革过程中纷繁复杂的新型劳动关系, 及时化解了企业改革和发展中出现的矛盾和问题。"

"According to *Beijing Evening News/Beijing Daily*, Wang Village Coal Mine owed Zheng Pingjun and others, a group of 20 people, wages of more than 30,000 Yuan. Approaching the Spring Festival, the migrant workers wanted to visit home and asked several times for their wages, but the coal mine refused due to lack of money. The migrants had no alternative but to go to Beijing city court, demanding to be compensated for their work.

To the benefit of the workers, the court took their case very seriously, speeded up the process, and waived the application fee. Due to the hard work of the judges, the case was resolved through mediation. The migrants received partial compensation on the same day, and they had enough money to travel home for New Year.

According to statistics, since my country's [National] Labor Law was passed in 1995, the number of accepted cases in the whole nation was 425,726. These disputes' rightful, timely, and proper application were beneficial to protecting the legitimate rights of the large working population. The court guided and shaped the complicated labor relations during the reform process, as well as solved the problems and contradictions arising during the reform and development of enterprises."

Original source: People's Daily, March 21, 2002. "为了员工的合法权益: 人民法院积极处理劳动纠纷案件纪实"; http://www.people.com.cn/GB/paper464/5760/582877.html

Length: 315 characters.

Tone: +3 (assessed relying on LLCATA measure of tone; see Appendix D for details).

Commercialized Frame:

"据(北京晚报/北京日报), 刘定伟、李德敏、陈潜、李庆参等19人均系四川省南充市嘉陵区的农民。2005年7月22日至12月1日在成都某通信有限公司承建的某网络优化网工地务工, 该工程承包方是成都某通信公司。在施工过程中, 该通信公司将上述工程承包给自然人邹某, 邹某接到工程后, 遂请刘定伟等19人负责建设施工, 工作时间及工资标准由邹某决定, 工作过程中邹某只给这些农民工发过一些生活费, 每个农民工均不同程度地被拖欠工资, 经统计这19名农民工共被拖欠工资26050元。

刘定伟等人曾多次向何某、邹某追索未果, 于2007年2月12日到省法律援助中心申请法律援助。工作站刘红、邓冰二位律师及工作人员杜伟数次前往通信公司, 与其进行积极协调、沟通, 最终于日前达成协议, 由通信公司支付劳动报酬23000元。"

"According to *Beijing Evening News/Beijing Daily*, Liu Dingwei, Li Demin, and Chen Qian belong to a group of nineteen farmers in the city of Nanchong city Xi dictrict in Sichuan province. Between July and December 2005, they worked at a construction site of TongXin Company in Chengdu. Throughout the process, the company outsourced to Mr. Zou. After arriving at the construction site, Mr. Zou asked Liu Dingwei and the other eighteen to hurry up. Working hours and wages were decided by Mr. Zou. While working at the site, Mr. Zou only gave these migrant workers a small sum to pay for living expenses. Each migrant's wages were delayed to a different extent. In total, wages in the amount of 26,050 Yuan were not paid.

Liu Dingwei and the others asked several times for their wages, but without any result, although Mr. Zou said he would inquire about the reasons for the delay. In February, the workers asked the provincial legal aid center for help. Together with two lawyers and staff, they contacted TongXin Company and, after positive coordination and communication, eventually received compensation of 23,000 Yuan."

Original source: Chengdu Evening News, September 18, 2007. "免费为民工维权 律师不必白干了"; http://cdwb.newssc.org/system/2007/09/18/010483069.shtml

Length: 328 characters.

Tone: +1 (assessed relying on LLCATA measure of tone; see Appendix D for details).

Appendix D

Data Coding, Statistical Models, and Robustness Test Results

Computer-Aided Text Analysis (CATA)

Content analysis is often criticized for vagueness of categorization, especially so far as the tone of content is concerned. To clarify measurement and ensure consistency, I relied on Yoshikoder, which is, according to my knowledge, the only content analysis software program that can recognize Chinese characters. Dictionaries for content analysis were carefully pretested and improved based on qualitative reading of the text, as discussed in detail in the USCATA data documentation available at www.daniestockmann.net. Measurement validity tests are discussed in the second half of Appendix D. For a detailed explanation of the advantages and disadvantages of Yoshikoder and CATA, as well as measurement, see Stockmann (2010b). Dictionaries with lists of keywords are available at www.daniestockmann.net.

Labor Law Computer-Aided Text Analysis (LLCATA), 2005

Newspaper Selection: Chongqing Daily, Chongqing Times, and *People's Daily.* Based on the following criteria: (1) categorization of newspapers by media practitioners in Chapter 2; (2) readership size based on LLM and CTR market research data (see Online Appendix); (3) availability of electronic search engines. Articles in *Chongqing Daily* were transcribed from hardcopy into electronic format.

Time Period: January 1, 2005 – April 26, 2005 (four months prior to the end of LLM).

Sampling: All articles mentioning "[National] Labor Law" (*laodongfa*) or "labor contract" (*laodong hetong*). To increase the number of articles in *Chongqing Daily*, additional keywords included "labor dispute" (*laodong jiufen*) and "Law for Protection of Work Related Injury" (*zhiyebing fangzhifa*).

Measuring Tone: The number of negative words was subtracted from the number of positive words within a semantic space of eight words before and after keywords for a concept of interest. Because the number of matching synonyms for each concept affects the number of negative and positive words found in the text, I divided the resulting number by the number of times a concept of interest was mentioned. Slightly changing the size of the semantic space does not significantly change the results.

Measuring Sensitivity: Dummy variable indicating whether the article mentioned a slightly, medium, or highly sensitive keyword.

United States Computer-Aided Text Analysis (USCATA), 2001–2003

Newspaper Selection: People's Daily, Beijing Evening News. Criteria for selection were the same as in the case of LLCATA.

Time Period: Ten constructed weeks in 1999 and ten constructed weeks in 2003.

Sampling: All articles mentioning the term "United States" (*Meiguo*) at least twice. For more details on constructed week sampling and proof of representativeness for one year of news reporting on the United States, see Stockmann (2010b).

Measuring Tone: I examined the number of negative and positive words within a semantic space of eight words before and after keywords representing "United States." The number of negative words was subtracted from the number of positive words. To facilitate interpretation of the results, tone was not normalized, as the length of the article was controlled for in the regression analysis.

Measuring the People's Daily: Dummy variable coded 1 for the *People's Daily* and 0 for the *Beijing Evening News.*

Measuring Year: Dummy variable coded 1 for 2003 and 0 for 1999.

Measuring Political Leader: Dummy variable for mentioning a Chinese, American, or international leader.

Measuring Politics: Number of times Chinese, American, international leaders, or political institutions were mentioned. Logged and recoded to run from 0 to 1. Figures 5.3a and 5.3b display references to keywords, not the coding of the variable politics in Table 5.2.

Measuring Article on China and the United States: Dummy variable for mentioning China.

Measuring Issue Sensitivity: Articles that mentioned a highly sensitive keyword were coded as 3, those with a medium sensitive keyword as 2, and those with somewhat sensitive keywords as 1; 0 indicates that none of the keywords were mentioned. For OLS regression analysis, the variable was recoded to run from 0 to 1.

Measuring Sensitivity Over Time: Proportion of Xinhua articles in the newspaper on the same day. For a discussion of measurement validity, see
Stockmann (2010b).

Measuring Length: Total number of words in the article, recoded to run
from 0 to 1.

Measuring Xinhua: Dummy variable for reprinted Xinhua report.

Survey Data and Question Wording

Survey nonresponses ("don't know" and "no answer") were deleted from the
analysis. To facilitate interpretation, all independent variables were recoded to
run from 0 to 1.

Survey of Labor Law Mobilization (LLM), 2005

Effectiveness: "Have you heard about the [National] Labor Law?" If yes,
respondent was asked: "In general, is the implementation of the [National]
Labor Law very effective, somewhat effective, not so effective, or not at
all effective in protecting workers' rights?" For ordinal probit regression,
the variable was coded from 1 to 4 such that higher numbers represent
perceiving the Labor Law to be more effective. A total of 910 respondents
were excluded from the analysis (see Chapter 2, footnote 33). For probit
regression, the variable was coded 1 if the respondent had heard about
the National Labor Law and thought it was somewhat or very effective,
otherwise it was coded 0.

Willingness to Take Action: "Old Chen works at a company; his labor
contract ends in 5 years. After 3 and a half years, the company was not
performing very well and dismissed Old Chen without severance pay. Do
you think the company's action was legal?" If the respondent answered
illegal, she was asked "If you were Old Chen, what would you do? Would
you take action to resolve the dispute or would you do nothing?" If yes,
"Would you use mediation/arbitration/litigation to solve the problem?"

Newspaper/TV/Internet/Radio Use/Alternative Media Exposure: "How frequently do you (read/watch/listen) (newspapers/magazines/television/radio
broadcasting/Internet) to understand the news about society and life –
Often, sometimes, or never?" If a respondent indicated consuming media
sources frequently, she was asked which two newspapers/magazines/TV
channels/radio channels/websites she used. Up to two media sources
were reported. Dummy variables were created for individual newspapers,
which roughly match the readership percentages reported by CTR market research data (see Online Appendix). Dummy variables for official
paper use and nonofficial paper use were created based on media practitioners' categorization of newspapers, correlating with the newspaper's
founding year. Based on information about the sponsoring institution and

the founding year, newspaper types were estimated for Shenyang, Wuxi, and Foshan (see Appendix B).

Attention: Scale based on knowledge questions (correct answers in parentheses): (1) "Old Chen works at a company; his labor contracts end in five years. After three and a half years, the company was not performing very well and dismissed Old Chen without severance pay. Do you think the company's action was legal?" If the respondent answered "illegal:" "Why was it not legal? – "I have a feeling that it's illegal, but cannot tell the specific reason," "It's illegal, because the company cannot determine the contract ahead of time," "It's illegal, because the company can determine the contract ahead of time, but has to pay severance pay (true)." (2) "Imagine a work unit that often asks workers to work on holidays. The payment is the same as normal wages. What do you think about this remuneration? – "The work unit's behavior is legal, there is nobody to blame"; "The work unit's behavior is legal, but unfair"; "The work unit's behavior is illegal, but having some remuneration is better than having none"; "The work unit's behavior is illegal, it should pay 150 percent of regular wages as overtime bonus (true)." (3) "Based on your knowledge, how many hours per day/month are the maximum hours for an employee's work as stipulated by the Labor Law?" (8 hours). (4) "What is the standard for this city's minimum wage?" (coded right if the respondent's answer is within 1.5 standard deviations below and 0.5 standard deviations above the actual minimum wage range). (5) "According to your understanding, how long is the period in which a labor dispute can be brought forward?" (60 days). (6) "During arbitration, if one side is dissatisfied with the results of the arbitration, can he go to court?" (yes).

Cadre/Party or State Unit: Dummy variables based on profession.

Disputant: "Within the past 10 years, have you ever encountered a labor-related problem about the following issues? A labor-relations problem is a problem whereby the employer and employee disagree about a labor contract, working hours, income, work-related injury, wages, social security, or traineeship." "Has the issue about, for example, labor contract, working hours, income, work-related injury, wages, social security, or traineeship ever become a labor dispute because the problem could not be resolved?" Dummy variable coded 1 if labor-relations problem developed into a labor dispute.

Propaganda: "Have you now or some time in the past heard about the [National] Labor Law through propaganda at the work unit?" Dummy variable.

Union Participation: "Are you or have you been a member of a trade union?" If yes, "Have you resolved any of the following problems through your work unit? – working conditions, implementing labor contracts, problems related to wages and benefits, solving problems with co-workers, solving problems with leaders of the work unit, other." Dummy variable.

Worker: "Which type of work have you done or are you currently doing at the work unit?" Dummy variable coded 1 if respondents selected "worker," "regular employee," or "other," specifying being a worker.

SOE: "Which type of work unit are you currently working at/have you been working at in the past?" Dummy variable.

Urban Resident: "Do you currently have a residency permit for the non-countryside (city) or for the countryside?" Dummy variable for urban *hukou.*

Unemployed/Retired: "Do you have work?" If no, are you currently a laid-off SOE worker (*xiagang*), unemployed, on extended leave, early and involuntarily retired, or retired?" Dummy variable for being unemployed include the first two categories, and for being retired the last two categories.

Income: Based on self-reported income and estimated income group, a measure for the respondents' personal income level was developed (logged).

Education: Education levels were tapped by years of education (logged).

Age +39: Dummy variable based on age.

Male: Dummy variable.

Beijing Area Studies Survey of Beijing Residents (BAS), 2004

Positivity (Amity)/Feeling Thermometer/Negativity: "This is a card; on the front there is a thermometer scale. We use it to rate people's feelings toward countries. If you have a positive feeling for a country, you can indicate a value between 50 and 100. If you have a negative feeling for a country, you can indicate a value between 1 and 50. If you are somewhere in the middle, please select 50. Now let's see what your feeling is toward (country name); please select the value on the thermometer scale on the card." Variable *Negativity* was recoded into a 0 to 1 scale such that higher values represent colder feelings toward Japan or the United States.

Newspaper/Internet Use/Reading the News Online/Exposure to Official Messages: "Do you often (read newspapers/access news websites when surfing the Internet)?" If yes, "Which of these (newspaper/news website) do you (read/surf) frequently?" Respondents were provided with a card of the most popular newspapers or news websites. Respondents could also choose the answer category "other" and specify the name of a media source. Because empirical data were not available when the survey questions were developed, I chose these cases based on a list developed in consultation with local media practitioners and scholars. Because *Beijing Times* had only been founded recently at the time of the questionnaire development, it was not included on the card, leading to underestimated consumption rates. A detailed comparison of the BAS with CTR data is included in the Online Appendix. Coding of newspaper types was based on categorization by media practitioners as laid out in Chapter 2. Coding of exposure to official messages is explained in detail in Chapter 9. Low numbers reflect being, on average, exposed to commercialized messages and high numbers reflect being, on average, exposed to official messages.

Press Restrictions/Post-April 9 Interview/Official Events: Based on the date on which the interview was conducted. The press restrictions treatment was coded 0 before April 10, and 1 after April 9. The official events treatment was coded 0.5 during Lien's visit (April 27 to May 3), and 1 during Song's visit (May 4 to May 15).

Attention: "Do you pay attention to the news about the United States when reading newspapers, watching news on TV, or surfing the Internet? Do you pay much attention, little, so-so, not so much, or absolutely not?"

Cadre/Party or State Unit/Neighborhood Committee Worker: Dummy variables based on profession. Neighborhood committee worker was assessed if respondent was a social service worker (which included but was not limited to residential service), a woman, and earning below RMB 2000 per month.

Zero Political Confidence: "The Chinese central government and the local government are responsible for providing the public pension system, and enterprises are responsible for implementing the private pension system. We would like to learn about your level of confidence in these systems. Are you not very confident, not so confident, somewhat confident, or very confident in the central government, the local government, and private enterprises?" Low political confidence was coded as dummy variable, whereby 1 indicates respondents did not feel very confident in the local and the central government.

National Identity: Scale based on strong agreement, agreement, disagreement, strong disagreement with two statements: "I would prefer to be a citizen of China more than any other country in the world." "Generally speaking, China is a better country than most other countries." Higher values indicate a stronger national identity. Cronbach's alpha = 0.67.

Threat Perceptions of the United States/Japan: "Which factor(s) on this list is a threat that China might be facing at the moment? Please select a suitable degree on a scale of 5, whereby 1 indicates "no threat," and 5 "serious threat." – Taiwanese independence; the return of Japanese militarism; global economic decline; domestic social disorder; the strength of the US military; the strength of the European Union's military; other, such as crime, drugs, HIV-AIDS, pollution, etc."

Personal Contact/Travel to EU/US: "Have you traveled abroad?" If yes, "where?" "Are you in touch with Americans in daily life?" "Do you have frequent contact with Americans at work?" Based on three items mentioning the United States or Americans, I created, I created a scale for personal contact with Americans; higher values indicate more personal contact. Cronbach's alpha = 0.62. Dummy variable for travel to EU/US was coded 1 if respondent had traveled to the United States or Europe.

Exposure to Entertainment (Movie Liking): "Do you like to watch American movies? Do you like them very much, quite a lot, so-so, not so much, or not at all?"

Years Studying English/Having Studied Some English: "Have you studied English?" If yes, "how many years?" (logged). Having studied some English is a dummy variable for answering yes to the first question.

Years lived in Beijing: How many years have you lived in Beijing?

Retired: Are you currently working, studying, doing housework, unemployed, retired, or something else? Dummy variable.

Family Income/Personal Income: "How much was your whole 12-month family income during (past year)?" Based on self-reported family and personal income during the past year (logged).

Education: Education levels are tapped by total years of education (logged).

Age/Generation: Based on age. Generation was coded as a dummy variable for those born between 1951 and 1967 (21 years or younger during Sino-US rapprochement between 1972 and 1989).

Tension: During the spring of 2005, China went through a period of confrontation with Japan and tension in international relations. I created a dummy variable for interviews taking place after April 9, 2005 – the day the first anti-Japanese protest occurred in Beijing (38.09 percent of the sample).

Female: Dummy variable.

Cross-Regional and Cross-Country Comparison

China Regional Media Data, 2007

All independent variables were coded to run from 0 to 1 to facilitate interpretation.

Cases: All regions sampled in the World Values Survey (WVS) 2007 in China (n = 24).

Newspaper/ Television Credibility: Regional means of WVS 2007: "What is your degree of confidence toward the organizations below? – A great deal, quite a lot, not very much, none at all." Relevant answer categories included the press (*xinwen chubanye*), television (*dianshitai*), the central government (*zhongyang zhengfu*), political party/ies (*zhengdang*), and the National People's Congress (*renmin daibiao dahui*). Based on the last three items, I created a scale for political trust (Cornbach's alpha = 0.865). To assess media credibility, I subtracted the average level of political trust among respondents within a region from their average level of trust in the press or television. Coding is consistent with the Media and Authoritarianism Data and runs from −1 (media much less trustworthy) to +1 (media much more trustworthy). The minimum for regional averages of newspaper credibility was −0.33; the maximum +0.17; the mean +0.115. The minimum for regional averages of television credibility was −0.33; the maximum +0.18; the mean +0.117.

Media Marketization: Due to multicollinearity, I created an index between advertising income and percentage of Internet users as reported by the *China Advertising Yearbook* for 2008 and the China Internet Network Information Center for the end of 2007. The results remain stable when using each variable independently, as shown in the Online Appendix.

Ratio of Rural Population: Based on percentage of the population in villages and townships as reported in the *China Statistical Yearbook 2008*.

Ratio of Han Chinese: Based on 2000 census data.

Economic Development: Based on gross regional product per capita reported for 2007 in the *China Statistical Yearbook 2009* (logged).

Municipality/Autonomous Region: Dummy variables.

Media and Authoritarianism Data Set, 2001–2009

All independent variables were coded to run from 0 to 1 to facilitate interpretation. To explore the relationship between media marketization and diversity of information, independent and control variables were lagged by one year.

Cases: States were incorporated when receiving a Freedom House ranking of partially free or not free (+3 and above) and when included in IREX (n = 132). Countries include Armenia, Azerbaijan, Bahrain, Belarus, Burkina Faso, Burundi, Cameroon, Chad, Egypt, Ethiopia, Georgia, Guinea, Jordan, Kazakhstan, Kenya, Kuwait, Libya, Mauritania, Morocco, Mozambique, Oman, Qatar, Russia, Rwanda, Saudi Arabia, Sudan, Syria, Tajikistan, Tanzania, Togo, Tunisia, Uganda, Ukraine, United Arab Emirates, Uzbekistan, Yemen, Zambia, Zimbabwe.

Diversity of Information: Runs from 0 to 4, whereby low values present low diversity and high values high diversity, defined as "state or public media reflect the views of the political spectrum, are nonpartisan, and serve the public interest." Because IREX does not provide results for expert scores on individual indicators, I estimated whether the results were below or above average based on the description of the results in the IREX reports. For example, in 2006, Botswana received a plurality score of 2.53, but the report states that "panelists felt that a broad spectrum of social interests is not reflected in the media, and therefore it scored that indicator roughly three-quarters of a point lower than the average." Accordingly, I recoded the variable for diversity of political information as 1.78. For more details, see: http://www.Irex.org/resource/media-sustainability-index-msi-methodology, accessed January 12, 2012.

Media Credibility: Based on country mean of WVS waves 2000 and 2005: "What is your degree of confidence toward the organizations below? – A great deal, quite a lot, not very much, none at all. Relevant answer categories included the press, television channels, government, political parties, and parliament/legislature. Coding is consistent with the China Regional Media Data and runs from −1 (media much less trustworthy) to +1 (media much more trustworthy).

Media Marketization: Based on IREX local expert ratings of how well the country fulfilled seven indicators: media outlets and supporting firms operate as efficient, professional, and profit-generating businesses; media receive revenue from a multitude of sources; advertising agencies and related industries support an advertising market; advertising revenue as a percentage of total revenue is in line with accepted standards at commercial outlets; independent media do not receive government subsidies; market research is used to formulate strategic plans, enhance advertising revenue, and tailor products to the needs and interests of audiences; broadcast ratings and circulation figures are reliably and independently produced. Higher values indicate higher levels of media marketization.

One-Party Rule: Based on coding by Barbara Geddes and Jason Brownlee. For years not contained in these data sets, I checked whether the state had undergone transition since, using Geddes' coding for regime length. For a discussion of problems associated with this coding, see Brownlee (2007).

Level of Economic Development: Real gross domestic product per capita (Constant Prices: Chain series) based on the Penn World Tables version 6.2 (logged).

Oil Reserves: Same measure as Egorov et al. (2009) based on oil reserves in billion barrels (logged); collected from the Statistical Review of World Energy at www.bp.com, accessed January 12, 2012.

Regime Length: Runs from 8–59 years. Following Geddes' approach: the end of an authoritarian regime comes about when (1) the dictator and his supporters have been ousted from office, or (2) a negotiated transition results in "reasonably fair, competitive elections and a change in the party or individual occupying the executive office."

Freedom House Ranking: Runs from 3 to 7, whereby a higher score indicates *lower* political liberalization. Results do not significantly change when using Polity (see robustness test results).

Population: Based on World Development Indicators (logged).

Statistical Models for Chapters 8, 9, and 11

Estimating selection effects (Chapter 8)
  Basic Treatment Model without Interaction Terms (Equ.8.1):

$$Y = \beta_0 + \beta_1 X + \beta_2 Z + \beta_3 U + \beta_4 A + \beta_5 \text{Controls} + u$$

Whereby X represents a dummy variable for press restrictions; Z represents a categorical variable for official events; U indicates utility; A represents availability.
  Commitment Model with interaction term between credibility and commitment (Equ.8.2):

$$Y = \beta_0 + \beta_1 X + \beta_2 Z + \beta_3 XV + \beta_4 V + \beta_5 \text{Controls} + u$$

Whereby X represents a dummy variable for press restrictions; Z represents a categorical variable for official events; V stands for commitment about the issue on which dissonance is created, in this case, negativity toward Japan.
  Political Confidence Model with interaction term between utility and political confidence (Equ.8.3):

$$Y = \beta_0 + \beta_1 X + \beta_2 Z + \beta_3 ZW + \beta_4 W + \beta_5 \text{Controls} + u$$

Whereby X represents a dummy variable for press restrictions; Z represents a categorical variable for official events; W stands for zero political confidence.
  Official Paper Use Model (Equ.8.4):

$$Y = \beta_0 + \beta_1 U + \beta_2 A + \beta_3 \text{Controls} + u$$

Whereby U indicates utility; A represents availability.

Estimating Media Effects (Chapter 9)

Novel Issue Model with linear relationship between attention and attitudes (Equ.9.1):

$$Y = \beta_0 + \beta_1 X + \beta_2 Z + \beta_3 XZ + \beta_4 \text{Controls} + u$$

Whereby X represents a dummy variable for exposure to individual newspapers or newspaper types; Z stands for attention to the dependent variable Y, in this case the perceived effectiveness of the National Labor Law.
  Controversial Issue Model with nonlinear relationship between attention and attitudes (Equ.9.2):

$$Y = \beta_0 + \beta_1 X + \beta_2 Z + \beta_3 Z^2 + \beta_4 XZ + \beta_5 X^2 Z + \beta_6 \text{Controls} + u$$

Whereby X represents a dummy for exposure to individual newspapers or newspaper types, or a continuous variable for being, on average, exposed to official messages; Z stands for attention paid to the news about the dependent variable Y, in this case, positivity toward the United States.

Estimating Diversity of Information and Media Credibility (Chapter 11)

Diversity of Information Random Effects Model with time-invariant variables, allowing regime type and media marketization to interact (Equ.11.1):

$$Y_t = \beta_0 + \beta_1 X_{t-1} + \beta_2 Z_{t-1} + \beta_3 XZ_{t-1} + \beta_4 \text{Controls}_{t-1} + u$$

Whereby X represents a dummy variable for one-party rule; Z constitutes a continuous variable for media marketization; Y stands for diversity of information; and Year lay out yearly dummy variables for each year included in the cross-sectional time-series data.

Diversity of Information Fixed Effects Model by Regime Type whereby media marketization is regressed on diversity of information, once among all one-party regimes and once among all other regimes (Equ.11.2):

$$Y_t = \beta_0 + \beta_1 Z_{t-1} + \beta_2 \text{Controls}_{t-1} + \beta_3 \text{Year 2002} + \cdots$$
$$+ \beta_8 \text{Year 2009} + \beta_9 \text{Country}_1 + \cdots + \beta_n \text{Country}_n + u$$

Whereby Z constitutes media marketization; Y stands for diversity of information; Year lay out yearly dummy variables for each year (except 2006 since IREX collected one combined score for 2006 and 2007) and Country dummy variables for each country included in cross-sectional time-series data.

Media Credibility Model (Equ.11.3):

$$Y = \beta_0 + \beta_1 Z + \beta_2 \text{Controls} + u$$

Whereby Z indicates media marketization; Y stands for media credibility.

Robustness Test Results

Estimating Tone of News Reporting, Chapter 5

Measurement Error: The dictionary to assess the dependent variable, tone, is composed of a translation of the *General Inquirer* and a collection of colloquial terms used on the Internet. Its validity was pretested using a method to extract positivity/negativity from radicals in Chinese characters (Stone et al. 1966; Ku et al. 2005). Although a mainland version would be desirable, results from the Taiwanese version generally accurately match my own and Chinese native speakers' qualitative reading of mainland Chinese texts. CATA's assumption that co-occurrences of positive and negative words surrounding a keyword correspond to relationships of valence words to the keyword does sometimes lead to inaccurate measurement of tone in individual sentences. However, the average tone of the article picked up by the software program corresponds to my own and native speakers' qualitative reading of the text, even if the qualitative assessment of individual sentences occasionally differs. For further discussion see Stockmann (2010b).

To assess sensitivity, I rely on multiple measures: one was developed based on my qualitative interviews with media practitioners, suggesting that articles become more sensitive as they become more relevant to Chinese officials; the other is based on three lists of keywords frequently censored by website administrators. These lists differ in degree of sensitivity and contain terms referring to specific names and events associated with, for example, the 1989 student demonstrations, as well as general topics, including such terms as, for example, "human rights," "democracy," or "freedom." These two indicators are correlated with one another. In the case of LLCATA, articles mentioning Chinese officials also tended to mention sensitive keywords. In the case of USCATA, sensitivity increases as articles become more relevant to China or Chinese officials involved in foreign policy making.

When assessing the sensitivity of the topic based on the number of times names of Chinese central-level officials, the number of times Chinese political institutions, or the number of times China is mentioned in the text, correlation with tone of news reporting is positive and statistically significant. The coefficients are largest for references to Chinese leaders, followed by political institutions, and references to China. For detailed results, see Online Appendix.

Omitted Variable Bias: The results remain stable when adding control variables for the number of times the United States is referenced in the text, a dummy variable for the article referencing Xinhua, and the variable "issue sensitivity" based on sensitive keywords frequently censored by web administrators. When adding a dummy variable for Iraq, the results remain stable except that the dummy variable for 2003 becomes statistically significant due to the prevalence of reporting on Iraq in 2003. However, the dummy variable for Iraq is negatively correlated with tone and substantially and statistically significant. For detailed results, see Online Appendix. For further discussion, see Online Appendix to Stockmann (2011c).

Estimating Media Selection, Chapter 8

Measurement Error: People may not accurately report their habits of newspaper consumption, and their responses may differ when question wording changes. Yet readership rates are almost identical when comparing readership of individual newspapers in the BAS and LLM with data from CTR market research, despite different question wordings (see Online Appendix). For an in-depth discussion of measurement validity of self-reported newspaper use in China, see Stockmann (2009).

A second problem may be the coding of individual newspaper's degree of marketization. Coding was based on media practitioners' subjective categorization of newspapers. Critics may doubt that these evaluations accurately measure differences in the degree of marketization across papers. However, this critique is less worrisome for two reasons: First, I used this typology mainly to assess varying perceptions of newspapers that are closely related to different stages of media reform (media labels). Second, I also repeated the analysis based on objective indicators for individual newspapers, such as effective advertising income and investment, which I collected during my fieldwork. The results closely paralleled those reported in the figures and tables in this book. However, these objective measures are potentially unreliable because newspapers tend to overreport advertising income (see Appendix A).

Omitted Variable Bias: To test whether the regression results of newspaper use and official paper use suffered from omitted variables, I repeated the analysis with additional control variables. These included: positivity toward the United States/Japan/perceptions of effectiveness of the National Labor Law; attention paid to the news about the United States and the National Labor Law; having been socialized during the Cultural Revolution (ages 46–64); being interviewed in Haidian district (interviews in Haidian were delayed due to reasons unrelated to the anti-Japanese protests); being retired and therefore having less access to official papers; percentage of life spent in Beijing; having traveled to Europe or North America; exposure to other media types; whether the respondent had experienced a labor dispute; age; gender. Reporting test results across different combinations of these controls would fill numerous tables and figures. For economy of presentation, I present the results of the probit regression of some extended models in the Online Appendix. When including more control variables, the treatment effects remain substantially significant. The coefficients do not change much when additional variables are included in the model. Statistically significant coefficients stay statistically significant.

Estimating Media Effects on Perceived Effectiveness of the Labor Law, Chapter 9

Measurement Error: First, I repeated the analysis relying on alternative measures for the dependent variable – perceived effectiveness of the National Labor Law. Apart from a question about the effectiveness of the National Labor Law, the LLM included a vignette – a short story about a case in which an employee was dismissed without severance pay before the labor contract was terminated. Respondents were asked whether they thought the company's action was legal or illegal. If they perceived the action as illegal, they were asked whether they would take action and pursue a labor dispute or would do nothing. If a respondent indicated that she was willing to take action, she was asked whether she would use mediation, arbitration, or litigation. Based on these questions, I created two alternative measures of the dependent variable. The result is a dummy variable that was coded 1 if the respondent was willing to take action and 0 for everyone else. This variable assumes that a person who is willing to take action to solve a labor dispute also perceives the National Labor Law as effective. The results resembled the pattern displayed in Table 9A.1 in Appendix E. Further results are displayed in the Online Appendix.

In addition, I also relied on different measures for the main independent variables. Results do not differ much when measuring the use of individual newspapers. Statistical results for exposure to *Chongqing Daily* and *Chongqing Times* are shown in the Online Appendix.

Another concern is associated with the knowledge scale as a measure of attention in the Chinese context. Based on the BAS data, I found some indication that knowledge-based measurement of attention might not be as reliable as, for example, it is in the American context. However, in the LLM, the knowledge scale serves as an alternative indicator of news reception (see Stockmann, 2009, footnote 11, p. 154). I also repeated the analysis with an alternative indicator for news media reception about the National Labor Law. The LLM included a question that asked whether a person had heard about the National Labor Law. The coefficients worked in the anticipated direction: When respondents had heard about the National Labor Law and read nonofficial newspapers, they were more likely to take action; when respondents had heard about the National Labor Law and read official papers, they were less likely to take action.

Omitted Variable Bias: The most important alternative explanations of perceptions of the labor law are a person's personal experience with labor disputes, alternative sources of information, a person's social standing, and socialization in reference groups. To test whether the regression results were biased due to omitted variables, I repeated the analysis with additional control variables. These included the following: consumption of alternative media sources, including magazines, television, the Internet, and radio broadcasting; participation in a trade union[1]; employment in a state-owned enterprise (SOE); being unemployed or being retired; level of personal income; gender.

When including more control variables, the effects of newspaper consumption remain impressive. The coefficients do not change much when additional variables are included in the model, and the variance and standard errors decrease, thus increasing the statistical significance. The statistical results for a number of extended models are shown in the Online Appendix.

Estimating Media Effects on Views about the United States, Chapter 9

Measurement Error: As in the case of the labor law, I repeated the analysis relying on alternative measures for the dependent variable – attitudes toward the United States. Apart from a feeling thermometer, the BAS included a series of questions that asked respondents to rank an object on dimensions expressed by two adjectives expressing opposites (semantic differentials). Respondents were asked to rank the United States on four dimensions on a 7-point scale: being peaceful versus warlike, having a positive versus negative effect, being modest versus arrogant, and being sincere versus hypocritical. Similar questions were asked regarding Americans as a people. Based on these semantic differentials, I created a series of alternative measures for the dependent variable. First, I repeated the analysis with respect to each individual dimension, for both Americans as a people and the United States as a country. Second,

---

[1] Trade unions in China are not independent from the state and are charged with educating workers in the law and communicating Party policy. Formal membership is required in most enterprises that have a (legal) trade union. Because trade unions aim to transmit state policies, active participation in a trade union should be positively related to the perceived effectiveness of the labor law.

based on the respondents' rankings on the various dimensions, I created two scales, one for overall perceptions of Americans and one for overall perceptions of the United States. The results closely resembled the pattern displayed Figure 9.2. The results are shown in the Online Appendix.

Furthermore, I also created a series of variables intended to measure identity difference. In the BAS, respondents were asked to rank Chinese as a people and China as a country on the same dimensions as Americans and the United States. By subtracting each respondent's ranking of Chinese/China from Americans/United States, I created indicators for perceived differences between Chinese and Americans as well as China and the United States. Again, the results closely paralleled the pattern observed in Figure 9.2. The results are shown in the Online Appendix.

Finally, I also relied on different measures for the main independent variable, newspaper consumption. However, the results do not differ much when using different measures.[2] In addition to the measures used in the robustness testing in Chapter 8, I also employed an alternative measure for the scale for exposure to official messages. A potential problem of this scale is that it averages across newspaper types, weighting each newspaper equally. However, some newspapers devote more space to international news than others. I therefore accounted for these possibilities by creating an alternative indicator that assigned weights to newspapers depending on the number of pages devoted to international news. To count the pages, I picked a random date in 2005 or 2006. The nature of the relationships estimated based on the weighted measures closely paralleled Figure 9.2. Statistical results for exposure to *Beijing Youth Daily* and *People's Daily* are shown in the Online Appendix.

Omitted Variable Bias: The most important alternative explanations of perceptions of foreign countries are national identity, personal contact with foreigners, socialization in reference groups, and education. To test whether the regression results were biased due to omitted variables, I repeated the analysis with additional control variables. These included exposure to news reporting on television and the Internet; threat perceptions of the United States; exposure to American entertainment; years of studying English; tension in international relations at the time when the interview was conducted; gender.

When including more control variables, the effects of newspaper consumption remain substantially significant. The coefficients do not change much when additional variables are included in the model, and the variance and standard errors decrease, thus increasing the t-ratios (but still not always to the 95 percent confidence level). Statistical results for a number of extended models are shown in the Online Appendix.

---

[2] Newspapers that differed from the basic pattern are the *Beijing Daily* (official paper), the *Beijing Yule Xinbao* (commercialized paper), and the *Legal Evening News* (commercialized paper). Apart from these three exceptions, in the ten other cases examined, the pattern was observed.

Estimating Effects of Media Marketization on Credibility across Chinese Regions, Chapter 10

Measurement Error: As a result of multicollinearity, advertising income and the percentage of Internet users could not be included separately in the same statistical model. The results remain stable when inserting these measures individually into the model. For results, see the Online Appendix. Similarly, the findings do not change when advertising income per province is normalized by gross regional product, as reported by the *China Statistical Yearbook 2009* for the year 2007.

Estimating Effects of Media Marketization on Diversity of Information across Authoritarian Regimes, Chapter 11

Table 11.1 presents two methods to estimate the relationship between media marketization and diversity of information based on panel data, characterized by greater N (38 countries) compared with smaller T (2–7 years) properties. The use of a pooled OLS regression with such unbalanced, short panel data raises specific problems. As observations are usually not independent across panels, standard assumptions of classical OLS regressions are violated. Although, in principle, most of these problems can be accounted for, techniques for doing so imply theoretical and econometric trade-offs (see, for example, Kennedy 2003; Franzese 2005; and contributions to *Political Analysis* 19[2] 2011). Due to the limited sample properties of the data, many advanced techniques cannot be applied or do not improve the statistical results. Therefore, I am only presenting fixed-effects and random-effects models here.

Although fixed-effect models control for a certain type of omitted variable, they only use a small part of the information in the sample, producing, most of the time, an unbiased but less efficient estimate of the common slope. In addition, fixed-effects models do not allow an estimation of time-invariant variables (in this case one-party rule, Middle East/North Africa, Sub-Saharan Africa). Therefore, I divided the sample into countries ruled by one-party and other authoritarian regimes, which further reduces efficiency. Results for the dummy variables for year and country are not presented in Table 11.1.

In comparison to fixed-effect models, random-effects models produce more efficient estimates for the slope coefficients and allow for estimation of time-invariant variables. However, random-effects models produce biased estimates if the assumption is violated such that the explanatory variable is uncorrelated with the composite error. The random-effects model presented here is what Clark and Linzer (2012) call a "sluggish case," whereby most of the variation in the independent variable is between rather than within units. Their simulations demonstrate that when there are few data that are sluggish and correlation between the composite error and the explanatory variable is low, the random-effects estimator will result in some degree of bias, but more efficient estimates. In the model presented here, the correlation between the explanatory variables and the composite error is 0.18. In this case, and when the number of units (N) is about 40 and the number of observations (T) is about 5, the random-effects estimates of the coefficient are, on average, slightly biased compared with the fixed estimates, but the total root-mean-square error (RSME) is significantly lower in comparison, according to Clark and Linzer's simulations.

Measurement Error: As argued in Chapter 2, press freedom is not equivalent to diverse information flows. It is possible to increase press freedom and still derive a roughly uniform news product. Therefore, Freedom House Press Ratings do not measure the same concept as the dependent variable "diversity of information." Nevertheless, the results remain stable when "diversity of information" is measured by the Freedom House Press Ratings. However, the positive coefficient for media marketization becomes statistically insignificant. The results are displayed in the Online Appendix.

When measuring political liberalization by POLITY instead of the Freedom House Rankings, the results remain stable. The coefficients remain similar in direction, size, and significance, although the statistical significance decreases slightly.

Omitted Variable Bias: At the time of the data analysis, the measure for levels of economic development controlled for in the Media Credibility Model (Equ.11.3) only extended until 2004, which did not match the data used for the fixed and random effects (Equ.11.1 and 11.2). When using a different measure for levels of economic development based on gross domestic product per capita (purchasing power parity) from the World Development Indicators, the cases are lost due to a lack of data. When including this measure as a control variable, the size and direction of the coefficients remain stable, but the statistical significance decreases.

Appendix E

Additional Tables and Figures

Chapter 8

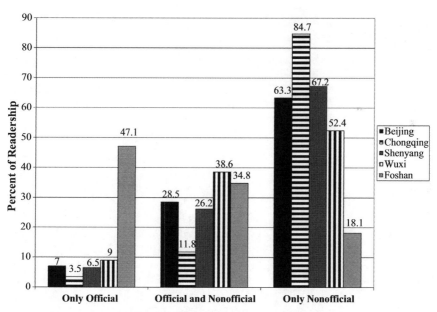

FIGURE 8A.1. Percent of Readership of Newspaper Types Among Readers in Beijing, Chongqing, Shenyang, Wuxi, and Foshan. *Source:* BAS 2005 and LLM 2005.

TABLE 8A.1. *Consumption of Newspaper Types Among Frequent Readers in Beijing (n = 498).*[a]

Newspaper Type	Official	Semiofficial	Commercialized	All Three Types
Official	7% (35)			
Semiofficial	16.3 % (81)	36.8 % (183)		
Commercialized	2.8 % (14)	20.1 % (100)	6.4 % (32)	
All three types				9.4 % (47)

[a] Frequencies are in parentheses.
Source: BAS 2004.

TABLE 8A.2. *Average Demographic Characteristics of Respondents by Control and Treatment Groups.*[a]

	Whole Survey	Control Group	Press Restrictions Treatment	Official Events Treatment (Zhan)	Official Events Treatment (Song)
Years of education	11.34 (3.17)	11.07 (3.08)	12.03 (3.04)	11.66 (3.09)	11.97 (3)
Personal income	2212.28 (5918.01)	2,067.1 (6,709.74)	2,548.68 (4,409.72)	2,099.97 (3.067.17)	5,227.42 (9,747.61)
Female	0.43 (0.5)	0.47 (0.5)	0.38 (0.49)	0.5 (0.5)	0.36 (0.49)
Age	47 (9.78)	48.29 (9.35)	45.21 (9.6)	45.41 (10.54)	42.33 (12.07)
N	617	385	232	58	33

[a] Standard deviations are in parentheses.
Source: BAS 2004.

TABLE 8A.3. *Multiple Probit Regression on Newspaper Use in Beijing (Equ. 8.1 and Equ. 8.2).*[a]

Independent Variables:	Dependent Variable: Newspaper Use	
	Coefficient (s.e.)	Coefficient (s.e.)
Press restrictions	−0.132	0.568
	(0.144)	(0.465)
Negativity * press restrictions	–	−1.048*
		(0.617)
Negativity toward Japan	–	0.645*
		(0.333)
Official events	0.304	0.343
	(0.285)	(0.287)
Cadre	0.969**	0.968**
	(0.433)	(0.449)
Party or state unit	0.341	0.52
	(0.314)	(0.349)
Neighborhood committee worker	0.149	0.2
	(0.413)	(0.419)
Travel to EU/US	−0.620**	−0.609**
	(0.293)	(0.297)
Internet use	0.104	0.072
	(0.193)	(0.196)
Education	2.520***	2.621***
	(0.645)	(0.659)
Personal income	0.492*	0.408
	(0.276)	(0.281)
Constant	−1.519***	−1.971***
	(0.53)	(0.609)
N	605	598
Pseudo R-squared	0.08	0.08

* $z < 0.1$; ** $z < 0.05$; *** $z < 0.01$.

[a] Negativity toward Japan has been recoded from the original feeling thermometer into a 0 to 1 scale, whereby higher values represent colder feelings toward Japan. To simplify interpretation of the results, I calculated the corresponding degrees on the feeling thermometer (variable Positivity) in Figure 8.3.

Source: BAS 2004.

TABLE 8A.4. *Multiple Probit Regression on Use of Official Papers Among Readers in Beijing (Equ. 8.1 and Equ. 8.3).*

Independent Variables:	Dependent Variable: Use of Official Papers	
	Coefficient (s.e.)	Coefficient (s.e.)
Press restrictions	−0.47***	−0.44***
	(0.15)	(0.15)
Official events	0.53**	0.42
	(0.27)	(0.29)
Official events * zero political confidence	–	0.70
		(0.73)
Zero political confidence	–	0.42**
		(0.19)
Cadre	0.19	0.18
	(0.21)	(0.21)
Party or state unit	0.60***	0.58
	(0.22)	(0.22)
Neighborhood committee worker	0.68*	0.70*
	(0.38)	(0.38)
Education	1.07	1.06
	(0.73)	(0.74)
Personal income	0.46	0.40
	(0.31)	(0.31)
Constant	−1.51**	−1.53**
	(0.62)	(0.62)
N	492	492
Pseudo R-squared	0.05	0.06

* $z < 0.1$; ** $z < 0.05$; *** $z < 0.01$.

Source: BAS 2004.

TABLE 8A.5. *Multiple Probit Regression on Use of Commercialized Papers Among Readers of Nonofficial Papers in Beijing (Equ. 8.1).*[a]

Independent Variables:	Dependent Variable: Use of Commercialized Papers Coefficient (s.e.)
Press restrictions	0.1
	(0.17)
Official visits	−0.68**
	(0.34)
Having studied some English	0.27
	(0.17)
Years lived in Beijing	−0.53
	(0.42)
Reading the news online	0.61***
	(0.20)
Education	−1.87*
	(1.10)
Personal income	−0.47
	(0.95)
Constant	1.72**
	(0.95)
N	314
Pseudo R-squared	0.05

* z < 0.1; ** z < 0.05; *** z < 0.01.
[a] A dummy variable for having traveled to countries located in Europe or North America was dropped from the analysis because it predicted the use of commercialized papers perfectly. The results are available from the author upon request.
Source: BAS 2004.

TABLE 8A.6. *Multiple Probit Regression on Use of Official Papers Among Frequent Readers (Equ. 8.4).*

Independent Variables:	Dependent Variable: Use of Official Papers Coefficient (s.e.)
Cadre	0.332**
	(0.141)
Party or state unit	0.272*
	(0.153)
Urban resident	0.005
	(0.395)
Education	2.343***
	(0.733)
Age	0.41**
	(0.173)
Foshan	1.875***
	(0.189)
Wuxi	0.96***
	(0.125)
Shenyang	0.442***
	(0.123)
Constant	−3.032***
	(0.64)
N	2,369
Pseudo R-squared	0.18

* z < 0.1; ** z < 0.05; *** z < 0.01.
Source: LLM, 2005.

Chapter 9

TABLE 9A.I. *Ordinal Probit Results on Perceived Effectiveness of Labor Law Among Frequent Readers (Equ. 9.1).*

Independent Variables:	Dependent Variable: Effectiveness of Labor Law Coefficient (s.e.)
Official papers	0.393**
	(0.19)
Attention	0.784***
	(0.196)
Official papers * attention	−0.704**
	(0.299)
Disputant	−0.458**
	(0.183)
Propaganda at work unit	0.275***
	(0.051)
Worker	−0.101*
	(0.053)
Urban resident	−0.118
	(0.111)
Education	−0.615*
	(0.326)
Foshan	0.103
	(0.085)
Wuxi	0.390***
	(0.07)
Shenyang	0.181**
	(0.071)
Cut 1	−1.812***
	(0.296)
Cut 2	−0.278
	(0.293)
Cut 3	1.464***
	(0.294)
N	2,049
Pseudo R-squared	0.02

* $z < 0.1$; ** $z < 0.05$; *** $z < 0.01$.
Source: LLM, 2005.

TABLE 9A.2. *Multiple Probit Regression of Reading Official Papers on Perceived Effectiveness of the Labor Law as Attention Changes Among Frequent Readers in Chongqing.*[a]

	Dependent Variable: Effectiveness of Labor Law	
	Reading One Paper Coefficient	*Reading Two Papers* Coefficient
Independent Variables:	(s.e.)	(s.e.)
Official papers	0.459	1.157
	(1.094)	(0.756)
Attention	2.428***	1.402***
	(0.584)	(0.495)
Official papers * attention	−1.375	−2.157*
	(1.842)	(1.188)
Disputant	−0.057	−0.751
	(0.873)	(0.469)
Propaganda at work unit	0.374**	0.406***
	(0.19)	(0.145)
Worker	−0.092	−0.093
	(0.206)	(0.147)
Urban resident	−0.496	−0.032
	(0.318)	(0.264)
Education	0.25	−1.343
	(1.141)	(0.87)
Constant	−1.37	0.356
	(0.98)	(0.712)
N	205	360
Pseudo R-squared	0.1	0.04

* $z < 0.1$; ** $z < 0.05$; *** $z < 0.01$.

[a] Because the parallel regression assumption was violated, the dependent variable was recoded, with 1 representing a person's opinion that the labor law was very effective or somewhat effective, and 0 otherwise.

Source: LLM 2005.

TABLE 9A.3. *Ordinal Probit Regression of Reading Official, Nonofficial, and Both Types of Papers on Perceived Effectiveness of the Labor Law as Attention Changes Among Frequent Readers.*

Independent Variables:	Dependent Variable: Effectiveness of the Labor Law	
	Coefficient (s.e.)	Coefficient (s.e.)
Attention	0.569***	0.610***
	(0.174)	(0.162)
Official and nonofficial papers * attention	−0.332	–
	(0.334)	
Official and nonofficial papers	0.182	−0.022
	(0.212)	(0.061)
Only official papers	−0.068	0.419
	(0.085)	(0.256)
Only official papers * attention	–	−0.823**
		(0.407)
Disputant	−0.441**	−0.451**
	(0.183)	(0.184)
Propaganda at work unit	0.271***	0.273***
	(0.051)	(0.051)
Worker	−0.105**	−0.100*
	(0.053)	(0.053)
Urban resident	−0.112	−0.116
	(0.111)	(0.111)
Education	−0.606*	−0.606*
	(0.326)	(0.326)
Foshan	0.112	0.115
	(0.088)	(0.088)
Wuxi	0.386***	0.389***
	(0.07)	(0.07)
Shenyang	0.173**	0.179**
	(0.071)	(0.071)
Cut 1	−1.934***	−1.909***
	(0.291)	(0.289)
Cut 2	−0.403	−.375
	(0.288)	(0.286)
Cut 3	1.337***	1.366***
	(0.288)	(0.286)
N	2,049	2,049
Pseudo R-squared	0.02	0.02

* $z < 0.1$; ** $z < 0.05$; *** $z < 0.01$.
Source: LLM 2005.

TABLE 9A.4. *OLS Regression of Attention on Positivity toward the United States as Exposure to Official Messages Changes Among Readers (Equ. 9.2).*

Independent Variables:	Dependent Variable: Positivity Toward the US Coefficient (s.e.)
Attention	−92.676**
	(38.978)
Attention squared	106.965***
	(38.31)
Exposure to official messages	−10.54
	(15.992)
Exposure to official messages * attention	127.604*
	(71.822)
Exposure to official messages * attention squared	−153.769**
	(72.429)
National identity	−17.751***
	(4.127)
Personal contact	34.129***
	(11.718)
Generation	4.269**
	(2.101)
Education (logged)	16.942
	(13.692)
Tension	−9.119***
	(2.144)
Constant	47.394***
	(14.866)
N	482
R-squared	0.12

* $p < 0.1$; ** $p < 0.05$; *** $p < 0.01$.
Source: BAS 2005.

TABLE 9A.5. *OLS Regression of Attention on Positivity toward the United States as Exposure to Official Messages Changes Among Readers.*

Independent Variables:	Dependent Variable: Positivity Toward the US	
	Reading One Paper Coefficient (s.e.)	*Reading Two Papers* Coefficient (s.e.)
Attention	−71.47	−128.505*
	(57.607)	(70.848)
Attention squared	72.114	130.338*
	(59.31)	(72.792)
Exposure to official messages	−13.743	−20.391
	(22.096)	(26.277)
Exposure to official messages* attention	(119.145)	(177.331)
	(111.523)	(130.498)
Exposure to official messages* attention squared	−115.101	−212.749
	(119.08)	(143.074)
National identity	−20.158***	−11.287
	(7.339)	(7.741)
Personal contact	46.709	39.232
	(43.072)	(28.887)
Generation	1.777	3.413
	(3.447)	(3.954)
Education (logged)	−6.261	68.641**
	(22.357)	(27.174)
Tension	−9.770***	−10.725***
	(3.562)	(3.963)
Constant	68.301***	12.08
	(22.413)	(28.975)
N	175	135
R-squared	0.08	0.15

* $p < 0.1$; ** $p < 0.05$; *** $p < 0.01$.
Source: BAS 2005.

TABLE 9A.6. *OLS Regression Results for Reading Official, Nonofficial, and Both Types of Papers on Positivity toward the United States.*[a]

Independent Variables:	Dependent Variable: Positivity toward the US		
	Paying Moderate Attention Coefficients (s.e)	*Paying Much Attention* Coefficients (s.e)	*All Levels of Attention* Coefficients (s.e)
Reading only official papers	−4.32 (6.59)	−4.2 (7.81)	−4.9 (4.7)
Reading official *and* nonofficial papers	9.98 (7.51)	8.46 (8.69)	9.21* (5.38)
Reading only nonofficial papers	−3.95 (3.21)	2.48 (4)	−0.9 (2.38)
Constant	18.71* (11.07)	51.89*** (16.27)	26.84*** (7.98)
N	286	265	601
R-squared	0.06	0.11	0.06

* $p < 0.1$; ** $p < 0.05$; *** $p < 0.01$.

[a] Exposure to paper type was coded 1 if the paper contained an international news section. Otherwise, exposure was coded as 0. OLS regression model controlling for personal contact, national identity, education, and generation.

Source: BAS 2004.

TABLE 9A.7. *OLS Regression Results for Exposure to Commercialized Messages on Positivity toward Japan before and after Press Restrictions Among Readers.*[a]

Independent Variables:	Dependent Variable: Positivity toward Japan Coefficient (s.e.)
Exposure to commercialized messages	−14.33**
	(7.1)
Exposure to commercialized messages * post-April 9 interview	6.33
	(10.68)
Post-April 9 interview	−9.62*
	(5.85)
National identity	−12.5***
	(3.94)
Threat perceptions of Japan	−8.36***
	(3.18)
Constant	50.66***
	(13.19)
N	481
R-squared	0.11

* $p < 0.1$; ** $p < 0.05$; *** $p < 0.01$.

[a] Exposure to commercialized messages is the same variable as exposure to official messages, only recoded in the reverse direction to facilitate interpretation. Low numbers reflect being, on average, exposed to official messages and high numbers reflecting being, on average, exposed to commercialized messages. Table 9A.7 does not display results for additional control variables. For information about the statistical model, question wording, variable coding, and complete probit regression results, see Daniela Stockmann, "Who Believes Propaganda? Media Effects During the Anti-Japanese Protests in Beijing," *China Quarterly* 202 (2010a).

Source: BAS 2004.

References

Aaker, David A. *Managing Brand Equity: Capitalizing on the Value of a Brand Name.* New York: Free Press, 1991.

Abelson, Robert P. "Conviction." *American Psychologist* 43 (1988): 267–75.

Acemoglu, Daron, and James A. Robinson. *Economic Origins of Dictatorship and Democracy.* New York: Cambridge University Press, 2006.

Amin, Hussein. "Freedom as a Value in Arab Media: Perceptions and Attitudes among Journalists." *Political Communication* 19, no. 2 (2002): 125–35.

Anderson, Benedikt. *Imagined Communities.* London: Verso, 1983.

Anderson, Christopher J., Andre Blais, Shaun Bowler, Todd Donovan, and Ola Listhaug. *Losers' Consent: Elections and Democratic Legitimacy.* Oxford: Oxford University Press, 2005.

Attaway-Fink, Betty. "Market-Driven Journalism: Creating Special Sections to Meet Reader Interests." *Journal of Communication Management* 9, no. 2 (2005): 145–54.

Ayish, Muhammad. "Political Communication on Arab World Television: Evolving Patterns." *Political Communication* 19, no. 2 (2002): 137–54.

Ball-Rokeach, Sandra, and Melvin DeFleur. "A Dependency Model of Mass Media Effects." *Communications Research* 3, no. 1 (1976): 2–21.

Bandurski, David. "China's Guerrilla War for the Web." *Far Eastern Economic Review* 171, no. 6 (July 2008), www.feer.com.

Baum, Matthew A. "Sex, Lies, and War: How Soft News Brings Foreign Policy to the Inattentive Public." *American Political Science Review* 96, no. 1 (2002): 91–109.

Baum, Matthew A., and Tim Groeling. "Shot by the Messenger: Partisan Cues and Public Opinion Regarding National Security and War." *Political Behavior* 31, no. 2 (2009): 157–86.

Baum, Matthew A., and Phil Gussin. "In the Eye of the Beholder: How Information Shortcuts Shape Individual Perceptions of Bias in the Media." *Quarterly Journal of Political Science* 3, no. 1 (2007): 1–31.

Beijing Academic Association of Journalism. *Beijing Duzhe, Tingzhong, Guanzhong Diaocha (Survey of Beijing Newspaper, Radio, and Television Audiences).* Beijing: Gongren Chubanshe, 1984.

Bennett, Lance W. "The Media and Democratic Development: The Social Basis of Political Communication." In *Communicating Democracy: The Media and Political Transitions,* edited by Patrick H. O'Neil, 195–206. Boulder: Lynne Rienner, 1998.

Bennett, Lance W., Regina G. Lawrence, and Steven Livingston. *When the Press Fails: Political Power and the News Media from Iraq to Katrina.* Chicago: University of Chicago Press, 2007.

Blecher, Marc J. "Hegemony and Workers' Politics in China." *China Quarterly* 170 (2002): 283–303.

Bo, Zhiyue, and Gang Chen. "Bo Xilai and the Chongqing Model." *East Asian Policy* 1, no. 3 (2009): 42–49.

Boix, Carles. *Democracy and Redistribution.* New York: Cambridge University Press, 2003.

Bondes, Maria. "Chinas Virtülle Jasminblüte – Eine Internetbasierte Analyse Der Jüngsten Protestereignisse (China's Virtual Jasmine Blossoming – An Internet-Based Analysis of Recent Protests." *Asien* 120 (2011): 73–81.

Bovitz, Gregory, James N. Druckman, and Arthur Lupia. "When Can a News Organization Lead Public Opinion?" *Public Choice* 113, no. 1–2 (2002): 127–55.

Brady, Anne-Marie. *Marketing Dictatorship: Propaganda and Thought Work in Contemporary China.* Lanham: Rowman & Littlefield, 2008.

Brambor, Thomas, William Roberts Clark, and Matt Golder. "Understanding Interaction Models: Improving Empirical Analyses." *Political Analysis* 14, no. 1 (2006): 63–82.

Brehm, Jack Williams, and Arthur Robert Cohen. *Explorations in Cognitive Dissonance.* New York: Wiley, 1962.

Brownlee, Jason. *Authoritarianism in an Age of Democratization.* New York: Cambridge University Press, 2007.

Bueno de Mesquita, Bruce, Alastair Smith, Randolph M. Siverson, and James D. Morrow. *The Logic of Political Survival.* Cambridge: The MIT Press, 2003.

Burns, John P. "Strengthening Central CCP Control of Leadership Selection: The 1990 Nomenklatura." *China Quarterly* 138 (1994): 458–91.

Burns, Nancy, and Donald R. Kinder. "Conviction and Its Consequences." Unpublished manuscript. Ann Arbor, Center for Political Studies, University of Michigan, 2005.

Cao, Peng. *Zhongguo Baoye Jituan Fazhan Yanjiu (China Newspaper Group Development Research).* Beijing: Xinhua Chubanshe, 1999.

Carmines, Edward G., and James A. Stimson. *Issue Evolution: Race and the Transformation of American Politics.* Princeton: Princeton University Press, 1989.

Carothers, Thomas. "The End of the Transition Paradigm." *Journal of Democracy* 13, no. 1 (2002): 5–21.

Chaffee, Steven H., Melissa Nichols Saphir, Joseph Graf, Christian Sandvig, and Kyu Sup Hahn. "Attention to Counter-Attitudinal Messages in a State Election Campaign." *Political Communication* 18 (2001): 247–72.

Chan, Alex. "Guiding Public Opinion through Social Agenda-Setting: China's Media Policy since the 1990s." *Journal of Contemporary China* 16, no. 53 (2007): 547–59.

Chan, Hon. "Cadre Personnel Management in China: The Nomenklatura System, 1990–1998." *China Quarterly* 179 (2004): 703–34.

Chan, Joseph Man. "Commercialization without Independence: Trends and Developments of Media Commercialization in China." In *China Review 1993,* edited by Joseph Cheng, 25.1–25.21. Hong Kong: Chinese University Press, 1993.

Chang, Yu-tzung, Yun-han Chu, and Chong-Min Park. "Authoritarian Nostalgia in East Asia." *Journal of Democracy* 18, no. 3 (2007): 66–80.

Chen, Chongshan, and Xiuling Mi. *Zhongguo Chuanbo Xiaoguo Toushi (A Perspective on Media Effects in China)*. Shenyang: Shenyang Chubanshe, 1989.

Chen, Chongshan, and Wusan Sun. *Meijie–Ren–Xiandaihua (The Media–People–Modernization)*. Beijing: Zhongguo Shehui Kexue Chubanshe, 1995.

Chen, Chongshan, Jian-Hua Zhu, and Wei Wu. "The Chinese Journalist." In *The Global Journalist: News People around the World*, edited by David H. Weaver and Wei Wu, 9–30. Cresskill: Hampton Press, 1998.

Chen, Lidan. *Makesi Zhuyi Xinwen Sixiang Gailun (Introduction to Marxist News Thought)*. Shanghai: Fudan Daxue Chubanshe, 2003b.

——— *Makesi Zhuyi Xinwenxue Cidian (Dictionary of Marxian Journalism)*. Beijing: Zhongguo Guangbo Dianshi Chubanshe, 2002.

——— "Open Information System and Crisis Communication in China." *Chinese Journal of Communication* 1, no. 1 (2008): 38–54.

——— "Yong Shishi Shuo Hua Shi Xuanchuan Fangfa Er Bu Shi Xinwen Xiezuo Guilu (Using Facts to Write News Is a Propaganda Method and Not a Rule to Write News Reports), 2003a." http://www.people.com.cn/GB/14677/22100/28502/28503/1939459.html, accessed July 20, 2012.

Chen, Ni. "Institutionalizing Public Relations: A Case Study of Chinese Government Crisis Communication on the 2008 Sichuan Earthquake." *Public Relations Review* 35 (2009): 187–98.

Chen, Wei. *Baozhi Faxing Yingxiao Daolun (Introduction to Marketing Newspaper Distribution)*. Shanghai: Fudan Daxue Chubanshe, 2004.

Chen, Xueyi, and Tianjian Shi. "Media Effects on Political Confidence and Trust in the People's Republic of China in the Post-Tiananmen Period." *East Asia: An International Quarterly* 19, no. 3 (2001): 84–118.

China News Analysis. "The Press and Its Market after the Fourth Plenum." *China News Analysis* 1531 (1995): 1–10.

Chinese Advertising Yearbook 2004 *(Zhongguo Guanggao Nianjian 2004)*. Beijing: Xinhua Chubanshe, 2004.

Chu, Leonard L. "Continuity and Change in China's Media Reform." *Journal of Communication* 44, no. 3 (1994): 4–21.

Clark, Tom S., and Drew A. Linzer. "Should I Use Fixed or Random Effects?" *Working Paper Series, The Society for Political Methodology*. Atlanta: Emory University, 2012. http://polmeth.wustl.edu/mediaDetail.php?docId=1315.

Converse, Philip. "Changing Conceptions of Public Opinion in the Political Process." *Public Opinion Quarterly* 51, pt. 2 (1987): 12–24.

——— "Information Flow and the Stability of Partisan Attitudes." *Public Opinion Quarterly* 26, no. 4 (1962): 578–99.

——— "The Nature of Belief in Mass Publics." In *Ideology and Discontent*, edited by David Apter, 206–61. New York: Free Press, 1964.

Cook, Thomas D., and Donald T. Campbell. *Quasi-Experimentation: Design & Analysis Issues for Field Settings*. Chicago: Rand McNally, 1979.

Cook, Timothy E. *Governing with the News: The News Media as a Political Institution*. Chicago: University of Chicago Press, 1998.

CPCR. "Zhongguo Shichanghua Baokan Guanggao Toufang Cankao 2005 (I) (Market Intelligence Report on China's Print Media Retail Distribution)." Beijing: CPCR Kaiyuan Celüe (Opening Strategy Consultation), 2005.

Curtis, Gerald. *The Japanese Way of Politics*. New York: Columbia University Press, 1988.

Dalton, Russell J., Paul A. Beck, and Robert Huckfeldt. "Partisan Cues and the Media: Information Flows in the 1992 Presidential Election." *American Political Science Review* 92, no. 1 (1998): 111–26.

De Burgh, Hugo. "Kings without Crowns? The Re-Emergence of Investigative Journalism in China." *Media, Culture, and Society* 25 (2003): 801–20.

Diamond, Larry J. "Elections without Democracy: Thinking about Hybrid Regimes." *Journal of Democracy* 13, no. 2 (2002): 21–35.

––––––– "Liberation Technology." *Journal of Democracy* 21, no. 3 (2010): 69–83.

Dickson, Bruce J. "Populist Authoritarianism: The Future of the Chinese Communist Party." In *Chinese Leadership, Politics, and Policy*. Carnegie Endowment for International Peace, 2005.

Ditto, Peter H., and David E. Lopez. "Motivated Skepticism: Use of Differential Decision Criteria for Preferred and Nonpreferred Conclusions." *Journal of Personality and Social Psychology* 63, no. 4 (1992): 568–84.

Ditto, Peter H., James A. Scepansky, Geoffrey D. Munro, and Anne Marie Apanovitch. "Motivated Sensitivity to Preference-Inconsistent Information." *Journal of Personality and Social Psychology* 75, no. 1 (1998): 53–69.

Downs, Anthony. *An Economic Theory of Democracy*. New York: Harper Books, 1957.

Druckman, James N., and Arthur Lupia. "Preference Formation." *Annual Review of Poitical Science* 3, no. 1 (2000): 1–24.

Durante, Ruben, and Brian Knight. "Partisan Control, Media Bias, and Viewer Responses: Evidence from Berlusconi's Italy." In *Working Paper Series, National Bureau of Economic Research*, 14762 (2009). http://www.nber.org/papers/w14762.

Eagly, Alice, Wendy Wood, and Shelly Chaiken. "Causal Inferences about Communicators and Their Effects on Opinion Change." *Journal of Personality and Social Psychology* 36, no. 4 (1978): 424–35.

Economy, Elizabeth. *The River Runs Black: The Environmental Challenge to China's Future*. Ithaca: Cornell University Press, 2004.

Edin, Maria. "State Capacity and Local Agent Control in China: CCP Cadre Management from a Township Perspective." *China Quarterly* 173 (2003): 35–52.

Egorov, Gregory, Sergei Guriev, and Konstantin Sonin. "Why Resource-Poor Dictators Allow Freer Media: A Theory and Evidence from Panel Data." *American Political Science Review* 103, no. 4 (2009): 645–68.

Ehteshami, Anoushiravan, and Emma C. Murphy. "Transformation of the Corporatist State in the Middle East." *Third World Quarterly* 17, no. 4 (1996): 753–72.

Eickelman, Dale F., and Jon W. Anderson. *New Media in the Muslim World: The Emerging Public Sphere*. 2nd ed, Indiana Series in Middle East Studies. Bloomington: Indiana University Press, 2003.

Ekiert, Grzegorz. "Conditions of Political Obedience and Stability in State-Socialist Societies: The Inapplicability of Weber's Concept of Legitimacy." In *Working Paper Series, Center for Research on Politics and Social Organization*, 28. Cambridge: Harvard University, 1988.

Esarey, Ashley. "Cornering the Market: State Strategies for Controlling China's Commercial Media." *Asian Perspective* 29, no. 4 (2005): 37–83.

———— "Speak No Evil: Mass Media Control in Contemporary China." *Freedom House Special Report*, 1–12. Washington, DC: Freedom House, 2006.

Esarey, Ashley, and Qiang Xiao. "Digital Communication and Political Change in China." *International Journal of Communication* 5 (2011): 298–319.

Exner, Mechthild. "The Convergence of Ideology and the Law: The Functions of the Legal Education Campaign in Building a Chinese Legal System." *Issues and Studies* 31, no. 8 (1995): 68–102.

Ezrow, Lawrence. "The Variance Matters: How Party Systems Represent the Preferences of Voters." *Journal of Politics* 69, no. 1 (2007): 182–92.

Fang, Hanqi, and Changfeng Chen. *Zhongguo Dangdai Xinwen Shiye (China's Contemporary News Industry)*. Beijing: Renmin Chubanshe, 2002.

Fang, Xiaohong. *Dazhong Chuanmei Yu Nongcun (Mass Media and the Countryside)*. Beijing: Zhonghua Shuju, 2002.

Farquhar, Peter H. "Managing Brand Equity." *Journal of Advertising Research* 30, no. 4 (1990): RC7–RC12.

Feldman, Stanley. "Answering Survey Questions: The Measurement and Meaning of Public Opinion." In *Political Judgment: Structure and Process*, edited by Milton Lodge and Kathleen McGraw, 249–70. Ann Arbor: University of Michigan Press, 1995.

Festinger, Leon. *Conflict, Decision, and Dissonance*, Stanford Studies in Psychology 3. Stanford: Stanford University Press, 1964.

———— *A Theory of Cognitive Dissonance*. Evanston: Row Peterson, 1957.

Fewsmith, Joseph. "Assessing Social Stability on the Eve of the 17th Party Congress." *China Leadership Monitor* 20 (2007).

Fewsmith, Joseph, and Stanley Rosen. "The Domestic Context of Chinese Foreign Policy." In *The Making of Chinese Foreign and Security Policy in the Era of Reform, 1978–2000*, edited by David M. Lampton, 151–87. Stanford: Stanford University Press, 2001.

Finnemore, Martha. *National Interest in International Security*, Cornell Studies in Political Economy. Ithaca: Cornell University Press, 1996.

Fiorina, Morris. "Parties, Participation, and Representation in America: Old Theories Face New Realities." In *Political Science: The State of the Discipline*, edited by Ira Katznelson and Helen Milner, 510–41. New York: W.W. Norton & Company, 2002.

Fischer, Peter, Eva Jonas, Dieter Frey, and Stefan Schulz–Hardt. "Selective Exposure to Information: The Impact of Information Limits." *European Journal of Social Psychology* 35 (2005): 469–92.

Franzese, Robert J. "Empirical Strategies for Various Manifestations of Multilevel Data." *Political Analysis* 13, no. 4 (2005): 430–46.

Fraser, Nancy. "Rethinking the Public Sphere: A Contribution to the Critique of Actually Existing Democracy." In *Habermas and the Public Sphere*, edited by Craig Calhoun, 56–80. Cambridge: The MIT Press, 1993.

Freeman, Laurie Anne. *Closing the Shop: Information Cartels and Japan's Mass Media*. Princeton: Princeton University Press, 2000.

Frey, Dieter. "Amount of Available Information and Selective Exposure." Christian-Albrechts-University, Kiel (Cited in Dieter Frey, "Recent Research on Selective Exposure to Information." In *Advances in Experimental Social Policy*, edited by L. Berkowitz. New York: Academic Press, 1986a).

———— "The Effect of Negative Feedback about Oneself and Cost of Information on Preferences for Information about the Source of this Feedback." *Journal of Experimental Social Psychology* 17, no. 1 (1981c): 42–50.

_____ "Postdecisional Preferences for Decision-Relevant Information as a Function of the Competences of Its Source and the Degree of Familiarity with this Information." *Journal of Experimental Psychology* 17 (1981a): 621–26.

_____ "Recent Research on Selective Exposure to Information." *Advances in Experimental Social Psychology* 19 (1986b): 41–80.

_____ "Reversible and Irreversible Decisions: Preference for Consonant Information as a Function of Attractiveness of Decision Alternatives." *Personality and Social Psychology Bulletin* 7 (1981b): 621–26.

Frey, Dieter, and Robert A. Wicklund. "A Clarification of Selective Exposure: The Impact of Choice." *Journal of Experimental Psychology* 14 (1978): 132–39.

Friedrich, Carl J., and Zbigniew Brzezinski. *Totalitarian Dictatorship and Autocracy.* Cambridge: Harvard University Press, 1956.

Gallagher, Mary E. "'Use the Law as Your Weapon!' The Rule of Law and Labor Conflict in the PRC." In *Engaging the Law in China: State, Society, and Possibilities for Justice,* edited by Neil J. Diamant, Stanley B. Lubman, and Kevin J. O'Brien, 54–83. Stanford: Stanford University Press, 2005.

Gandhi, Jennifer. *Political Institutions under Dictatorship.* New York: Cambridge University Press, 2008.

Gandhi, Jennifer, and Adam Przeworski. "Authoritarian Institutions and the Survival of Autocrats." *Comparative Political Studies* 40, no. 11 (2007): 1279–1301.

Geddes, Barbara. "What Causes Democratization?" In *The Oxford Handbook of Comparative Politics,* edited by Charles Boix and Susan C. Stokes, 317–39. Oxford: Oxford University Press, 2007.

_____ "What Do We Know about Democratization after Twenty Years?" *Annual Review of Political Science* 2 (1999): 115–44.

Geddes, Barbara, and John Zaller. "Sources of Popular Support for Authoritarian Regimes." *American Journal of Political Science* 33, no. 2 (1989): 319–47.

Gibson, Edward L. "Boundary Control: Subnational Authoritarianism in Democratic Countries." *World Politics* 58, no. 1 (2005): 101–32.

Gibson, James L., and Amanda Gows. *Overcoming Intolerance in South Africa: Experiments in Democratic Persuasion.* New York: Cambridge University Press, 2003.

Giles, John, Albert Park, and Fang Cai. "How Has Economic Restructuring Affected China's Urban Workers?" *China Quarterly* 185 (2006): 62–95.

Gilley, Bruce, and Heike Holbig. "The Debate on Party Legitimacy in China: A Mixed Quantitative/Qualitative Analysis." *Journal of Contemporary China* 18, no. 59 (2009): 339–58.

Goldman, Merle, and Elizabeth J. Perry, eds. *Changing Meanings of Citizenship in Modern China.* Cambridge: Harvard University Press, 2002.

Graber, Doris. "The Media and Democracy: Beyond Myths and Stereotypes." *Annual Review of Political Science* 6 (2003): 139–60.

_____ "Seeing Is Remembering: How Visuals Contribute to Learning from Television News." *Journal of Communication* 40, no. 3 (1990): 134–55.

Grzymala-Busse, Anna. "The Best Laid Plans: The Impact of Informal Rules on Formal Institutions in Transitional Regimes." *Studies in Comparative International Development* 45, no. 3 (2010): 311–33.

_____ *Rebuilding Leviathan.* Cambridge: Cambridge University Press, 2007.

Grzymala-Busse, Anna, and Pauline Jones Luong. "Reconceptualizing the State: Lessons from Post-Communism." *Politics and Society* 30, no. 4 (2002): 529–54.

Gunther, Albert C. "Attitude Extremity and Trust in Media." *Journalism Quarterly* 65, no. 2 (1988): 279–87.

Habermas, Jürgen. *Strukturwandel Der Oeffentlichkeit: Untersuchungen Zu Einer Kategorie Der Bürgerlichen Gesellschaft*. Frankfurt am Main: Suhrkamp, 1962 [1990].

––––––– *Theorie Des Kommunikativen Handelns*. Frankfurt am Main: Suhrkamp, 1995 [2009].

Hamilton, James. *All the News That's Fit to Sell: How the Market Transforms Information into News*. Princeton: Princeton University Press, 2004.

Hans-Bredow-Institut. *Internationales Handbuch Medien (International Handbook Media)*. Baden-Baden: Nomos Verlagsgesellschaft, 2002.

Hardin, Russell. "Compliance, Consent, and Legitimacy." In *The Oxford Handbook of Comparative Politics*, edited by Carles Boix and Susan Stokes, 236–55. Oxford: Oxford University Press, 2007.

Hartford, Kathleen. "Dear Mayor: Online Communications with Local Governments in Hangzhou and Nanjing." *China Information* 19, no. 2 (2005): 217–60.

Hassid, Jonathan. "China's Contentious Journalists: Reconceptualizing the Media." *Problems of Post-Communism* 55, no. 4 (2008): 52–61.

––––––– "Four Models of the Fourth Estate: A Typology of Contemporary Chinese Journalists." *China Quarterly* 208 (2012): 813–32.

Havel, Vaclav. "The Power of the Powerless." In *Open Letters: Selected Writings 1965–190*, edited by Vaclav Havel, 125–214. London: Faber & Faber, 1978.

He, Jing. "Shishang Xiaofei Lei Zazhi Dui Bentu Zhongceng Jieji De Xingxiang Jiangou (The Construction of Images of Local Middle Class by Lifestyle Magazines)." *Xinwen yu Chuanbo Yanjiu (Research in Journalism and Communications)* 3 (2006): 80–96.

He, Qinglian. *Zhongguo Zhengfu Ruhe Kongzhi Meiti: Zhongguo Renquan Yanjiu Baogao (Media Control in China: A Report by Human Rights in China)*. New York: Human Rights in China, 2003.

He, Zhou. "Chinese Communist Press in a Tug of War: A Political Economy Analysis of the Shenzhen Special Zone Daily." In *Power, Money, and Media: Communication Patterns and Bureaucratic Control in Cultural China*, edited by Chin-chuan Lee, 112–51. Evanston: Northwestern University Press, 2000.

Heurlin, Christopher. "Responsive Authoritarianism: Protest and Policy Change in Rural and Urban China." PhD diss., University of Washington, 2011.

Hicken, Allen. "Party Fabrication: Constitutional Reform and the Rise of Thai Rak Thai." *Journal of East Asian Studies* 6, no. 3 (2006): 381–407.

Hildebrandt, Timothy. *Social Organizations and the Authoritarian State in China*. New York: Cambridge University Press, 2013.

Hirschman, Albert O. *Exit, Voice, and Loyalty: Responses to Decline in Firms, Organizations and States*. Cambridge: Harvard University Press, 1970.

Ho, Virginia Harper. *Labor Dispute Resolution in China: Implications for Labor Rights and Legal Reform*. Berkeley: Institute of East Asian Studies, University of California, 2003.

Hollander, Paul. *Anti-Americanism: Critiques at Home and Abroad, 1965–1990*. New York: Oxford University Press, 1992.

Hong, Junhao. "The Resurrection of Advertising in China: Developments, Problems, and Trends." *Asian Survey* 34, no. 4 (1994): 326–42.

Houn, Franklin W. "Chinese Communist Control of the Press." *Public Opinion Quarterly*, no. 22 (1958–59): 435–48.

Howard, Philip N. *The Digital Origins of Dictatorship and Democracy: Information Technology and Political Islam.* New York: Oxford University Press, 2010.

Howard, Philip N., and Muzammil M. Hussain. "The Role of Digital Media." *Journal of Democracy* 22, no. 3 (2011): 35–48.

Hu, Chunlei. "Zhongguo Baoye Jingji Fazhan Jin 20 Nian Chengjiu (The Achievement of the Chinese Newspaper Industry in the Course of the Past 20 Years)." In *Zhongguo Baoye Nianjian (China Newspaper Industry Yearbook)*, 7–17. Beijing: Zhonghua Gongshang Lianhe Chubanshe, 2004.

Hu, Zhengrong. "The Post-WTO Restructuring of the Chinese Media Industries and the Consequences of Capitalization." *Javnost/The Public* 20, no. 4 (2003): 19–36.

Hua, Xu. "Morality Discourse in the Marketplace: Narratives in the Chinese Television News Magazine Oriental Horizon." *Journalism Studies* 1, no. 4 (2000): 637–47.

Huang, Chengju. "The Development of a Semi-Independent Press in Post-Mao China: An Overview and a Case Study of Chengdu Business News." *Journalism Studies* 1, no. 4 (2000): 649–64.

Huang, Jinghua, Jun Zhang, Jun Xie, and Limei Shao. "Quan Guo Chengshi Jumin Meijie Jiechu Yu Shiyong Xingwei Diaocha Baogao (Survey Report on Urban Residents' Media Contact and Consumption Behavior in All of China)." In *Zhongguo Xinwen Nianjian (China Journalism Yearbook)*, edited by Zhongguo Shehui Kexue Xinwen Yu Chuanbo Yanjiusuo (Chinese Academy of Social Science Journalism and Communications Research Institute), 27–190. Beijing: Zhongguo Xinwen Nianjian She, 2004.

Hughes, Christopher. *Chinese Nationalism in the Global Era.* New York: Routledge, 2006.

Hui, Dennis Lai Hang. "Research Note: Politics of Sichuan Earthquake, 2008." *Journal of Contingencies and Crisis Management* 17, no. 2 (2009): 137–40.

Huntington, Samuel. "Democracy's Third Wave." In *The Global Resurgence of Democracy*, edited by Larry J. Diamond and Marc F. Plattner, 3–35. Baltimore: Johns Hopkins University Press, 1996.

———— *Political Order in Changing Societies.* New Haven: Yale University Press, 1968.

Hurst, William. *The Chinese Worker after Socialism.* New York: Cambridge University Press, 2009.

International Federation of Journalists (IFJ). *Zhongguo Xinwen Ziyou 2010 (Press Freedom in China in 2010).* 2010. http://asiapacific.ifj.org/en/pages/ifj-asia-pacific-reports, accessed July 20, 2012.

Iyengar, Shanto. *Is Anyone Responsible? How Television Frames Political Issues.* Chicago: University of Chicago Press, 1991.

Iyengar, Shanto, and Kyu S. Hahn. "Red Media, Blue Media: Evidence of Ideological Selectivity in Media Use." *Journal of Communication* 59, no. 1 (2009): 19–39.

Iyengar, Shanto, and Donald R. Kinder. "Psychological Accounts of Agenda-Setting." In *Mass Media and Political Thought*, edited by Sidney Kraus and Richard Perloff, 117–40. Beverly Hills: Sage, 1985.

Johnston, Alastair Iain, and Daniela Stockmann. "Chinese Attitudes toward the United States and Americans." In *Anti-Americanisms in World Politics*, edited by Peter Katzenstein and Robert Keohane, 157–95. Ithaca: Cornell University Press, 2007.

Jost, John T. "Negative Illusions: Conceptual Clarification and Psychological Evidence Concerning False Consciousness." *Political Psychology* 16, no. 2 (1995): 397–424.

Ju, Honglei. "Zhongguo Baoye De Fagui Yu Zhengce (Law and Policies Relevant to the Chinese Newspaper Industry)." In *Zhongguo Baoye Nianjian (China Newspaper Industry Yearbook)*, 18–25. Beijing: Zhonghua Gongshang Lianhe Chubanshe, 2004.

Kahneman, Daniel, Paul Slovic, and Amos Tversky. *Judgment under Uncertainty: Heuristics and Biases*. New York: Cambridge University Press, 1982.

Kang, Yin. *Xinwen Yu Zhengzhi Yaolüe (Summary of News and Politics)*. Beijing: Beijing Guangbo Xueyuan Chubanshe, 2001.

Katzenstein, Peter. *The Culture of National Security: Norms and Identity in World Politics*. New York: Columbia University Press, 1996.

Ke, Huixin. *Meijie Yu Aoyun: Yige Chuanbo Xiaoguo De Shizheng Yanjiu (The Media and the Olympics: A Quantitative Study of Media Effects)*. Beijing: Zhongguo Chuanmei Daxue Chubanshe, 2004.

Kennedy, John James. "Maintaining Popular Support for the Chinese Communist Party: The Influence of Education and the State-Controlled Media." *Political Studies* 57, no. 3 (2009): 517–36.

Kennedy, Peter. *A Guide to Econometrics*. Cambridge: MIT Press, 2003.

Kern, Holger Lutz, and Jens Hainmüller. "Opium for the Masses: How Foreign Media Can Stabilize Authoritarian Regimes." *Political Analysis* 17, no. 4 (2009): 377–99.

Kinder, Donald R. "Belief Systems Today." *Critical Review* 18, no. 1–3 (2006): 197–216.

King, Gary, Christopher J. L. Murray, Joshua A. Salomon, and Ajay Tandon. "Enhancing the Validity and Cross-Cultural Comparability of Measurement in Survey Research." *American Political Science Review* 98, no. 1 (2004): 191–207.

King, Gary, Michael Tomz, and Jason Wittenberg. "Making the Most of Statistical Analyses: Improving Interpretation and Presentation." *American Journal of Political Science* 44, no. 2 (2000): 347–61.

Kitschelt, Herbert. *The Radical Right in Western Europe*. Ann Arbor: University of Michigan Press, 1995.

Knobloch-Westerwick, Silvia, Francesca Dillman Carpentier, Andree Blumhoff, and Nico Nickel. "Selective Exposure Effects for Positive and Negative News: Testing the Robustness of the Informational Utility Model." *Journalism & Mass Communication Quarterly* 82, no. 1 (2005): 181–95.

Kotler, Philip. *Marketing Management: Analysis, Planning and Control*. Englewood Cliffs: Prentice Hall, 1991.

Krauss, Ellis S. "The Mass Media and Japanese Politics: Effects and Consequences." In *Media and Politics in Japan*, edited by Susan J. Pharr and Ellis S. Krauss, Honolulu: University of Hawai'i Press, 1996.

Ku, Lun-wei, Tung-ho Wu, Li-ying Lee, and Chen-Hsin-hsi. "Construction of an Evaluation Corpus for Opinion Extraction." Paper presented at *NTCIR-5 Workshop*, Tokyo, Japan, 2005.

Kuran, Timur. "Now Out of Never: The Element of Surprise in the East European Revolution of 1989." *World Politics* 44, no. 1 (1991): 7–48.

Lacy, Stephen, Daniel Riffe, Staci Stoddard, Hugh Martin, and Kuang-Kuo Chang. "Sample Size for Newspaper Content Analysis in Multi-Year Studies." *Journalism and Mass Communication Quarterly* 78, no. 4 (2001): 836–45.

Landry, Pierre F. "The Institutional Diffusion of Courts in China: Evidence from Survey Data." In *Rule by Law: The Politics of Courts in Authoritarian Regimes*, edited by Tom Ginsburg and Tamir Moustafa, 207–34. New York: Cambridge University Press, 2008b.

_____ *Decentralized Authoritarianism in China: The Communist Party's Control over Local Elites in the Post-Mao Era*. New York: Cambridge University Press, 2008a.

Latham, Kevin. "Nothing but the Truth: News Media, Power and Hegemony in South China." *China Quarterly* 163 (2000): 633–54.

Lawson, Chappell. *Building the Fourth Estate: Democratization and the Rise of a Free Press in Mexico*. Berkeley and Los Angeles: University of California Press, 2002.

Lee, Ching *Against the Law: Labor Protests in China's Rustbelt and Sunbelt*. Berkeley and Los Angeles: University of California Press, 2007.

Lee, Taeku. *Mobilizing Public Opinion: Black Insurgency and Racial Attitudes in the Civil Rights Era*. Chicago: University of Chicago Press, 2002.

Lerner, Daniel. *The Passing of Traditional Society: Modernizing the Middle East*. Glencoe: Free Press of, 1964.

Levitsky, Stephen. *Transforming Labor-Based Parties in Latin America*. New York: Cambridge University Press, 2003.

Levitsky, Stephen, and Lucan A. Way. "Elections without Democracy: The Rise of Competitive Authoritarianism." *Journal of Democracy* 13, no. 2 (2002): 51–65.

Lewis, John W., and Litai Xue. "Social Change and Political Reform in China: Meeting the Challenge of Success." *China Quarterly* 176 (2003): 926–42.

Li, Cheng. "Introduction: The Rise of the Middle Class in the Middle Kingdom." In *China's Emerging Middle Class: Beyond Economic Transformation*, edited by Cheng Li, 3–31. Washington, DC: Brookings Institution Press, 2010.

Li, Chin-chuan, Zhou He, and Huang Yu. "'Chinese Party Publicity Inc.' Conglomerated: The Case of the Shenzhen Press Group." *Media, Culture & Society* 28, no. 4 (2006): 581–602.

Li, Lianjiang. "Political Trust in Rural China." *Modern China* 30, no. 2 (2004): 228–58.

Li, Lianjiang, and Kevin J. O'Brien. "Villagers and Popular Resistance in Contemporary China." *Modern China* 22, no. 1 (1996): 28–61.

Li, Yanhong. "Zhengzhi Xinwen De Mohu Biaoshu: Cong Zhongguo Dalu Liang Jia Baozhi Dui Kelindun FangHua De Baodao Kan Shichanghua De Yingxiang (The Blurred State of Political News: Looking at the Impact of Commercialization through the Lens of News Reports about Clinton's Visit by Two Newspapers from Mainland China)." *Xinwenxue Yanjiu (Research in Journalism)* 73 (2003): 169–99.

Liao, Shengqin, Xiaojing Li, and Guoliang Zhang. "Zhongguo Dalu Dazong Chuanmei Gongxinli De Shizheng Yanjiu (An Empirical Study of Mass Media Public Credibility in Mainland China)." Paper presented at the 8th National Conference on Communication Studies, Tsinghua University, Beijing, 2004.

Lieberthal, Kenneth. *Governing China: From Revolution through Reform*. 2nd ed. New York: W. W. Norton, 2004.

Lieberthal, Kenneth, and David M. Lampton, eds. *Bureaucracy, Politics, and Decision Making in Post-Mao China*, Studies on China. Berkeley: University of California Press, 1992.

Liebman, Benjamin J. "Changing Media, Changing Courts." In *Changing Media, Changing China*, edited by Susan Shirk, 150–74. Oxford: Oxford University Press, 2011a.

_____ "The Media and the Courts: Towards Competitive Supervision?" *China Quarterly* 208 (2011b): 833–50.

_____ "Watchdog or Demagogue? The Media in the Chinese Legal System." *Columbia Law Review* 101, no. 1 (2005): 1–107.

Lin, Fen. "A Survey Report on Chinese Journalists in China." *China Quarterly* 202 (2010): 421–34.

Liu, Haitao, Jinxiong Zheng, and Rong Shen. *Zhongguo Xinwen Guansi Ershi Nian, 1987–2007 (Twenty Years of Chinese News Lawsuits, 1987–2007)*. Beijing: Zhongguo Guangbo Dianshi Chubanshe, 2007.

Lodge, Milton, Marco Steenbergen, and Shawn Brau. "The Responsive Voter: Campaign Information and the Dynamics of Candidate Evaluation." *American Political Science Review* 89 (1995): 309–36.

Lohmann, Susanne. "Collective Action Cascades: An Informational Rationale for the Power in Numbers." *Journal of Economic Surveys* 14, no. 5 (2002): 655–84.

Lorentzen, Peter L. "Deliberately Incomplete Press Censorship." Working Paper, Berkeley: University of California-Berkeley, 2010.

Loveless, Matthew. "Media Dependency: Mass Media as Sources of Information in the Democratizing Countries of Central and Eastern Europe." *Democratization* 15, no. 1 (2008): 162–83.

Lowin, Aaron. "Further Evidence for an Approach-Avoidance Interpretation of Selective Exposure." *Journal of Experimental Social Psychology* 5, no. 3 (1969): 265–71.

Lupia, Arthur. "Shortcuts versus Encyclopedias: Information and Voting Behavior in California Insurance Reform Elections." *American Political Science Review* 88 (1994): 63–76.

Lynch, Marc. "After Egypt: The Limits and Promise of Online Challenges to the Authoritarian Arab State." *Perspectives on Politics* 9, no. 2 (2011): 301–10.

_____ *Voices of the New Arab Public: Iraq, Al-Jazeera, and Middle East Politics Today.* New York: Columbia University Press, 2006.

MacFarquhar, Roderick. "A Visit to the Chinese Press." *China Quarterly* 53 (1973): 144–52.

Magaloni, Beatriz. "Credible Power-Sharing and the Longevity of Authoritarian Rule." *Comparative Political Studies* 41, no. 4/5 (2008): 715–41.

_____ *Voting for Autocracy: Hegemonic Party Survival and Its Demise in Mexico.* New York: Cambridge University Press, 2006.

Magaloni, Beatriz, and Ruth Kricheli. "Political Order and One-Party Rule." *Annual Review of Political Science* 13 (2010): 123–43.

Manion, Melanie. *Corruption by Design: Building Clean Government in Mainland China and Hong Kong.* Cambridge: Harvard University Press, 2004.

Mann, Michael. "Infrastructural Power Revisited." *Studies in Comparative International Development* 43, no. 3–4 (2008): 355–65.

Marletti, Carlo, and Franca Roncarolo. "Media Influence in the Italian Transition from a Consensual to a Majoritarian Democracy". In *Democracy and the Media: A Comparative Perspective*, edited by Richard Gunther and Anthony Mughan. New York: Cambridge University Press, 2000.

Maryland Study. "Perspectives towards the United States in Selected Newspapers of the People's Republic of China." Report for the U.S. China Security Review Commission, 2002.

McCroskey, James. "Scales for the Measurement of Ethos." *Speech Monographs* 33, no. 1 (1966): 65–72.

Meguid, Bonnie M. "Competition between Unequals: The Role of Mainstream Party Strategy in Niche Party Success." *American Political Science Review* 99, no. 3 (2005): 347–59.

Mertha, Andrew. "'Fragmented Authoritarianism 2.0': Political Pluralization in the Chinese Policy Process." *China Quarterly* 200 (2009): 995–1012.

Mickiewicz, Ellen. *Television, Power, and the Public in Russia.* New York: Cambridge University Press, 2008.

Miller, Arthur G., John W. McHoskey, Cynthia M. Bane, and Timothy G. Dowd. "The Attitude Polarization Phenomenon: Role of Response Measure, Attitude Extremity, and Behavioral Consequences of Reported Attitude Change." *Journal of Personality and Social Psychology* 64, no. 4 (1993): 561–74.

Miller, Joanne, and Jon Krosnick. "News Media Impact on the Ingredients of Presidential Evaluations: Politically Knowledgeable Citizens Are Guided by a Trusted Source." *American Journal of Political Science* 44, no. 2 (2000): 301–15.

Mishler, William, Richard Rose, and Neil Munro. *Russia Transformed.* New York: Cambridge University Press, 2006.

Moehler, Devra C., and Naunihal Singh. "Whose News Do You Trust? Explaining Trust in Private versus Public Media in Africa." *Political Research Quarterly* 64, no. 2 (2009): 276–92.

Morozov, Evgeny. *The Net Delusion: How Not to Liberate the World.* London: Penguin Books, 2011.

Mowlana, Hamid. *International Flow of Information: A Global Report and Analysis.* Reports and Papers on Mass Communication, No. 99. Paris: UNESCO, 1985.

Mulgan, Geoff. *Communication and Control: Networks and the New Economies of Communication.* New York: Guilford Press, 1991.

Mulligan, Casey B., Richard Gil, and Xavier Sala-i-Martin. "Do Democracies Have Different Public Policies Than Nondemocracies?" *Journal of Economic Perspectives* 18, no. 1 (2004): 51–74.

Mutz, Diana C., and Robin Pemantle. "The Perils of Randomization Checks in the Analysis of Experiments." University of Pennsylvania, 2011.

Nathan, Andrew. "Changing of the Guard: Authoritarian Resilience." *Journal of Democracy* 14, no. 1 (2003): 6–17.

Norris, Pippa. *Digital Divide: Civic Engagement, Information Poverty, and the Internet Worldwide*, Communication, Society, and Politics. New York: Cambridge University Press, 2001.

————— "The Role of the Free Press in Promoting Democratization, Good Governance, and Human Development." Paper presented at Annual Meeting of the Midwest Political Science Association. Chicago, 2006.

Norris, Pippa, and Ronald Inglehart. *Cosmopolitan Communications: Cultural Diversity in a Globalized World.* New York: Cambridge University Press, 2009.

O'Brien, Kevin J., and Lianjiang Li. *Rightful Resistance in Rural China.* New York: Cambridge University Press, 2006.

Oi, Jean. "Realms of Freedom in Post-Mao China." In *Realms of Freedom in Modern China*, edited by William C. Kirby, 264–84. Stanford: Stanford University Press, 2004.

Olson, Mancur. "Dictatorship, Democracy, and Development." *American Political Science Review* 87, no. 3 (1993): 567–76.

Olukotun, Ayo. "Authoritarian State, Crisis of Democratization and the Underground Media in Nigeria." *African Affairs* 101, no. 404 (2002): 317–42.

Oyedeji, Tayo. "The Credible Brand Model: The Effects of Ideological Congruency and Consumer-Based Brand Equity on News Credibility." *American Behavioral Scientist* 54, no. 2 (2010): 83–99.

Paek, Hye-Jin, and Zhongdang Pan. "Spreading Global Consumerism: Effects of Mass Media and Advertising on Consumerist Values in China." *Mass Communication and Society* 7, no. 4 (2004): 491–515.

Park, Myung-Jin, and James Curran. *De-Westernizing Media Studies*. London: Routledge, 2000.

Peffley, Mark, James M. Avery, and Jason E. Glass. "Public Perceptions of Bias in the News Media: Taking a Closer Look at the Hostile Media Phenomenon." Paper presented at the Annual Meeting of the Midwest Political Science Association, Chicago, 2001.

Perry, Elizabeth J. "From Mass Campaigns to Managed Campaigns: 'Constructing a New Socialist Countryside'." In *Mao's Invisible Hand: The Political Foundations of Adaptive Governance in China*, edited by Sebastian Heilmann and Elizabeth J. Perry, 30–61. Cambridge: Harvard University Press, 2011.

———— "Studying Chinese Politics: Farewell to Revolution?" *China Journal* 57 (2007): 1–22.

———— "Trends in the Study of Chinese Politics: State–Society Relations." *China Quarterly* 139 (1994): 704–13.

Petty, Richard, and Duane Wegener. "Attitude Change: Multiple Roles for Attitude Change." In *The Handbook of Social Psychology*, edited by Daniel Gilbert, Susan Fiske and Gardner Lindzey. Vol. 2, 323–90. Boston: McGraw-Hill, 1998.

Popkin, Samuel L. *The Reasoning Voter: Communication and Persuasion in Presidential Campaigns*. Chicago: University of Chicago Press, 1991.

Price, Vincent. "The Impact of Varying Reference Periods in Survey Questions about Media Use." *Journalism Quarterly* 70, no. 3 (1993): 615–27.

Prior, Markus. "The Immensely Inflated News Audience: Assessing Bias in Self-Reported News Exposure." *Public Opinion Quarterly* 73, no. 1 (2009): 130–43.

———— "News Vs. Entertainment: How Increasing Media Choice Widens Gaps in Political Knowledge and Turnout." *American Journal of Political Science* 49, no. 3 (2005): 577–92.

Przeworski, Adam. *Democracy and Development: Political Institutions and Material Well-Being in the World, 1950–1990*, Cambridge Studies in the Theory of Democracy. Cambridge: Cambridge University Press, 2000.

———— *Democracy and the Market: Political and Economic Reforms in Eastern Europe and Latin America*, Studies in Rationality and Social Change. New York: Cambridge University Press, 1991.

Qian, Gang, and David Bandurski. "China's Emerging Public Sphere: The Impact of Media Commercialization, Professionalism, and the Internet in an Era of Transition." In *Changing Media, Changing China*, edited by Susan Shirk, 38–76. Oxford: Oxford University Press, 2011.

Qiu, Jack Linchuan. *Working-Class Network Society: Communication Technology and the Information Have-Less in Urban China*. Cambridge: MIT Press, 2009.

Rawnsley, Gary D., and Ming-Yeh T. Rawnsley. "Regime Transition and the Media in Taiwan." In *Democratization and the Media*, edited by Vicky Randall, 106–24. London: Frank Cass, 1998.

Reilly, James. "China's History Activism and Sino-Japanese Relations." *China: An International Journal* 4, no. 2 (2006): 189–216.

———— "China's History Activists and the War of Resistance against Japan." *Asian Survey* 44, no. 2 (2004): 276–94.

———— *Strong State, Smart State: The Rise of Public Opinion in China's Japan Policy.* New York: Columbia University Press, 2012.

Ren, Liying. "Surveying Public Opinion in Transitional China: An Examination of Survey Responses." PhD diss., University of Pittsburgh, 2009.

Rose, Richard, William Mishler, and Christian Haerpfer. *Democracy and Its Alternatives: Understanding Post-Communist Societies.* Baltimore: Johns Hopkins University Press, 1998.

Rosen, Stanley. "Is the Internet a Positive Force in the Development of Civil Society, a Public Sphere, and Democratization in China?" *International Journal of Communication* 4 (2010): 509–16.

Ross, Michael. "Does Oil Hinder Democracy?" *World Politics* 53, no. 3 (2001): 325–61.

Rubin, Alan M., and Sven Windahl. "The Uses and Dependency Model of Mass Communication." *Critical Studies in Mass Communication* 3 (1986): 184–99.

Saich, Tony. "Is SARS China's Chernobyl or Much Ado about Nothing?" In *SARS in China: Prelude to Pandemic?*, edited by Arthur Kleinman and James L. Watson, 71–104. Stanford: Stanford University Press, 2006.

Schedler, Andreas. "Authoritarianism's Last Line of Defense." *Journal of Democracy* 21, no. 1 (2010): 69–80.

———— "The Menu of Manipulation." *Journal of Democracy* 13, no. 2 (2002): 36–50.

Schell, Orville. "Maoism Vs. Media in the Marketplace." *Media Studies Journal* 9, no. 3 (1995): 33–42.

Schiller, Herbert I. *Mass Communications and American Empire.* New York: A. M. Kelley, 1969.

Schoenhals, Michael. *Doing Things with Words in Chinese Politics: Five Studies.* Berkeley: Institute of East Asian Studies, University of California, 1992.

Schwarz, Norbert, Dieter Frey, and Martin Kumpf. "Interactive Effects of Writing and Reading a Persuasive Essay on Attitude Change and Selective Exposure." *Journal of Experimental Psychology* 16 (1980): 1–17.

Scott, James. *Seeing Like a State: How Certain Schemes to Improve the Human Condition Have Failed.* New Haven: Yale University Press, 1998.

———— *Weapons of the Weak.* New Haven: Yale University Press, 1985.

Sears, David O. "Political Behavior." In *Handbook of Social Psychology*, edited by Gardner Lindzey and Elliot Aronson, 415–16. Reading: Addison-Wesley, 1969.

Sears, David O., and Jonathan L. Freedman. "Selective Exposure to Information: A Critical Review." In *The Process and Effects of Mass Communication*, edited by Wilbur Schramm, and Donald F. Roberts, 209–34. Urbana: University of Illinois Press, 1971.

Semetko, Holli, and Patti M. Valkenburg. "Framing European Politics: A Content Analysis of Press and Television News." *Journal of Communication* 49, no. 1 (2000): 93–109.

Shadish, William R., Thomas D. Cook, and Donald Thomas Campbell. *Experimental and Quasi-Experimental Designs for Generalized Causal Inference.* Boston: Houghton Mifflin Company, 2002.

Shambaugh, David L. *Beautiful Imperialist: China Perceives America, 1972–1990.* Princeton: Princeton University Press, 1991.

———— "China's Propaganda System: Institutions, Processes, and Efficacy." *China Journal* 57 (2007): 25–58.

Shentu, Qingnan. "2004 Nian Baoye Touzi Xin Tedian (New Characteristics of Investment in the Newspaper Industry in 2004)." In *Zhongguo Baoye Nianjian (China Newspaper Industry Yearbook)*, 41–42. Beijing: Zhonghua Gongshang Lianhe Chubanshe, 2004.

Shepsle, Kenneth A. *Models of Multiparty Electoral Competition.* New York: Harwood Academic Publishing, 1991.

Shi, Tianjian. *Political Participation in Beijing.* Cambridge: Harvard University Press, 1997.

——— "Survey Research in China." In *Research in Micropolitics: Rethinking Rationality*, edited by Michael X. Delli Carpini, Leonie Huddy, and Robert Y. Shapiro, 213–50. Greenwich: JAI Press, 1996.

Shi, Tianjian, John Aldrich, and Jie Lu. "Bifurcated Images of the U.S. in Urban China and the Impact of Media Environment." *Political Communication* 28, no. 3 (2011): 1–20.

Shi, Tianjian, and Jie Lu. "The Shadow of Confucianism." *Journal of Democracy* 21, no. 4 (2010): 123–30.

Shih, Victor. "'Nauseating' Displays of Loyalty: Monitoring the Factional Bargain Through Ideological Campaigns in China." *Journal of Politics* 70, no. 4 (2008): 1177–92.

Shirk, Susan. "Changing Media, Changing Foreign Policy." *Japanese Journal of Political Science* 8, no. 1 (2007): 43–70.

Shue, Vivienne. "Legitimacy Crisis in China?" In *State and Society in 21st Century China*, edited by Peter Hays Gries and Stanley Rosen, 24–49. New York: Routledge Curzon, 2004.

Siebert, Fred S., Theodore Peterson, and Wilbur Schramm. *Four Theories of the Press: The Authoritarian, Libertarian, Social Responsibility, and Soviet Communist Concepts of What the Press Should Be and Do.* Freeport: Books for Libraries Press, 1956 [1973].

Slater, Dan. "Can Leviathan Be Democratic? Competitive Elections, Robust Mass Politics, and State Infrastructural Power." *Studies in Comparative International Development* 43, no. 3–4 (2008): 252–72.

Solinger, Dorothy J. *Contesting Citizenship in Urban China: Peasant Migrants, the State, and the Logic of the Market.* Berkeley: University of California Press, 1999.

Solnick, Steven L. "The Breakdown of Hierarchies in the Soviet Union and China: A Neoinstitutional Perspective." *World Politics* 48, no. 2 (1996): 209–38.

Song, Yongjun. "Zhongguo Baoye Jituanhua Zhuyao Moshi Ji Xianshi Wenti Fenxi (Analysis of the Main Pattern and Practical Problems of China's Newspaper Conglomeration)" and "Zhongguo Baoye Jituan Jianjie (Introduction to Chinese Newspaper Conglomerates)." In *Zhongguo Baoye Nianjian (China Newspaper Industry Yearbook)*, 370–405. Beijing: Zhonghua Gongshang Lianhe Chubanshe, 2004.

Stempel, Guido H. "Sample Size for Classifying Subject Matter in Dailies." *Journalism Quarterly* 29, no. 3 (1952): 333–34.

Stern, Rachel E., and Jonathan Hassid. "Amplifying Silence: Uncertainty and Control Parables in Contemporary China." *Comparative Political Studies* 45, no. 10 (2012): 1230–54.

Stockmann, Daniela. "Greasing the Reels: Advertising as a Means of Campaigning on Chinese Television." *China Quarterly* 208 (2011d): 851–69.

——— "Information Overload? Collecting, Managing, and Analyzing Chinese Media Content." In *Sources and Methods in Chinese Politics*, edited by Allen Carlson, Mary

Gallagher, and Melanie Manion, 107–25. New York: Cambridge University Press, 2010b.

———. "Media Influence on Ethnocentrism towards Europeans in China." In *Chinese Views of the EU: Public Support for a Strong Relation*, edited by Lisheng Dong, Zhengxu Wang, and Henk Dekker. London: Routledge, In Press.

———. "One Size Doesn't Fit All: Measuring News Reception East and West." *The Chinese Journal of Communication* 2, no. 2 (2009): 140–57.

———. "Race to the Bottom: Media Marketization and Increasing Negativity toward the United States in China." *Political Communication* 28, no. 3 (2011c): 268–90.

———. "What Information Does the Public Demand? Getting the News During the 2005 Anti-Japanese Protests." In *Changing Media, Changing China*, edited by Susan Shirk, 175–201. Oxford: Oxford University Press, 2011a.

———. "Who Believes Propaganda? Media Effects during the Anti-Japanese Protests in Beijing." *China Quarterly* 202 (2010a): 269–89.

Stockmann, Daniela, Ashley Esarey, and Jie Zhang. "Advertising Chinese Politics: How Public Service Advertising Prime and Alter Political Trust in China." Paper presented at the Annual Meeting of the American Political Science Association, Seattle, WA, 2011.

Stockmann, Daniela, and Mary E. Gallagher. "Remote Control: How the Media Sustains Authoritarian Rule in China." *Comparative Political Studies* 44, no. 4 (2011): 436–67.

Stokes, Susan. "Perverse Accountability: A Formal Model of Machine Politics with Evidence from Argentina." *American Political Science Review* 99, no. 3 (2005): 215–25.

Stone, Philip J., Dexter C. Dunphy, Marshall S. Smith, and Daniel M. Ogilvie. *The General Inquirer: A Computer Approach to Content Analysis*. Cambridge: MIT Press, 1966.

Stoner-Weiss, Kathryn. "Central Governing Incapacity and the Weakness of Political Parties: Russian Democracy in Disarray." *Publius: The Journal of Federalism* 32, no. 2 (2002): 125–46.

Sun, Longji. *Zhongguo Wenhua De Shenceng Jiegou (The Deep Structure of Chinese Culture)*. Guilin: Guangxi Shifan Daxue Chubanshe, 2004.

Sun, Xupei. *Zhongguo Chuanmei De Huodong Kongjian (China's Space for Media Activity)*. Beijing: Renmin Chubanshe, 2004.

Svolik, Milan W. "Power Sharing and Leadership Dynamics in Authoritarian Regimes." *American Journal of Political Science* 53, no. 2 (2009): 477–94.

Tajfel, Henri. *Social Identity and Intergroup Relations*, European Studies in Social Psychology. Cambridge: Cambridge University Press, 1982.

Tang, Wenfang. *Public Opinion and Political Change in China*. Stanford: Stanford University Press, 2005.

Tang, Wenfang, and William L. Parish. *Chinese Urban Life under Reform: The Changing Social Contract*, Cambridge Modern China Series. New York: Cambridge University Press, 2000.

Tanner, Murray Scot. "China Rethinks Unrest." *The Washington Quarterly* 27, no. 3 (2004): 137–56.

Tironi, Eugenio, and Guillermo Sunkel. "The Modernization of Communications: The Media in the Transition to Democracy in Chile." In *Democracy and the Media: A Comparative Perspective*, edited by Richard Gunther and Anthony Mughan, 165–93. New York: Cambridge University Press, 2000.

Tsfati, Yariv, and Joseph N. Cappella. "Do People Watch What They Do Not Trust? Exploring the Association between News Media Skepticism and Exposure." *Communication Research* 30, no. 5 (2003): 504–29.

Turner, John C. *Rediscovering the Social Group: A Self-Categorization Theory*. Oxford: B. Blackwell, 1987.

Tyler, Tom. "Psychological Perspectives on Legitimacy and Legitimation." *Annual Review of Psychology* 57 (2006): 375–400.

Vallone, Robert, Less Ross, and Mark Lepper. "The Hostile Media Phenomenon: Biased Perception and Perceptions of Media Bias in Coverage of the Beirut Massacre." *Journal of Personality and Social Psychology* 49 (1985): 577–88.

Vossen, Koen. "Populism in the Netherlands after Fortuyn: Rita Verdonk and Geert Wilders Compared." *Perspectives on European Politics and Society* 11, no. 1 (2010): 22–38.

Vreese, Cleas de. *Framing Europe: Television News and European Integration*. Amsterdam: Aksant, 2003.

Wan, Ming. *Sino-Japanese Relations: Interaction, Logic, and Transformation*. Stanford: Stanford University Press, 2006.

Wang, Cungang. "Gongzhong Dui Zhongguo Waijiao De Canyu Jiqi Yingxiang: Jiyu 2003 Nian De San Ge Anli De Yanjiu (The Participation and Influence of the Public on Chinese Foreign Affairs: Three Case Studies from 2003)." *Waijiao Pinglun (Commentary on Foreign Affairs)* 3 (2010): 74–96.

Wang, Jianying, and Deborah Davis. "China's New Upper Middle Class: Heterogenous Composition and Multiple Identities." In *China's Emerging Middle Class: Beyond Economic Transformation*, edited by Cheng Li, 157–76. Washington, DC: Brookings Institution Press, 2010.

Wang, Jing. *Brand New China: Advertising, Media and Commercial Culture*. Cambridge: Harvard University Press, 2008.

Wang, Mulin, and Ming Jing. "Waishi Caifang Baodao (Foreign Affairs Interview Reports)." In *Zhuanye Caifang Baodaoxue (Studies of Professional Interview Reports)*, edited by Hongwen Lan, 53–75. Beijing: Renmin Chubanshe, 2003.

Wang, Zhengxu. "Explaining Regime Strength in China." *China: An International Journal* 4, no. 2 (2006): 217–37.

Way, Lucan A. "Authoritarian Failure: How Does State Weakness Strengthen Electoral Competition?" In *Electoral Authoritarianism: The Dynamics of Unfree Competition*, edited by Andreas Schedler, 167–80. Boulder: Lynne Rienner, 2006.

——— "Authoritarian State Building and the Sources of Regime Competitiveness in the Fourth Wave: The Cases of Belarus, Moldova, Russia, and Ukraine." *World Politics* 57, no. 2 (2005): 231–61.

——— "A Reply to My Critics." *Journal of Democracy* 20, no. 1 (2009): 90–97.

Weatherford, Stephen. "Economic Stagflation and Public Support for the Political System." *British Journal of Political Science* 14, no. 2 (1984): 187–205.

Weber, Max. *Wirtschaft Und Gesellschaft*. Tübingen: Mohr, 1921 [1980].

Weingast, Barry R. "The Political Foundations of Democracy and the Rule of Law." *American Political Science Review* 91, no. 2 (1997): 245–63.

Weiss, Jessica C. "Powerful Patriots: Nationalism, Diplomacy and the Strategic Logic of Anti-Foreign Protest." PhD diss., University of California, San Diego, 2008.

Weller, Robert P. "Responsive Authoritarianism." In *Political Change in China: Comparisons with Taiwan*, edited by Bruce Gilley and Larry Diamond, 117–33. Boulder: Lynne Rienner, 2008.

West, Mark. "Validating a Scale for the Measurement of Credibility: A Covariance Structure Modeling Approach." *Journalism Quarterly* 71, no. 1 (1994): 159–68.

White, Stephen, Sarah Oates, and Ian McAllister. "Media Effects and Russian Elections, 1999–2000." *British Journal of Political Science* 35 (2005): 191–208.

Whiting, Susan H. *Power and Wealth in Rural China: The Political Economy of Institutional Change*, Cambridge Modern China Series. New York: Cambridge University Press, 2001.

Whyte, Martin King. *Myth of the Social Volcano: Perceptions of Inequality and Distributive Injustice in Contemporary China*. Stanford: Stanford University Press, 2010.

Willnat, Lars, Zhou He, and Xiaoming Hao. "Foreign Media Exposure and Perceptions of Americans in Hong Kong, Shenzhen, and Singapore." *Journalism and Mass Communication Quarterly* 74, no. 4 (1997): 738–56.

Wintrobe, Ronald. *The Political Economy of Dictatorship*. New York: Cambridge University Press, 1998.

Wong, Cara. *Boundaries of Obligation in American Politics*. New York: Cambridge University Press, 2010.

Wright, Joseph. "Do Authoritarian Institutions Constrain? How Legislatures Affect Economic Growth and Investment." *American Journal of Political Science* 52, no. 2 (2008): 322–43.

―――― "How Foreign Aid Can Foster Democratization in Authoritarian Regimes." *American Journal of Political Science* 53, no. 3 (2009): 552–71.

Wu, Guoguang. "Command Communication: The Politics of Editorial Formulation in the People's Daily." *China Quarterly* 137 (1994): 194–211.

Wu, Xu. *Chinese Cyber Nationalism*. Lanham: Lexington Books, 2007.

Xiao, Qiang. "The Rise of Online Public Opinion and Its Political Impact." In *Changing Media, Changing China*, edited by Susan Shirk, 202–24. Oxford: Oxford University Press, 2011.

Xin, Xin. "A Developing Market in News: Xinhua News Agency and Chinese Newspapers." *Media, Culture & Society* 28, no. 1 (2006): 45–66.

Xu, Guangqiu. "The Rise of Anti-Americanism in China." *Asian Thought and Society* 12, no. 66 (1997): 208–26.

Xue, Ke, and Mingyang Yu. *Meiti Pinpai (Media Brand)*. Shanghai: Shanghai Jiaotong Daxue Chubanshe, 2008.

Yang, Dali L. "Economic Transformation and Its Political Discontents in China: Authoritarianism, Unequal Growth, and the Dilemmas of Political Development." *Annual Review of Political Science* 9 (2006): 143–64.

Yang, Zhaiqin, and Xinqing Zhang. "Fazhi Caifang Baodao (Legal System Interview Reports)." In *Zhuanye Caifang Baodaoxue (Studies of Professional Interview Reports)*, edited by Hongwen Lan, 76–98. Beijing: Renmin Daxue Chubanshe, 2003.

Yu, Guoming. *Biange Chuanmei: Jiexi Zhongguo Chuanmei Zhuanxing Wenti (Reforming the Media: Analyzing the Chinese Media's Pattern of Transformation)*. Beijing: Huaxia Chubanshe, 2005.

―――― *Jiegou Minyi: Yige Yulunxuezhe De Shizheng Yanjiu (Public Opinion Analysis: A Quantitative Approach to the Study of Public Opinion)*. Beijing: Huaxia Chubanshe, 2001.

―――― *Jiexi Chuanmei Bianju: Laizi Zhongguo Chuanmeiye Diyi Xianchang De Baogao (Analyzing the Situation of the Media under Reform: A First-Hand Report)*. Guangzhou: Nanfang Ribao Chubanshe, 2002.

_____ *Meijie De Shichang Dingwei: Yige Chuanboxuezhe De Shizheng Yanjiu (The Position of the Media Market: A Quantitative Approach to the Study of Communications)*. Beijing: Beijing Guangbo Xueyuan Chubanshe, 2000.

_____ *Yu Guoming Zixuanji: Bie Wu Xuanze: Yige Chuanmeixueren De Lilun Gaobai (Collection of Self-Selected Works by Yu Guoming: Others Don't Have a Choice: A Report on Theory by an Expert in Communications)*. Shanghai: Fudan Chubanshe, 2004.

_____ *Zhongguo Dazhong Meijie De Chuanbo Xiaoguo Yu Gongxingli Yanjiu (Study on Communication Effects and Credibility of Chinese Mass Media)*. Beijing: Jingji Kexue Chubanshe, 2009.

Yu, Haiqing. *Media and Cultural Transformation in China*. New York: Routledge, 2009.

Yu, Jianrong. *Diceng Lichang (The Perspective of the Lower Class)*. Shanghai: Shanghai Sanlian Shudian, 2011.

Zaller, John. *The Nature and Origins of Mass Opinion*. New York: Cambridge University Press, 1992.

Zeng, Fanxu. "Guojia Kongzhi Xia De NGO Yiti Jiangou: Yi Zhongguo Yiti Wei Li (NGO's Media Agenda Building under State Control: The Case of China)." *Chuanbo Yu Shehui Xuekan (Chinese Journal of Communication and Society)* 8 (2009): 19–53.

Zhai, Zheng. "Zhongmei Liang Guo Zai Duifang Zhuyao Meiti Zhong De Xiezhao – Dui Renmin Ribao He Niuyue Shibao 1998 Nian Baodao De Duibi Fenxi (The Mutual Portrayal of China and the US in Important Media – Comparative Analysis of 1998 Reporting in the *People's Daily* and the *New York Times*)." 2002. http://www.edu.cn/20030728/3088768.shtml, accessed July 20, 2012.

Zhan, Jiang. "Environmental Journalism in China." In *Changing Media, Changing China*, edited by Susan Shirk, 115–27. Oxford: Oxford University Press, 2011.

Zhang, Jie. "Cong Meijie Fazhan Jiaodu Lun Guojia Yulun Anquan (A Discussion of National Public Opinion Security Based on the Development of the Mass Media)." PhD diss., Peking University, 2006.

Zhang, Mingxin. "The Present Situation and Analysis of Mass Media Use & Media Credibility in Countryside of Mid-China: The Case of Hubei Province." *China Media Research* 2, no. 4 (2006): 37–47.

Zhang, Xiaoling. "Reading between the Headlines: SARS, Focus and TV Current Affairs Programmes in China." *Media, Culture & Society* 28, no. 5 (2006): 715–37.

Zhang, Xuehong. "Wo Guo Nongcun Xinwen Chuanbo Xianzhuang Yanjiu (A Study of Media Communication in China's Rural Regions)." In *Zhongguo Chuanbo Xiaoguo Toushi (A Perspective on Media Effects in China)*, edited by Chongshan Chen and Xiuling Mi, 146–66. Shenyang: Shenyang Chubanshe, 1989.

Zhao, Dingxin. *The Power of Tiananmen: State-Society Relations and the 1989 Beijing Student Movement*. Chicago: University of Chicago Press, 2001.

Zhao, Min. "Zhongguo Ren Kan Meiguo (The Chinese People Viewing America)." In *Zhongmei Changqi Duihua (China-United States Long-Term Dialogue)*, edited by Meixin Tao and Min Zhao, 3–20. Beijing: Chinese Academy of Social Sciences Press, 2001.

Zhao, Suisheng. "A State-Led Nationalism? The Patriotic Education Campaign in Post-Tiananmen China." *Communist and Post-Communist Studies* 31, no. 3 (1998): 287–302.

Zhao, Xuebo. *Zhandi Jizhe Shu Lun (Commentary and Discussion on Journalists on the Battlefield)*. Beijing: Zhongguo Guangbo Dianshi Chubanshe, 2007.

Zhao, Ying. "Two Circulation Audit Cases in China – Circulation Audit Development in China and Its Future." *China Media Research* 3, no. 1 (2007): 73–80.

Zhao, Yuezhi. *Communication in China: Political Economy, Power, and Conflict.* Lanham: Rowman & Littlefield, 2008.

―――― "'Enter the World': Neo-Liberal Globalization, the Dream for a Strong National, and Chinese Press Discourses on Wto." In *Chinese Media, Glo Contexts*, edited by Chin Kwan Lee, 32–56. New York, NY: Routledge, 2003.

―――― *Media, Market, and Democracy in China: Between the Party Line and the Bottom Line.* Urbana: University of Illinois Press, 1998.

―――― "The State, the Market, and Media Control in China." In *Who Owns the Media: Global Trends and Local Resistance*, edited by Pradip Thomas and Zaharom Nain, 179–212. Penang: Southbound, 2005.

―――― "Underdogs, Lapdogs and Watchdogs." In *Chinese Intellectuals between the State and the Market*, edited by Edward Gu and Merle Goldman, 43–74. New York: Routledge, 2004.

Zhao, Yuezhi, and Wusan Sun. "Public Opinion Supervision: The Role of the Media in Constrainting Local Officials." In *Grassroots Political Reform in China*, edited by Elizabeth J. Perry and Merle Goldman, 300–24. Cambridge: Harvard University Press, 2007.

Zhao, Zonghe, and Fei Cai. "Maohe Er Shenli: Cong Chuanbo Neirong De Jiaodu Kan Xinwen Yu Xuanchuan De Chayi (Apparently Harmonious but Actually Different: Difference between News and Propaganda from the Perspective of Communication Content)." Paper presented at the 8th National Conference on Communication Studies, Tsinghua University, Beijing, 2004.

Zheng, Baowei. *Lun Meijie Jingji Yu Chuanmei Jituanhua Fazhan (Discussing the Development of Conglomeration of the Economy and the Media).* Beijing: Renmin Daxue Chubanshe, 2003.

Zhou, Xiaohong, and Chen Qin. "Globalization, Social Transformation, and the Construction of China's Middle Class." In *China's Emerging Middle Class: Beyond Economic Transformation*, edited by Cheng Li, 84–103. Washington, DC: Brookings Institution Press, 2010.

Zhu, Adam. "In Search of China." PBS Home Video, 2000.

Index

21st Century Economic Report, 71, 120, 171. *See also* newspaper types

anti-foreign sentiment. *See* nationalism; United States; Japan

Arab spring. *See* Jasmine revolution; Middle East and North Africa

Armenia, 246, 247. *See also* Post-Soviet region

Asia, 2, 6, 28, 238, 246. *See also* Taiwan; Japan

attention, 43, 46, 204, 205, 206–207, 208, 210–211, 213–214, 215–216, 217, 221, 233–234. *See also* issue publics; political information and knowledge; persuasion
  definition of, 204
  indicators of, 208, 213–214

authoritarian regimes, 3, 41, 48, 204, 237–248, 257. *See also* responsive authoritarianism; regime stability; political liberalization; authoritarian resilience; totalitarian regimes
  definition of, 14
  military regimes, 239, 245–252
  one-party regimes, 14, 237–253:
    dominant-party regimes, definition of, 238–239; single-party regimes, definition of, 238–239
  personalist regimes, 239, 241, 245–252

authoritarian resilience, 3–5, 239–240, 254, 256. *See also* political liberalization; political change; regime stability; responsive authoritarianism

authoritarian states. *See* authoritarian regimes

autonomy. *See* media independence

awareness. *See* attention

Beijing, 1, 22, 46, 62, 64, 70–73, 77–103, 115–128, 137, 142, 143, 152–154, 163–168, 173–179, 180–183, 186–202, 212–220, 225, 226–227, 266–269. *See also* Beijing Daily; Beijing Evening News; Beijing News; Beijing Times; Beijing Youth Daily; Beijing Area Studies Survey (BAS); interviews; generalizability; Chongqing; Shenyang; Wuxi; Shanghai

Beijing Area Studies Survey (BAS), 19–20, 46–47, 66, 84, 101, 115, 122, 131, 138, 178, 181, 186, 189, 190–191, 193, 200, 213–215, 232, 266, 268–270. *See also* surveys

Beijing Daily, 52, 71, 115–116, 176, 178, 185, 237. *See also* Beijing; newspaper types

Beijing Evening News, 71, 115–116, 117, 121, 122, 125, 126, 153, 175–176, 177, 193. *See also* Beijing; newspaper types; content analysis, research method

Beijing News, 19, 71, 169. *See also* newspaper types; Beijing

Beijing Times, 19, 62, 71, 152. *See also* newspaper types; Beijing

Beijing Youth Daily, 19, 68, 71, 72, 85, 98, 117, 147, 169, 172, 185, 188–189, 216. *See also* newspaper types; Beijing

Belarus, 246, 247. *See also* Post-Soviet Region

Bo Xilai, 86, 113, 142. *See also* political elites

boundaries for news reporting. *See* sensitivity

Burkina Faso, 251. *See also* Sub-Saharan Africa

Bush, George W., 116, 120, 128, 206. *See also* political elites; United States; Sino-US relations

newspaper types; media marketization, pattern of; persuasion; media credibility; media labels
indicators of, 190–191, 207–208, 213
selective exposure, 41, 183–186, 218–220
media coverage, 95–96, 100–101, 104–106, 152–154, 174–176. *See also* Space for news reporting; Japan; labor law; United States; diversity of information
and crisis communication, 112–115, 119, 143–144, 148–152
and events, 81, 91, 93, 100–101, 112–113, 119, 126–170, 190, 261
framing/style 171. *See also* framing; media credibility; persuasion; experiments; media labels; media branding
and Labor law, 95–96, 107–115, 174–175, 176, 271–272. *See also* Labor law
and the United States, 99–101, 118–129, 152–154, 175. *See also* United States
tone and selection, 107–111, 118–128, 188–189. *See also* labor law; United States; Japan; media bias
trend over time, 152–154. *See also* Political change; political liberalization; diversity of information
media credibility, 5, 10, 12, 15, 39, 46, 134–135, 136, 150, 161–185, 194–200, 205–207, 210, 211–213, 220–245, 250–252, 255–256. *See also* Media labels; media consumption; persuasion; media citizenship
and audience demands, 185, 190, 191, 197, 199, 200–201
definition of, 161–163
gap between Chinese regions, 223–229. *See also* generalizability; Beijing; Chongqing; Wuxi; Shenyang; Guangdong; Shanghai
and identity, 228, 231. *See also* media consumption
and issue publics, 232–234. *See also* issue publics
levels in authoritarian regimes, 250–252. *See also* authoritarian regimes; generalizability
and space for news reporting, 13, 39–40. *See also* media labels
media effects. *See* persuasion
media, functions of, 13–14, 25, 201. *See also* media labels; feedback; mouthpiece; critical journalism; public opinion guidance
media independence, 3, 5, 30–31, 32, 33, 34, 36, 51, 63, 66, 71, 73, 133, 137, 151,

153, 156, 243, 255, 256, 258, 261. *See also* diversity of information; Media credibility; freedom of press; space for news reporting
media influence. *See* persuasion
media labels, 38–43, 146, 163–179, 205–206, 245. *See also* media branding; media credibility; shortcuts
definition of, 39, 163
media law and courts, 54–61, 80, 86–87, 88–89, 111–112, 152, 258–259, 260. *See also* labor law; legal dissemination campaign; legal evening news
media marketization, pattern of, 1–2, 8–10, 30–32, 50–73, 222, 223–226, 246. *See also* production of news; newspaper types; space for news reporting; media credibility; media consumption; persuasion; media coverage
definition of, 7–8
media practitioners, 19, 35, 36, 58–61, 67–73, 80–103, 110, 111, 115, 130, 132–138, 172. *See also* interviews; media coverage; professionalism; nomenklaura Lists; space for news reporting
media reform. *See* media marketization, pattern of
media selection. *See* media consumption
metro papers. *See* newspaper types
Mexico, 6, 241, 249–258, 259
middle class, 194, 229–231. *See also* identity; migrants; political elites
Middle East and North Africa, 2, 10, 14, 102, 237, 238, 245, 246, 248, 252, 281. *See also* Jasmine Revolution; Egypt; Jordan; Kuwait; Morocco; Qatar; Saudi-Arabia; United Arab Emirates; Tunisia; generalizability
migrants, 15–16, 26, 96, 97, 108, 154, 155, 174, 176, 181, 230, 231. *See also* labor law; residency permit; protest; middle class; issue publics; political elites
and surveys, 19, 138. *See also* Beijing Area Studies Survey (BAS); Survey of Labor Law Mobilization (LLM); generalizability
military regimes. *See* authoritarian regimes
Morocco, 2, 8, 251. *See also* Middle East and North Africa
mouthpiece, 6, 12, 13, 22, 25, 38–39, 42, 51, 52, 61, 71, 100, 106, 128, 153–154, 172, 173, 185, 201, 257. *See also* media, functions of; media labels; newspaper types

political elites, 3, 7, 15, 24–29, 50–51, 77–80,
105, 116, 132–139, 141–143, 147–152,
153–155, 193, 196, 199, 203, 239–240,
256–257, 259. *See also* authoritarian
regimes; Chinese Communist Party
(CCP); Propaganda Department; General
Administration of Press And Publications
(GAPP); State, definition of; fragmented
authoritarianism; responsive
authoritarianism
political information and knowledge, 78,
105–107, 116, 130, 137–138, 204–205.
See also attention; sensitivity; persuasion;
exposure-acceptance model
political interest, 137–139, 145. *See also*
sensitivity
political liberalization, 2–3, 5, 9, 29, 32, 155,
242, 256–260. *See also* political change;
regime stability; freedom of
press
political organ papers. *See* newspaper
types
political sensitivity. *See* sensitivity; social
desirability bias
political trust, 143, 167, 200, 250. *See also*
legitimacy; regime support; public opinion
definition of, 34
Post-Soviet Region, 14, 29, 41, 241, 242, 246,
281. *See also* Soviet Union; Russia;
Gorbachev, Mikhail; Putin, Vladimir;
Georgia; Armenia; Belarus; Kazakhstan;
Kyrgyzstan; Tajikistan; Ukraine;
Uzbekistan; generalizability
press freedom. *See* freedom of press
privatization, 8, 62–63. *See also* media
marketization, pattern of
production of news, 32–37, 77–139, 156. *See
also* sensitivity; space for news reporting;
diversity of information; media
marketization, pattern of
professionalism, 132–139, 258. *See also*
Critical Journalism; media practitioners;
space for news reporting; sensitivity;
socialization of journalists
propaganda authorities. *See* Propaganda
Department
propaganda, definition of, 13–14, 164. *See
also* persuasion; media labels; media
credibility; media, functions of; public
opinion guidance
Propaganda Department, 53–54, 65–66,
77–95, 132–136, 140–141, 153, 156,
244–245, 257, 259. *See also* institutions;

sensitivity; space for news reporting;
media, functions of
directives by, 77–80, 82, 83–85, 86, 94, 95,
99, 133, 142, 145, 150, 169, 188
protest, 25, 26–27, 44, 112–115, 119–121,
143–144, 151, 154, 175, 187–190,
219–220, 232–234, 237–238, 252–253,
259. *See also* regime stability;
authoritarian resilience; issue publics;
public opinion crisis
and labor, 15–16, 89–90. *See also* Labor
law
and nationalism, 16–17. *See also* United
States
public discourse, 27, 38–39, 100, 144–145,
155, 229, 231, 233, 234, 235, 243, 252,
254, 259. *See also* space for news reporting
definition of, 27
layers of, 38, 39. *See also* media labels
public opinion, 4, 6–7, 228, 234. *See also*
Political culture; Surveys; political trust;
regime support; issue publics; attention;
political interest; political information
and knowledge; feedback; social
desirability bias
definition of, 27
and public evaluations of Labor law, 15–16,
108–179, 207–213. *See also* labor law;
Survey of Labor Law Mobilization (LLM)
and public sentiment toward the United
States, 17–18, 122, 214–218. *See also*
nationalism; United States; Beijing Area
Studies Survey (BAS)
public opinion crisis, 143–144, 148–152. *See
also* protest; regime stability; regime
support
public opinion guidance, 11, 13, 14, 26,
235–236, 255–256. *See also* public
opinion; media, functions of; Jiang Zemin;
persuasion; propaganda, definition of
public opinion supervision. *See* critical
journalism
public sphere, 3. *See also* public discourse
pufa. *See* legal dissemination campaign
Putin, Vladimir, 2, 241. *See also* Russia;
Gorbachev, Mikhail; Soviet Union

Qatar, 246. *See also* Middle East and North
Africa
quasi-experiment, 20, 161, 173–179,
186–202, 219–220, 266–267. *See also*
experiments
definition of, 20, 186–187